TOOLKIT FOR INTERMEDIATE ACCOUNTING
EIGHTH CANADIAN EDITION

SUMMARY OF KEY RATIOS

Use this summary whenever evaluating a financial issue where financial information is given about the company. You should select the key ratios relevant to the company and … nd that certain ratios are more important than others in certain situations.

A Summary of Financial Ratios

RATIO	FORMULA	
I. Liquidity		
1. Current ratio	$\frac{\text{Current assets}}{\text{Current liabilities}}$	Measures short-term debt-paying ability
2. Quick or acid-test ratio	$\frac{\text{Cash, marketable securities, and receivables (net)}}{\text{Current liabilities}}$	Measures immediate short-term liquidity
3. Current cash debt coverage ratio	$\frac{\text{Net cash provided by operating activities}}{\text{Average current liabilities}}$	Measures a company's ability to pay off its current liabilities from the excess cash provided from its operations
II. Activity		
4. Receivable turnover	$\frac{\text{Net sales}}{\text{Average trade receivables (net)}}$	Measures liquidity of receivables
5. Inventory turnover	$\frac{\text{Cost of goods sold}}{\text{Average inventory}}$	Measures liquidity of inventory
6. Asset turnover	$\frac{\text{Net sales}}{\text{Average total assets}}$	Measures how efficiently assets are used to generate sales
III. Profitability		
7. Profit margin on sales	$\frac{\text{Net income}}{\text{Net sales}}$	Measures net income generated by each dollar of sales
8. Rate of return on assets	$\frac{\text{Net income}}{\text{Average total assets}}$	Measures overall profitability of assets
9. Rate of return on common share equity	$\frac{\text{Net income minus preferred dividends}}{\text{Average common shareholders' equity}}$	Measures profitability of owners' investment
10. Earnings per share	$\frac{\text{Net income minus preferred dividends}}{\text{Weighted shares outstanding}}$	Measures net income earned on each common share
11. Price earnings ratio	$\frac{\text{Market price of shares}}{\text{Earnings per share}}$	Measures the number of times that the E.P.S. has to be paid to buy one share
12. Payout ratio	$\frac{\text{Cash dividends}}{\text{Net income}}$	Measures percentage of earnings distributed in the form of cash dividends
IV. Coverage		
13. Debt to total assets	$\frac{\text{Total debt}}{\text{Total assets or equities}}$	Measures the percentage of total assets provided by creditors
14. Times interest earned	$\frac{\text{Income before interest expense and taxes}}{\text{Interest expense}}$	Measures the ability of a company to generate enough income so that it can meet interest payments
15. Cash debt coverage ratio	$\frac{\text{Net cash provided by operating activities}}{\text{Average total liabilities}}$	Measures a company's ability to repay its total liabilities in a given year from its operations
16. Book value per share	$\frac{\text{Common shareholders' equity}}{\text{Outstanding shares}}$	Measures the amount each share would receive if the company were liquidated at the amounts reported on the balance sheet

TOOLKIT FOR INTERMEDIATE ACCOUNTING
EIGHTH CANADIAN EDITION

STUDY STEPS

This framework has been incorporated into each chapter to provide a consistent approach to the study of the material. Students should follow this whenever studying a new topic or attempting to analyse a new issue.

1. Understanding transaction/arrangement—business content

Tips!

- **Draw a diagram that shows parties involved and details of the transactions—legal form.**
- **On a very basic level, know what is *given up* and what is *received by* the company.**
- **Attempt to prepare a rough journal entry. You may not be able to do this at this point especially since you might not have the numbers. This is useful at this stage however, as it often will draw your attention to an issue.**
- **Try to determine the economic substance of the transaction—consider intent.**

Note: This analysis is essential when identifying and analyzing complex transactions where the issue is not evident.

2. Understanding how the transaction fits into the financial reporting model and conceptual framework—analysis

Tips!

- **List "recognition," "measurement," and "presentation/disclosure" down the left hand side of the page and fill in principles/concepts/definitions/criteria that you think are relevant beside each one. Use the other charts and exhibits at the front and in various chapters of the Study Guide for a complete list of principles/concepts/definitions/criteria.**
- **Try to identify any problems/issues that might be encountered in analyzing the topic. These are usually the result of the nature of the transaction. You may have already identified these as part of Step 1 above.**
- **Try to identify where professional judgement will be required.**

Note: This process also helps establish a framework for case analysis for more complex transactions.

3. Becoming proficient in any required calculations—skills

Tips!

- **In many of the more complex areas, accountants have developed worksheets that are invaluable in doing the calculations. These must be mastered. Consider them an additional skill to carry forward in your accounting career.**
- **There are many methods that have been developed over the years to account for certain things such as amortization and bad debt expense. These have been separately summarized in the TOOLKIT and also are reviewed in more detail in the main body of the Study Guide chapters.**
- **In order to master the calculations, you should do as many of the exercises and problems as you can. There are many problems included in the Study Guide with answers. There are also numerous exercises and problems in the text as well as on the Student Website. These are the minimum numbers that should be done.**
- **When doing the exercises and problems, attempt them first without an answer since this helps you to identify your weaknesses. Afterwards, look at the answer. There is no point in doing these if you are not checking your answers.**

STUDY GUIDE TO ACCOMPANY

Intermediate Accounting

VOLUME 1: CHAPTERS 1 - 12

Donald E. Kieso, PhD, CPA
KPMG Peat Marwick Emeritus Professor of Accounting
Northern Illinois University
DeKalb, Illinois

Jerry J. Weygandt, PhD, CPA
Arthur Andersen Alumni Professor of Accounting
University of Wisconsin
Madison, Wisconsin

Terry D. Warfield, PhD
PricewaterhouseCoopers Research Scholar
University of Wisconsin
Madison, Wisconsin

Nicola M. Young, MBA, FCA
Saint Mary's University
Halifax, Nova Scotia

Irene M. Wiecek, FCA
University of Toronto
Toronto, Ontario

Study Guide prepared by Peter J. Thomas

BICENTENNIAL 1807 WILEY 2007 BICENTENNIAL

John Wiley & Sons Canada, Ltd.

Library and Archives Canada Cataloguing in Publication

Thomas, Peter J. (Peter John)
Study guide to accompany Intermediate accounting, eighth Canadian edition / Peter J. Thomas.

ISBN 978-0-470-15313-0 (v. 1)
ISBN 978-0-470-15314-7 (v. 2)

1. Accounting—Problems, exercises, etc. I. Title.
HF5635.I573 2007 Suppl. 1 657'.044 C2007-901337-6

Production Credits
Editorial Manager: Karen Staudinger
Publishing Services Director: Karen Bryan
Marketing Manager: Aida Krneta
Media Editor: Elsa Passera Berardi
Developmental Editor: Daleara Hirjikaka
Graphic Designer: Natalia Burobina
Wiley Bicentennial Logo: Richard J. Pacifico
Printing & Binding: Webcom Inc.

Printed and bound in Canada
10 9 8 7 6 5 4 3 2 1

John Wiley & Sons Canada, Ltd.
6045 Freemont Blvd.
Mississauga, Ontario L5R 4J3

Visit our website at: www.wiley.com/canada

CONTENTS

PREFACE

To the Student

The purpose of this *Study Guide* is to help you to improve your success rate in solving accounting homework assignments and in answering accounting exam questions. For each chapter we include the following:

OVERVIEW	To briefly introduce the chapter topics and their importance.
STUDY STEPS	To discuss the business transactions or issues pertinent to the chapter topics, including an analysis of the key recognition, measurement, and disclosure issues.
TIPS	To alert you to common pitfalls and misconceptions and remind you of important terminology, concepts, and relationships that are relevant to answering specific questions or solving certain problems. To help you to understand the intricacies of a problematic situation and tell you what to do in similar circumstances.
EXERCISES	To provide you with a selection of problems representative of homework assignments that an intermediate accounting student may encounter.
MULTIPLE CHOICE	To provide you with a selection of multiple-choice questions that are representative of common exam questions covering topics in the chapter.
PURPOSES	To identify the essence of each question or exercise and link it to the text material.
SOLUTIONS	To show you the appropriate solution for each exercise and multiple-choice question presented.
EXPLANATIONS	To give you the details of how selected solutions were derived and explain why things are done as shown.
APPROACHES	To coach you on the particular model, computational format, or other strategy to be used to solve particular problems. To teach you how to analyze and solve multiple-choice questions.

This book will be a welcome teaching/learning aid because it provides you with the opportunity to solve accounting problems in addition to the ones assigned by your instructor without having to rely on your teacher for solutions. Many of the exercises and questions contained herein are very similar to items in your intermediate accounting textbook; the difference is, the ones in this book are accompanied with detailed, clearly laid out solutions.

The use of the multiple-choice questions in this volume and the related suggestions on how to approach them can easily increase your ability (and confidence in your ability) to deal with exam questions of this variety.

HOW TO STUDY ACCOUNTING

The successful study of accounting requires a different approach than most other subjects. In addition to reading a chapter, applying the material through the completion of exercises or problems is necessary to developing a true and lasting understanding of the concepts introduced in the text chapter. The study of accounting principles is a combination of theory and practice; theory describes what to do and why, and practice is the application of guidelines to actual situations. We use illustrations to demonstrate how theory works and we use theory to explain why something is done in practice. Therefore, it is impossible to separate the two in the study of accounting.

Learning accounting is a cumulative process. It is difficult to master Chapter 4 until you are thoroughly familiar with Chapters 1-3, and so on. Therefore, it is imperative that you keep up with class assignments. And, because accounting is a technical subject, you must pay particular attention to terminology.

Accounting is the language of business. It is an exciting subject that provides a challenge for most business majors. Your ultimate success in life may well depend on your ability to grasp financial data. The effort you expend now will provide rewards for years to come.

We encourage you to follow the four steps for study outlined below to give yourself the best possible chance for a successful learning experience and to make the most efficient use of your time. These steps provide a system of study for each new chapter in your text.

Step 1

- Scan the learning objectives at the beginning of each chapter.
- Scan the chapter (or chapter section) rather quickly.
- Glance over the questions at the end of the chapter.

The first step will give you an overview of the material to be mastered.

Step 2

- Read the assigned pages slowly.
- Study carefully, and mark for later attention any portions not clearly understood.
- Pay particular attention to examples and illustrations.
- Try to formulate tentative answers to end-of-chapter questions.

During this phase, you will be filling in the "outline" you formed in Step 1. Most of the details will fall into place during this part of your study. The remaining steps are necessary, however, for a keen understanding of the subject.

Step 3

- Carefully read the **Overview**, **Study Steps**, and **Tips** sections of this *Study Guide*.
- Do the **Exercises** and **Cases** in this *Study Guide* that pertain to the same topics as your homework assignments.
- Review the relevant **Illustrations** in this book.
- Do the **Multiple-Choice Questions** in the *Study Guide* that pertain to the same concepts as your homework assignments.
- Refer back to the sections of the chapter in the text that you marked as unclear, if any. It is likely that any confusion or questions on your part will have been cleared up through your work in the *Study Guide*. If a section remains unclear, carefully reread it and rework relevant pages of the *Study Guide*.
- Repeat this process for each assigned topic area.

Step 4

- Write out formal answers to homework assignments in the text.

This step is crucial because you find out whether you can independently apply the material you have been studying to fresh situations. You may find it necessary to go back to the text and/or the *Study Guide* to restudy certain sections. This is common and merely shows that the study assignments are working for you.

Additional comments to help you get the most out of this *Study Guide* are as follows:

The **Study Steps** and **Tips**, along with the **Illustrations**, will aid your understanding and retention of the material. **Exercises** provide examples of application of the text material. These should be very valuable in giving you guidance in completing homework assignments that are often similar in nature and content.

The **Approach** stated for an exercise or question is likely the most valuable feature of this *Study Guide* because it tells you how to think through the situation at hand. This thought process can then be used for similar situations. It is impossible to illustrate every situation you may encounter. You can, however, handle new situations by simply applying what you know and making modifications where appropriate. Many students make the mistake of attempting to memorize their way through an accounting book. That, too, is an impossible feat. **Do not rely on memorization.** If this material is going to be useful to you, you must think about what you are reading and always be thinking of why things are as they are. If you know the reasoning for a particular accounting treatment, it will be much easier to remember that treatment and reconstruct it even weeks after your initial study of it.

Explanations are provided for exercises and questions. These are very detailed so that you will thoroughly understand what is being done and why. These details will serve you well when you complete your homework assignments.

Always make an honest effort to solve the exercises and answer the questions contained in this *Study Guide* **before** you look at the solutions. Answering the questions on your own will maximize the benefits you can expect to reap from this book.

The **Multiple-Choice Questions** are self-tests to give you immediate feedback on how well you understand the material. Study the **Approaches** suggested for answering these questions in the *Study Guide*. Practice them when answering the multiple-choice questions in the text. Apply them when taking examinations. By doing so, you will learn to calmly, methodically, and successfully process examination questions. This will definitely improve your exam scores. When you work an **Exercise** or **Case** in the *Study Guide* or in the text, always read the instructions **before** you read all of the given data. This allows you to determine what you are to accomplish. Therefore, as you now tread through the data, you can begin to process it because you can determine its significance and relevance. If you read the data before the instructions, you are likely to waste your time because you will have to reread the facts once you find out what you are to do with them. Also, more importantly, you are likely to begin to anticipate what the problem is about, which will often cause you to do things other than what is requested in the questions.

Good luck and best wishes for a positive learning experience!

Chapter 1

The Canadian Financial Reporting Environment

Overview

Accounting is the language of business. As such, accountants collect and communicate economic information about business enterprises or other entities to a wide variety of persons. To be useful, financial statements must be clearly understandable and comparable, so that users may compare the performance of one business with the performance of the same business for a prior period, or with the performance of another similar business. Therefore, all general purpose financial statements should be prepared in accordance with the same uniform guidelines, specifically, Canadian Generally Accepted Accounting Principles (GAAP).

It is an exciting time in Canada, with the decision now made to move to International Accounting Standards by 2011. Of course it is "business as usual" until then, but users, preparers, and standard setters must prepare for this change over the next few years.

Study Steps

Understanding the Reporting Environment

It is important to recognize both the preparer and user perspective on financial statements. One must acknowledge that financial statements are prepared by people, for people for decision-making purposes. Financial statements should provide useful information.

It is not necessary to memorize lists of potential users and what their information needs are; however, an understanding of this relationship is critical. There is no need to present information in the financial statements that is not useful.

For example, investors need information about the past performance of a company in order to determine whether they should invest in the company. Financial statements should provide information about the company's profitability, whether it has paid dividends in the past, and if it can stay solvent.

GAAP, the GAAP Hierarchy, and Professional Judgment

Generally accepted accounting principles (GAAP) provide guidance to accountants in meeting the objective of providing useful information in most situations. GAAP act as a constraint to ensure that certain reporting standards are met. It is codified in the *CICA Handbook* (**Canadian Institute of Chartered Accountants**), which is prepared by professional accountants.

Since no specific rule can be phrased to suit every situation, the recommendations in the *CICA Handbook* are quite often general in nature and usually give a basic principle. For instance, in determining when revenue should be recognized from sale of goods, the *CICA Handbook* suggests recognition when the risks and rewards of ownership have passed. This is a general statement that applies to numerous situations even though it requires some interpretation. A basic principle is preferable to having a rule such as all revenue must be recognized when goods are shipped. While the latter is easy to follow and very clear, it may result in inappropriate accounting (e.g., what if the goods are shipped on consignment?).

Therefore, although GAAP provide guidance, it is often of a general nature, requiring interpretation, which in turn requires professional judgment. The recommendations in the *CICA Handbook* do not fit every situation, and there may be situations that are not covered specifically. In the latter case, *CICA Handbook* Section 1100 has a specific hierarchy to follow.

According to Section 1100 of the *CICA Handbook*, the primary sources of GAAP are as follows:

(a) *CICA Handbook* Sections 1300-4460, including Appendices and Board Notices;

(b) Accounting Guidelines, including Appendices and Board Notices;

(c) Background Information and Basis for Conclusions documents including Appendices;
(d) Abstracts of Issues discussed by the Emerging Issues Committee (EIC Abstracts), including Appendices;
(e) Illustrative Examples of those pronouncements noted above;
(f) Implementation Guides authorized by the Board.

Other sources noted in Section 1100 include:

- pronouncements by accounting standard-setting bodies in other jurisdictions;
- research studies;
- accounting textbooks, journals, studies, and articles;
- other.

In general, primary sources must be looked to first. Where primary sources do not deal with the specific issue at hand, the entity should adopt accounting policies that are consistent with the primary sources as well as the concepts laid out in Section 1000 (the conceptual framework).

As the transition to International Standards continues, preparers are encouraged to look to these standards for guidance when the *CICA Handbook* is silent.

Bias in Reporting and Ethical Considerations

Another key thing to remember is that financial statements are prepared by people, often the management of the company. Therefore, there are behavioural aspects to financial reporting. People are not perfect and often act in a self-serving manner. For instance, if a manager knows that his performance will be evaluated by the shareholders based on how well the company has done, he might be motivated to make the financial statements look better than they really are.

Reporting bias defeats the whole purpose of financial reporting since, in the case above, the manager's real performance might be obscured and the shareholders may make an incorrect decision based on the information presented. Where GAAP is a constraint, this problem may not be as severe, since the manager will have to follow GAAP (i.e., GAAP will constrain his choices). But to the extent that GAAP requires judgment, there will always be some leeway. Many companies require that an outside auditor review the financial statements for fairness. This alleviates some of the problem since the **auditor** is unbiased. **External auditors** often review financial statements to ensure that the information is presented fairly in accordance with GAAP.

Any good analysis of financial reporting issues should consider the issues from an ethical viewpoint. Who is affected (stakeholders) and how are they affected? In an ethical conflict, there is usually no correct answer and, therefore, the compromise solution that is best for most stakeholders should be selected.

Tips on Chapter Topics

TIP! The accounting profession has adopted a common set of standards and procedures called generally accepted accounting principles (often referred to as GAAP). The term "generally accepted" can either mean that an authoritative accounting rule-making body has established a principle of reporting in a given area or that over time a given practice has been accepted as appropriate because of its universal application.

TIP! Because most business owners (shareholders of corporations) are not involved with the operation of the business, the stewardship function—measuring and reporting data to absentee owners—has emerged as a critical role for accounting. This situation greatly increases the need for accounting standards.

TIP! The financial statements most frequently provided by an entity (often called the basic financial statements or general purpose financial statements) are: (1) the income statement, (2) the statement of owners' equity (or statement of shareholders' equity), (3) the balance sheet, and (4) the statement of cash flows. In addition, note disclosures and other supporting schedules are an integral part of the financial statements.

TIP! The primary focus of this textbook concerns the development of two types of financial information which are governed by generally accepted accounting principles: (1) the basic financial statements and (2) the related note disclosures.

TIP! The terms principles and standards are used interchangeably in practice and throughout this book.

TIP! The accrual basis of accounting is used in preparing the basic financial statements. The accrual basis provides for (1) reporting revenues in the period they are earned (which may not be the same period in which the related cash is received), and (2) reporting expenses in the period they are incurred (which may not be the same period in which the related cash is paid).

TIP! Accounting is a constantly changing and evolving entity, which continues to change to meet the needs and demands of its users; thus the principles of GAAP will continue to evolve over time.

TIP! Potential management bias may play a key role in the development and choice of accounting principles chosen by management. These should always be kept in mind when analyzing a set of financial statements. This may take the form of overstating assets/revenues or understating liabilities/expenses.

TIP! There exist over 150 different GAAPs around the world. Each country has their own GAAP to meet the unique needs (objectives) and conditions of that country or group of countries. GAAP of one country may or may not be the same for the same situation. Harmonization of GAAP is a main focus of many accounting standard setters to eliminate barriers and improve comparability.

TIP! To address this issue, the International Accounting Standards Board was created. It quickly became the model for many countries, with over 100 countries adopting the standards as of 2005. The standards are referred to as International Financial Reporting Standards (IFRS).

Canada has made a decision to adopt these standards for public companies, effective in 2011. Private companies and not-for-profit entities will be considered in the future as to how this change will affect them. **TIP!**

For the short term, however, existing Canadian GAAP will continue to apply. The convergence continues in a way that by 2011, the *CICA Handbook* will be the *IFRA Handbook*! **TIP!**

Accounting decisions are not made in a "vacuum". Many things influence the decision of how to account for a particular transaction, including who makes the decision, who uses the resulting material, and how similar transactions are accounted for. **TIP!**

Accounting is not always "black and white". There are many "grey" areas that require professional judgment. **TIP!**

Standard setting is a political process and therefore GAAP is sometimes a compromise. This means that a treatment prescribed in the *CICA Handbook* may not necessarily agree with the conceptual framework as described in Section 1000. **TIP!**

Consider the motivations of those who are involved in preparing financial statements. They might not always be pure. **TIP!**

Auditors add value because they perform an independent review of the financial statements, ensuring that GAAP has been followed. **TIP!**

Case 1-1

PURPOSE: This case will review the meaning of generally accepted accounting principles and their significance.

All publicly held companies must have their annual financial statements audited by an independent accountant. In accordance with generally accepted auditing standards (which you will study in an auditing class), the auditor expresses an opinion regarding the fairness of the financial statements, which are to be in conformity with generally accepted accounting principles.

Instructions

(a) Define generally accepted accounting principles.
(b) List the primary sources of Canadian GAAP.

Solution to Case 1-1

(a) The accounting profession has adopted a common set of standards and procedures called **generally accepted accounting principles** (often referred to as GAAP). The word "principles" refers to methods or procedures or standards. The phrase "generally accepted" means having "substantial authoritative support." A method has substantial authoritative support if it has been approved by a rule-making body or if it has gained acceptance over time because of its universal application.

(b) The GAAP hierarchy is addressed in Section 1100 of the *CICA Handbook*. The primary sources (where one should look first) are summarized below:

(i) *CICA Handbook* Sections 1300-4460, including Appendices and Board Notices;
(ii) Accounting Guidelines, including Appendices and Board Notices;
(iii) Background Information and Basis for Conclusions documents including Appendices;
(iv) Abstracts of Issues discussed by the Emerging Issues Committee (EIC Abstracts), including Appendices;
(v) Illustrative Examples of those pronouncements noted above;
(vi) Implementation Guides authorized by the Board.

Other sources noted in Section 1100 include:

- pronouncements by accounting standard-setting bodies in other jurisdictions;
- research studies;
- accounting textbooks, journals, studies, and articles;
- other.

Where these sources do not deal with the particular issue, it is recommended that one look to standards of other accounting bodies (for example **FASB** in the United States).

Analysis of Multiple-Choice Questions

Question

1. The process of identifying, measuring, analyzing, and communicating financial information needed by management to plan, evaluate, and control an organization's operations is called:
   a. financial accounting.
   b. managerial accounting.
   c. tax accounting.
   d. auditing.

EXPLANATION: Define each answer selection. Select the answer item for which your definition matches the stem of the question. **Financial accounting** is the process that culminates in the preparation of financial reports for the enterprise as a whole for use by parties both internal and external to the enterprise. (Users of these financial reports include investors, creditors, managers, unions, and government agencies.) **Managerial accounting** is the process of identifying, measuring, analyzing, and communicating financial information needed by management to plan, evaluate, and control an organization's operations. (These reports are only for the use of parties internal to the enterprise.) **Tax accounting** usually refers to tax planning, advising on tax matters, and/or preparing tax returns. **Auditing** refers to the examination of financial statements by a certified accountant (CA or CGA depending on jurisdiction) in order to express an opinion on their fairness. An auditor attests to the fairness of financial statements and their conformity to generally accepted accounting principles. (Solution = b.)

Question

2. One objective of financial reporting is to provide:
   a. information about the investors in the business entity.
   b. information about the liquidation values of the resources held by the enterprise.
   c. information that is useful in resource allocation decisions.
   d. information that will attract new customers.

EXPLANATION: Before you read the possible answers, mentally list the objectives of financial reporting or write down the key words of each objective. Then carefully read the suggested answers. As you read an answer choice, note whether it is a match to an item in your list or not. The objectives of financial reporting are to communicate information that is useful to investors, members, contributors, creditors, and other users in making their resource allocation decisions and/or assessing management stewardship. Consequently, financial statements provide information about:

(i) an entity's economic resources, obligations, and equity/net assets;
(ii) changes in an entity's economic resources, obligation, and equity/net assets; and
(iii) the economic performance of the entity. (Solution = c.)

Question

3. The measuring and reporting of data to absentee owners of a corporation is referred to as management's:
   a. fiduciary responsibility.
   b. stewardship function.
   c. accounting standard-setting function.
   d. audit function.

EXPLANATION: Management's responsibility to manage assets with care and trust is its **fiduciary responsibility**. Management does not set accounting standards. Audits are conducted by independent accountants, not management. The **stewardship function** involves measuring and reporting data to absentee owners. (Solution = b.)

Question

4. The most significant current source of generally accepted accounting principles in the non-governmental sector is the:
   a. Securities Commissions and Stock Exchanges.
   b. FASB.
   c. IASB.
   d. CICA.

EXPLANATION: The mission of the AcSB of the CICA is to develop and maintain GAAP in Canada. The Securities and Stock Exchanges have an influence on the standard setting and control the stock exchanges. FASB is the primary standard setting organization in the United States (CICA counterpart in the United States), while the IASB is an international organization involved in harmonization of accounting principles. For the present time, the CICA is still the most current source of accounting principles.(Solution = d.)

Question

5. Accounting assists in the efficient use of scarce resources by providing information that is:
   i. timely.
   ii. reliable.
   iii. relevant.

   a. i only.
   b. i and ii.
   c. i and iii.
   d. all of the above.

EXPLANATION: Think about how accounting information can be used to provide information to aid in the decision making of scarce resources. An effective process of capital allocation promotes productivity, encourages innovation, and provides an efficient and liquid market for buying and selling securities and debt. Unreliable and irrelevant information can lead to poor capital allocation. To be useful, information must be relevant to the decision maker, it must be received in a timely manner, and it must be reliable. (Solution = d.)

Question

6. Management bias can occur by all of the following except:
   a. increasing reported revenues.
   b. decreasing reported expenses.
   c. increasing reported debt.
   d. increasing reported assets.

EXPLANATION: Management is responsible for the preparation of the financial statements of an enterprise. Companies that are trying to present their company in the best light will tend to use more aggressive accounting methods, which will tend to overstate revenues/assets and understate expenses/liabilities, hence increasing reported debt would be considered more conservative. (Solution = c.)

Question

7. All of the following organizations are directly involved in the development of financial accounting standards (GAAP) in Canada, except the:
   a. Canada Revenue Agency (CRA).
   b. Accounting Standards Board (AcSB).
   c. Canadian Institute of Chartered Accountants (CICA).
   d. Provincial Securities Commissions (SEC).

EXPLANATION: The Canada Revenue Agency (CRA) is responsible for federal income tax rules and administration. Although the CRA influences accounting practice, they are not directly involved in the development of accounting standards (for financial statements) as are the other organizations listed. (Solution = a.)

Question

8. Which of the following steps is not typical in the evolution of an addition or amendment to the *CICA Handbook*?
   a. Task force established to study the issue.
   b. Topic identified and placed on the Board's agenda.
   c. Exposure draft produced and posted on CICA website.
   d. Discussion with government for final approval of addition or amendment.

EXPLANATION: Think about the steps involved in the process of the evolution of an addition or amendment:
   i. topics identified and placed on Board's agenda;
   ii. task force established to study issue;

iii. research and analysis conducted;
iv. Exposure Draft produced and posted for comment on CICA website;
v. Board evaluates responses and changes exposure draft, if necessary. Final standard issued. The CICA has the responsibility in Canada for the development and maintenance of GAAP. It does not have to consult with the government prior to final approval of an addition or amendment to Canadian GAAP. (Solution = d.)

Question

9. The essential characteristics of accounting involve:
   a. identification and measurement of financial information relating to an economic entity.
   b. identification, measurement, and communication of financial information about an economic entity to interested persons.
   c. identification, measurement, and communication of financial information about an economic entity to management.
   d. identification and communication of financial information about an economic entity to management.

EXPLANATION: Accounting involves identification, measurement, and communication of relevant information to all interested decision makers whether they are internal or external. (Solution = b.)

Question

10. Major financial statements involve:
    a. balance sheet, income statement, statement of cash flows, statement of shareholders' equity, and notes.
    b. balance sheet, income statement, and cash flow statement.
    c. balance sheet and income statement.
    d. balance sheet, income statement, and notes.

EXPLANATION: A complete set of financial statements, to be in accordance with GAAP, must include a balance sheet, income statement, statement of cash flows, statement of shareholders' equity, and notes. (Solution = a.)

Question

11. Explain the meaning of **stakeholder** within the context of financial reporting.
    a. A stakeholder is someone who has something at stake when a decision is being made.

b. A stakeholder includes only parties external to the company.
c. A stakeholder includes only those parties who own or work for a company.
d. A stakeholder has no vested interest in the decision being made.

EXPLANATION: **Stakeholders** are interested parties who have something to gain or lose: i.e., an auditor stands to lose his reputation, an investor stands to increase his investment, etc. Therefore, they are not restricted to those internal to the company. (Solution = a.)

Question

12. Which of the following statements best describes the notion of management bias within the context of financial reporting?
    a. Management bias involves management consciously misstating the financial statement for personal gain.
    b. Management bias results in financial statements that are not neutral and, therefore, not useful.
    c. Management bias is unavoidable.
    d. Management bias involves management consciously misstating the financial statements so that the company can raise funds in capital markets.

EXPLANATION: Recall that the bias of a preparer may affect the quality (and, therefore, usefulness) of the information being prepared. Biased information by definition is not useful. Management bias is avoidable with the proper control environment and transparent financial reporting. (Solution = b.)

Question

13. Explain the significance of professional judgment in applying GAAP.
    a. The use of professional judgment does not exist in GAAP since it erodes the concept of comparability.
    b. Professional judgment allows management to contradict the *CICA Handbook*.
    c. Professional judgment is rarely used in applying GAAP.
    d. Professional judgment is fairly pervasive in Canada since GAAP consists of general principles that need to be interpreted.

EXPLANATION: The use of professional judgment is necessary and allows flexibility. However, if there is already a principle articulating a specific accounting treatment in the *CICA Handbook*, the latter would take precedence. Professional judgment should not be misconstrued to mean that, at all costs, management's objectives in financial reporting will be met. (Solution = d.)

Chapter 2

Conceptual Framework Underlying Financial Reporting

Overview

Financial statements are needed for decision making. In order to make informed decisions, a financial statement user must understand both the financial information conveyed and how it is derived. To be useful, financial statements must be clearly understandable and comparable, so that users may compare the performance of one business with the performance of the same business for a prior period, or with the performance of another similar business. Therefore the financial statements need relevant and reliable information, and all general purpose financial statements should be prepared in accordance with the same uniform guidelines. This is referred to as first principles and forms the cornerstone of accounting theory. This chapter also presents a framework within which accounting decisions are made.

Study Steps

Understanding the Importance of a Conceptual Framework

A conceptual framework establishes the following:

- The objectives of good financial reporting (i.e., to provide useful information to users).
- What useful information means.
- What basic elements should be included (i.e., assets, liabilities, etc.).
- How transactions and balances should be measured and when they should be recognized.

The conceptual framework ensures consistent, comparable financial statements and acts as a model to allow for the development of future GAAP that is consistent. It encompasses first principles as an integral part of the decision-making process.

Becoming Proficient in Using the Conceptual Framework in Analysis of Financial Reporting Issues

Review **Illustrations 2-1**, **2-2**, and **2-3** to assist in this step. However, memorizing the framework is only a means to an end, the end being that you develop sufficient professional judgment to be able to make an acceptable accounting decision within the context of the framework. With no framework, it is very difficult to make sound accounting decisions.

This is the first stage of solid case analysis. Many students are not able to identify issues in cases. The primary problem is that they don't know what they are looking for. If you are looking to see whether a transaction should be recorded or not, the definitions and principles in the conceptual framework will often give you the key. Liabilities are defined as financial statement elements that evidence an obligation or duty to another party that may not be avoided. If you know this definition, you can look for situations where a company might have a duty or obligation that they can't avoid.

Tips on Chapter Topics

Although it can sometimes be confusing, accountants often use the terms **assumptions, concepts, principles, conventions, constraints,** and **standards** interchangeably. Regardless of the particular term used, they are all a part of GAAP (Generally Accepted Accounting Principles). **TIP!**

The revenue recognition principle is applied before the matching principle is applied. **The revenue recognition** principle gives guidance in determining what revenues to recognize in a given period. The matching principle then gives guidance as to what expenses to recognize during the period. According to the **revenue recognition principle**, revenues are to be recognized in the period earned. Per the **matching principle**, expenses are to be recognized in the same period as the revenues they helped generate. **TIP!**

The **matching principle**, however, is in a period of transition in Canadian GAAP. It is no longer considered acceptable to "match" if the resulting cost deferral does not result in a "real" asset. Hence, more emphasis is put on the **balance sheet** aspect of the entry, and not on the **income statement** impact, as has been the case for many years. **TIP!**

Furthermore, future standards will address the balance sheet aspect of **revenue recognition**. Specifically, when is an asset created (such as a valid accounts receivable) versus the existing view of earnings process. **TIP!**

The term **recognition** refers to the process of formally recording or incorporating an item in the accounts and financial statements of an entity. **TIP!**

Accounting assumptions underlie the more detailed accounting principles or standards. These assumptions include the **economic entity assumption**, the **going concern assumption**, the **monetary unit assumption**, and the **periodicity assumption**. They are the foundation for the basic principles that include the **historical cost principle**, the **revenue recognition principle**, the **matching principle**, and the **full disclosure principle**. For example, the historical cost principle and the matching principle would not be appropriate if it were not for the going concern assumption. If an entity is not expected to continue in business, then plant assets would be reported on the balance sheet at their liquidation or net realizable value (estimated selling price less estimated cost of disposal) rather than at their cost, and amortization of these assets would not be appropriate. **TIP!**

A recent change in Canadian GAAP is the requirement for management to assess the ability of an entity to continue as a **going concern**. They are required to take into account information at least twelve months from the balance sheet date in making this assessment. **TIP!**

There are three common bases of expense recognition: (1) cause and effect (matched against revenue in the period), (2) systematic and rational allocation, and (3) immediate expense recognition. You should be able to explain and give examples for each of these. (See **Case 2-3**) **TIP!**

This material is **essential** in any financial reporting issues analysis. You will find that these definitions and principles continually come up in discussions of many different issues. **TIP!**

Illustration 2-1

Conceptual Framework for Financial Reporting

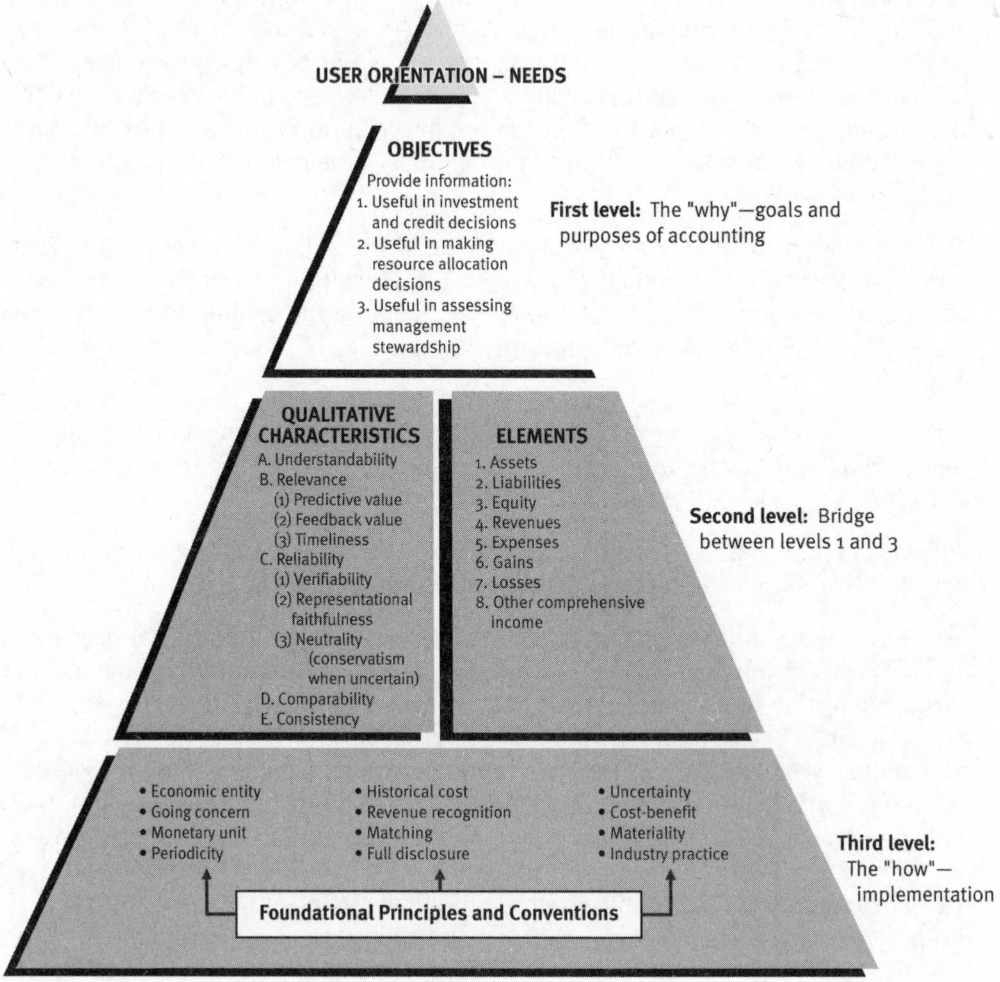

At the first level, the **objectives** identify the goals and purposes of financial accounting and are the building blocks for the conceptual framework. At the second level are the **qualitative characteristics** that make financial accounting information useful and the **elements of financial statements** (assets, liabilities, and so on). At the final, or third level, are the **foundational principles and conventions** that accountants use in establishing and applying financial accounting standards. These include **assumptions**, **principles**, and **constraints** that describe the present reporting environment.

Case 2-1

PURPOSE: This exercise is designed to review the qualitative characteristics that make accounting information useful for decision-making purposes.

The qualitative characteristics that make accounting information useful for decision making are as follows:

- Understandability
- Verifiability
- Relevance
- Representational faithfulness
- Reliability
- Neutrality
- Predictive value
- Comparability
- Feedback value
- Consistency
- Timeliness

Instructions

Fill in the blank to identify the appropriate qualitative characteristic(s) being described in each of the statements below. A qualitative characteristic may be used more than once.

____________________ 1. Two qualitative characteristics that make accounting information useful for decision-making purposes.

____________________ 2. Information that is capable of making a difference in a decision is said to have this qualitative characteristic.

____________________ 3. Information that is verifiable and reasonably free of error and bias is said to have this primary qualitative characteristic.

____________________ 4. Two qualitative characteristics that are related to both relevance and reliability.

____________________ 5. An entity is to apply the same accounting methods to similar events for successive accounting periods; that is, when an entity selects one method from a list of alternative acceptable methods, that same method is used period after period.

____________________ 6. Information is measured and reported in a similar manner for different enterprises.

____________________ 7. Neutrality is an ingredient of this qualitative characteristic of accounting information.

__________________ 8. Requires that information cannot be selected to favour one set of interested parties over another.

__________________ 9. Predictive value is an ingredient of this qualitative characteristic of information.

__________________ 10. When information provides a basis for forecasting annual earnings for future periods, it is said to have this qualitative characteristic of accounting information.

__________________ 11. Quality of information that confirms or corrects users' prior expectations.

__________________ 12. Information must be available to decision makers before it loses its capacity to influence their decisions.

__________________ 13. Imperative for providing comparisons of a single firm from period to period.

__________________ 14. Qualitative characteristic being employed when companies in the same industry are using the same accounting principles.

__________________ 15. A company cannot suppress information just because such disclosure is embarrassing or damaging to the entity.

__________________ 16. The amounts and descriptions in financial statements agree with the elements or events that these amounts and descriptions purport to represent.

__________________ 17. Independent measurers, using the same measurement methods, obtain similar results.

__________________ 18. The numbers and descriptions in financial statements represent what really existed or happened.

__________________ 19. Requires information to be free of personal bias.

__________________ 20. Requires a high degree of consensus among individuals on a given measurement.

__________________ 21. Financial information is a tool and, like most tools, cannot be much direct help to those who are unable or unwilling to use it, or who misuse it.

Solution to Case 2-1

1. Relevance and reliability
2. Relevance
3. Reliability
4. Comparability and consistency
5. Consistency
6. Comparability
7. Reliability
8. Neutrality
9. Relevance
10. Predictive value
11. Feedback value
12. Timeliness
13. Consistency
14. Comparability
15. Neutrality
16. Representational faithfulness
17. Verifiability
18. Representational faithfulness

19. Neutrality
20. Verifiability
21. Understandability

APPROACH: Before beginning to fill in the 21 blanks required, visualize the diagram for the hierarchy of accounting qualities **(Illustration 2-1)**. Also, take a few minutes to individually consider the characteristics listed and think of the key phrases involved in describing those items. Such as:

- **Understandability**: Information provided by financial reporting should be comprehensible to those who have a reasonable understanding of business and economic activities and are willing to study the information with reasonable diligence.
- **Relevance**: Capable of making a difference in a decision.
- **Reliability**: Users can depend on information to be verifiable, reasonably free of error and bias, and to represent what it purports to represent.
- **Predictive value**: Helps users make predictions about the outcome of past, present, and future events.
- **Feedback value**: Helps to confirm or correct prior expectations.
- **Timeliness**: Information must be available to decision makers before it loses its capacity to influence their decisions.
- **Verifiability**: Is demonstrated when a high degree of consensus can be secured among independent measurers using the same measurement methods.
- **Representational faithfulness**: Correspondence or agreement between the accounting numbers and descriptions and the resources or events that these numbers and descriptions purport to represent.
- **Neutrality**: Information is not to be selected to favour one set of interested parties over another and is to be free from bias towards a predetermined result.
- **Comparability**: Information that has been measured and reported in a similar manner for different enterprises is considered comparable.
- **Consistency**: A company is to apply the same methods to similar accountable events from period to period.

Illustration 2-2

Elements of Financial Statements

ASSETS: Probable future economic benefits obtained or controlled by a particular entity as a result of past transactions or events.

LIABILITIES: Probable future sacrifices of economic benefits arising from present duty or responsibility to others, as a result of past transactions or events, where there is little or no discretion to avoid the obligation.

EQUITY/NET ASSETS: Residual interest in the assets of an entity that remains after deducting its liabilities. In a business enterprise, the equity is the ownership interest.

REVENUES: Increases in economic resources, either by inflows or other enhancements of assets of an entity or settlement of its liabilities resulting from ordinary activities of the entity.

EXPENSES: Decreases in economic resources, either by outflows or reductions of assets or incurrence of liabilities resulting from an entity's ordinary revenue-generating activities.

GAINS: Increases in equity (net assets) from peripheral or incidental transactions of an entity and from all other transactions and other events and circumstances affecting the entity during a period, except those that result from revenues or investments by owners.

LOSSES: Decreases in equity (net assets) from peripheral or incidental transactions of an entity and from all other transactions and other events and circumstances affecting the entity during a period except those that result from expenses or distributions to owners.

Illustration 2-3

Basic Accounting Assumptions, Principles, and Constraints

ECONOMIC ENTITY ASSUMPTION: States that economic events can be identified with a particular unit of accountability. The activities of an accounting entity can be and should be kept separate and distinct from its owners and all other accounting entities. The entity concept does not necessarily refer to a legal entity.

GOING CONCERN ASSUMPTION: Assumes that the enterprise will continue in operation long enough to carry out its existing objectives and commitments. It assumes the entity will continue in operation long enough to recover the cost of its assets. This assumption serves as a basis for basic principles such as the historical cost principle. Because of this assumption, liquidation values of assets are not relevant. As noted in TIPS, management must make this assessment and consider available information up to tweleve months from the balance sheet date.

MONETARY UNIT ASSUMPTION: States that only transaction data capable of being expressed in terms of money should be included in the accounting records of the economic entity. All transactions and events can be measured in terms of a common denominator—units of money. A corollary is the added assumption that the unit of measure remains constant from one period to the next (some people call the corollary the "stable dollar assumption").

PERIODICITY ASSUMPTION: Assumes that the economic life of a business can be divided into artificial time periods. Although some companies choose to subdivide the business life into months or quarters, others report financial statements only for an annual period.

HISTORICAL COST PRINCIPLE: States that assets should initially be recorded and subsequently accounted for at acquisition cost. The principle also states that cost is measured by the fair market value (cash equivalent value) of the consideration given or the fair market value (cash equivalent value) of the consideration received, whichever is the more objectively determinable. In addition, the cost of an asset includes all costs necessary to acquire the item and get it in the place and condition for its intended use.

REVENUE RECOGNITION PRINCIPLE: Dictates that revenue should be recognized when (1) **realized** or **realizable** and (2) **earned**. Revenues are **realized** when products (goods or services, merchandise, or other assets) are exchanged for cash or claims to cash. Revenues are realizable when assets received or held are readily convertible into cash or claims to cash. Assets are readily convertible when they are saleable or interchangeable in an active market at readily determinable prices without significant additional cost. Revenues are considered **earned** when the entity has substantially accomplished what it must do to be entitled to the benefits represented by the revenues. The revenue generating process for most entities includes a number of steps. As a result, revenue is **earned** when the "critical point" in the earnings process is reached. This critical point is different for different circumstances as the following examples illustrate.

(1) When a sale is involved, the point of sale is the critical event.

(2) When long-term construction contracts are involved, progress toward completion is the critical event.

(3) When products are saleable in an active market at readily determinable prices without significant additional cost, the completion of production is the critical event.

(4) When uncertainty about the collection of receivables exists for credit sales of goods and services, the receipt of cash is the critical event.

In example (1), the sales basis is used for revenue recognition. In example (2), the percentage-of-completion method is appropriate for revenue recognition. In example (3), recognition of revenue at the end of production is justified. In example (4), the instalment method is used.

MATCHING PRINCIPLE: Dictates that expenses be matched with revenues whenever it is reasonable and practical to do so ("let the expense follow the revenue"). Expenses (efforts) are recognized in the same period as the related revenue (accomplishment) is recognized. Thus, a factory worker's wages are not recognized as an expense when cash is paid or when the work is performed, or when the product is produced; they are recognized as an expense when the labour (service) or the product actually makes its contribution to the revenue generating process (which is when the related product is sold). However, the matching principle **may not be** appropriate should it result in a cost deferral that does not meet the **definition of an asset**. The balance sheet would be the more important primary statement in making this decision. This reflects the ongoing emphasis on the balance sheet for standard setters, instead of the income statement as was the case for many years.

FULL DISCLOSURE PRINCIPLE: Dictates that information should be provided when the information is important enough to influence the judgment and decisions of an informed user. An entity is to disclose, through the data contained in the financial statements and the information in the notes that accompany the statements, all information necessary to make the statements not misleading. To be recognized in the main body of the financial statements, an item should meet the definition of one of the basic elements, be measurable with sufficient certainty, and be relevant and reliable. The notes to financial statements generally amplify or explain the items presented in the body of the statements. Information in the notes does not have to be quantifiable, nor does it need to qualify as an element. A trade-off exists between sufficient detail and sufficient condensation.

COST-BENEFIT RELATIONSHIP: States that the costs of providing the information must be weighed against the benefits that can be derived from using the information. In order to justify requiring a particular measurement or disclosure, the benefits perceived to be derived from it must exceed the costs perceived to be associated with the measurement or disclosure. When the perceived costs exceed the perceived benefits, a measurement or disclosure may be foregone based on its lack of practicality.

MATERIALITY CONSTRAINT: Dictates that an immaterial item need not be given strict accounting treatment; it can be given expedient treatment. An item is material if its inclusion or omission would influence or change the judgment of a reasonable person. The point involved here is one of relative size and importance. If the amount involved is significant when compared with other revenues and expenses, assets and liabilities, or net income of the entity, it is a material item and generally acceptable standards should be followed. If the amount is so small that it is quite unimportant when compared with other items, strict treatment is of less importance. The nature of an item may also affect the judgement of its materiality. A misclassification affecting cash has a lower threshold of materiality than the same dollar amount of a misclassification affecting plant assets.

INDUSTRY-PRACTICES CONSTRAINT: States that the peculiar nature of some industries and business concerns sometimes requires departure from what would normally be considered good accounting practice. For example, current assets usually appear first on a balance sheet; however, for a public utility, it is an acceptable industry practice to report plant assets (non-current items) first on the balance sheet to highlight the entity's capital-intensive nature. However, care must be taken here. The *CICA Handbook* in Section 1100 makes it clear that an accounting practice that has become common in the "industry" does not automatically make it acceptable under GAAP.

TIP!

Accounting constraints are justifications for departure from the basic accounting principles in certain situations. They are sometimes referred to as "exception principles". For example, the cost of an item that will benefit operations for five years should be initially recorded as an asset and amortized (expensed) over the related five-year period as dictated by the matching principle. However, if the item is a recycling container that cost $20, the amount is deemed to be insignificant and the whole amount is handled with expedience; that is, it is expensed in the period the container is acquired. This departure from the matching principle is justified by the materiality constraint. For another example, if the market value (replacement value) of inventory is below the cost of inventory, the inventory is to be reported at the market value (the lower value). Thus, there is a departure from the historical cost principle with the justification being the conservatism constraint.

Case 2-2

PURPOSE: This exercise will test your comprehension of the essence and significance of basic accounting assumptions, principles, and constraints.

Instructions

For each of the following statements, identify (by letter) the basic accounting assumption, principle, or constraint that is **most directly** related to the given phrase. Each code letter may be used more than once.

Assumptions, Principles, and Constraints

a. Economic entity assumption
b. Going concern assumption
c. Monetary unit assumption
d. Periodicity assumption
e. Historical cost principle
f. Revenue recognition principle
g. Matching principle
h. Full disclosure principle
i. Cost-benefit relationship
j. Materiality constraint
k. Industry-practices constraint

TIP!

Before you begin to read and answer the items listed, it would be helpful to briefly think about what you know about each of the assumptions, principles, and constraints. An explanation of each appears in **Illustration 2-3**.

Statements

_____ 1. Revenue should be recognized when it is earned, which is usually at the point of sale.

_____ 2. All information necessary to ensure that the financial statements are not misleading should be reported.

_____ 3. This concept eliminates the "liquidation concept" in viewing business affairs.

_____ 4. Measurement of the standing and progress of entities should be made at regular intervals rather than at the end of the business' life.

_____ 5. Although an item such as a wastebasket may be of service for eight years, the total cost of the item may be expensed when it is purchased, because the amount is too insignificant to warrant the strict treatment of depreciation over the eight years.

_____ 6. The recorded amount of an acquired item should be the fair market value of what was given or the fair market value of what was received in the exchange, whichever can be more objectively determined.

_____ 7. There must be complete and understandable reporting on financial statements.

_____ 8. The president of a business should not loan his spouse the company's credit card for personal gasoline purchases.

_____ 9. Expenses should be recognized in the same period that the related revenues are recognized, provided the balance sheet is not misstated as a result.

_____ 10. This concept is often exemplified by numerous notes to the financial statements.

_____ 11. If revenue is deferred to a future period, the related costs of generating that revenue should be deferred to the same future period, provided the resultant cost deferral meets the definition of an asset.

_____ 12. This concept includes a set of rules concerning when to recognize revenue and how to measure its amount.

_____ 13. All transactions and events are expressed in terms of a common denominator.

_____ 14. It is assumed that an organization will remain in business long enough to recover the cost of its assets.

_____ 15. Changes in the purchasing power of the dollar are so small from one period to the next that they are ignored in preparing the basic financial statements.

_____ 16. Items whose amounts are very small in comparison to other amounts on the financial statements may be accounted for in the most expedient manner, rather than requiring strict accounting treatment under GAAP.

_____ 17. The cost of an item should be measured by the amount of the resources expended to acquire it.

_____ 18. Accruals are often necessary in order to report expenses in the proper time periods.

_____ 19. Each accounting unit is considered separate and distinct from all other accounting units.

_____ 20. An accountant assumes that a business will continue indefinitely.

_____ 21. Assets that have appreciated in value are not reported at their current worth subsequent to acquisition because of this principal.

_____ 22. Amortization of a long-term tangible asset is based on the asset's original acquisition cost rather than the asset's current market value.

_____ 23. If an item will not affect any business decisions, it need not be separately reported in the financial statements.

_____ 24. In order to justify requiring a particular measurement or disclosure, the benefits perceived to be derived from it must exceed the costs expected to be associated with it.

_____ 25. Externally acquired intangible assets with a finite life are capitalized and amortized over the periods benefited.

_____ 26. Repair tools are expensed when purchased even though they may be of use for more than one period.

_____ 27. Brokerage firms use market value for purposes of valuation of all marketable securities. Changes in those market values are recognized in the income statement in the periods the changes occur.

_____ 28. All significant post balance sheet events are reported in the notes to the financial statements.

_____ 29. Revenue for a retail establishment is recorded at the point of sale.

_____ 30. All important aspects of bond indentures (contracts) are presented in the financial statements.

_____ 31. Reporting must be done at defined time intervals. The time intervals are of equal length.

_____ 32. An allowance for doubtful (uncollectible) accounts is established.

_____ 33. All payments out of petty cash are charged to Miscellaneous Expense, even though some expenditures will benefit the following period. (Do not use conservatism.)

_____ 34. A company charges its sales commission costs to expense in the same period that the sale is made.

_____ 35. When the liquidation of an enterprise looks imminent, this assumption is inapplicable, and thus the historical cost principle does not apply. Rather, assets are reported at their net realizable values.

_____ 36. The initial note to financial statements is usually a summary of significant accounting policies.

Solution to Case 2-2

1. f	10. h	19. a	28. h
2. h	11. g	20. b	29. f
3. b	12. f	21. e	30. h
4. d	13. c	22. e*	31. d
5. j	14. b	23. j	32. g
6. e	15. c	24. i	33. j
7. h	16. j	25. g	34. g
8. a	17. e	26. j	35. b
9. g	18. g	27. k	36. h

*An argument could be made for answer "g."

Case 2-3

PURPOSE: This case is designed to review the three methods of matching expenses with revenues with examples of each.

An unexpired cost represents **probable future benefits** and hence is accounted for as an asset. An expired cost represents an expiration of benefits and hence is accounted for as an expense or a loss. There are three common bases of expense recognition: (1) cause and effect, (2) systematic and rational allocation, and (3) immediate recognition.

Instructions

Describe each of the three bases of expense recognition and give a few examples of each for a retail establishment.

Solution to Case 2-3

1. **CAUSE AND EFFECT:** When there is a direct association between the expiration of a cost and a particular revenue transaction, the expense recognition should accompany the revenue recognition; that is, the cost is expensed in the same time period that the related specific revenue is recognized.

   Examples: Cost of goods sold, sales commissions, transportation-out.

2. **SYSTEMATIC AND RATIONAL ALLOCATION:** This basis is used when, although a cost benefits the revenue generating process of two or more accounting periods, the cost cannot be related to particular revenue transactions. Even though a close cause-and-effect relationship between revenue and cost cannot be determined, this relationship is assumed to exist. The definition of asset must be met. Arbitrary cost deferrals for the sake of "matching" are not considered acceptable under GAAP. The cost is initially accounted for as an asset and then allocated to the periods benefited (as an expense) in a systematic and rational manner. The allocation method used should appear reasonable to an unbiased observer and should be consistently applied from period to period.

   Examples: Amortization of plant assets, amortization of intangibles, amortization of prepaids (such as rent and insurance).

3. **IMMEDIATE RECOGNITION:** This basis is used for costs that fall into the following categories:
   (a) Their incurrence during the period provides no discernible future benefits.
   (b) They must be incurred each accounting period, and no buildup of expected future benefits occurs.

(c) By their nature, they relate to current revenues even though they cannot be directly associated with any specific revenues.
(d) The amount of cost to be deferred can be measured only in an arbitrary manner or great uncertainty exists regarding the realization of future benefits.
(e) Uncertainty exists regarding whether allocating them to current and future periods will serve any useful purpose.
(f) They are measures of asset costs recorded in prior periods from which no future benefits are now discernible.

Examples: Sales salaries, office salaries, utilities, repairs, advertising, accounting and legal, research and development, postage, write-off of worthless patent.

TIP!

Costs incurred by a manufacturing company are often classified into two groups: product costs and period costs. **Product costs** such as material, labour, and manufacturing overhead attach to the product and are carried into future periods (as a balance in inventory) if the product remains unsold at the end of the current period; therefore, the revenue recognition is deferred to the period of sale. This is an acceptable treatment under GAAP provided that the future benefit exceeds the amounts deferred. Product costs are expensed in the period of sale in accordance with the cause and effect basis of expense recognition. **Period costs** such as officers' salaries and other administrative items are expensed immediately, even though benefits associated with these costs may occur in the future, because no direct relationship between cost and revenue can be determined and it is highly uncertain what, if any, benefits relate to the future.

TIP!

For a manufacturing company, amortization of the office building is determined and expensed based on a systematic and rational allocation. On the other hand, amortization of factory machinery is a component of manufacturing overhead; thus, it is an element of product cost. The amount of amortization that pertains to the products produced during a period is first determined by use of the selected amortization method. The amount of amortization that ends up being reflected as an expense on the income statement for the same period depends on the number of products sold (not produced) during the period; it is included as a part of cost of goods sold expense.

Analysis of Multiple-Choice Questions

Question

1. The objectives of financial reporting include all of the following except to provide information that:
   a. is useful to Canada Revenue Agency in allocating the tax burden to the business community.
   b. is useful to those making investment and credit decisions.

c. is helpful in assessing future cash flows.
d. identifies the economic resources (assets), the claims to those resources (liabilities), and the changes in those resources and claims.

EXPLANATION: Financial reporting is for the use of investors, potential investors, management, and other interested parties. It is not for the CRA. The information required to be reported to the CRA is provided by the reporting entity on tax forms and is referred to as income tax accounting as opposed to financial reporting. (Solution = a.)

Question

2. According to the Conceptual Framework for Financial Reporting, timeliness is an ingredient of:

	Relevance	Reliability
a.	Yes	Yes
b.	Yes	No
c.	No	No
d.	No	Yes

EXPLANATION: In answering this question, read the above statement and answer "Yes" (true) or "No" (false) when completing it with the word **relevance**. Then reread the statement and answer "Yes" or "No" when completing it with the word **reliability**. Then look for the corresponding combination of "Yes" and "No" to select your answer. In the diagram of the hierarchy of accounting qualities, timeliness is linked to relevance and not reliability. Therefore, we want to respond "Yes" to the relevance column and "No" to the reliability column. (Solution = b.)

Question

3. According to The Conceptual Framework for Financial Reporting, neutrality is an ingredient of the qualitative characteristics of:

	Relevance	Reliability
a.	Yes	Yes
b.	Yes	No
c.	No	No
d.	No	Yes

EXPLANATION: In answering this question, read the question and answer "Yes" (true) or "No" (false) when completing the statement with the word **relevance**. Then reread the question and answer "Yes" or "No" when completing the statement with the word **reliability**. Then look for the corresponding combination of "Yes" and "No" to select your answer. In the diagram of the hierarchy of accounting qualities, neutrality is linked to reliability and not relevance. Therefore, we want to respond "No" to the relevance column and "Yes" to the reliability column. (Solution = d.)

Question

4. If the FIFO inventory method was used last period, it should be used for the current and following periods because of:
   a. materiality.
   b. verifiability.
   c. timeliness.
   d. consistency.

EXPLANATION: In reading the question, cover up the answer selections. Anticipate the correct answer by attempting to complete the statement given. This process should yield the answer of "consistency". If you cannot think of the word to complete the statement, then take each answer selection and write down what each means. You should then be able to match up the question with answer selection "d."

Selection "d" is correct because consistency is a qualitative characteristic of accounting information. To be useful, financial statements should reflect consistent application of generally accepted accounting principles. This means that a company should apply the same methods to similar accountable events from period to period. Selection "a" is incorrect because materiality refers to a constraint whereby an item is to be given strict accounting treatment unless it is insignificant. Selection "b" is incorrect because verifiability refers to an ingredient of reliability (it is demonstrated when a high degree of consensus can be secured among independent measurers using the same measurement methods). Selection "c" is incorrect because timeliness is an ingredient of relevance which indicates that for information to be relevant, it must be prepared on a timely basis. (Solution = d.)

Question

5. Which of the following transactions does not represent a gain to the organization:
   a. a bookstore selling a computer for a profit.
   b. a consulting company selling a block of land it was holding for future expansion.
   c. the Ottawa Senators selling season tickets.
   d. a lawyer selling a pair of theatre tickets for more than she paid for them.

EXPLANATION: Define or explain "gain" before you read the answer selections. Select the answer that best fits your description. The *CICA* defines a gain as an increase in equity from a peripheral or incidental transaction. Ask yourself whether the revenue earned in each situation would be in the normal course of business for the enterprise or is it incidental or a peripheral transaction. Bookstores are not in the business of regularly selling computers. Land held for expansion would not represent a normal transaction for a consulting firm and a lawyer does not regularly sell theatre tickets as a scalper. The Ottawa Senators however would try to sell season tickets in the normal course of business. (Solution = c.)

Question

6. Which of the following does not represent a liability to the organization?
   a. Salaries earned for work performed last week by employees.
   b. Money received by Northern Air in advance of a flight to take place next week.
   c. Inventory purchased but not paid for.
   d. Owner of a company decides to buy a car next week and goes to the lot to pick out the car she wants.

EXPLANATION: Define the term liability. Compare your definition of liability against the possible choices available. A liability represents a probable future sacrifice of economic benefits arising from a present duty or responsibility to others, as a result of a past transaction or event, where there is little or no discretion to avoid the obligation. In all cases, this will probably represent a future sacrifice to the organization of economic benefits (monetary in "a", "c", and "d", and a service to be provided in "b"). Situations "a", "b", and "c" all represent past transactions, while "d" represents an event which has not yet taken place as she has not purchased the vehicle and certainly has the ability to change her mind; thus there is the possibility to avoid the transaction. (Solution = d.)

Question

7. The assumption that an enterprise will remain in business indefinitely and will not liquidate in the near future is called the:
   a. economic entity assumption.
   b. going concern assumption.
   c. monetary unit assumption.
   d. periodicity assumption.

EXPLANATION: Read the question (while covering up the answer selections) and attempt to complete the statement. Compare your attempt with the selections. Hopefully, you anticipated the correct answer. If your attempt does not match any of the selections given, take each selection and write down the key words in the definitions of the term. This process should lead you to the correct response.

Answer selection "b" is correct because the going concern assumption implies that an enterprise will continue in business and will not liquidate within the foreseeable future. Selection "a" is incorrect because the economic entity assumption indicates that the activities of an accounting entity should be kept separate and distinct from all other accounting entities. Selection "c" is incorrect because the monetary unit assumption indicates that all transactions and events can be measured in terms of a common denominator—units of money. Selection "d" is incorrect because the periodicity assumption indicates that the economic activities of an enterprise can be divided into equally spaced artificial time periods. (Solution = b.)

Question

8. Pluto Magazine Company sells space to advertisers. The company requires an advertiser to pay for services one month before publication. Advertising revenue should be recognized when:
   a. an advertiser places an order.
   b. a bill is sent to an advertiser.
   c. the related cash is received.
   d. the related ad is published.

EXPLANATION: Read the last sentence of the question. We want to know the point at which revenue should be recognized. Write down what you know from the revenue recognition principle. Revenue is generally recognized when (1) realized or realizable, and (2) earned. Read the stem and think of how to apply the revenue recognition principle to the facts given. At the points when an order is placed and a bill is sent to an advertiser, revenue has neither been realized nor earned. At the point when the cash is received in advance of the publication, the revenue is realized but not earned. The revenue is earned when the related ad is published and, thus, should be recognized then. (Solution = d.)

Question

9. The historical cost principle provides that:
   a. items whose costs are insignificant compared to other amounts on the financial statements may be accounted for in the most expedient manner.
   b. assets and equities be expressed in terms of a common denominator.
   c. the recorded amount of an acquired item should be the fair market value of what is given or the fair market value of what is received in the exchange, whichever is more objectively determinable.
   d. the expenses of generating revenue should be recognized in the same period that the related revenue is recognized.

EXPLANATION: Briefly define the historical cost principle before you read the answer selections. See **Illustration 2-3**. Answer selection "a" describes the materiality constraint. Selection "b" describes the monetary unit assumption. Selection "d" relates to the matching principle. (Solution = c.)

Question

10. If revenue is received in the current period, but it is not earned until a future period, the related expenses of generating the revenue should **not** be recognized until that future period. This guideline is an application of the:
    a. revenue recognition principle.

b. full disclosure principle.
c. matching principle.
d. conservatism constraint.

EXPLANATION: The revenue recognition principle dictates that revenue be recognized (recorded and reported) in the period it is realized (or realizable) and earned. The matching principle dictates that expenses be recognized in the same period as the revenue that they helped to generate is recognized. Thus, if revenue is deferred, the related expenses should also be deferred. This is required provided the resultant cost deferral meets the definition of an asset (inventory, for example). (Solution = c.)

Question

11. The process of reporting an item in the financial statements of an enterprise is:
    a. recognition.
    b. realization.
    c. allocation.
    d. incorporation.

EXPLANATION: The term recognition refers to the process of formally recording or incorporating an item in the accounts and financial statements of an entity. An item that gets recorded in the accounts eventually gets reported in the financial statements of the enterprise. Realization is the process of converting non-cash resources and rights into money and is most precisely used in accounting and financial reporting to refer to sales of assets for cash or claims to cash. The term allocation refers to the process or result of allocating (assigning costs or systematically spreading costs). The term incorporation refers to the process of establishing a business in the corporate form of organization. (Solution = a.)

Question

12. Revenue is to be recognized when it is realized (or realizable) and earned. This statement refers to the:
    a. revenue recognition principle.
    b. matching principle.
    c. going concern assumption.
    d. consistency concept.

EXPLANATION: Briefly define each of the answer selections. Choose the item for which your definition most closely agrees with the question. See **Illustration 2-3**. The revenue recognition principle dictates that revenue be recognized (recorded and reported) in the period it is realized (or realizable) and earned. The matching principle dictates that expenses be recognized in the same period as the revenue that they helped to generate is recognized. The going concern assumption implies that an enterprise will continue in business indefinitely. The consistency concept or characteristic dictates that, for financial information to be useful, an entity is to apply the same accounting methods to similar events for successive accounting periods. (Solution = a.)

Question

13. In matters of doubt and great uncertainty, accounting issues should be resolved by choosing the alternative that has the least favourable effect on net income, assets, and owners' equity. This guidance comes from the:
    a. materiality constraint.
    b. industry practices constraint.
    c. conservatism constraint.
    d. full disclosure principle.

EXPLANATION: See **Illustration 2-4**. In matters of doubt and uncertainty, the accountant is conservative and chooses the accounting alternative that is the least likely to cause an overstatement of net income, assets, and owners' equity. (Solution = c.)

Question

14. When an entity charges the entire cost of an electric pencil sharpener to expense in the period when it was purchased, even though the appliance has an estimated life of five years, we have an application of the:
    a. matching principle.
    b. materiality constraint.
    c. historical cost principle.
    d. conservatism constraint.

EXPLANATION: When an item benefits operations of more than one period, the matching principle will dictate that the cost of the item be allocated (spread) systematically over the periods benefited. However, the materiality constraint dictates that an immaterial item need not be given strict accounting treatment; it can be given expedient treatment. The cost of a pencil sharpener would obviously be small and thus immaterial. Consequently, the materiality constraint is justification for departure from the matching principle in accounting for the cost of the pencil sharpener. (Solution = b.)

Question

15. The value of a conceptual framework is the fact that:
    a. it provides the correct answer for every financial reporting problem.
    b. it reduces the use of professional judgement and therefore management bias.

c. it does not allow choice.
d. it provides an established and accepted body of concepts and objectives that may be applied to any situation.

EXPLANATION: The conceptual framework improves consistency and comparability yet still allows professional judgement to be used. It does not provide a correct answer to every problem. (Solution = d.)

Question

16. The main decisions being made by external users of financial statements involve:
   a. resource allocation.
   b. stewardship assessment.
   c. both a. and b.
   d. neither a. nor b.

Explanation: Although many users have many differing needs, most users are concerned with resource allocation decisions and assessing management stewardship. (Solution = c.)

Question

17. Identify the traits that make information useful.
   a. comparability and consistency
   b. reliability and relevance
   c. understandability
   d. all of the above

EXPLANATION: Information must be understandable, relevant, reliable, comparable, and consistent to be useful. (Solution = d.)

Question

18. Which of the following best describes the periodicity assumption?
   a. The lifespan of the business is the only relevant period to consider in financial reporting.
   b. It is relevant to divide the lifespan of the business into smaller units so that the company may report to users on a more frequent basis.
   c. Dividing the lifespan of a business into smaller units creates too many allocation problems and, therefore, the periodicity assumption precludes its use.
   d. The only relevant reporting period is the fiscal year.

EXPLANATION: Users need timely information, whether it is daily, monthly, quarterly, or annually. Therefore, it is necessary to divide the lifespan into units (usually monthly, quarterly, and annually) to allow users to analyze the information on a regular basis. (Solution = b.)

Question

19. It is not always possible to incorporate all the concepts or ideas in the conceptual framework since some are in conflict with each other. Identify the conflicting concepts in the following scenario. It normally takes three months for the company to finalize its year-end numbers. By the time the auditor has audited the financial statements, it is five months into the next year.
    a. cost/benefit versus timeliness
    b. materiality versus reliability
    c. reliability versus timeliness
    d. timeliness versus consistency

EXPLANATION: The longer the company takes to ensure that the numbers are accurate, the more reliable they will be. They lose relevance, however, the less timely they are. (Solution = c.)

Question

20. Identify which concepts are in conflict in the following scenario. Unsure as to whether to book revenues now or when greater certainty exists with respect to collectibility, the company decides to recognize revenues in the period that the goods are delivered.
    a. revenue recognition versus conservatism
    b. revenue recognition versus materiality
    c. matching versus revenue recognition
    d. full disclosure versus revenue recognition

EXPLANATION: The revenue recognition principle dictates that revenues be recognized when earned, which is often when the risks and rewards of ownership pass. This, along with accrual accounting, would dictate earlier recognition. However, conservatism dictates that when the accountant is unsure as to how to handle a transaction, the option that does not overstate income is the more conservative choice and should be selected. (Solution = a.)

The Accounting Information System

Chapter 3

Overview

Accounting information must be accumulated and summarized before it can be communicated and analyzed. In this chapter, we will discuss the steps involved in the accounting cycle. We will emphasize the subject of adjusting entries. Throughout an accounting period, cash receipts and cash disbursements are recorded. At the end of the accounting period, adjusting entries are required so that revenues and expenses are reflected on the accrual basis of accounting. Adjusting entries are simply entries required to bring account balances up to date. The failure to record proper adjustments will cause errors on both the income statement and the balance sheet.

Study Steps

Understanding the Importance of Debits and Credits and the Accounting Cycle

Do not underestimate the importance of being able to journalize a transaction and prepare financial statements. Many students struggle through intermediate accounting without being able to master it because they do not have the fundamental bookkeeping skills.

Debits and credits are a fundamental building block in understanding financial reporting.

The best approach to this material is to attempt as many problems as possible and to verify answers against the solutions provided. This will reinforce the mechanics involved, the importance of balancing, and the dual-entry bookkeeping system. Again, it would normally be assumed that this material would have been covered in a previous course and, therefore, you should be proficient in this area. If you have not taken introductory accounting recently, a review of this material would be beneficial.

The accounting cycle involves capturing data, journalizing and posting it to the general ledger, taking a trial balance, making adjustments to the trial balance, summarizing and classifying accounts for inclusion into financial statements, and closing income statement accounts.

Adjustments to the trial balance are usually made at month-end, when financial statements are prepared. They involve corrections to accounts (often due to reconciliations with external information or subledgers), accruals, and entries to adjust the value of assets and liabilities to ensure that they are properly valued.

The preparation of financial statements requires grouping trial balance accounts into similar accounts. This reduces the amount of information that is presented since too much detail on the statements makes them difficult to interpret. This step requires significant professional judgment: some companies like to provide more detail and some less. Materiality is another consideration. That is, if an account is considered to be so insignificant that it would not affect decisions made by users, the amount is not shown separately.

GAAP requires the use of accrual accounting for the balance sheet and income statement since it provides more useful information to users. Under the accrual method, transactions are generally booked as soon as they can be estimated with any degree of reliability. Therefore, information is more complete and timely.

Becoming Proficient in Using a Work Sheet and the Accounting Equation

The accounting equation is a simple formula that encapsulates the relationships between financial statement elements.

Use the accounting equation to review the incremental impact of a transaction on the financial statements.

The work sheet is a mechanism for capturing unadjusted information and required adjustments to produce complete and accurate information.

Study the material in the text and complete as many exercises as possible using a worksheet. Mechanical proficiency is very important. Review the following illustrations and exercises until that proficiency has been achieved.

Tips on Chapter Topics

TIP! This chapter is an extremely important one. A good understanding of this chapter and an ability to think and work quickly with the concepts incorporated herein are necessary for comprehending subsequent chapters. Although adjusting entries were introduced in your principles course, you are likely to discover new dimensions to this subject in your intermediate accounting course: Pay close attention when studying this chapter!

TIP! When you encounter a transaction, always analyze it in terms of its effects on the elements of the basic accounting equation (or balance sheet equation). For your analysis to be complete, it must maintain balance in the basic accounting equation. The **basic accounting** equation is as follows:

ASSETS = LIABILITIES + OWNERS' EQUITY

or

A=L+OE

TIP! Assets are economic resources. Liabilities and owners' equity are sources of resources; liabilities are creditor sources, and owners' equity represents owner sources (owner investments and undistributed profits). The basic accounting equation simply states that the total assets (resources) at a point in time equal the total liabilities plus total owners' equity (sources of resources) at the same point in time.

TIP! **An understanding of the following terms is important.** (1) **Event**: A happening of consequence. An event generally is the source or cause of changes in assets, liabilities, and equity. Events may be external or internal. (2) **Transaction**: An external event involving a transfer or exchange between two or more entities. (3) **Account**: A systematic arrangement that shows the effect of transactions and other events on a specific asset or equity. A separate account is kept for each type of asset, liability, revenue, and expense, and for capital (owners' equity). (4) **Permanent and Temporary accounts**: Permanent (real) accounts are asset, liability, and equity accounts; they appear on the balance sheet. Temporary (nominal) accounts are revenue, expense, and dividend accounts; except for dividends, they appear on the income statement. Temporary accounts are periodically closed; permanent accounts are left open. (5) **Ledger**: The book (or computer printouts) containing the accounts. Each account usually has a separate page. A general ledger is a collection of all the asset, liability, owners' equity, revenue, and expense accounts. A subsidiary ledger contains the details related to a given general ledger account. (6) **Journal**: The book of original entry where transactions and selected other events are initially recorded. (7) **Posting**: The process of transferring the essential facts and figures from the book of original entry to the ledger accounts. (8) **Trial balance:** A list of all open accounts in the ledger and their balances. A trial balance may be prepared at any

TIP! time. (9) **Adjusting entries**: Entries made at the end of an accounting period to bring all accounts up to date on an accrual accounting basis so that correct financial statements can be prepared. (10) **Financial statements**: Statements that reflect the accounting data's collection, tabulation, and final summarization. Financial statements consist of the balance sheet, the income statement, the statement of cash flows, and the statement of retained earnings. (11) **Closing entries**: The formal process by which all temporary accounts are reduced to zero, and the net income or net loss is determined and transferred to the appropriate owners' equity account.

TIP! **Transactions** are the economic events of an entity recorded by accountants. Some events (happenings of consequence to an entity) are not measurable in terms of money and do not get recorded in the accounting records. Hiring employees, placing an order for supplies, greeting a customer, and quoting prices for products are examples of activities that do not by themselves constitute transactions.

TIP! In accordance with the **revenue recognition principle**, revenue is to be recognized (reported) in the period in which it is realized (or realizable) and earned. In accordance with the **matching principle**, the expenses incurred in generating revenues should be recognized in the same period as the revenues they helped to generate. First, the revenue recognition principle is applied to determine in what period(s) to recognize revenue. Then, the matching principle is applied to determine in what period(s) to recognize expense.

TIP! Adjusting entries are often required so that revenues and expenses are reflected on an accrual basis of accounting (revenues recognized when earned and expenses recognized when incurred) rather than on a cash basis of accounting. Therefore, adjusting entries reflect the accruals and prepayments of revenues and expenses and also estimated expenses. Adjusting entries are simply entries required to bring account balances up to date before financial statements can be prepared. The failure to record proper adjustments will cause errors in both the income statement and the balance sheet.

TIP! **Prepayments** result from **cash** flows that occur **before** expense or revenue recognition. That is, cash is paid for expenses that apply to more than one accounting period or cash is received for revenue that applies to more than one accounting period. The portion of the expense that applies to future periods is deferred by reporting a prepaid expense (asset) or the portion of the revenue that applies to future periods is deferred by reporting unearned revenue (liability) on the balance sheet.

TIP! **Accruals** result from **cash** flows that occur **after** expense or revenue recognition. That is, cash is to be paid or received in a future accounting period for an expense incurred or a revenue earned in the current period:

TIP! Notice that **none** of the adjusting entries discussed in Chapter 3 involves the **Cash** account. Therefore, if you are instructed to record **adjusting entries**, double check your work when it is completed. If you have used the Cash account in any adjusting entry, it is very likely in error. (The only time Cash belongs in an adjusting entry is when a bank reconciliation discloses a need to adjust the Cash account—this will be explained in Chapter 7—or when an error has been made that involves the Cash account, in which case a correcting entry is required).

TIP! Notice that each adjusting entry discussed in this chapter involves a balance sheet account **and** an income statement account.

When preparing homework assignments, working through the **Study Guide**, and answering exam questions, pay careful attention to whether a prepayment situation relates to a **cash inflow** or **cash outflow** for the entity in question. Be sure you then use the proper related account for recording the cash receipt or disbursement and correct terminology in explaining the scenario. If cash is **received** in a rental situation, the amount will be recorded (by a credit) in either an earned rent revenue account or an unearned rent revenue account, **not** in an expense or a prepaid expense account. If cash is **paid** in a rental situation, the amount will be recorded (by a debit) in either an expense or a prepaid expense account: **TIP!**

In an adjusting entry for an accrual (accrued revenue or accrued expense), the word "accrued" is **not** needed in either account title. If you choose to use the word "accrued" in an account title, it is appropriate to do so **only** in the balance sheet account title. For example, the entry to record accrued salaries of $1,000 is as follows: **TIP!**

Salaries Expense	1,000	
Salaries Payable		1,000

The word "accrued" is not needed in either account title, but it could be used in the liability account title if desired (the account title would then be Accrued Salaries Payable). It would be wrong to insert the word "accrued" in the expense account title. Some people simply call the credit account "Accrued Salaries" (rather than "Salaries Payable") but we advise that you include the key word "Payable" and omit the unnecessary word "Accrued". **TIP!**

An unadjusted trial balance is referred to as either "unadjusted trial balance" or simply "trial balance". An adjusted trial balance is referred to as either "adjusted trial balance" or the "adjusted trial". **TIP!**

Closing entries are necessary at the end of an accounting period to prepare the temporary accounts (revenues, expenses, gains, and losses) for the recording of transactions for the next accounting period. Closing entries are prepared after the temporary account balances have been used to prepare the income statement. Only temporary accounts are closed. Permanent accounts are never closed; their balances continue into the next accounting period. **Temporary** accounts are often called **nominal** accounts; **permanent** accounts are often called **real** accounts. **TIP!**

A temporary account with a credit balance is closed by a debit to that account and a credit to Income Summary. A temporary account with a debit balance is closed by a credit to that account and a debit to Income Summary. The Income Summary account is closed to an owners' equity account (Retained Earnings for a corporation) and is often called the Revenue and Expense Summary. **TIP!**

If a separate account is used to record owner withdrawals or owner distributions (such as Dividends Declared for a corporation or Owner's Drawings for a proprietorship or partnership), this account is also closed at the end of the accounting period, but it is not closed to the Income Summary account because it is not a component of the net income calculation. Rather, it is closed directly to Retained Earnings (for a corporation) or to Owner's Capital (for a proprietorship or partnership). **TIP!**

A **post-closing trial balance** contains only permanent accounts because the temporary accounts all have a zero balance after the closing process. A post-closing trial balance is prepared to check on the equality of debits and credits after the closing process. **TIP!**

TIP! In preparing a 10-column work sheet, the debit and credit columns for every column pair must be equal before you can proceed to the next column pair. (This pertains to the first three column pairs). All five pairs of columns must balance for a work sheet to be complete.

TIP! You should be able to define the following four terms and describe the related adjusting entry for each; they are:

1. A **prepaid expense** is an expense that has been paid but has not been incurred. An adjusting entry for a deferred expense involves an EXPENSE account and an ASSET (prepaid expense) account. Ex: Prepaid rent, rent expense,

2. An **unearned revenue** is a revenue that has been collected but has not been earned. An adjusting entry for an unearned revenue involves a LIABILITY (unearned revenue) account and a REVENUE account. Ex: Cash collected for a magazine subscription. When the magazine is mailed to the customer, the unearned revenue would be earned.

3. An **accrued expense** is an expense that has been incurred but has not been paid. An adjusting entry for an accrued expense involves an EXPENSE account and a LIABILITY (payable account). Ex: Wages payable, wages expense.

4. An **accrued revenue** is a revenue that has been earned but has not been received. An adjusting entry for accrued revenue involves an ASSET (receivable) account and a REVENUE account. Ex: A painter that has painted a house, but has not received payment yet.

TIP! An **unearned revenue** may be called a **deferred revenue** because the recognition of revenue is being deferred to a future period; thus, a credit is carried on the balance sheet now and will be released to the income statement in a future period when the related revenue is earned.

TIP! An adjusting entry for prepaid insurance expense (expense paid but not incurred) involves an expense account and an asset account. The expense account is often called Insurance Expense or Expired Insurance. Possible titles for the asset account include Prepaid Insurance, Deferred Insurance Expense, Prepaid Insurance Expense, Deferred Insurance, and Unexpired Insurance.

TIP! An adjusting entry for unearned rent revenue (revenue collected but not earned) involves a liability account and a revenue account. Possible titles for the liability account include Unearned Rent Revenue, Unearned Rent, Deferred Rent Revenue, Rent Revenue Received in Advance, and Rental Income Collected in Advance. The use of Prepaid Rent Revenue as an account title is **not** appropriate because the term prepaid usually refers to the payment of cash in advance, not the receipt of cash in advance. The revenue account is often called Rent Revenue or Rental Income or Rent Earned.

TIP! In an adjusting entry to record accrued interest revenue (revenue earned but not received), the debit is to an asset account and the credit is to a revenue account. Possible names for that asset account are Interest Receivable and Accrued Interest Receivable. Possible names for the revenue account include Interest Revenue, Interest Income, and Interest Earned.

TIP! In an adjusting entry to record accrued salaries expenses (expense incurred, but not paid) the debit is to an expense account and the credit is to a liability account. The expense account is usually titled Salaries Expense. Possible names for the liability account include Salaries Payable and Accrued Salaries Payable.

TIP! The ability to capture information completely and accurately is an essential and fundamental skill.

Illustration 3-1

Double-Entry (Debit and Credit) Accounting System

The debit and credit rules are summarized below:

Asset Accounts	
Debit	Credit
Increase	Decrease
+	–

Liability Accounts	
Debit	Credit
Decrease	Increase
–	+

Dividends Account	
Debit	Credit
Increase	Decrease
+	–

Shareholders' Equity Accounts	
Debit	Credit
Decrease	Increase
–	+

Expense Accounts	
Debit	Credit
Increase	Decrease
+	–

↑ **Normal Balance** (left side: Debit)

Revenue Accounts	
Debit	Credit
Decrease	Increase
–	+

↑ **Normal Balance** (right side: Credit)

Notice that the accounts above are arranged in such a way that all of the increases ("+" signs) are on the outside and all of the decreases ("–" signs) are on the inside of this diagram.

TIP! An **account** is an individual accounting record of increases and decreases in a specific asset, liability, or stockholders' equity item. In its simplest form, an account consists of three parts: (1) the title of the account, (2) a left or debit side, and (3) a right or credit side. Because the alignment of these parts of an account resembles the letter T, it is often referred to as a **T-account**.

TIP! "Credit" does **not** always mean favourable or unfavourable. In accounting, "debit" and "credit" simply mean left and right, respectively. "Debit" is a term that refers to the left side of any account. Thus, the debit side of an account is always the left side. "Credit" is a word that simply refers to the right side of an account. Thus, the credit side of an account is always the right side of the account. The phrase "to debit an account" means to enter an amount on the debit (left) side of an account. Debit can be abbreviated as "Dr." and credit is abbreviated as "Cr."

TIP! A "+" indicates an increase and a "–" indicates a decrease. Therefore, a transaction which causes an increase in an asset is recorded by a debit to the related asset account; a transaction which causes a decrease in the same asset is recorded by a credit to the same account.

TIP! The normal balance of an account is the side where increases are recorded. Therefore, the normal balance of an asset account is a debit balance; the normal balance of a liability account is a credit balance.

TIP! A separate account should exist in the general ledger for each item that will appear on the financial statements.

TIP! At this stage of your study of accounting, you should be able to quickly and correctly identify the debit and credit rules for any given account. If you are slow at this process, drill on the rules until you improve. If you memorize the rules for an asset account, you can figure out the rules for all other types of accounts by knowing which rules are the opposite of the rules for assets and which are the same. Increases in assets are recorded by debits. Because liabilities and owners' equity are on the other side of the equals sign in the basic accounting equation, they must have debit and credit rules opposite of the rules for assets. Therefore, a liability or an owners' equity account is increased by a credit entry. Revenues earned increase owners' equity (retained earnings for a corporate form of organization) so the rules to record increases in revenue are the same as the rules to record increases in an owners' equity account (increases are recorded by credits). Because expenses and owners' withdrawals reduce owners' equity, they have debit/credit rules which are opposite of the rules for an owners' equity account.

TIP! In the double-entry system of accounting, for every debit there must be a credit(s) of equal amount, and vice versa.

Exercise 3-1

PURPOSE: This exercise will test your understanding of the debit and credit rules.

Instructions

For each account listed below, put a check mark (√) in the appropriate column to indicate if it is increased by an entry in the debit (left) side of the account or by an entry in the credit (right) side of the account. The first one is done for you.

	Account	Debit	Credit
1.	Cash	√	
2.	Sales Revenue		✓
3.	Commissions Expense	✓	
4.	Advertising Expense	✓	
5.	Salaries Payable		✓
6.	Prepaid Insurance	✓	
7.	Property Taxes Payable		✓
8.	Property Tax Expense	✓	
9.	Dividends Declared		✓
10.	Interest Revenue	✓	
11.	Salaries Expense	✓	
12.	Commissions Revenue	✓	
13.	Unearned Rent Revenue	✓	
14.	Equipment	✓	
15.	Note Payable		✓
16.	Building	✓	
17.	Accounts Payable		✓
18.	Supplies on Hand	✓	
19.	Accounts Receivable	✓	
20.	Common Shares		✓
21.	Retained Earnings		✓
22.	Mortgage Payable	✓	
23.	Loan Receivable	✓	
24.	Bank Loan Payable		✓
25.	Audit Fees Incurred	✓	
26.	Dividend Income		✓
27.	Fees Incurred	✓	
28.	Fees Earned		✓
29.	Utilities Expense	✓	
30.	Utilities Payable		✓

TIP! In essence, you are being asked to identify the normal balance of each of the accounts listed. The normal balance of an account is the side where increases are recorded.

Solution to Exercise 3-1

APPROACH: Determine the classification of the account (asset, liability, owners' equity, revenue, or expense). Think about the debit and credit rules for that classification. Refer to **Illustration 3-1** and the related **TIPS** for those rules. In determining the classification of an account, look for the key words, if any, in each individual item. For example: (1) the words Revenue, Earned, or Income are often associated with a revenue account, (2) the words Expense, Incurred, or Expired are often associated with an expense account, (3) the words Receivable or Prepaid Expense refer to types of asset accounts, and (4) the words Payable or Unearned Revenue refer to types of liabilities.

	Debit	Credit	Classification
1. Cash	√		Asset
2. Sales Revenue		√	Revenue
3. Commissions Expense	√		Expense
4. Advertising Expense	√		Expense
5. Salaries Payable		√	Liability
6. Prepaid Insurance	√		Asset
7. Property Taxes Payable		√	Liability
8. Property Tax Expense	√		Expense
9. Dividends Declared	√		Owners' Equity (Owners' Withdrawals)
10. Interest Revenue		√	Revenue
11. Salaries Expense	√		Expense
12. Commissions Revenue		√	Revenue
13. Unearned Rent Revenue		√	Liability
14. Equipment	√		Asset
15. Note Payable		√	Liability
16. Building	√		Asset
17. Accounts Payable		√	Liability
18. Supplies on Hand	√		Asset
19. Accounts Receivable	√		Asset
20. Common Stock		√	Owners' Equity (Owners' Investments)
21. Retained Earnings		√	Owners' Equity (Earned Capital)
22. Mortgage Payable		√	Liability
23. Loan Receivable	√		Asset
24. Bank Loan Payable		√	Liability
25. Audit Fees Incurred	√		Expense
26. Dividend Income		√	Revenue
27. Fees Incurred	√		Expense
28. Fees Earned		√	Revenue
29. Utilities Expense	√		Expense
30. Utilities Payable		√	Liability

Exercise 3-2

PURPOSE: This exercise will review how to record transactions in the general journal.

Transactions for the Motorboat Repair Shop, Inc. for August 2008 are listed below.

1. August 1 — Joan and Phillip began the business by each depositing $2,500 of personal funds in the business bank account in exchange for common shares of the newly formed corporation.
2. August 2 — Joan rented space for the shop behind a strip mall and paid August rent of $800 out of the business bank account.
3. August 3 — The shop purchased supplies for cash, $3,000.
4. August 4 — The shop paid *Cupboard News*, a local newspaper, $300 for an ad appearing in the Sunday edition.
5. August 5 — The shop repaired a boat for a customer. The customer paid cash of $1,300 for services rendered.
6. August 13 — The shop purchased supplies for $900 by paying cash of $200 and charging the rest on account.
7. August 14 — The shop repaired a boat for Zonie Kinkennon, a champion skier, for $3,600. Phillip collected $1,000 in cash and put the rest on Zonie's account.
8. August 24 — The shop collected cash of $400 from Zonie Kinkennon.
9. August 28 — The shop paid $200 to Mini Maid for cleaning services for the month of August.
10. August 31 — The board of directors of the corporation declared and paid a dividend of $400 in cash to its shareholders.

Instructions

(a) Explain the impact of each transaction on the elements of the basic accounting equation and translate that into debit and credit terms.

(b) Journalize the transactions listed above. Include a brief explanation with each journal entry.

Solution to Exercise 3-2

(a)	1.	Increase in Cash. Increase in Common Shares.	Debit Cash. Credit Common Shares.
	2.	Increase in Rent Expense. Decrease in Cash.	Debit Rent Expense. Credit Cash.

3.	Increase in Supplies on Hand. Decrease in Cash.	Debit Supplies on Hand. Credit Cash.
4.	Increase in Advertising Expense. Decrease in Cash.	Debit Advertising Expense. Credit Cash.
5.	Increase in Cash. Increase in Service Revenue.	Debit Cash. Credit Service Revenue.
6.	Increase in Supplies on Hand. Decrease in Cash. Increase in Accounts Payable.	Debit Supplies on Hand. Credit Cash. Credit Accounts Payable.
7.	Increase in Cash. Increase in Accounts Receivable. Increase in Service Revenue.	Debit Cash. Debit Accounts Receivable. Credit Service Revenue.
8.	Increase in Cash. Decrease in Accounts Receivable.	Debit Cash. Credit Accounts Receivable.
9.	Increase in Cleaning Expense. Decrease in Cash.	Debit Cleaning Expense. Credit Cash.
10.	Decrease in Retained Earnings. Increase in Dividends Payable.	Debit Retained Earnings. Credit Dividends Payable.

APPROACH: Write down the effects of each transaction on the basic accounting equation. Think about the individual asset, liability, or shareholders' equity accounts involved. Apply the debit and credit rules to translate the effects into a journal entry. Refer to **Illustration 3-1** for the debit and credit rules for each type of account.

GENERAL JOURNAL **J1**

Date		Account Titles and Explanations	Ref.	Debit	Credit
(b)					
2008					
1.	Aug. 1	Cash		5,000	
		Common Shares			5,000
		(Issued shares of stock for cash.)			
2.	2	Rent Expense		800	
		Cash			800
		(Paid August rent.)			
3.	3	Supplies on Hand		3,000	
		Cash			3,000
		(Purchased supplies for cash.)			

4.	4	Advertising Expense	300	
		Cash		300
		(Paid *Cupboard News* for advertising.)		
5.	5	Cash	1,300	
		Service Revenue		1,300
		(Received cash for service fees earned.)		
6.	13	Supplies on Hand	900	
		Cash		200
		Accounts Payable		700
		(Purchased supplies for cash and on credit.)		
7.	14	Cash	1,000	
		Accounts Receivable	2,600	
		Service Revenue		3,600
		(Performed services for customer for cash and on credit.)		
8.	24	Cash	400	
		Accounts Receivable		400
		(Received cash from Zonie Kinkennon on account.)		
9.	28	Cleaning Expense	200	
		Cash		200
10.	31	Retained Earnings (or Dividends Declared)	400	
		Dividends Payable		400

Exercise 3-3

PURPOSE: This exercise will provide you with examples of adjusting entries for the accrual of expenses and revenues.

The following information relates to the Yuppy Clothing Sales Company at the end of 2007. The accounting period is the calendar year. This is the company's first year of operations.

1. Employees are paid every Friday for the five-day work week ending on that day. Salaries amount to $2,400 per week. The accounting period ends on a Thursday.
2. On October 1, 2005, Yuppy borrowed $8,000 cash by signing a note payable due in one year at 8 percent interest. Interest is due when the principal is paid.

3. A note for $2,000 was received from a customer in a sales transaction on May 1, 2007. The note matures in one year and bears 12 percent interest per annum. Interest is due when the principal is due.
4. A portion of Yuppy's parking lot is used by executives of a neighbouring company. A person pays $6 per day for each day's use, and the parking fees are due by the fifth business day following the month of use. The fees for December 31, 2007, amount to $1,260.

Instructions

Using the information given above, prepare the necessary adjusting entries at December 31, 2007.

Solution to Exercise 3-3

1. Salaries Expense	1,920	
Salaries Payable		1,920
($2,400 ÷ 5 = $480); ($480 x 4 = $1,920 accrued salaries.)		
2. Interest Expense	160	
Interest Payable		160
($8,000 x 8% x 3/12 = $160 accrued interest.)		
3. Interest Receivable	160	
Interest Revenue		160
($2,000 x 12% x 8/12 = $160 accrued interest.)		
4. Parking Fees Receivable	1,260	
Parking Fees Revenue		1,260

EXPLANATION: Write down the definitions for accrued expense and accrued revenue. Think about what is to be accomplished by each of the adjustments required in this exercise. An **accrued expense** is an expense that has been incurred but not paid. The "incurred" part results in an increase in Expense (debit) and the "not paid" part results in an increase in Payable (credit). An **accrued revenue** is a revenue that has been earned but not received. The "earned" part results in an increase in Revenue (credit) and the "not received" part results in an increase in Receivable (debit).

Exercise 3-4

PURPOSE: This exercise will provide you with examples of adjusting entries for prepaid expenses and unearned revenues (that is, for the deferral of expenses and revenues).

The following information relates to the "I AM" Magazine Company at the end of 2008. The accounting period is the calendar year.

1. An insurance premium of $8,000 was paid on April 1, 2008, and was charged to Prepaid Insurance. The premium covers a 24-month period beginning April 1, 2008.
2. The Office Supplies on Hand account showed a balance of $3,500 at the beginning of 2008. Supplies costing $12,000 were purchased during 2008 and debited to the asset account. Supplies of $2,200 were on hand at December 31, 2008.
3. On July 1, 2008, cash of $48,000 was received from subscribers (customers) for a 36-month subscription period beginning on that date. The receipt was recorded by a debit to Cash and a credit to Unearned Subscription Revenue.
4. At the beginning of 2008, the Unearned Advertising Revenue account had a balance of $75,000. During 2008, collections from advertisers of $800,000 were recorded by credits to Advertising Revenue. At the end of 2008, revenues received but not earned are computed to be $51,000.

Instructions

Using the information given above, prepare the necessary adjusting entries at December 31, 2008.

Solution to Exercise 3-4

1. Insurance Expense	3,000	
Prepaid Insurance		3,000
($8,000 x 9/24 = $3,000 expired cost.)		
2. Supplies Expense	13,300	
Office Supplies on Hand..		13,300
($3,500 + $12,000 – $2,200 = $13,300 supplies consumed.)		
3. Unearned Subscription Revenue	8,000	
Subscription Revenue		8,000
($48,000 x 6/36 = $8,000 earned revenue.)		

4. Unearned Advertising Revenue	24,000	
Advertising Revenue		24,000
($75,000 – $51,000 = $24,000 earned revenue.)		

EXPLANATION: Write down the definitions for prepaid expense and unearned revenue. Think about what is to be accomplished by each of the adjustments required in this exercise. A **prepaid expense** is an expense that has been paid but not incurred. In a case where the prepayment was recorded as an increase in an asset account (such as Prepaid Expense or Supplies on Hand), the adjusting entry will record the increase in Expense (debit) and a decrease in the recorded Asset (credit) due to the consumption of the benefits yielded by the earlier prepayment. An **unearned revenue** is a revenue that has been received but not earned. In a case where the cash receipt was recorded as an increase in a liability account (such as Unearned Revenue), the adjusting entry will record a decrease in the recorded liability Unearned Revenue (debit) and an increase in Earned Revenue (credit) due to the earning of all or a portion of the revenue represented by the earlier cash receipt.

It is helpful to sketch a T-account for the related asset or liability account. Enter the amounts reflected in that account before adjustment, enter the desired ending balance, and notice how the required adjustment is then obvious from facts reflected in your T-account. The T-accounts would appear as follows:

1.

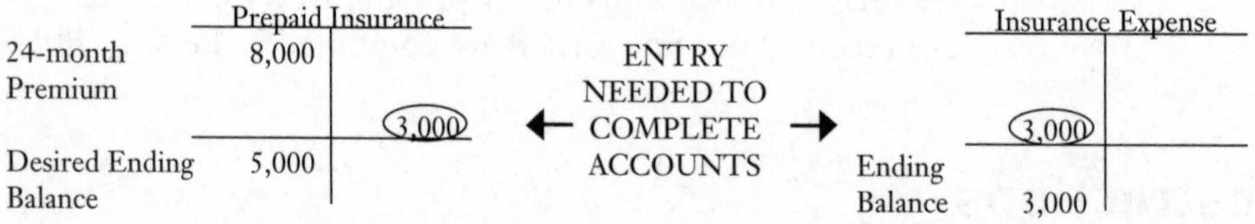

2.

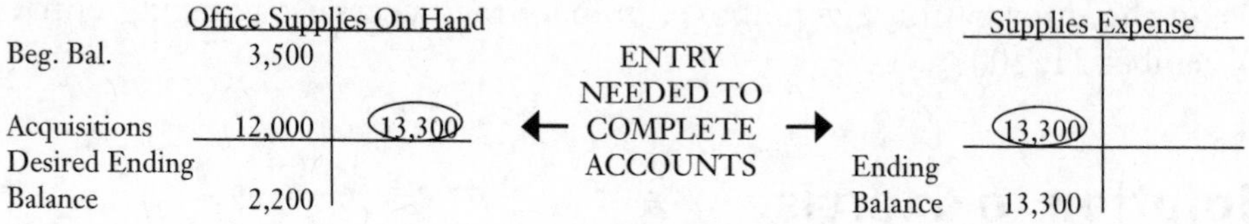

3.

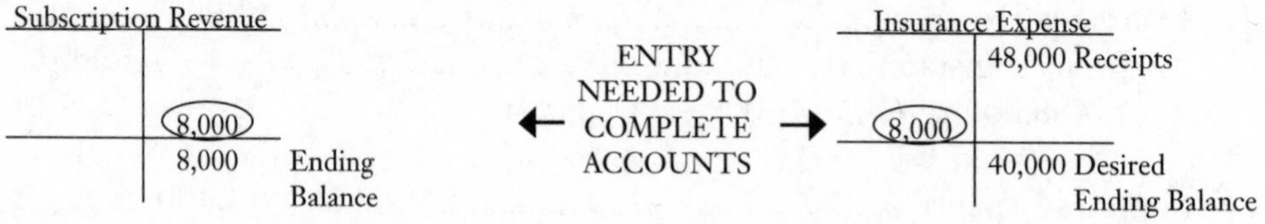

4.

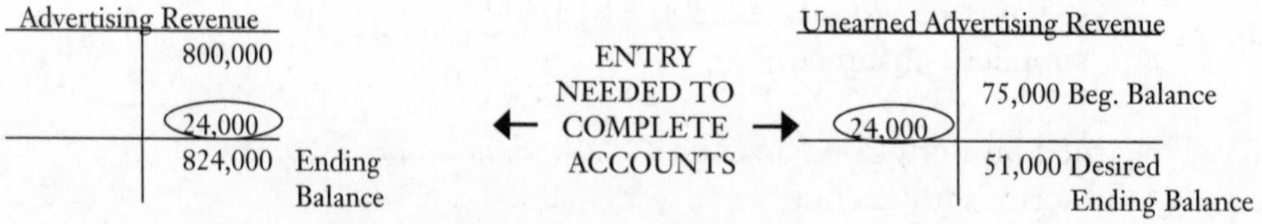

Illustration 3-2

Summary of Adjustment Relationships and Explanations

Type of Adjustment	Account Relationship	Reason for Adjustment	Account Balances Before Adjustment	Adjusting Entry
1. Prepaid Expense	Asset and Expense	(a) Prepaid expense initially recorded in asset account has been consumed; or,	Asset overstated Expense understated	Dr. Expense Cr. Asset
		*(b) Prepaid expense initially recorded in expense account has not been consumed.	Asset understated Expense overstated	Dr. Asset Cr. Expense
2. Unearned Revenue	Liability and Revenue	(a) Unearned revenue initially recorded in liability account has been earned; or,	Liability overstated Revenue understated	Dr. Liability Cr. Revenue
		*(b) Unearned revenue initially recorded in revenue account has not been earned.	Liability understated Revenue overstated	Dr. Revenue Cr. Liability
3. Accrued Expense	Expense and Liability	Expense incurred has not been billed nor paid nor recorded.	Expense understated Liability understated	Dr. Expense Cr. Liability
4. Accrued Revenues	Asset and Revenue	Revenue earned has not been billed nor collected nor recorded.	Asset understated Revenue understated	Dr. Asset Cr. Revenue
5. Estimated Item	Asset and Expense	(a) A previously recorded long-lived asset has now been partially consumed; or,	Asset overstated Expense understated	Dr. Expense Cr. Contra Asset
		(b) An existing asset is not fully realizable.	Asset overstated Expense understated	Dr. Expense Cr. Contra Asset

EXPLANATION:

1. When expenses are paid for before they are incurred, the payment may either be recorded by a debit to an asset account (prepaid expense) or by a debit to an expense account. At the end of the accounting period, the accounts are adjusted as needed. If the prepayment was initially recorded by use of a prepaid (asset) account, the consumed portion is transferred to an expense account in the adjusting entry. Whereas, if the prepayment was initially recorded by use of an expense account, an adjusting entry is required only if a portion of the expense remains prepaid at the end of the accounting period (in which case the unconsumed portion is transferred to an asset account). (See **Illustration 3-3** for an example).

2. When revenues are received before they are earned, the receipt may either be recorded by a credit to a liability account (unearned revenue) or by a credit to a revenue account. At the end of the accounting period, the

accounts are adjusted as needed. If the collection was initially recorded by a credit to a liability account (unearned revenue), the earned portion is transferred to a revenue account in the adjusting entry. Whereas, if the collection was initially recorded by use of a revenue account, an adjusting entry is required only if a portion of the revenue remains unearned at the end of the accounting period (in which case the unearned portion is transferred to a liability account). (See **Illustration 3-3** for an example).

3. Expenses are often incurred before they are paid. An expense incurred but not yet paid is called an **accrued expense**. If at the end of an accounting period this accrued expense has not been recorded (which is often the case because it usually has not been billed yet by the vendor), it must be recorded by way of an adjusting entry. Expense that accrues with the passage of time (such as interest expense) is a good example of a reason to need an accrued expense (or accrued liability) type adjusting entry.

4. Revenues are often earned before they are collected. Revenue earned but not received is called an **accrued revenue**. If at the end of an accounting period this accrued revenue has not been recorded (which is often the case because it usually has not been billed yet), it must be recorded by way of an adjusting entry. Revenue that accrues with the passage of time (such as interest revenue) is a good example of a reason to need an accrued revenue (or accrued asset) type adjusting entry.

5. The cost of most long-lived tangible assets is allocated to expense in a systematic and rational manner. The entry to record the expiration of cost due to the consumption of benefits yielded by the asset is a debit to Amortization Expense and a credit to Accumulated Amortization. The amortization of intangibles is treated in a similar manner. A reduction in the net realizable value of accounts receivable or inventories is recorded in an adjusting entry by a charge to expense and a credit to a contra asset account.

TIP! Examine each type of adjustment explained above and notice the logic of the resulting entry. For example, an adjustment to recognize supplies used (when the supplies were recorded in an asset account when purchased) should reduce assets and increase expenses.

TIP! Keep in mind that for accrued items (accrued revenues and accrued expenses), the related cash flow follows the period in which the relevant revenue or expense is recognized; whereas, with prepayment type items (unearned revenues and prepaid expenses), the related cash flow **precedes** the period in which the relevant revenue or expense is recognized.

TIP! For example, assume the accounting period is the calendar year. Consider an accrued expense such as accrued salaries at the end of 2008. An adjusting entry will be recorded at the end of 2008, so the expense will get reported on the 2008 income statement. The related cash payment to employees will take place in the following accounting period (2009, in this case). For another example, consider a prepaid expense such as the prepayment of rent in December 2008 for January 2009 occupancy. The cash payment occurs in December 2008. The expense is incurred and recognized in the following accounting period (January 2009).

Illustration 3-3

Alternative Treatments of Prepaid Expenses and Unearned Revenues

When a company writes a cheque to pay for an item that affects expense in at least two different time periods (such as for an insurance premium or a licence or dues), the bookkeeper may record the payment in one of two ways: as a prepaid expense (asset) or as an expense. The first way is used most often in introductory accounting textbooks; the second is used most often in the real world. Regardless of the way the payment is recorded, an appropriate adjusting entry will be made at the end of the accounting period so that correct balances appear on the income statement and the balance sheet. For example, a $1,200 payment is made on April 1, 2008, for a 12-month insurance premium covering the time between April 1, 2008, and March 31, 2009. (Assume a calendar-year reporting period). A comparison of the two possible approaches appears below.

Prepayment (Cash Paid) Initially Debited to Asset Account				**OR**	**Prepayment (Cash Paid) Initially Debited to Expense Account**			
4/1	Prepaid Insurance	1,200			4/1	Insurance Expense	1,200	
	Cash		1,200			Cash		1,200
12/31	Insurance Expense	900			12/31	Prepaid Insurance	300	
	Prepaid Insurance		900			Insurance Expense		300

After posting the entries, the accounts appear as follows:

Prepaid Insurance (asset approach)

Debit		Credit	
4/1	1,200	12/31 Adj.	900
12/31 Bal.	300		

Prepaid Insurance (expense approach)

Debit		Credit	
12/31 Adj.	300		

Insurance Expense (asset approach)

Debit		Credit	
12/31 Adj.	900		

Insurance Expense (expense approach)

Debit		Credit	
4/1	1,200	12/31 Adj.	300
12/31 Bal.	900		

Notice that regardless of the path, you end up at the same place—with a balance of $300 in Prepaid Insurance and a balance of $900 in Insurance Expense. That was your objective—to report balances in accordance with the accrual basis of accounting.

TIP! Reversing entries are never required. But if it is company policy to use reversing entries where appropriate, either or both of the above adjusting entries illustrated in the left column would **not** get reversed since to do so would result in re-establishing an asset amount that the adjusting entry indicated had expired. The adjusting entry illustrated in the right column **can be** reversed since a reversing entry will record $300 of insurance expense in the new accounting period (2009), which is the period we expect the remaining $300 of premium to pertain to.

When a company receives cash from a customer in advance of earning the related revenue, the bookkeeper may record the receipt in one of two ways. Either as an unearned revenue (liability) or as an earned revenue. The first way is used most often in introductory accounting textbooks; the second is used most often in the real world. Regardless of the way the receipt is recorded, an appropriate adjusting entry will be made at the end of the accounting period so that correct balances appear on the income statement and the balance sheet. For example, $1,200 is received on May 1, 2008, for a 12-month magazine subscription covering the time between May 1, 2008, and April 30, 2009. (Assume a calendar-year reporting period). A comparison of the two possible approaches appears below:

Unearned Revenue (Cash Received) Initially Credited to Liability Account				OR	Unearned Revenue (Cash Received) Initially Credited to Revenue Account			
5/1	Cash	1,200			5/1	Cash	1,200	
	Unearned Sub. Rev.		1,200			Subscription Revenue		1,200
12/31	Unearned Sub. Rev.	800			12/31	Subscription Revenue	400	
	Subscription Revenue		800			Unearned Sub. Rev.		400

After posting the entries, the accounts appear as follows:

Unearned Subscription Revenue (left)

12/31 Adj.	800	5/1	1,200
		12/31 Bal.	400

Unearned Subscription Revenue (right)

		12/31 Adj.	400

Subscription Revenue (left)

		12/31 Adj.	800

Subscription Revenue (right)

12/31 Adj.	400	5/1	1,200
		12/31 Bal.	800

Notice that the balances in the accounts are the same regardless of the approach used; that is, Unearned Subscription Revenue is $400, and Subscription Revenue is $800 at December 31, 2008.

TIP! The adjusting entry illustrated in the left column would not be subject to reversal; a reversing entry can be used with the approach illustrated in the right column.

Exercise 3-5

PURPOSE: This exercise will provide you with examples of adjusting entries for:

(1) Prepaid expenses when cash payments are recorded in an asset (permanent) account.

(2) Prepaid expenses when cash payments are recorded in an expense (temporary) account.

(3) Unearned revenues when cash receipts are recorded in a liability (permanent) account.

(4) Unearned revenues when cash receipts are recorded in a revenue (temporary) account.

Thus, this exercise will review the alternative treatments of prepaid expenses and unearned revenues discussed in **Illustration 3-3**.

Each situation described below is **independent** of the others.

(1) Office supplies are recorded in an asset account when acquired. There were $400 of supplies on hand at the beginning of the period. Cash purchases of office supplies during the period amount to $900. A count of supplies at the end of the period shows $320 worth to be on hand.

(2) Office supplies are recorded in an expense account when acquired. There were $400 of supplies on hand at the beginning of the period. Cash purchases of office supplies during the period amount to $900. A count of supplies at the end of the period shows $320 worth to be on hand. No reversing entries are used.

(3) Receipts from customers for magazine subscriptions are recorded as a liability when cash is collected in advance of delivery. The beginning balance in the liability account was $6,700. During the period, $54,000 was received for subscriptions. At the end of the period, it was determined that the balance of the Unearned Subscription Revenue account should be $8,000.

(4) Receipts from customers for magazine subscriptions are recorded as revenue when cash is collected in advance of delivery. The beginning balance in the liability account was $6,700. During the period, $54,000 was received for subscriptions. At the end of the period, it was determined that the balance of the Unearned Subscription Revenue account should be $8,000. No reversing entries are used.

Instructions

For each of the **independent** situations above:

(a) Prepare the appropriate adjusting entry in general journal form.

(b) Indicate the amount of revenue or expense that will appear on the income statement for the period.

(c) Indicate the balance of the applicable asset or liability account at the end of the period.

(d) Indicate the amount of cash received or paid during the period.

(e) Indicate the change in the applicable asset or liability account from the beginning of the period to the end of the period.

TIP! It would be helpful to draw T-accounts for each situation. Enter the information given as it would be, or needs to be, reflected in the accounts. Solve for the adjusting entry that would be necessary to "reconcile" the facts given.

Solution to Exercise 3-5

(1)	a. Office Supplies Expense	980	
	Office Supplies on Hand		980
	b. Office Supplies Expense	$980	
	c. Office Supplies on Hand	$320	
	d. Cash paid	$900	
	e. Decrease in Office Supplies on Hand	$ 80	

APPROACH:

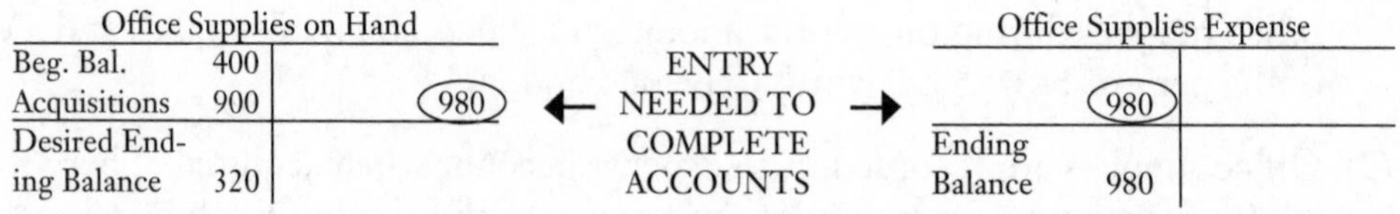

(2)	a. Office Supplies Expense	80	
	Office Supplies on Hand		80
	b. Office Supplies Expense	$980	
	c. Office Supplies on Hand	$320	
	d. Cash paid	$900	
	e. Decrease in Office Supplies on Hand	$ 80	

APPROACH:

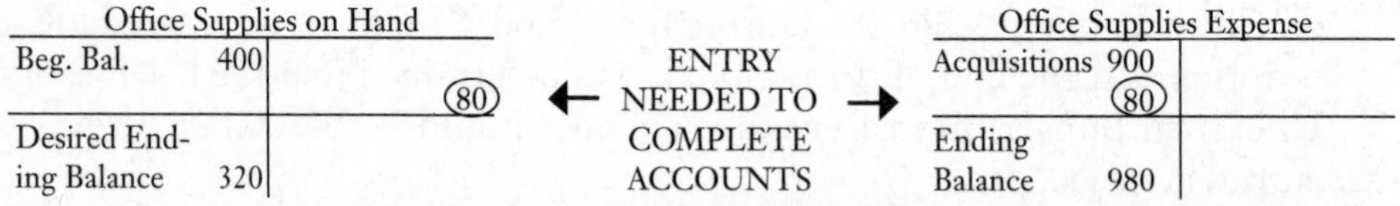

TIP! Compare situation (1) with situation (2). Notice the facts are the same **except** for the account debited for acquisitions of office supplies. The solution is then the same except for the adjusting entry required.

(3)	a. Unearned Subscription Revenue	52,700	
	Subscription Revenue		52,700
	b. Subscription Revenue	$52,700	
	c. Unearned Subscription Revenue	$ 8,000	
	d. Cash received	$54,000	
	e. Increase in Unearned Subscription Revenue	$ 1,300	

APPROACH:

Subscription Revenue			Unearned Subscription Revenue	
		ENTRY		Beg. Bal. 6,700
	(52,700)	← NEEDED TO →	(52,700)	Receipts 54,000
	Ending Balance 52,700	COMPLETE ACCOUNTS		Desired Ending Bal. 8,000

(4) a. Subscription Revenue 1,300
Unearned Subscription Revenue 1,300
b. Subscription Revenue $52,700
c. Unearned Subscription Revenue $ 8,000
d. Cash received $54,000
e. Increase in Unearned Subscription Revenue $ 1,300

APPROACH:

Unearned Subscription Revenue			Subscription Revenue	
	Beg. Bal. 6,700	ENTRY		Receipts 54,000
	(1,300)	← NEEDED TO →	(1,300)	
	Desired Ending Bal. 8,000	COMPLETE ACCOUNTS		Ending Balance 52,700

TIP!

Compare situation (3) with situation (4). Notice the facts are the same except for the account credited for receipt of revenue in advance of the period in which the revenue is earned. The solution is the same **except** for the adjusting entry required.

You should be able to handle what for most students can be the most challenging situations. Refer back to the descriptions of situations (2) and (4). Redo them, assuming that reversing entries are used. Reversing entries are described in Appendix 3-A in the text. Those new solutions should appear as follows.

(2) Assuming reversing entries **are** used.
a. Office Supplies on Hand....:................................ 320
Office Supplies Expense.......................... 320
b. Office Supplies Expense $980
c. Office Supplies on Hand $320
d. Cash paid $900
e. Decrease in Office Supplies on Hand $ 80

APPROACH:

Office Supplies Expense			Office Supplies on Hand	
Reversing 400		ENTRY	Beg. Bal. 400	
Acquisitions 900	(320)	← NEEDED TO →	(320)	Reversing 400
Ending Bal. 980		COMPLETE ACCOUNTS	Desired Ending Bal. 320	

(4) Assuming reversing entries **are** used.
a. Subscription Revenue 8,000
Unearned Subscription Revenue......... 8,000
b. Subscription Revenue $52,700

c. Unearned Subscription Revenue $ 8,000
d. Cash received $54,000
e. Increase in Unearned Subscription Revenue $ 1,300

APPROACH:

Unearned Subscription Revenue			Subscription Revenue	
	Beg. Bal. 6,700	ENTRY		Receipts 6,700
Reversing 6,700	(8,000)	← NEEDED TO →	(8,000)	Receipts 54,000
	Desired Ending Bal. 8,000	COMPLETE ACCOUNTS		Ending Balance 52,700

Exercise 3-6

PURPOSE: This exercise will illustrate the preparation of adjusting entries from an unadjusted trial balance and additional data.

The following list of accounts and their balances represents the unadjusted trial balance of Tami Corp. at December 31, 2007.

	Dr.	Cr.
Cash	$ 15,000	
Accounts Receivable	122,500	
Allowance for Doubtful Accounts		$ 1,875
Inventory	162,500	
Prepaid Insurance	7,350	
Prepaid Rent	33,000	
Investment in Lamb Corp. Bonds	45,000	
Land	25,000	
Plant and Equipment	260,000	
Accumulated Amortization		45,000
Accounts Payable		23,275
Bonds Payable		125,000
Discount on Bonds Payable	3,750	
Common Shares		250,000
Retained Earnings (January 1, 2007)		201,650
Sales		533,275
Rent Revenue		25,500
Cost of Goods Sold	410,250	
Transportation-out	22,500	
Salaries and Wages	87,500	
Interest Expense	9,000	
Miscellaneous Expense	2,225	
	$1,205,575	$1,205,575

ADDITIONAL INFORMATION:

1. On March 31, 2007, Tami rented a warehouse for $2,750 per month, paid $33,000 in advance, and debited Prepaid Rent to record the payment.
2. On September 1, 2007, Tami received $25,500 rent from its lessee for a 12-month lease on a parking lot, beginning on that date. The receipt was recorded by a credit to Rent Revenue.
3. Tami estimates that 1 percent of the credit sales made during 2007 will result in accounts receivable that will ultimately become uncollectible. All sales are made on credit (on account).
4. Prepaid Insurance contains the $7,350 premium cost of a policy that is for a 2-year term and was taken out on May 1, 2007.
5. On April 1, 2007, Tami issued 125, $1,000, 8 percent bonds, maturing on April 1, 2017, at 97 percent of par value. Interest payment dates are April 1 and October 1. The straight-line method is used to amortize any bond premium or discount. Amortization is recorded only at year end.
6. The regular rate of amortization is 10 percent of acquisition cost per year. Acquisitions and retirements during a year are depreciated at half this rate. Assets costing $16,000 were retired during the year. On December 31, 2006, the balance of Plant and Equipment was $230,000.
7. On September 1, 2007, Tami purchased 45, $1,000, 10 percent Lamb Corp. bonds, at par. The bonds mature on August 31, 2009. Interest is to be received every August 31 and February 28.

Instructions

Prepare the year-end adjusting entries in general journal form using the information above. (Round amounts to the nearest dollar.)

Solution to Exercise 3-6

1. Rent Expense..	24,750	
Prepaid Rent		24,750
($33,000 x 9/12 = $24,750 expired rent)		
2. Rent Revenue	17,000	
Unearned Rent Revenue		17,000
($25,500 x 8/12 = $17,000 unearned revenue)		
3. Bad Debt Expense	5,333	
Allowance for Doubtful Accounts		5,333
($533,275 x 1% = $5,333 bad debt expense)		

TIP!

If the estimate for uncollectible accounts receivable is to be based on a percentage of net sales, the expense figure is a percentage of net sales and any existing balance in the Allowance account will **not** affect the amount of the adjusting entry. If the estimate for uncollectible accounts receivable is to be based on an aging of accounts receivable or a percentage of accounts receivable existing at the balance sheet date, the desired ending balance for the Allowance account is determined and any existing balance in the Allowance account will affect the amount of the adjusting entry. (This subject will be more thoroughly reviewed in Chapter 7).

4. Insurance Expense	2,450	
Prepaid Insurance		2,450
($7,350 x 8/24 = $2,450 expired insurance)		
5. a. Interest Expense	2,500	
Interest Payable		2,500
($125,000 x 8% x 3/12 = $2,500 accrued interest)		

TIP! An interest rate is an annual rate unless otherwise indicated. For preparing an adjusting entry involving interest, calculate interest assuming the rate given is for a whole year, unless it is evident that this is not the case. Also, assume a 360-day year, unless otherwise indicated.

b. Interest Expense	281	
Discount on Bonds Payable		281
(125 x $1,000 x 97% = $121,250)		
[(125 x $1,000) - $121,250 = $3,750]		
($3,750 x 9/120 = $281 discount amortization)		
6. Amortization Expense	24,500	
Accumulated Amortization		24,500
($230,000 – $16,000 assets retired = $214,000 assets used for full year)		
($214,000 x 10% = $21,400 amortization on assets held for full year)		
($16,000 x 10% x 1/2 = $800 amortization on assets disposed of during the year)		
($260,000 – $214,000 = $46,000 assets acquired during the year)		
($46,000 x 10% x 1/2 = $2,300 amortization on assets acquired during the year)		
($21,400 + $800 + $2,300 = $24,500 total amortization for the year)		
7. Interest Receivable	1,500	
Interest Revenue		1,500
($45,000 x 10% x 4/12 = $1,500 accrued interest)		

EXPLANATION: Identify each item as involving: (1) a prepaid expense, (2) an accrued expense, (3) an unearned revenue, (4) an accrued revenue, or (5) an estimated item. From the facts, determine the existing account balances. Read the facts carefully to determine the desired account balances for financial statements in accordance with generally accepted accounting principles (historical cost principle, revenue recognition principle, matching principle, etc.). Determine the adjusting entries necessary to bring existing account balances to the appropriate account balances.

1. This situation involves a prepaid expense. The advance payment was for twelve months and was recorded in an asset account. At December 31, 2007, nine months have passed for which the rent was paid, so the

expired portion of the rent must be removed from the Prepaid Rent (asset) account and put into the Rent Expense account.

2. This situation involves unearned revenue. On September 1, 2007, cash was received and recorded as follows:

Cash	25,500	
Rent Revenue..		25,500

At December 31, 2007, before adjustment, there is no Unearned Rent Revenue account on the trial balance. We need a balance of $17,000 ($25,500 x 8/12) in Unearned Rent Revenue at the balance sheet date. Therefore, in an adjusting entry, Unearned Rent Revenue is credited for $17,000. The other half of an adjusting entry dealing with Unearned Rent Revenue always has to be Rent Revenue. The debit to Rent Revenue in this exercise will reduce the balance in the earned revenue account to the amount actually earned during 2007 ($8,500).

3. This situation involves an estimated expense. The bad debt expense for the year is estimated to be 1 percent of credit sales and all sales are on account. Thus, an expense of $5,333 (1 percent of $533,275 sales) is recorded and a valuation account to Accounts Receivable is credited. The $1,875 balance in that valuation account (Allowance for Doubtful Accounts) before adjustment does not affect the amount required in the adjusting entry in this case.

4. This item involves a prepaid expense. Before adjustment, the total cost of the insurance premium is in the Prepaid Insurance account. The expired portion must be taken out of Prepaid Insurance (credit) and put into Insurance Expense (debit).

5. This situation involves an accrued expense and amortization of a related discount. Interest must be accrued since the last interest payment date (October 1) so three months of interest belong in the accrual entry. The discount (3 percent of the par value) is to be amortized on a straight-line basis from the date of issuance (April 1, 2007) to the date of maturity (April 1, 2017), which is a 10-year period.

6. Of the $260,000 ending balance in Plant and Equipment, $230,000 represents items held during the whole year. There were retirements of $16,000 during the year so we can compute the $46,000 amount of acquisitions. (Acquisitions and retirements are to be amortized for only one-half of a year—that is, at a 5 percent rate). A 10 percent rate of amortization per year is equivalent to amortizing assets over a 10-year period using the straight-line method.

7. This situation involves an accrued revenue. Interest must be accrued since the last interest payment date, which is four months. The 10 percent interest rate stated is expressed on an annual basis.

Exercise 3-7

PURPOSE: This exercise will review the preparation of closing entries.

The adjusted trial balance for the Motorboat Repair Corporation at December 31, 2008 appears as follows:

Motorboat Repair Corporation
ADJUSTED TRIAL BALANCE
December 31, 2008

	Debit	Credit
Cash	$ 2,600	
Accounts Receivable	2,200	
Supplies on Hand	2,100	
Accounts Payable		$ 700
Utilities Payable		80
Common Shares		3,000
Retained Earnings (January 1, 2008)		1,300
Service Revenue		4,900
Rent Expense	800	
Advertising Expense	300	
Cleaning Expense	200	
Utilities Expense	80	
Supplies Expense	1,700	
	$ 9,980	$ 9,980

Instructions

(a) Prepare the appropriate closing entries at December 31, 2008.
(b) Explain why closing entries are necessary.

Solution to Exercise 3-7

(a) Service Revenue	4,900	
Income Summary		4,900
(To close the revenue account to Income Summary.)		

Income Summary	3,080	
Rent Expense		800
Advertising Expense		300
Cleaning Expense		200
Utilities Expense		80
Supplies Expense		1,700
(To close expense accounts to Income Summary.)		

Income Summary	1,820	
Retained Earnings		1,820
(To close Income Summary to Retained Earnings.) ($4,900 total revenues - $3,080 total expenses = $1,820 credit balance in Income Summary before closing.)		

(b) The major reason closing entries are needed is that they prepare the temporary (nominal) accounts for the recording of transactions of the next accounting period.

Closing entries produce a zero balance in each of the temporary accounts so that they can be used to accumulate data pertaining to the next accounting period. Because of closing entries, the revenues of 2008 are not commingled with the revenues of the prior period (2007). A second reason closing entries are needed is that the Retained Earnings account will reflect a true balance only after closing entries have been completed. Closing entries formally recognize in the ledger the transfer of net income (or loss) and dividends declared to retained earnings as indicated in the statement of retained earnings.

TIP!

The Income Summary account is used only in the closing process. Before it is closed, the balance in this account must equal the net income or net loss figure for the period.

Where do you look for the accounts (and their amounts) to be closed? If a work sheet is used, you can use the amounts listed in the Income Statement column pair and the balance of the Dividends Declared (or Owner's Drawing) account. If a work sheet is not used, you must refer to the temporary accounts (after adjustment) in the ledger to determine the balances to be closed.

Exercise 3-8

PURPOSE: This exercise will allow you to quickly check your knowledge of how items are extended on a 10-column work sheet.

Instructions

The last six columns of an incomplete 10-column work sheet are illustrated below. Place an "X" in the appropriate columns to indicate the proper work sheet treatment of the balance in each of the accounts listed. (The accounts are **not** listed in their usual order, the work sheet is **only partially** illustrated, and the Trial Balance and Adjustments columns have been **omitted**.)

Handy Dandy Hardware
WORK SHEET
For the Year Ended December 31, 2008

Account	Adjusted Trial Balance		Income Statement		Balance Sheet	
	Debit	Credit	Debit	Credit	Debit	Credit
Advertising Expense						
Amortization Expense						
Land						
Store Equipment						
Wages and Salaries Expense						
Mortgage Payable						
Cash						
Salaries Payable						
Prepaid Insurance						
Delivery Equipment						
Accumulated Amortization						
Revenue Received in Advance						
Rent Expense						
Sales Revenue						
Prepaid Rent						
Dividends Declared						
Repairs Expense						
Wages Payable						
Interest Receivable						
Accounts Receivable						
Net Income						
Retained Earnings						

Handy Dandy Hardware
WORK SHEET
For the Year Ended December 31, 2008

Account	Adjusted Trial Balance		Income Statement		Balance Sheet	
	Debit	Credit	Debit	Credit	Debit	Credit
Advertising Expense	×		×			
Amortization Expense	×		×			
Land	×				×	
Store Equipment	×				×	
Wages and Salaries Expense	×		×			
Mortgage Payable		×				×
Cash	×				×	
Salaries Payable		×				×
Prepaid Insurance	×				×	
Delivery Equipment	×				×	
Accumulated Amortization		×				×
Revenue Received in Advance		×				×
Rent Expense	×		×			
Sales Revenue		×		×		
Prepaid Rent	×				×	
Dividends Declared	×				×	
Repairs Expense	×		×			
Wages Payable		×				×
Interest Receivable	×				×	
Accounts Receivable	×				×	
Net Income			×			×
Retained Earnings		×				×

The amount shown for Retained Earnings on the work sheet above is the balance of that account **before** considering dividends declared during the period (determined by the facts that a separate Dividends Declared account appears on the same work sheet) and **before** considering net income for the period.

TIP!

TIP! Every amount appearing in the Adjusted Trial Balance column pair must be extended to one of the four statement (income statement or balance sheet) columns. Debit amounts go to a debit column further to the right and credit amounts go to a credit column further to the right of the adjusted trial balance column pair.

TIP! When a dollar amount is added to balance the income statement column pair of columns, the same amount must be added in an opposite debit or credit column in the balance sheet column pair. This amount in a balance sheet column indicates the impact of net income (or net loss) on owners' equity.

Exercise 3-9

PURPOSE: This exercise reviews the procedures involved in the accounting cycle when two optional steps, a work sheet and reversing entries, are employed.

Instructions

Ten steps in the accounting cycle for a company, which uses a work sheet and reversing entries, are listed below in random order. Arrange the 10 procedures carried out in the accounting cycle in the order in which they should be performed by numbering them "1," "2," and so forth in the spaces provided.

_______ a. Journalize and post closing entries.
_______ b. Prepare financial statements from the work sheet.
_______ c. Prepare a post-closing trial balance.
_______ d. Balance the ledger accounts and prepare a trial balance on the work sheet.
_______ e. Journalize and post adjustments made on the work sheet.
_______ f. Record transactions in the journals.
_______ g. Journalize and post reversing entries.
_______ h. Post from journals to the ledgers.
_______ i. Complete the work sheet (adjusting entries, adjusted trial balance, and extend amounts to the appropriate financial statement columns).
_______ j. Identify and analyze business transactions and events.

Solution to Exercise 3-9

a. 8	c. 9	e. 7 (or 6)	g. 10	i. 5
b. 6 (or 7)	d. 4	f. 2	h. 3	j. 1

APPROACH: As you work through this exercise, concentrate on the logical progression and the flow of information in the data gathering process. Think about the purpose served by each step involved in the process of identifying, recording, classifying, summarizing, reporting, and interpreting transactions and other events relating to enterprises. This process is summarized below, and first assumes no work sheet is used. Then differences introduced by use of a work sheet are discussed.

EXPLANATION:

(1) Transactions and other events that are to be recognized (recorded) are first **identified** and **analyzed**. Many happenings (such as interviews of prospective employees and the order for placement of an advertisement in a local newspaper) are not recorded. However, the payment or accrual for salaries to employees and amounts owed to vendors of services are recordable events.

(2) Transactions and other events are **recorded** chronologically in the journal(s). A transaction can be viewed in its entirety in a journal.

(3) Transactions and events are **classified** by posting from the journal(s) to the ledger(s).

(4) All transactions and events affecting individual accounts are summarized by balancing the accounts (determining the balances of all accounts).

(5) Adjusting entries are recorded in the general journal and posted to the general ledger to update the accounts for accruals, deferrals, and estimated items. An adjusted trial balance is prepared to prove the maintenance of the equality of total debits and total credits after the adjustments.

(6) The **income statement** is prepared using the balances of accounts for revenues, expenses, gains, and losses (temporary or nominal accounts).

(7) **Closing entries** are recorded in the general journal and posted to the general ledger. Closing entries are necessary to prepare the temporary (nominal) accounts for recordings of the subsequent period. Closing entries also update the balance of the Retained Earnings account for the balance sheet.

(8) The statement of retained earnings is prepared to report the changes in retained earnings during the period. It uses the net income figure as one reason for change.

(9) The **balance sheet** is prepared. It reports the balances of assets, liabilities, and owners' equity.

(10) A **post-closing** trial balance is prepared.

(11) **Reversing entries** may be recorded and posted to facilitate certain recordings in the subsequent period.

(12) Financial statements are **interpreted** by users after careful analysis of all items reported.

TIP!

A work sheet is usually prepared to facilitate the process of adjusting the accounts and accumulating the balances needed for the financial statements. When a work sheet is employed, the adjusting entries and the adjusted trial balance are entered directly on the work sheet. The adjusted account balances are then sorted on the work sheet and all balances needed for the financial statements are accumulated in one handy place (on the work sheet). The actual journalizing and posting of adjusting entries and closing entries are then normally done after the financial statements are completed.

Exercise 3-10

PURPOSE: This exercise will provide practice in determining which adjusting entries may be reversed.

Instructions

The following represent adjusting entries prepared for the Bent Tree Company at December 31, 2008 (end of the accounting period). The company has the policy of using reversing entries when appropriate. For each adjusting entry below, indicate if it would be appropriate to reverse it at the beginning of 2009. Indicate your answer by circling "yes" or "no."

Yes No	1. Deferred Advertising Expense	4,500	
	Advertising Expense		4,500
Yes No	2. Interest Expense.......................................	800	
	Discount on Bonds Payable............		800
Yes No	3. Interest Receivable	690	
	Interest Revenue		690
Yes No	4. Unearned Rental Income.......................	900	
	Rental Income................................		900
Yes No	5. Insurance Expense	1,600	
	Prepaid Insurance...........................		1,600
Yes No	6. Salaries Expense......................................	1,100	
	Salaries Payable		1,100

Solution to Exercise 3-10

1. Yes	3. Yes	5. No
2. No	4. No	6. Yes

TIP! A reversing entry is an entry made at the very beginning of an accounting period that is the exact opposite of an adjusting entry made at the end of the previous period. The recording of reversing entries is an **optional** step in the accounting cycle. The **purpose** of a reversing entry is to simplify the recording of transactions in the new accounting period. The use of reversing entries does not change the amounts reported in financial statements.

EXPLANATION: Write down what the related reversing entry would look like and then (1) think about the effects that the reversing entry would have on the account balances in the accounting period that follows the one for which the adjustment was made, and (2) think about whether those effects are appropriate or not. It is appropriate to reverse an adjusting entry involving a prepaid expense or unearned revenue **only if** the adjustment increases (rather than decreases) a balance sheet account. It is **always** appropriate to reverse an adjusting entry involving an accrual. It is **never** appropriate to reverse an adjusting entry for depreciation or amortization or bad debts.

1. An adjustment for a deferred expense can be reversed if the (original) adjustment increases an asset or liability account. This adjustment increases a prepaid expense (asset) account.
2. Never reverse an adjustment for amortization of a discount or premium.
3. An accrual-type adjustment can always be reversed.
4. A reversal of this entry would put back into the Unearned Rental Revenue account the amount that the adjustment indicated has been earned.
5. An adjustment for a deferral can be reversed only if it increases a balance sheet account. This adjustment decreases an asset account.
6. An accrual-type adjustment can always be reversed. You can tell the adjusting entry is for an accrued expense because the debit is to an expense account and the credit is to a payable account.

Exercise 3-11

PURPOSE: This exercise will give you practice in identifying adjusting entries that may be reversed.

Instructions

Refer to **Exercise 3-6** and the **Solution to Exercise 3-6**. Indicate the adjusting entries that can be reversed.

Solution to Exercise 3-11

EXPLANATION: Think of the types of adjustments and whether they can be reversed. Accrual-type adjusting entries can always be reversed. Therefore, items 5a and 7 can be reversed. Estimated items such as amortization of plant assets, the recognition of bad debts, and amortization of intangibles and discounts and premiums on receivables and payables should never be reversed. Therefore, items 3, 6, and 5b should **not** be reversed. Adjustments involving deferrals can be reversed **if** the original cash entry involved a temporary account (revenue or expense account) rather than a prepaid or unearned account (a permanent account) and the adjustment **increases** a prepaid expense or unearned revenue account. Therefore, item 2 **can be** reversed but items 1 and 4 should **not** be reversed.

Illustration 3-4

Reversing Entries for Accrued Expenses Illustrated and Comparison of System Using Reversing Entries with Systems Where no Reversals Are Used

An entity can choose to use or not use reversing entries. The advantage of using reversing entries is that the reversal of an adjustment for accrued expense (or accrued revenue) facilitates the recording of the subsequent payment (or receipt) of cash. The subsequent payment (or receipt) can then be recorded to a temporary account rather than a permanent account.

When an entity chooses **not** to use a reversing entry for an adjustment for accrued expense (or accrued revenue) at the end of Year 1 and the entity wishes to record the subsequent payment (or receipt) of cash in Year 2 to a temporary account rather than a permanent account, the adjustment process at the end of Year 2 can accommodate the situation.

Assume the following data applies to GuardDog Corp.:

1. The company began operations in 2007.
2. During 2007, interest of $80,000 was paid.
3. At the end of 2007, accrued interest on a note payable amounted to $5,500.
4. During 2008, interest of $50,000 was paid.
5. At the end of 2008, accrued interest amounted to $8,200.
6. During 2009, interest of $65,000 was paid.
7. At the end of 2009, accrued interest amounted to $3,000.

There are three paths the information could take through the accounting records. Regardless of the path taken, the true amount of expense incurred should be reported on the income statement each year, and the amount incurred but not paid should be reported on the balance sheet at the end of each period.

Examine each path below.

	Reversing entries	Payment entries recorded to
PATH A	Yes	temporary account
PATH B	No	permanent and temporary account
PATH C	No	temporary account

The individual effects that the above events have on the accounts, depending on the path chosen, are illustrated on the following pages. The description of the flow of data through the accounting records is organized into the following sections:

I. The journal entries required to reflect the transactions in the accounts in 2007–2009.
II. The postings of journal entries to T-accounts in 2007 and 2008.
III. The resulting account balances at the end of 2007 and 2008.

I. The journal entries required to reflect the transactions in the accounts in 2007–2009.

		PATH A			PATH B			PATH C		
		Reversing entries are made.			Reversing entries are **not** made.			Reversing entries are **not** made.		
		Payment entries are charged to **temporary** account (Interest Expense).			Payment entries are allocated to a **permanent account** (Interest Payable) and to a **temporary** account (Interest Expense).			Payment entries are charged to a **permanent** account (Interest Expense).		
Date	EVENT									
During 2007	(1) Paid $80,000 interest	Interest Expense Cash	80,000	 80,000	Interest Expense Cash	80,000	 80,000	Interest Expense Cash	80,000	 80,000
12/31/07	(2) Adjusting entry—$5,500 accrued interest	Interest Expense Interest Payable	5,500	 5,500	Interest Expense Interest Payable	5,500	 5,500	Interest Expense Interest Payable	5,500	 5,500
12/31/07	(3) Closing entry	Income Summary Interest Expense	85,000	 85,000	Income Summary Interest Expense	85,000	 85,000	Income Summary Interest Expense	85,000	 85,000
1/1/08	(4) Reversing entry	Interest Payable Interest Expense	5,500	 5,500	NONE			NONE		
During 2008	(5) Paid $50,000 interest	Interest Expense Cash	50,000	 50,000	Interest Payable Interest Expense Cash	5,500 44,500	 50,000	Interest Expense Cash	50,000	 50,000
12/31/08	(6) Adjusting entry — $8,200 accrued interest	Interest Expense Interest Payable	8,200	 8,200	Interest Expense Interest Payable	8,200	 8,200	Interest Expense Interest Payable	2,700	 2,700
12/31/08	(7) Closing entry	Income Summary Interest Expense	52,700	 52,700	Income Summary Interest Expense	52,700	 52,700	Income Summary Interest Expense	52,700	 52,700
1/1/09	(8) Reversing entry	Interest Expense Interest Payable	8,200	 8,200	NONE			NONE		
During 2009	(9) Paid $65,000 interest	Interest Expense Cash	65,000	 65,000	Interest Payable Interest Expense Cash	8,200 56,800	 65,000	Interest Expense Cash	65,000	 65,000
12/31/09	(10) Adjusting entry — $3,000 accrued interest	Interest Expense Interest Payable	3,000	 3,000	Interest Expense Interest Payable	3,000	 3,000	Interest Expense Interest Payable	5,200	 5,200
12/31/09	(11) Closing entry	Income Summary Interest Expense	59,800	 59,800	Income Summary Interest Expense	59,800	 59,800	Income Summary Interest Expense	59,800	 59,800

II. The postings of journal entries to T-accounts in 2007–2009.

	PATH A	PATH B	PATH C
	Reversing entries are made.	Reversing entries are **not** made.	Reversing entries are **not** made.
	Payment entries are charged to **temporary** account (Interest Expense).	Payment entries are allocated to a **permanent** account (Interest Payable) **and** to a **temporary** account (Interest Expense).	Payment entries are charged to a **temporary** account (Interest Expense).

The T-accounts would appear as follows:	Interest Expense (Dr)	Interest Expense (Cr)	Interest Payable (Dr)	Interest Payable (Cr)	Interest Expense (Dr)	Interest Expense (Cr)	Interest Payable (Dr)	Interest Payable (Cr)	Interest Expense (Dr)	Interest Expense (Cr)	Interest Payable (Dr)	Interest Payable (Cr)
(1) During 2007	80,000				80,000				80,000			
(2) 12/31/07 Adj.	5,500			5,500	5,500			5,500	5,500			5,500
Balances 12/31/07	85,500			5,500	85,500			5,500	85,500			5,500
(3) 12/31/07 Closing		85,500				85,500				85,500		
(4) 1/1/08 Reversing		5,500	5,500									
(5) During 2008	50,000				44,500		5,500		50,000			
(6) 12/31/08 Adj.	8,200			8,200	8,200			8,200	2,700			2,700
Balances 12/31/08	52,700			8,200	52,700			8,200	52,700			8,200
(7) 12/31/08 Closing		52,700				52,700				52,700		
(8) 1/1/09 Reversing		8,200	8,200									
(9) During 2009	65,000				56,800		8,200		65,000			
(10) 12/31/09 Adj.	3,000			3,000	3,000			3,000		5,200	5,200	
Balances 12/31/09	59,800			3,000	59,800			3,000	59,800			3,000
(11) 12/31/09 Closing		59,800				59,800				59,800		

III. The account balances resulting at the end of 2007–2009.

AMOUNT OF ITEM	PATH A	PATH B	PATH C
Interest Expense on Income Statement for year ending Dec. 31, 2007	$85,500	$85,500	$85,500
Interest Payable on Balance Sheet at December 31, 2007	$ 5,500	$ 5,500	$ 5,500
Interest paid on Statement of Cash Flows for year ending Dec. 31, 2007	$80,000	$80,000	$80,000
Interest Expense on Income Statement for year ending Dec. 31, 2008	$52,700	$52,700	$52,700
Interest Payable on Balance Sheet at Dec. 31, 2008	$ 8,200	$ 8,200	$ 8,200
Interest paid on Statement of Cash Flows for year ending Dec. 31, 2008	$50,000	$50,000	$50,000
Interest Expense on Income Statement for year ending Dec. 31, 2009	$59,800	$59,800	$59,800
Interest Payable on Balance Sheet at Dec. 31, 2009	$ 3,000	$ 3,000	$ 3,000
Interest paid on Statement of Cash Flows for year ending Dec. 31, 2009	$65,000	$65,000	$65,000

Illustration 3-5

Reversing Entries (Comparison of System Using Reversing Entries with Systems Where No Reversals Are Used)

JOURNAL ENTRIES	**Accounting System Where Reversing Entries ARE Used**			**Accounting System Where Reversing Entries ARE NOT Used**
(1) During 2007	(1) Interest Expense	80,000		(1) Interest Expense
	Cash		80,000	Cash
(2) 12/31/07 Adjusting	(2) Interest Expense	5,500		(2) Interest Expense
	Interest Payable		5,500	Interest Payable
(3) 12/31/07 Closing	(3) Income Summary	85,500		(3) Income Summary
	Interest Expense		85,500	Interest Expense
(4) 1/1/08 Reversing	(4) Interest Payable	5,500		(4) No Entry
	Interest Expense		5,500	
(5) 1/1/08 Payment	(5) Interest Expense	6,000		(5) Interest Expense
				Interest Payable
	Cash		6,000	Cash

LEDGER ACCOUNT POSTINGS	**Interest Expense**		**Interest Payable**		**Interest Expense**	
(1) During 2007	80,000				80,000	
(2) 12/31/07 Adjusting	5,500			5,500	5,500	
(3) 12/31/07 Closing		85,000				85,000
(4) 1/1/08 Reversing		5,500	5,500			
(5) 1/1/08 Payment	6,000				500	

FINANCIAL STATEMENTS

Interest Expense for the year 2007	$85,500
Interest Paid in 2007	$80,000
Balance of Interest Payable at close of business on 12/31/07	$5,500
Interest Expense for the day 1/1/08	$ 500
Balance of Interest Payable at close of business on 1/1/08	$ 0

Analysis of Multiple-Choice Questions

Question

1. Which of the following is a temporary account?
   a. Prepaid Insurance
   b. Unearned Revenue
   c. Insurance Expense
   d. Interest Receivable

EXPLANATION: Read the question. Before looking at the answer selections, write down the meaning of the term "temporary account." Then answer "true" or "false" as you ask whether each answer selection is a temporary account. A temporary account is an account whose balance is closed at the end of an accounting period. Revenue and expense accounts are closed; permanent accounts (including asset and liability accounts) are never closed. Prepaid Insurance and Interest Receivable are asset accounts. Unearned Revenue is a liability account. Insurance Expense is a temporary account. (Solution = c.)

Question

2. Which of the following errors will cause an imbalance in the trial balance?
   a. Omission of a transaction in the journal.
   b. Posting an entire journal entry twice to the ledger.
   c. Posting a credit of $720 to Accounts Payable as a credit of $720 to Accounts Receivable.
   d. Listing the balance of an account with a debit balance in the credit column of the trial balance.

EXPLANATION: Analyze each error (answer selection) and write down whether or not the error will cause the trial balance to be out of balance. Look for the selection that will cause an imbalance (selection "d"). Selections "a," "b," and "c" do not cause an imbalance in the trial balance. (Solution = d.)

Question

3. Which of the following statements is associated with the accrual basis of accounting?
   a. The timing of cash receipts and disbursements is emphasized.
   b. A minimum amount of record keeping is required.
   c. This method is used less frequently by businesses than the cash method of accounting.
   d. Revenues are recognized in the period they are earned, regardless of the time period the cash is received.

EXPLANATION: Mentally define the accrual basis of accounting. Write down the key words and phrases of your definition. Compare each answer selection with your definition and choose the one that best matches. Using the **accrual basis of accounting**, events that change a company's financial statements are recorded in the periods in which the events occur. Thus, revenues are recognized in the period in which they are earned, and expenses are recognized in the period in which they are incurred, regardless of when the related cash is received or paid. Answer selections "a" and "b" refer to the cash basis of accounting that is not GAAP. (Solution = d.)

Question

4. An accrued expense is an expense that:
   a. has been incurred but has not been paid.
   b. has been paid but has not been incurred.
   c. has been incurred for which payment is to be made in instalments.
   d. will never be paid.

EXPLANATION: Write down a definition for **accrued expense**. Compare each answer selection with your definition and choose the best match. Expenses may be paid for in the same period in which they are incurred or they may be paid for in the period before or in the period after the one in which they are incurred. An **accrued expense** refers to an expense that has been incurred but has not yet been paid. It will be paid for in a period subsequent to the period in which it was incurred. (Solution = a.)

Question

5. In reviewing some adjusting entries, you observe an entry which contains a debit to Prepaid Insurance and a credit to Insurance Expense. The purpose of this journal entry is to record a(n):
   a. accrued expense.
   b. prepaid expense.
   c. expired cost.
   d. prepaid revenue.

EXPLANATION: Write down the entry so you can see what the entry does. Notice the entry records a prepaid expense (an asset). Then examine each answer selection one at a time. A debit to Prepaid Insurance records an increase in a prepaid expense. A prepaid expense is an expense that has been paid but has not been incurred. An accrued expense is an expense incurred, but not paid. An expired cost is an expense or a loss. Prepaid revenue is a bad term for unearned revenue (or deferred revenue). (Solution = b.)

Question

6. An adjusting entry to record an accrued expense involves a debit to a(n):
   a. expense account and a credit to a prepaid account.
   b. expense account and a credit to Cash.
   c. expense account and a credit to a liability account.
   d. liability account and a credit to an expense account.

EXPLANATION: Write down a definition for **accrued expense** and the types of accounts involved in an adjusting entry to accrue an expense. Find the answer selection that describes your entry.

Dr.	Expenses	
Cr.		Liabilities

Notice the logic of the entry. An **accrued expense** is an expense incurred but not yet paid. Thus, you record the incurrence by increasing an expense account and you record the "not paid" aspect by increasing a liability account. (Solution = c.)

Question

7. The failure to properly record an adjusting entry to accrue an expense will result in an:
   a. understatement of expenses and an understatement of liabilities.
   b. understatement of expenses and an overstatement of liabilities.
   c. understatement of expenses and an overstatement of assets.
   d. overstatement of expenses and an understatement of assets.

EXPLANATION: Write down the adjusting entry to record an accrued expense. Analyze the effects of the entry. This will help you to determine the effects of the failure to properly make that entry.

Dr.	Expenses		xx	
Cr.		Liabilities		xx

This entry increases expenses and liabilities. Therefore, the failure to make this entry would result in an understatement of expenses and an understatement of liabilities. (Solution = a.)

Question

8. Which of the following properly describes a prepayment for which an adjusting entry will typically have to be made at a future date?
   a. Cash is received after revenue is earned.
   b. Cash is received before revenue is earned.
   c. Cash is paid after expense is incurred.
   d. Cash is paid in the same time period that an expense is incurred.

EXPLANATION: Think about the nature of prepayments and the relative timing of revenue or expense recognition and the related cash flow. **Prepayments** result from cash flows that occur **before** expense or revenue recognition. That is, cash is paid for expenses that apply to more than one accounting period or cash is received for revenue that applies to more than one accounting period. The portion of the expense that applies to future periods is deferred by reporting a prepaid expense (asset) or the portion of the revenue that applies to future periods is deferred by reporting unearned revenue (liability) on the balance sheet.

Accruals result from cash flows that occur **after** expense or revenue recognition. That is, cash is to be paid or received in a future accounting period for an expense incurred or a revenue earned in the current period. Items "a" and "c" above are accrual situations. Item "d" is neither an accrual or deferral situation. (Solution = b.)

Question

9. An adjusting entry to allocate a previously recorded asset to expense involves a debit to an:
   a. asset account and a credit to Cash.
   b. expense account and a credit to Cash.
   c. expense account and a credit to an asset account.
   d. asset account and a credit to an expense account.

EXPLANATION: Write down the sketch of an adjusting entry to transfer an asset to expense. Compare each answer selection with your entry and choose the one that matches.

Dr.		Expenses	
	Cr.		Assets

(Solution = c.)

Question

10. Which of the following adjusting entries will cause an increase in revenues and a decrease in liabilities?
    a. Entry to record an accrued expense.
    b. Entry to record an accrued revenue.
    c. Entry to record the consumed portion of an expense paid in advance and initially recorded as an asset.
    d. Entry to record the earned portion of revenue received in advance and initially recorded as unearned revenue.

EXPLANATION: For each answer selection, write down the sketch of the adjusting entry described and the effects of each half of the entry. Compare the stem of the question with your analyses to determine the correct answer. (Solution = d.)

The entry to record an accrued expense is:

Dr.		Expenses	
	Cr.		Liabilities

The effects of the entry are to increase expenses and to increase liabilities.

The entry to record an accrued revenue is:

Dr.		Assets	
	Cr.		Revenues

The effects of the entry are to increase assets and to increase revenues.

The entry to record the consumed portion of a prepaid expense initially recorded as an asset is:

Dr.		Expenses	
	Cr.		Assets

The effects of the entry are to increase expenses and to decrease assets.

The entry to record the earned portion of unearned revenue initially recorded as a liability is:

Dr.		Liabilities	
	Cr.		Revenues

The effects of the entry are to decrease liabilities and to increase revenues.

Question

11. The Office Supplies on Hand account had a balance at the beginning of year 3 of $1,600. Payments for acquisitions of office supplies during year 3 amounted to $10,000 and were recorded by a debit to the asset account. A physical count at the end of year 3 revealed supplies costing $1,900 were on hand. The required adjusting entry at the end of year 3 will include a debit to:
    a. Office Supplies Expense for $300.
    b. Office Supplies on Hand for $300.
    c. Office Supplies Expense for $9,700.
    d. Office Supplies on Hand for $1,900.

EXPLANATION: Draw T-accounts. Enter the data given and solve for the adjusting entry. Compare each alternative answer to the adjusting entry you have sketched in the accounts. (Solution = c.)

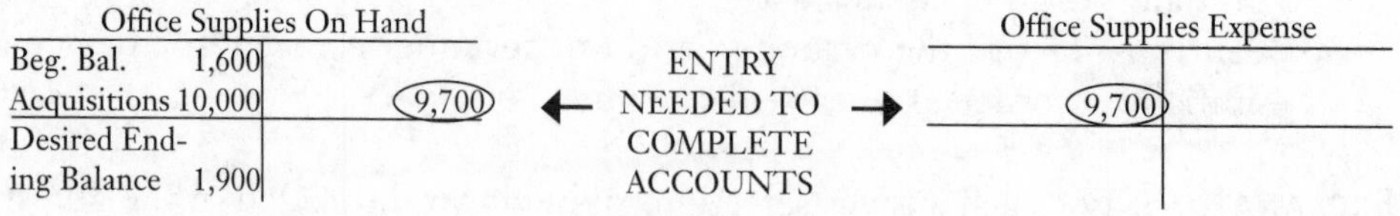

Question

12. The book value of a piece of equipment is the:
    a. original cost of the equipment.
    b. current replacement cost of the used equipment.
    c. current market value of the used equipment.
    d. difference between the original cost of the equipment and its related accumulated amortization.

EXPLANATION: Equipment benefits the operations of several accounting periods; thus, in compliance with the matching principle, a portion of the cost of a long-lived asset should be reported as an expense during each period of the asset's useful life. Amortization is the process of allocating the cost of an asset to expense over its useful life in a rational and systematic manner. The annual charge for amortization is recorded by a debit to Amortization Expense and a credit to Accumulated Amortization. The Accumulated Amortization—Office Equipment is a contra asset account and reflects the total amortization to date. The difference between the balance in the Equipment account (the original cost of the asset) and balance in the related Accumulated Amortization account at any given point in time represents the book value (often called carrying value or carrying amount) of the equipment. This amount will rarely equal the asset's current market value. (Solution = d.)

Question

13. The purpose of recording closing entries is to:
    a. reduce the number of temporary accounts.
    b. enable the accountant to prepare financial statements at the end of an accounting period.
    c. prepare revenue and expense accounts for the recording of the next period's revenues and expenses.
    d. establish new balances in some asset and liability accounts.

EXPLANATION: Cover up the answer selections while you read the question. Attempt to complete the statement started by the question. Think about when closing entries are made and what they do. Then go through the selections using a process of elimination approach. Closing entries clear out the balances of revenue and expense accounts so that the accounts are ready to accumulate data for a new accounting period. Selection "c" is correct. Selection "a" is incorrect; closing entries do not change the number of accounts. Selection "b" is incorrect; financial statements are prepared before closing entries are done. If closing entries were posted first, the income statement would include nothing but zero amounts. Selection "d" is incorrect; closing entries will affect only temporary accounts and owners' equity. (Solution = c.)

Question

14. The Office Supplies on Hand account had a balance at the beginning of year 3 of $1,600. Payments for acquisitions of office supplies during year 3 amounted to $10,000 and were recorded as a debit to the expense account. A physical count at the end of year 3 revealed supplies costing $1,900 were on hand. Reversing entries are used by this company. The required adjusting entry at the end of year 3 will include a debit to:
   a. Office Supplies Expense for $300.
   b. Office Supplies on Hand for $300.
   c. Office Supplies Expense for $9,700.
   d. Office Supplies on Hand for $1,900.

EXPLANATION: Draw T-accounts. Enter the data given and solve for the adjusting entry. Compare each alternative answer to the adjusting entry you have sketched in the accounts. (Solution = d.)

Office Supplies Expense (Debit)	Office Supplies Expense (Credit)
Reversing 1,600	
Acqstns. 10,000	(1,900)
Ending Bal. 9,700	

← ENTRY NEEDED TO COMPLETE ACCOUNTS →

Office Supplies on Hand (Debit)	Office Supplies on Hand (Credit)
Beg. Bal. 1,600	
(1,900)	Reversing 1,600
Desired Ending Bal. 1,900	

Question

15. The Office Supplies on Hand account had a balance at the beginning of year 3 of $1,600. Payments for purchases of office supplies during year 3 amounted to $10,000 and were recorded by a debit to an expense account. A physical count at the end of year 3 revealed supplies costing $1,900 were on hand. Reversing entries are **not used** by this company. The required adjusting entry at the end of year 3 will include a debit to:
   a. Office Supplies Expense for $300.
   b. Office Supplies on Hand for $300.
   c. Office Supplies Expense for $9,700.
   d. Office Supplies on Hand for $1,900.
   e. none of the above.

EXPLANATION: Draw T-accounts. Enter the data given and solve for the adjusting entry. Compare each alternative answer to the adjusting entry you have sketched in the accounts. (Solution = b.)

Office Supplies Expense (Debit)	Office Supplies Expense (Credit)
Acquisitions 10,000	
	(300)
Ending Bal. 9,700	

← ENTRY NEEDED TO COMPLETE ACCOUNTS →

Office Supplies on Hand (Debit)	Office Supplies on Hand (Credit)
Beg. Bal. 1,600	
(300)	
Desired Ending Bal. 1,900	

Question

16. John Chu Limited just purchased a car that will be used for its sales person. In order to capture this event, the company should record the transaction in the following manner:
    a. Prepare a journal entry and generate a journal and unadjusted trial balance.
    b. Prepare the journal entry and post to a journal/database.
    c. Prepare the journal entry but do not post until month end.
    d. Prepare the journal entry and also prepare financial statements.

EXPLANATION: A journal entry must be prepared to capture the transaction. The journal entry must then be posted either to a journal or into a database. The company would not generate a trial balance or financial statement until the end of a reporting period. (Solution = b.)

Chapter 4

Reporting Financial Performance

Overview

An income statement reports on the results of operations of an entity for a period of time. It is important to classify revenues, expenses, gains, and losses properly on the income statement. In this chapter, we discuss the income statement classifications and the content of the statement of retained earnings, along with related disclosure issues such as irregular items and earnings per share. It is imperative that charges and credits that represent elements of income determination be properly reflected in the financial statements. Errors in the determination of income cause errors on the income statement, statement of retained earnings, and balance sheet. The concepts of "Comprehensive Income" and "Other Comprehensive Income" are also discussed.

Tips on Chapter Topics

TIP! The **income statement** or **statement of income** is often referred to as the "statement of operations" or the "operating statement" because it reports on the results of operations for a period of time. Other names given to it include the "earnings statement," "statement of earnings," and "profit and loss statement" (or "P&L statement").

TIP! Canadian GAAP has added another element to the income statement—specifically the concept of **comprehensive income**. Comprehensive income will, by definition, include net income. Therefore, the concept of "**Other Comprehensive Income**" (OCI) is important. Items such as the unrealized gain or loss on an "Available for Sale" financial asset will be included in OCI.

TIP! The income statement is often referred to as a link between balance sheets because it explains one major reason why the balance of shareholders' equity changed during the period. Shareholders' equity (net assets) at the beginning of the period can be reconciled with ending shareholders' equity as follows:

	Shareholders' equity at the beginning of the period
-	Dividends paid
+/-	Results of operations for the period (net income or net loss)
=	Shareholders' equity at the end of the period

TIP! The above equation will now be affected by the presence of "**Accumulated Other Comprehensive Income**" (AOCI), which is the cumulative impact of "**Other Comprehensive Income**" (OCI) recognized each year.

TIP! To summarize, net income will "close" to retained earnings as usual. "Other Comprehensive Income" will "close" to Accumulated Other Comprehensive Income" in the equity section.

TIP! A comprehensive income statement will only be required if an entity has items that affect it. In other words, a comprehensive income statement is not required if it is zero.

TIP! The income statement is used by investors and creditors to (1) evaluate the enterprise's past performance; (2) provide a basis for predicting future performance; and (3) help assess the risk or uncertainty of achieving future cash flows.

TIP! The income statement is limited in its usefulness by the accounting policy choices, estimations, and assumptions, which are reflected in the numbers.

TIP! The higher the quality of information, the more useful the income statement is to users. High quality earnings are reflected in the choice of accounting policies and estimations that require less judgment, and reduce bias. Cash flows that are more closely correlated with the event in the same time period, and which have more predictive and feedback value and represent economic reality, all increase the quality of earnings.

TIP! A **contra revenue** item has the same effect on net income as that of an expense; it decreases net income. Contra revenue accounts include Sales Discounts and Sales Returns and Allowances.

TIP! The income tax consequences of all items appearing above the line "Income from continuing operations before income taxes" are summarized in the line "Income taxes." Revenues cause an increase in income taxes and expenses cause a decrease in income taxes. The income tax consequences of items appearing below the "income from continuing operations" line are reported right along with the items (hence, these items are reported "net of tax"). This procedure of allocating income taxes within a period is referred to as **intraperiod tax allocation**.

TIP! An extraordinary item is reported "net of tax" by deducting the tax effect from the related gain or loss. For example, if the tax rate is 30 percent, an extraordinary gain of $400,000 will be reported at $280,000 net of tax. Likewise, an extraordinary loss of $400,000 will be reported at $280,000 net of tax. The gain situation increases net income, whereas the loss reduces it.

TIP! Corrections for errors in the reporting of revenues and expenses in prior periods are accounted for as **prior period adjustments**. A prior period adjustment is reported as an adjustment (debit or credit, whichever is applicable) to the opening balance of Retained Earnings on the retained earnings statement for the current period (period in which the adjustment is made) and is shown net of any related income tax effect.

TIP! Net income minus preferred share dividend requirements (i.e., income applicable to common shareholders) is divided by the weighted average of common stock shares outstanding to arrive at earnings per share (EPS). This is a key ratio in financial analysis and must be disclosed on the face of the income statement. A per share amount must **always** be disclosed for "net income". Also, the following holds true:

(1) A company that reports discontinued operations must report a per share amount for that item.
(2) A company that reports an extraordinary item must report a per share amount for the extraordinary item.

TIP! In the EPS calculation, preferred dividends are deducted from net income if they were declared; however, if the preferred share is cumulative, the preferred dividend preference for the current period is deducted whether or not the dividends were declared. Dividends declared on common shares have no effect on the EPS calculation.

Study Steps

Understanding the Importance of the Income Statement in Financial Decision Making

Income statements tell a story about the company. Before looking at any financial reporting issues, briefly review the income statement to see if revenues and profits are increasing/decreasing and at what rate. Focus also on EPS. If these are decreasing, there may be some motivation to try to artificially increase them, perhaps by recognizing revenues more aggressively or by expense deferral.

Even before looking at the trends noted in the above tips, determine what the main (and ancillary) business of the company is. Where do they make their money and how? What are their major expenses? This will also give some insight into financial reporting issues that may be material. Many issues revolve around identifying the earnings process of the company and whether or not it is complete.

A quick study of earnings assessment will also give some insight into the company; i.e., are the earnings managed? Do they have predictive value?

Required disclosures

How information is presented on the income statement is often largely a matter of professional judgment. Be sensitive to what is required disclosure and whether a company is providing additional information or the minimum required under GAAP.

CICA Handbook Section 1520 requires at least a distinction between recurring, normal operating activities and non-recurring, non-operating activities. Also, there are certain minimum disclosure requirements such as revenues, income from leases, government assistance, and others.

The *CICA Handbook* also adopts the all-inclusive approach with a few exceptions (for example, error corrections) that would be booked through the statement of retained earnings. In practice, larger companies give a minimum level of detail and use a multiple-step approach. Remember that the required disclosures in the *CICA Handbook* may also be disclosed in the notes.

Components of the income statement and respective predictive value for users

Since recurring income or net income from continuing operations is a key number, care should be taken to ensure that items grouped as discontinued or extraordinary do indeed belong there. There may be a bias on the part of the preparer to classify a loss as extraordinary when it does not fully meet the criteria, or a gain in continuing operations when it may be clearly extraordinary.

Exercise 4-1

PURPOSE: This exercise reviews the basic accounting formula (Assets = Liabilities + Owners' Equity) and the connection between the income statement and the balance sheet (which is a change in owners' equity due to the net income or net loss for the period).

The following data were extracted from the records of Dora Loesing's Cookies, a sole proprietorship:

	Dr.	Cr.
Total assets, beginning of the period	$100,000	
Total liabilities, beginning of the period		36,000
Owner withdrawals during the period	30,000	
Total assets, end of the period	108,000	
Total liabilities, end of the period		38,000
Owner's contributions during the period		10,000

Instructions

Calculate the amount of net income (or loss) for the period. Show calculations.

Solution to Exercise 4-1

Beginning owners' equity	$ 64,000 [a]
Additional owner contributions	10,000
Owner withdrawals during the period	(30,000)
Subtotal	44,000
Net income (loss) for the period	X
Ending owner's equity	$ 70,000 [b]
Solving for X, net income =	$ 26,000

[a] A = L + OE
$100,000 = $36,000 + ?
Beginning owners' equity = $64,000

[b] A = L + OE
$108,000 = $38,000 + ?
Ending owners' equity = $70,000

APPROACH: The question asks you to solve for net income; however, no information is given regarding revenues and expenses for the period. Only balance sheet data and transactions affecting owners' equity are given. Net income (or net loss) for a period is one reason for a change in the balance of owners' equity. Write down the items that reconcile the beginning owners' equity balance with the ending owners' equity balance, enter the amounts known, calculate beginning and ending owners' equity balances by use of the basic accounting equation, and then solve for the amount of net income. Recall that assets - liabilities = net assets; that is, assets - liabilities = owners' equity at a point in time.

TIP!

The basic accounting equation (A = L + OE) is applied at a specific point in time. When you have the facts for the equation components at two different points in time for the same entity (such as amounts as of the beginning of a year and amounts as of the end of a year), you can modify the basic accounting equation to reflect that total changes in assets = total changes in liabilities + total changes in owners' equity. Using the symbol Δ to designate change, the following equation also holds true:

$$\Delta A = \Delta L + \Delta OE$$

Reasons for changes in owners' equity include:

(1) additional owner investments,
(2) owner withdrawals, and
(3) results of operations (net income or net loss).

TIP!

When using the **capital maintenance** (or **change in equity**) approach, the amount of owners' equity is determined at the beginning and at the end of the period (using the same valuation method). The difference between these two amounts, adjusted for owner withdrawals and additional owner investments during the same period, is the measure of net income for the period.

TIP! Net income (or net loss) is the change in owners' equity for a period of time, other than from capital transactions. Capital transactions are those that involve owners acting in their capacity of being owners of the entity.

Illustration 4-1

Elements of the Income Statement

REVENUES: Increases in economic resources either by way of inflows or enhancements of an entity's assets or settlement of liabilities resulting from its ordinary activities.

EXPENSES: Decreases in economic resources, either by outflows or reductions of assets or incurrence of liabilities, resulting from an entity's ordinary revenue-generating activities.

GAINS: Increases in equity (net assets) from peripheral or incidental transactions of an entity and from all other transactions or events and circumstances affecting the entity during a period except those that result from revenues or investments by owners.

LOSSES: Decreases in equity (net assets) from peripheral or incidental transactions of an entity and from all other transactions and other events and circumstances affecting the entity during a period except those that result from expenses or distributions to owners.

OTHER COMPREHENSIVE INCOME: Gains and losses which are recognized in comprehensive income but excluded from net income.

Revenues take many forms, such as sales revenue, fees earned, dividend income, and rents earned. Expenses also take many forms, such as cost of goods sold, rent, salaries, depreciation, interest, and taxes.

Revenues and gains are similar (they both increase net income), and expenses and losses are similar (they both decrease net income). However, these terms are dissimilar in the fact that they convey significantly different information about an enterprise's performance. Revenues and expenses result from an entity's ongoing major or central operations and activities—that is, from activities such as producing or delivering goods, rendering services, lending, insuring, investing, and financing. In contrast, gains and losses result from incidental or peripheral transactions of an enterprise with other entities and from other events and circumstances affecting it. Gains and losses often arise from the sale of investments;

disposal of plant assets; settlement of liabilities for an amount other than their book value; and writeoffs of assets due to obsolescence, casualty, or theft. Other comprehensive income includes unrealized gains and losses on certain securities, certain foreign exchange gains and losses, and other gains and losses.

Revenues and expenses are commonly displayed as **gross** inflows or outflows of net assets; while gains and losses are usually displayed as **net** inflows or outflows. For example, assume a company buys an inventory item for $6,000, sells it for $10,000, and pays a sales representative a $1,000 commission. Further, the same company sells for $20,000 a plant asset with a book value (carrying value) of $15,000 and pays an outside agency $2,100 for finding the buyer. The various flows associated with the first transaction (the company's major activity or regular operations) will be reported gross on its income statement, and the various elements of the second transaction (a peripheral transaction) will be reported net. Assuming these were the only two transactions completed during the period and ignoring income taxes, the income statement would reflect the following:

Sales revenue	$ 10,000
Cost of goods sold expense	6,000
Gross profit	4,000
Selling expense (sales commission)	1,000
Income from operations	3,000
Gain on sale of plant asset	2,900 [a]
Net income	$ 5,900

[a] $20,000 proceeds – $15,000 book value – $2,100 finders fee = $2,900 gain on sale.

TIP! Net income results from revenue, expense, gain, and loss transactions. These transactions are summarized in the income statement. This method of income measurement is called the **transaction approach** because it focuses on the income-related activities (broken down into completed transactions) that have occurred during the period.

TIP! Single-step income statement has only two groupings (Revenues and Expenses). It eliminates classification problems and is often used for simplicity.

Exercise 4-2

PURPOSE: This exercise will help you to determine which type of business activities should be classified as regular (normal operations) and which are irregular (unusual or extraordinary).

From the following list of activities, determine whether this would be classified as regular business activities, or unusual or extraordinary. Mark an (x) in the appropriate column:

		Continuing Operations	Extraordinary	Unusual
1.	Losses due to expropriation of assets in a foreign country			
2.	Revenues from Ottawa Senators selling pop and hot dogs			
3.	Loss due to hurricane at Jamaican subsidiary			
4.	Loss due to hurricane at Calgary subsidiary			
5.	Loss of inventory at a warehouse due to flood in Halifax			
6.	Toronto Maple Leafs selling hockey jerseys			
7.	Loss due to power outage caused by severe ice storm in Ottawa			
8.	Gain from winning a lawsuit against a major competitor			
9.	Loss due to a strike at a subsidiary			
10.	Gain of $2,000,000 from winning the Lotto 6-49 jackpot from a ticket purchased with company funds			

APPROACH: Define each of the terms "continuing operation" and "extraordinary item". A continuing operation results from activities in the normal course of operations for an enterprise. This will differ from one enterprise to another in different industries. An extraordinary item must meet all three criteria (infrequent in nature, atypical of normal business activities, and does not depend on decisions of management or owners).

1. Expropriation of assets does meet all three of the requirements of an extraordinary item.
2. Even though the Senators are a hockey team, vending sales would be part of the normal operations of the organization.
3. Losses due to a hurricane in Jamaica would be a fairly normal occurrence for the Caribbean and thus would be considered continuing operations. If the losses were severe, they may be classified as unusual in nature, but management was fully aware of the regular occurrence of hurricanes in the Caribbean when they established the business there.
4. A hurricane in Calgary, however, is not a regular occurrence and thus would be classified as an extraordinary event as this would not be anticipated by management as a regular occurrence.
5. The loss due to a flood would be determined as an extraordinary item depending on the regularity of flooding. If this were built on the flood plains of the Mississippi, it would be a normal occurrence and, hence, continuing operations; but since this is not a regular occurrence in Halifax, it would be considered extraordinary.
6. The Toronto Maple Leafs are a hockey team, but it is management's intention to make revenues selling hockey jerseys; thus this is considered regular income.
7. Again, the ice storm is a situation which does occur in Ottawa. The severity of the storm and materiality of the losses would determine whether this is classified as unusual or extraordinary.
8. A gain from a lawsuit would be considered to be an unusual item. It is a result of normal business operations, but investors would want to know that this is not considered a normal earnings stream for the company, and

thus it would be separated out on the income statement as unusual (depending on materiality).

9. A strike, unpleasant as it may be, is a normal occurrence in a business setting and thus would be considered to be continuing operations. The severity and materiality of losses occurring from the strike would need to be identified as to whether it is classified as unusual.
10. This, extraordinary as it may seem, would not be considered an extraordinary item. The definition of extraordinary requires the event not to be primarily dependant on decisions made by management. Management in this case purchased the ticket with the hope of winning, and thus it is a result of a management action. It would be classified as unusual so as to not let investors think this will be a normal revenue stream for the company.

Illustration 4-2

Sections of a Multiple-Step Income Statement

1. **Operating Section.** A report of the revenues and expenses of the company's principal operations. (This section may or may not be presented on a departmental basis.)
   (a) **Sales or Revenue Section:** A subsection presenting sales, discounts, allowances, returns, and other related information. Its purpose is to arrive at the net amount of sales revenue.
   (b) **Cost of Goods Sold Section:** A subsection that shows the cost of goods that were sold to produce the sales.
   (c) **Selling Expenses:** A subsection that lists expenses resulting from the company's efforts to make sales.
   (d) **Administrative or General Expenses:** A subsection reporting expenses of general administration.

2. **Non-operating Section.** A report of revenues and expenses resulting from secondary or auxiliary activities of the company. In addition, special gains and losses that are infrequent or unusual, but not both, are normally reported in this section. Generally these items break down into two main subsections:
   (a) **Other Revenues and Gains:** A list of the revenues earned or gains incurred, generally net of related expenses, from non-operating transactions.
   (b) **Other Expenses and Losses:** A list of the expenses or losses incurred, generally net of any related incomes, from non-operating transactions.

3. **Income Taxes.** A short section reporting federal and provincial taxes levied on income from continuing operations.

4. **DISCONTINUED OPERATIONS:** Material gains or losses resulting from the disposal of part of the business (net of tax).

5. **EXTRAORDINARY ITEMS:** Unusual and infrequent material gains and losses beyond the control of management (net of tax).

6. **EARNINGS PER SHARE**

7. **OTHER COMPREHENSIVE INCOME**

Exercise 4-3

PURPOSE: This exercise will allow you to contrast the multiple-step format and the single-step format for the income statement.

The accountant for Bubble Bath Products, Inc. has compiled the following information from the company's records as a basis for an income statement for the year ended December 31, 2008. (There was no change during the year in the 12,000 common shares outstanding.)

Net sales	$ 970,000
Amortization on plant assets (60% selling, 40% administrative)	70,000
Dividends declared	14,400
Rent revenue	30,000
Interest on notes payable	17,000
Market appreciation on land held as an investment	44,000
Merchandise purchases	421,000
Transportation-in—merchandise	37,000
Merchandise inventory, January 1, 2008	82,000
Merchandise inventory, December 31, 2008	81,000
Purchase returns and allowances	11,000
Wages and salaries—sales	95,000
Materials and supplies—sales	11,400
Income taxes	45,000
Wages and salaries—administrative	135,900
Other administrative expenses	46,700
Advertising expense	20,000
Express mail	6,000

Instructions

(a) Prepare a multiple-step income statement.
(b) Prepare a single-step income statement.

Solution to Exercise 4-3

(a)

Bubble Bath Products, Inc.
INCOME STATEMENT
For the Year Ending December 31, 2008

Sales Revenue			
Net sales revenue		$970,000	
Cost of Goods Sold			
Merchandise inventory, Jan. 1		$ 82,000	
Purchases	$ 421,000		
Less purchase returns & allowances	11,000		
Net purchases	410,000		
Transportation-in	37,000	447,000	
Total merchandise available for sale		529,000	
Less merchandise inventory, Dec. 31		81,000	
Cost of goods sold		448,000	
Gross profit		522,000	
Operating Expenses			
Selling expenses			
Wages and salaries	95,000		
Advertising	20,000		
Materials and supplies	11,400		
Amortization (60% x $70,000)	42,000		
Express mail	6,000	174,400	
Administrative expenses			
Wages and salaries	135,900		
Amortization (40% x $70,000)	28,000		
Other administrative expenses	46,700	210,600	385,000
Income from operations			137,000
Other Revenues and Gains			
Rent revenue			30,000
			167,000
Other Expenses and Losses			
Interest expense			17,000
Income before taxes			150,000
Income taxes			45,000
Net income			$105,000
Earnings per share ($105,000 ÷ 12,000)			$8.75

TIP! Dividends declared do not appear on the income statement. They are a distribution of corporate income—**not** a determinant of net income. Increases in the market value of assets (such as plant assets, and inventory) are not recognized in the accounts until they are realized through the sale of the assets. Hence, the market appreciation on the land held as an investment does not appear on the income statement. However, had this asset been a financial asset such as a marketable security, the gain would either be recognized in net income (if classified as held-for-trading) or other comprehensive income (if classified as available-for-sale). These are discussed further in Chapter 9.

(b)

Bubble Bath Products, Inc.
INCOME STATEMENT
For the Year Ending December 31, 2008

Revenues	
Net sales	$ 970,000
Rent revenue	30,000
Total revenue	1,000,000
Expenses	
Cost of goods sold	448,000
Selling expenses	174,400
Administrative expenses	210,600
Interest expense	17,000
Total expenses	850,000
Income before taxes	150,000
Income taxes	45,000
Net income	$ 105,000
Earnings per share	$8.75

TIP! In the single-step income statement, just two groupings exist: revenues and expenses. Expenses are deducted from revenues to arrive at net income or loss. The expression "single-step" is derived from the single subtraction necessary to arrive at net income. Frequently, however, income taxes are reported separately to indicate their direct relationship to income before income taxes.

TIP! In the multiple-step income statement, there are three major subtotals presented before arriving at net income. They are: net sales revenue, gross profit, and income from operations. These subtotals emphasize (1) a classification of expenses by function, such as merchandising or manufacturing (cost of goods sold), selling, and administration, and (2) a separation of operating and subordinate or non-operating activities of the company. The "other revenues and gains" and "other expenses and losses" sections include (1) investing and financing revenues and expenses such as interest revenue, dividend revenue (from dividends received), and interest expense, and (2) the results of non-operating items such as the sale of plant assets and investments.

TIP! The nature of an entity's typical operations is critical in determining whether the results of a transaction should be classified as an operating or a non-operating revenue, gain, expense, or loss. For example, consider rental activities. A business specializing in equipment rentals will classify rent revenue as an operating revenue. Whereas, a retail establishment that occasionally rents its temporarily idle assets to others will classify rent revenue as a non-operating (other) revenue. For a second example, consider the sale of an investment. An investment dealer will report the revenue from a sale as an operating revenue. Whereas, a retail entity that occasionally sells an investment will report the difference between the proceeds from the sale and the investment's carrying value as a non-operating gain or loss.

TIP! There is no specific order in which the individual selling expenses and administrative expenses are to be listed in the multiple-step income statement. Very often, they appear in order of decreasing magnitude.

TIP! Some accountants prefer to use a multiple-step income statement format because it discloses the amount of income from operations. Thus, by this disclosure, the difference between regular and irregular or incidental activities is highlighted. Irregular activities encompass transactions and other events that are derived from developments outside the normal operations of the business. Thus, they may not be expected to continue at the same level in future periods.

TIP! Some investors prefer a multiple-step income statement as it helps to identify specific types of revenues and expenses, which are primary or ancillary to normal business activities, as well as year over year comparisons. This helps determine repetitiveness and importance of earnings.

TIP! Within the income statement, net income from continuing operations (versus discontinued items or extraordinary items) is more important to many users since it provides the best indicator of future income.

TIP! Quality of earnings analysis assesses the quality of the information presented and recognizes that not all information presented is of equal utility in decision making. Users must be aware of any bias or objective the company may have in preparing the financials.

Exercise 4-4

PURPOSE: This exercise will give you practice in identifying components of net income and the order of items appearing on a single-step income statement and on a retained earnings statement.

Presented on the next page is the adjusted trial balance of Hip Corporation at December 31, 2008. The account titles and balances are **not** in the customary order.

Hip Corporation
ADJUSTED TRIAL BALANCE
December 31, 2008

	Debits	Credits
Sales		$ 958,500
Notes Receivable	$ 80,000	
Investments	88,500	
Accounts Payable		51,000
Accumulated Amortization—Equipment		31,500
Sales Discounts	10,500	
Sales Returns	17,500	
Purchase Discounts		8,000
Cash	190,000	
Accounts Receivable	95,000	
Rent Revenue		14,000
Retained Earnings		240,000
Salaries Payable		22,000
Notes Payable		75,000
Common Shares, $15 par		300,000
Income Tax Expense	68,000	
Cash Dividends Declared	70,000	
Allowance for Doubtful Accounts		6,500
Supplies on Hand	11,000	
Freight-In	16,000	
Selling Expenses	212,000	
Administrative Expenses	114,000	
Land	65,000	
Equipment	130,000	
Merchandise Inventory	79,000	
Building	104,000	
Purchases	500,000	
Dividend Income		10,000
Loss on Sale of Investment	13,000	
Interest Revenue		9,000
Interest Expense	12,500	
Bonds Payable		100,000
Gain on Sale of Land		24,500
Accumulated Amortization—Building		26,000
Totals	$ 1,876,000	$ 1,876,000

The company uses the periodic inventory system. A physical count of inventory on December 31 resulted in an inventory amount of $100,000.

Instructions

(a) Prepare an income statement for the year ending December 31, 2008, using the single-step form. Assume that 20,000 common shares were outstanding the entire year.

(b) Prepare a retained earnings statement for the year ending December 31, 2008. Assume that the only changes in retained earnings during the current year were from net income and dividends.

Solution to Exercise 4-4

(a)

Hip Corporation
INCOME STATEMENT
For the Year Ended December 31, 2008

Revenues	
Net sales *	$ 930,500
Gain on sale of land	24,500
Rent revenue	14,000
Dividend income	10,000
Interest revenue	9,000
Total revenues	988,000
Expenses	
Cost of goods sold**	487,000
Selling expenses	212,000
Administrative expenses	114,000
Loss on sale of investment	13,000
Interest expense	12,500
Total expenses	838,500
Income before taxes	149,500
Income taxes	68,000
Net income	$ 81,500
Earnings per common share ($81,500 ÷ 20,000)	$ 4.08

*Net sales:

Sales		$ 958,500
Less: Sales discounts	$ 10,500	
Sales returns	17,500	28,000
Net sales		$ 930,500

**Cost of goods sold:

Merchandise inventory, Jan. 1		$ 79,000
Purchases	$ 500,000	
Less purchase discounts	8,000	
Net purchases		492,000
Add freight-in		16,000
Merchandise available for sale		587,000
Less merchandise inventory, Dec.31		100,000
Cost of merchandise sold		$ 487,000

TIP! The solution presented here reports income taxes separately as the last item before net income to indicate their relationship to income before taxes. It is acceptable to list the income taxes in the expenses classification and omit the subtotal "income before taxes."

(b)

Hip Corporation
RETAINED EARNINGS STATEMENT
For the Year Ended December 31, 2008

Balance, January 1	$240,000
Add: Net income	81,500
	321,500
Less: Cash dividends declared	70,000
Balance, December 31	$251,500

APPROACH:

1. Go through the adjusted trial balance and lightly cross through any account title that does not pertain to the calculation of net income. With the exception of the balance of Merchandise Inventory (which is used to calculate cost of goods sold when a periodic inventory system is in use), balance sheet account balances are not used in determining net income.
2. Calculate intermediate subtotals for items such as (a) net sales, (b) cost of goods sold, (c) selling expenses, and (d) administrative expenses. Show your calculations for these subtotals. (In this particular exercise, selling expenses and administrative expenses are already summarized.)
3. Identify revenue and gain items.
4. Identify expense and loss items.
5. Identify income taxes for the period.
6. Identify any discontinued operations and extraordinary items.
7. Calculate net income.
8. Calculate earnings per share.
9. Identify the retained earnings balance at the beginning of the period.
10. Include any prior period adjustments on the statement of retained earnings (none are identified in this exercise).
11. Add net income for the period.
12. Deduct dividends declared.
13. Arrive at the retained earnings balance at the end of the period.

TIP! The account balances in the adjusted trial balance that are **not** used for the solution requested are as follows: Notes Receivable, Investments, Accounts Payable, Accumulated Amortization—Equipment, Cash, Accounts Receivable, Salaries Payable, Notes Payable, Common Shares, Allowance for Doubtful Accounts, Supplies on Hand, Land, Equipment, Building, Bonds Payable, and Accumulated Amortization—Building.

Exercise 4-5

PURPOSE: This exercise is designed to give you practice in preparing a condensed multiple-step income statement and a retained earnings statement when an extraordinary item and a change in accounting principle are to be reported.

Presented below is information related to Smith Corp., for the year 2009.

Net sales	$ 650,000
Cost of goods sold	400,000
Selling expenses	32,000
Administrative expenses	24,000
Dividend revenue	10,000
Interest revenue	7,000
Interest expense	15,000
Writeoff of goodwill due to impairment	25,000
Amortization expense omitted in 2007	35,000
Uninsured loss due to flood (unusual and infrequent)	60,000
Dividends declared	42,000
Retained earnings at December 31, 2008	1,800,000
Cumulative effect on prior years of change in accounting policy (credit)	75,000
Tax rate of 30% on all items	

Instructions

(a) Prepare a multiple-step income statement for 2009. Assume that 50,000 common shares were outstanding during 2009.

(b) Prepare a retained earnings statement for 2009.

Solution to Exercise 4-5

(a)

Smith Corp.
INCOME STATEMENT
For the Year Ended December 31, 2009

Net sales		$ 650,000
Cost of goods sold		400,000
Gross profit		250,000
Operating expenses		
Selling expenses	$ 32,000	
Administrative expenses	24,000	56,000
Income from operations		194,000
Other revenues and gains		
Dividend revenue	10,000	
Interest revenue	7,000	17,000
		211,000
Other expenses and losses		
Interest expense	15,000	
Loss due to writeoff of goodwill	25,000	40,000
Income before taxes and extraordinary item		171,000
Income taxes		51,300
Income before extraordinary item		119,700
Extraordinary item—loss from flood	60,000	
Less applicable income tax effect	18,000	42,000
Net income		$ 77,700

Per common share:	
Income before extraordinary item ($119,700 ÷ 50,000)	$2.39
Extraordinary item (net of tax) ($42,000 ÷ 50,000)	(.84)
Net income ($77,700 ÷ 50,000)	$1.55

TIP! The total income taxes pertaining to 2009 for this company was $33,300. This represents the $51,300 in tax on income before considering the loss from flood and the impact of the accounting change. The tax savings resulting from the flood are shown separately for accounting purposes but for tax return purposes will be netted to arrive at $33,300. The tax impact of the change in accounting policy involves future income taxes, which is discussed in Chapter 18.

(b)

Smith Corp.
RETAINED EARNINGS STATEMENT
For the Year Ended December 31, 2009

Retained earnings, Jan. 1, 2009, as previously reported		$1,800,000
Correction of an error in amortization in prior period (net of $10,500 income tax effect)*		(24,500)
Adjusted balance of retained earnings at Jan. 1, 2009		1,775,500
Net income		77,700
		1,853,200
Dividends declared		42,000
		$ 1,811,200
Retained earnings, December 31, 2009		
* Omitted Amortization	(35,000)	
less: tax savings (30%)	10,500	
net correction to retained earnings	(24,500)	

Illustration 4-3

Treatment Of Irregular Items

1. **DISCONTINUED OPERATIONS.** The results of operations (income or loss) of a component of a business that has been or will be disposed of are reported in a separate income statement category called "discontinued operations." This category appears **after** continuing operations but **before** extraordinary items. It is reported net of the related income tax effect.
2. **EXTRAORDINARY ITEMS.** Extraordinary items are reported individually in a separate category (immediately after discontinued operations, if any) net of any related income tax effect. Extraordinary items are defined as non-recurring (infrequent) material items that differ significantly from the entity's typical business activities. In addition to being material in amount, a transaction or event must meet all three of the following criteria to be classified as extraordinary:
   (a) **INFREQUENCY OF OCCURRENCE.** The underlying event or transaction should be of a type that would not reasonably be expected to recur in the foreseeable future, taking into account the environment in which the entity operates.
   (b) **UNUSUAL NATURE.** The underlying event or transaction should possess a high degree of abnormality and be of a type clearly unrelated to, or only incidentally related to, the ordinary and typical activities of the entity, taking into account the environment in which the entity operates.
   (c) **DETERMINATION BY MANAGEMENT.** The underlying event or transaction is not the result of actions or decisions taken by management or owners.

Examples of items that are **not** classified as extraordinary:

(a) Write down or writeoff of receivables, inventories, equipment leased to others, deferred research and development costs, or other intangible assets.

(b) Gains or losses from exchange or translation of foreign currencies, including those relating to major devaluations and revaluations.

(c) Gains or losses on disposal of a segment of a business.

(d) Other gains or losses from sale or abandonment of property, plant, or equipment used in the business.

(e) Effects of a strike, including those against competitors and major suppliers.

(f) Adjustment of accruals on long-term contracts.

Examples of items that **are** classified as extraordinary:

An event or transaction that clearly meets all criteria (unusual in nature and infrequent in occurrence and not the result of management or owner intervention) and gives rise to a gain or loss from the write down or writeoff of assets or to a gain or loss from disposal of assets and is a **direct result** of one of the following:

(a) A major casualty (such as an earthquake, tornado, hurricane, flood, or hail storm).

(b) An expropriation (such as the confiscation of assets by a government or the exercise of eminent domain or condemnation).

(c) A prohibition under a newly enacted law or regulation.

3. **UNUSUAL GAINS AND LOSSES.** A gain or loss that arises from a transaction that is unusual or infrequent, but not both, should be reported in the income statement as part of "income from continuing operations" (or "income before extraordinary items"). If the amount is material, it should be separately disclosed; if the amount is immaterial, it may be combined with other items on the income statement. In a multiple-step income statement, unusual gains and losses normally are classified in the "other revenues and gains" or "other expenses and losses" section, although a separate unusual items section may be displayed. Unusual gains and losses are **not** to be reported net of tax; rather, the tax consequences of these items are combined with the tax effects of all other components of income from continuing operations in the line called "income taxes".
4. **CHANGES IN ACCOUNTING POLICY.** A change in accounting policy occurs when a company changes from one generally accepted method to another generally accepted method. The initial adoption of an accounting policy is not considered a change in policy. Because such a change violates consistency and, therefore, reduces or destroys comparability of successive financial statements, a **voluntary** change in policy will only be allowed when the newly adopted policy results in financial information that is more **relevant** and **reliable** than the old method. This reasoning must also be disclosed in the notes. A change in policy to comply with a new GAAP standard (such as financial

instruments), is not subject to this rule. No other changes in accounting policy are permitted. A change in accounting policy is generally recognized through retrospective restatement. The financial statements for all prior periods that are presented for comparative purposes should be restated, except when that information may not be reasonably determined. If the impact cannot be determined, or all comparative years are not disclosed, a cumulative amount would be calculated and adjusted through opening retained earnings. (Discussed further in Chapter 21.)

5. **CHANGES IN ACCOUNTING ESTIMATE (Normal Recurring Corrections and Adjustments)**. A change from one good-faith estimate to another good-faith estimate because of new information or experience constitutes a change in accounting estimate. A change in an estimate will affect the amount of related revenue or expense reported in the period of change if the change affects only that period, or in the period of change (called the current period) and future periods if the change affects both. Examples are a change in the estimate of uncollectible accounts receivable (bad debts expense) and a change in the estimated service life of a plant (fixed) asset (amortization expense). A change in estimate is not considered a correction of an error (prior period adjustment); therefore, it is **not** handled retroactively. However, the impact of the change in estimate on net income should be disclosed. (Discussed further in Chapter 21.)

Exercise 4-6

PURPOSE: This exercise will test your knowledge of the elements and arrangement of the major sections of the income statement.

Instructions

The following list represents captions that would appear on an income statement (single-step format) for a company reporting an extraordinary gain, losses from discontinued operations, and a change in amortization method, as well as the results of continuing operations for the period. You are to "unscramble" the list and prepare a skeleton income statement using the captions given. (If you do not wish to write out each caption above, you may still test your knowledge by listing the appropriate letters in the correct order.)

(a) Income before extraordinary item
(b) Revenues
(c) Income taxes
(d) Discontinued operations
(e) Extraordinary gain (net of tax)
(f) Expenses
(g) Loss from disposal of discontinued component of business (net of tax)
(h) Net income

(i) Income from continuing operations before income taxes
(j) Loss from operations of discontinued component of business (net of tax)
(k) Income from continuing operations
(l) Other comprehensive income

Solution to Exercise 4-6

Company Name
INCOME STATEMENT
For the Year Ended December 31, 20XX

(b) Revenues
(f) Expenses
(i) Income from continuing operations before income taxes
(c) Income taxes
(k) Income from continuing operations
(d) Discontinued operations
(j) Loss from operations of discontinued component of business (net of tax)
(g) Loss from disposal of discontinued component of business (net of tax)
(a) Income before extraordinary item
(e) Extraordinary gain (net of tax)
(h) Net income
(l) Other comprehensive income.

TIP! The **current operating performance concept** would call for all irregular gains and losses and corrections of revenues and expenses of prior periods to be taken directly into the Retained Earnings account, rather than reported in the current period's income statement. The **all-inclusive concept** would call for these items to all be reported in the current period's income statement. Generally accepted accounting principles currently requires a **modified all-inclusive concept**. This means the corrections of revenues and expenses of prior periods go directly to Retained Earnings and, with minor exceptions, all other items (such as unusual gains and losses; discontinued operations and extraordinary items) are reported on the income statement.

Exercise 4-7

PURPOSE: This exercise will enable you to practice identifying the proper classification for items on an income statement. It will also give you an example of how the tax effects of various items are reflected in the income statement.

Margaret Moylan had the following selected transactions and events occur during 2008. The corporation is subject to a 30% tax rate on all items. All amounts are material. The corporation is engaged in the sale of energy products.

1. The corporation experienced an uninsured flood loss in the amount of $60,000 during the year. A flood is unusual and infrequent in the region where the corporation resides.
2. At the beginning of 2006, the corporation purchased an office machine for $108,000 (salvage value of $18,000) that has a useful life of six years. The bookkeeper used straight-line amortization for 2006 and 2007, but failed to deduct the salvage value in computing the amortizable base. The same amortization calculations were used for tax purposes.
3. Sale of securities held as a part of Moylan's portfolio resulted in a loss of $62,200 (pretax).
4. When its president died, the corporation realized $100,000 from an insurance policy. The cash surrender value of this policy had been carried on the books as an investment in the amount of $34,000 (the gain is non-taxable).
5. The corporation disposed of a component of business at a loss of $140,000 before taxes. Assume that this transaction meets the criteria for being classified as discontinued operations. There were no results of operations for this division during 2008.
6. The corporation had an unrealized gain of $ 40,000 on securities acquired during the year. These have been classified as available for sale.

Instructions

Describe how each of the items above will be reported in a multiple-step income statement for 2008. Indicate the amount that will be reported and the section of the income statement in which the amount will appear.

Solution to Exercise 4-7

1. A loss of $42,000 ($60,000 - 30% of $60,000) will be reported in the extraordinary items section of the income statement.
2. Amortization expense of $15,000 [($108,000 - $18,000) ÷ 6 years] will appear in the administrative expense (an operating expense) section of the 2008 income statement. The correction of prior periods' amortization (a prior

period adjustment) will not appear on the income statement. Rather, a credit of \$4,200 will appear on the statement of retained earnings for 2008 as an adjustment to the beginning balance of retained earnings. The prior period adjustment is reported net of tax.

Calculations:
\$108,000 ÷ 6 = \$18,000 amortization taken in 2006.
\$108,000 ÷ 6 = \$18,000 amortization taken in 2007.
(\$108,000 - \$18,000) ÷ 6 = \$15,000 correct annual depreciation.
\$15,000 x 2 = \$30,000 correct amortization for 2006 and 2007.
(\$18,000 + \$18,000) - \$30,000 = \$6,000 overstated expense in prior years.
\$6,000 - 30%(\$6,000) = \$4,200 addition to retained earnings.

3. A loss of \$62,200 will be reported in the other expenses and losses section of the income statement. It is **not** reported net of tax.
4. A gain of \$66,000 (\$100,000 - \$34,000) will appear in the other revenues and gains section of the income statement. It is **not** reported net of tax (in this case, it had no tax effect anyway). A good caption for this item is "Gain from proceeds of life insurance policy."
5. A loss of \$98,000 (\$140,000 - 30% of \$140,000) will appear as a "loss on disposal of assets of discontinued component" in the discontinued operations section of the income statement.
6. The unrealized gain of \$35,000 (\$50,000 - 30% of \$50,000) will be shown in Other Comprehensive Income. This will be reported separate from net income. This will also be "tracked" in Accumulated Other Comprehensive Income, an equity account. When realized, the amounts will move form OCI to net income.

TIP! Discontinued operations include **components** of an enterprise that have been disposed of (by sale, abandonment, or spin-off) or are classified as **held for sale.**

TIP! To be considered discontinued, the operations have been, or will be, eliminated and the enterprise will not have any continuing involvement.

TIP! A **component of an entity** occurs when the operations, cash flows, and financial elements are clearly distinguishable from the rest of the enterprise. This could be as small as one hotel being rented out or as large as a major subsidiary. It may be difficult at times to distinguish a **disposal of an asset** from the **disposal of a component**. The key distinction is whether the asset generates its own net cash flows and is a separate business. If so, it would be considered a separate component.

TIP! To be classified as held for sale, all of the following criteria must be met:

- an authorized plan to sell assets
- the asset is available for immediate sale in its current state
- an active program to find a buyer exists
- sale is probable within one year
- the asset is reasonably priced and actively marketed
- changes to the plan are unlikely

When an asset or component is **held for sale**, the asset would be remeasured to the lower of its carrying cost and fair value, less costs to sell. It would be separately presented on the balance sheet.

TIP!

For a **component**, the results of operations as well as any write down to the above remeasurement would be shown separately on the income statement, net of tax for both current and prior periods.

TIP!

Analysis of Multiple-Choice Questions

Question

1. In a multiple-step income statement, the excess of gross profit over operating expenses is called:
   a. net margin.
   b. income from operations.
   c. net profit.
   d. earnings.

EXPLANATION: Visualize a multiple-step income statement. Net sales less cost of goods sold yields gross profit (sometimes called gross margin). Gross profit less operating expenses equals income from operations. From there, other revenues and gains are added, other expenses and losses are deducted, and income tax expense is deducted to arrive at net income. Another popular name for net income is earnings. Net profit would likely refer to net income. Net margin is not a term applied to the income statement. (Solution = b.)

Question

2. The following expenses and loss were among those incurred by Mitzer Company during 2008:

Rent for office space	$ 660,000
Loss on sale of office furniture	55,000
Interest	132,000
Accounting and legal fees	352,000
Freight-out	70,000

   One-half of the rented premises is occupied by the sales department. How much of the items listed above should be classified as general and administrative expenses in Mitzer's income statement for 2008?
   a. $682,000
   b. $869,000
   c. $884,000
   d. $939,000

EXPLANATION: For each item listed, identify where it is reported. Then collect together the ones that you identify as general and administrative (G&A) expenses.

Rent for office space:	One-half selling; one-half G&A
Loss on sale of equipment:	Other expenses and losses
Interest:	Other expenses and losses
Accounting and legal fees:	G&A expenses
Freight-out:	Selling expenses

One-half of office space (0.5 x $660,000)	$330,000
Accounting and legal fees	352,000
General and administrative expenses	$682,000

(Solution = a.)

Question

3. Which of the following is **not** a selling expense?
   a. Advertising expense
   b. Office salaries expense
   c. Freight-out
   d. Store supplies consumed

EXPLANATION: Take each account and determine its classification. Items "a," "c," and "d" are selling expenses because they are associated with the sales function. Office salaries are related to normal operations, but they are not related to the sales function of the business. Therefore, they are not classified as a selling expense. (Solution = b.)

Question

4. The accountant for the Orion Sales Company is preparing the income statement for 2008 and the balance sheet at December 31, 2008. The January 1, 2008 merchandise inventory balance will appear:
   a. only as an asset on the balance sheet.
   b. only in the cost of goods sold section of the income statement.
   c. as a deduction in the cost of goods sold section of the income statement and as a current asset on the balance sheet.
   d. as an addition in the cost of goods sold section of the income statement and as a current asset on the balance sheet.

EXPLANATION: The January 1, 2008 inventory amount is the beginning inventory figure. Beginning inventory is a component of the cost of goods available for sale for the period, which is a component of cost of goods sold. (Solution = b.)

Question

5. The following amounts relate to the current year for the Ira Company:

Beginning inventory	$ 20,000
Ending inventory	28,000
Purchases	166,000
Purchase returns	4,800
Transportation-out	6,000

The amount of cost of goods sold for the period is:
a. $169,200.
b. $162,800.
c. $153,200.
d. $147,200.

EXPLANATION: Write down the calculation model for cost of goods sold. Enter the amounts given and solve for the unknown.

$	20,000		Beginning Inventory
+	166,000	+	Purchases
–	4,800	–	Purchase Returns and Allowances
		–	Purchase Discounts
		+	Freight-in
	181,200	=	Cost of Goods Available for Sale
–	28,000	–	Ending Inventory
$	153,200	=	Cost of Goods Sold

(Solution = c.)

TIP! Transportation-out is classified as a selling expense, not a component of cost of goods sold. "Transportation-out" is often called "freight-out"; "transportation-in" is another name for "freight in."

Question

6. A material loss should be presented separately, as a component of income from continuing operations, when it is:
   a. unusual in nature, infrequent in occurrence, and not a result of management decision.
   b. unusual in nature but not infrequent in occurrence.
   c. an extraordinary loss.
   d. a cumulative effect of a change in accounting policy.

EXPLANATION: Visualize an income statement and mentally identify the section that reports income from continuing operations. Read one answer at a time and determine if it correctly describes how the statement in the question stem can be completed. A material loss that is (1) unusual in nature and (2) infrequent in occurrence **and** (3) not a result of management decision should be reported as an extraordinary item. A loss that meets one or two of the criteria for being classified as extraordinary, but not all, should be separately disclosed as a component of income from continuing operations.

An extraordinary item is to be reported **after** (and not part of) income from continuing operations. (Solution = b.)

Question

7. During the year ended December 31, 2008, Schmelya Corporation incurred the following infrequent losses:
   1. A factory was shut down during a major strike by employees; costs were $120,000.
   2. A loss of $50,000 was incurred on the abandonment of computer equipment used in the business.
   3. A loss of $82,000 was incurred as a result of flood damage to a warehouse.

How much total loss should Schmelya report in the extraordinary item section of its 2008 income statement?

a. $82,000.
b. $120,000.
c. $202,000.
d. $252,000.

EXPLANATION: It is wise to review the list of items that are classified as extraordinary items and the list of items that are not extraordinary items (see **Illustration 4-3**) until you can readily recognize items that appear in the list. In the question at hand, the first two items are on the list of items that are **not** extraordinary. Therefore, the only possible one being extraordinary is the loss from flood damage. A flood would be considered infrequent in some locations but not others. The question indicates it is deemed infrequent for Schmelya. To be classified as extraordinary, an item needs to be unusual in nature, infrequent in occurrence and not a result of management decision. However, there are certain items that do **not** constitute extraordinary items. (Solution = a.)

Question

8. When a piece of office equipment is sold at a gain of $700,000 less related taxes of $280,000, and the gain is not considered unusual or infrequent, the income statement for the period would show these effects as:
   a. an extraordinary item net of applicable income taxes, $420,000.
   b. a prior period adjustment net of applicable income taxes, $420,000.
   c. another gain net of applicable income taxes, $420,000.
   d. another gain of $700,000 and an increase in income tax expense of $280,000 (i.e., not net).

EXPLANATION: A gain or loss on the disposal of property, plant, and equipment that is **not** unusual, infrequent, and a result of management decision is **not** to be classified as an extraordinary item. Therefore, a gain from such a disposal goes in the "other revenues and gains" classification. The related tax effect is reflected in the "income tax expense" figure. The only items reported net of tax are extraordinary items, discontinued operations, changes in accounting policy, and prior period adjustments. The tax effects of all other transactions are summarized in the amount captioned "income tax expense". (Solution = d.)

Question

9. A correction of an error in prior periods' income will be reported:

	In the income statement	Net of taxes
a.	Yes	Yes
b.	No	No
c.	Yes	No
d.	No	Yes

EXPLANATION: Write down what you know about the accounting for a correction of an error in calculating income in a prior period. Then answer "yes" or "no" to each question posed at the top of the appropriate column. Find the combination that matches yours. A correction of an error is a prior period adjustment; it is reported net of tax as an adjustment to the beginning retained earnings balance on the statement of retained earnings in the period the error is corrected. (Solution = d.)

Question

10. The OVA Company had the following errors occur in its financial statements:

	2007	2008
Ending inventory	\$12,000 Understated	\$18,000 Overstated
Amortization expense	\$24,000 Overstated	\$14,000 Overstated

Assuming that none of the errors were detected or corrected, by what amount will retained earnings at December 31, 2008 be misstated?

a. \$18,000 overstated.
b. \$20,000 understated.
c. \$32,000 understated.
d. \$14,000 understated.
e. None of the above.

EXPLANATION: Explain the effects of each error separately and then combine your results. The \$12,000 understatement of ending inventory for 2007 causes a \$12,000 understatement of net income for 2007 and a \$12,000 overstatement of net income for 2008 (because the ending inventory for 2007 is the beginning inventory for 2008); this nets to be a zero impact on the retained earnings balance at December 31, 2008. The \$24,000 overstatement of amortization expense in 2007 causes an understatement of net income for 2007 and a corresponding

$24,000 understatement of retained earnings at December 31, 2007 and at December 31, 2008. The $18,000 overstatement of ending inventory for 2008 causes an overstatement of net income for 2008 and an $18,000 overstatement of retained earnings at December 31, 2008. A $14,000 overstatement of amortization expense for 2008 causes a $14,000 understatement of net income for 2008 and a $14,000 understatement of retained earnings at December 31, 2008. The net effect on retained earnings at December 31, 2008 is, therefore, a $24,000 understatement + an $18,000 overstatement + a $14,000 understatement which equals a $20,000 understatement. (Solution = b.)

Question

11. When a component of a business has been discontinued during the year, that component's operating losses of the current year should be included in the:
    a. income statement as part of the income (loss) from operations of the discontinued component.
    b. income statement as part of the gain (loss) on disposal of the discontinued component.
    c. income statement as part of the income (loss) from continuing operations.
    d. statement of retained earnings as a direct decrease in retained earnings.

EXPLANATION: There are possibly two lines in the "discontinued operations" section of the income statement: (1) income (loss) from operations of discontinued component, and (2) gain or loss on disposal of discontinued component. The results of operations of the discontinued component for the year are to be reported in the first line. (Solution = a.)

TIP! Estimated future losses are not included in the loss from operations since they would be implicitly reflected in the fair value estimate of the assets held for sale or sold. (The second line of the discontinued operations presentation.)

Question

12. Which of the following statements is most true regarding the income statement?
    a. The income statement is accurate and very reliable as it is based on accrual accounting and is prepared by knowledgeable people (management).
    b. Care must be taken when reviewing an income statement of a company since it may be subject to bias.
    c. All income statements have the same information value as they have standard presentations and must adhere to the disclosure required by GAAP.
    d. The income statement is of little value when the cash flow statement is also prepared for the company.

EXPLANATION: The income statement, while providing good information for predicting future cash flows and assessing management stewardship, has many limitations, including the fact that the information may be biased. (Solution = b.)

Question

13. Revenues and gains are generally reported separately on the income statement for which one of the following reasons?
    a. More information and detail is always better than less.
    b. Users need to know how much a company is earning from its main or ordinary operations.
    c. Gains (and losses) are generally extraordinary items and are, therefore, required by the *CICA Handbook* to be disclosed separately.
    d. In order to adhere to the materiality concept.

EXPLANATION: Gains are often non-recurring and, by definition, do not arise from ordinary activities of the business. Gains are not always extraordinary, however, nor are they always material. Furthermore, more information is not always better than less. Although users appreciate a certain amount of detail, there comes a point where too much detail may obscure more important information. (Solution = b.)

Question

14. The following is a list of income statement components. Which of these items is not required to be disclosed by the *CICA Handbook*?
    a. Income or loss before discontinued operations and extraordinary items.
    b. Results from discontinued operations.
    c. Net income or loss for the period.
    d. Cost of goods sold.

EXPLANATION: Cost of good sold is desirable in terms of disclosure, however it is not required under *CICA Handbook* Section 1520. (Solution = d.)

Question

15. Basic and diluted EPS are required to be presented as follows:
    a. on the face of the income statement
    b. in the notes
    c. on the cash flow statement
    d. either in the notes or on the income statement

EXPLANATION: Basic and diluted EPS must be shown on the face of the income statement (*CICA Handbook* Section 3500.60). Where extraordinary items or discontinued operations exist, the EPS related to these line items may be shown either on the income statement or in the notes. (Solution = a.)

Financial Position and Cash Flows

Chapter 5

Overview

A balance sheet reports on the financial position of an entity at a point in time. A statement of cash flows reports reasons for cash receipts and cash payments during the period. In this chapter, we discuss the classifications of a balance sheet and a statement of cash flows along with related disclosure issues. It is extremely important that items are properly classified. Errors in classification will result in incorrect ratio analyses, which can lead to misinterpretations of the meaning of the information conveyed. This can affect the decisions that are being made based on that information.

Study Steps

Understanding the Usefulness and Limitations of the Balance Sheet and Cash Flow Statement

The balance sheet

The balance sheet gives information about liquidity and financial flexibility among other things. Liquidity is important since it shows the company's ability to continue to operate. Financial flexibility is important since it shows the company's ability (or inability) to adapt financially to changing situations. For instance, a highly levered company (i.e., with significant debt) with fixed debt repayment commitments is not as flexible, and may be more exposed in hard times since it must come up with the payments or presumably, in the worst scenario, go bankrupt.

Key balance sheet ratios are the current ratio (liquidity) and debt to equity (or total assets) ratio (solvency).

Importance of note disclosures to supplement the numbers

Like all statements, the balance sheet does not tell the whole story and, therefore, must be supplemented by note disclosures. For instance, a balance sheet might show long-term debt of $10 million. While this is useful information, it is insufficient for users for decision making because it does not answer such questions as: When is it due? What is the interest rate? Is it secured by the assets of the company? and so on. Therefore, the notes include additional information about the balances on the balance sheet and also additional information about things that are not included on the balance sheet, such as contingencies, commitments, subsequent events, and others. The notes should be referred to on the face of the balance sheet in order to direct the user's attention to them.

The notes are an integral part of the financial statements and the statements should never be read without reading the notes.

The notes often give essential information such as estimates in the balance sheet, how assets are valued, items that are not in the balance sheet due to inability to measure, etc.

The classified balance sheet

Most balance sheets are classified between assets and liabilities that are current and those that are non-current. A time frame of one year (or the operating cycle of the company) is used to distinguish between current and non-current. This classification allows users to assess the liquidity of the company.

Assets are generally listed in order of liquidity with cash being first. In specialized industries, this might not always be the case.

The cash flow statement

This statement looks at where a company gets its cash from and what it spends it on. It also classifies these sources and uses of cash between operating, investing, and financing activities.

One of the more important numbers on the statement is cash used in or provided from operations. This is important because, over the long run, a company's operations need to generate cash in order to keep the company solvent. A company whose operations are generating cash is a healthy company since the excess cash can be used for expansion, paying down debt, or paying dividends. Cash used in or provided from operations is calculated by converting the income statement from an accrual basis to a cash basis.

When performing any financial statement analysis, always look at cash from operating activities as a first step. This is a critical number and shows whether a company can generate cash from its main activities. If it cannot, then it will most likely not survive for long!

Ratio analysis

There are several common ratios identified in the illustrations below that you should familiarize yourself with. When determining how to account for an issue, always consider the impact of the alternatives on key ratios. Note that certain industries focus more on certain ratios due to the nature of the industry: e.g., the retail industry looks at gross profit as a key indicator of performance due to the importance of pricing, controlling inventory, and sourcing. The real estate industry might focus more on debt to equity or total assets ratio as this is a capital intensive industry (requires lots of financing to acquire and develop properties) and the risk that these companies may not be able to repay their often substantial debt is significant.

It is important to identify the important ratios in the case of the specific company being analyzed and then to benchmark against something such as an industry average or prior years.There are many different ratios and many different ways of calculating these ratios. It is not important to memorize every one and every calculation. A few basic ratios are all you need to do a basic financial analysis.

When looking at ratios calculated by analysts and companies, ensure that you understand how they have calculated the ratios. Ratios may be manipulated as well as earnings.

Tips on Chapter Topics

TIP! Financial statements are classified based on similar grouping characteristics and reported based on differing characteristics. Assets that differ in type or expected function should be reported separately. Assets and liabilities with different implications for the enterprise's financial flexibility should be reported separately, and assets and liabilities that differ in liquidity characteristics should be reported as separate items.

TIP! Memorize the definition of current assets. **Current assets** are cash and other assets that are expected to be converted into cash, sold, or consumed within the year or operating cycle that immediately follows the balance sheet date, whichever is longer. Think about how various examples of current assets meet this definition. Accounts receivable are current assets because they will be converted to cash shortly after the balance sheet date; inventory is a current asset because it will be sold within the year that follows the balance sheet date; prepaid insurance is a current asset because it will be consumed (used up) within the next year.

TIP! A normal **operating cycle** is the length of time required to go from release of cash back to receipt of cash. That is, for an entity, which sells products, the operating cycle is the time required to take cash out to buy (or to manufacture) inventory then sell the inventory and receive cash (either from a cash sale or the collection of an account receivable stemming from a credit sale). Thus, the length of an entity's operating cycle depends on the nature of its business. Unless otherwise indicated, always assume the operating cycle for an entity is less than a year so that the one-year test is used as the cut-off between current and non-current.

TIP! Memorize the definition of current liabilities. **Current liabilities** are obligations, which are expected to require the use of current assets or the incurrence of other current liabilities. A liability may be due within a year of the balance sheet and not be a current liability. An example is a debt due in six months that will be liquidated by use of a non-current asset.

TIP! In a classified balance sheet, any asset that is not classified as a current asset is a non-current asset. There are four non-current asset classifications: long-term investments; property, plant, and equipment; intangible assets; and other assets.

TIP! In a classified balance sheet, liabilities are classified either as current or non-current liabilities. The non-current liabilities are usually titled "long-term liabilities" or "long-term debt".

TIP! It is extremely important that items are properly classified on a balance sheet. Errors in classification can result in incorrect ratio analyses, which may lead to misrepresentations of the meaning of the information conveyed and can affect decisions that are based on those analyses.

TIP! Current assets are listed in the order of their liquidity, with the most liquid ones being listed first; property, plant, and equipment items are listed in order of length of life, with the longest life first. Current liabilities are not listed in any prescribed order; however, notes payable (short-term) is usually listed first followed by accounts payable (and the remainder of the current liabilities are often listed in descending order of amount).

TIP! **"Short-term"** is synonymous with **"current"**, and **"long-term"** is synonymous with "non-current". Therefore, "short-term debt" can be used to refer to "current liabilities". Asset classifications are typically titled current and non-current, whereas liability classifications are typically titled current and long-term.

All non-current assets (assets in classifications other than "current assets") are resources that are **not** expected to be converted into cash or fully consumed in operations within one year or the operating cycle, whichever is longer.

TIP! Investments in debt and equity securities are grouped into three separate portfolios for valuation and presentation purposes: (1) held-to-maturity securities; (2) trading securities; and (3) available-for-sale securities. Trading securities are current assets. Available-for-sale and held-to-maturity securities should be classified as current or non-current assets depending on the nature of the investment and management intent.

TIP! If an account title starts with "Allowance for...," then it generally is a contra balance sheet account.

TIP! If an account title starts with "Provision for...," it is generally an income statement account.

TIP! The balance of liabilities and the balance of owners' equity at a point in time simply serve as scorecards of the total amounts of unspecified assets, which have come about from creditor sources (liabilities) and owner sources (owners' equity). Thus, you **cannot** determine the amount of cash (or any other specific asset) held by an entity by looking at the balance of owners' equity or liabilities. You must look at the listing of individual assets on the balance sheet to determine the amount of cash owned.

TIP! A **reserve** is an appropriation of retained earnings. An appropriation of retained earnings refers to a portion of retained earnings, which for one reason or another is restricted, which simply means it cannot be used as a basis for the declaration of dividends.

TIP! A **valuation account** is an account whose balance is needed to properly value the item to which the valuation account relates. A **contra account** is a valuation account whose normal balance (debit versus credit) is opposite of the normal balance of the account to which the valuation account relates. An adjunct account is a valuation account whose normal balance is the same as the normal balance of the account to which it relates.

TIP! Interest on debt is due annually or more frequently (semi-annually or monthly, for example). Therefore, interest accrued on long-term debt is generally classified as a current liability. Likewise, interest receivable stemming from the accrual of interest on long-term receivables is generally classified as a current asset.

TIP! A fund can consist of restricted cash or non-cash assets such as shares and bonds of other companies. Funds are reported in the long-term investment classification. Other long-term investment classifications include investments in non-consolidated subsidiaries or affiliated companies, investments in securities, (such as bonds, common shares, or long-term notes), and investments in tangible fixed assets such as land held for speculation.

TIP! In answering questions regarding the classification of items on a balance sheet, always assume an individual item is material unless it is apparent otherwise.

Illustration 5-1

Balance Sheet Classifications

CURRENT ASSETS: includes cash, accounts receivable, inventory and other assets, which are expected to be realizable within the next year or operating cycle, whichever is longer.

SHORT-TERM INVESTMENTS: Investments in debt and equity securities are grouped into three separate portfolios for their valuation and presentation. **Held-to-maturity**: debt securities that the company intends to hold until maturity, and has an ability to do so. **Held-for-trading**: derivatives and any other investments the company has the intention of selling in the short term, not strategic investments noted below in long-term investments. **Available-for-sale**: debt and equity securities that are not classified as held for trading or held to maturity.

LONG-TERM INVESTMENTS: includes long-term receivables, restricted funds, investments in shares or debt of other companies (strategic investments), and land held for future plant site or for speculation. Note that **held-to-maturity** securities and **available-for-sale** securities may also be classified as long term (or non-current).

PROPERTY, PLANT, AND EQUIPMENT: includes long-lived tangible assets (land, building, equipment, and machinery) that are currently being used in operations to generate income. Assets in this category are often referred to as plant assets or fixed assets. They are not held for resale.

INTANGIBLE ASSETS: includes assets that lack physical substance, such as a patent, copyright, franchise, trademark, or trade names that give the holder exclusive right of use for a specified period of time. Their value to a company is generally derived from the rights or privileges granted by governmental or other authority.

OTHER ASSETS: includes assets that by common practice are not classified elsewhere.

CURRENT LIABILITIES: obligations that are due within a year and are expected to require the use of current assets or the incurrence of other current liabilities to liquidate them.

LONG-TERM LIABILITIES: obligations that do not meet the criteria to be classified as current liabilities.

CAPITAL SHARES: the exchange value of shares issued.

CONTRIBUTED SURPLUS: includes premiums on shares issued, capital donations, and other.

RETAINED EARNINGS: excess of net incomes over net losses and dividend distributions since inception of the business. An appropriation of retained earnings is a restricted portion of the total retained earnings figure. Sometimes referred to as earned surplus.

ACCUMULATED OTHER COMPREHENSIVE INCOME: includes (primarily) unrealized gains/losses on available-for-sale securities. May contain other items as appropriate, for example, the cumulative translation gain/loss of self-sustaining foreign operations and certain gains/losses on hedging transactions.

Exercise 5-1

PURPOSE: This exercise lists examples of balance sheet accounts and enables you to practice determining where they are classified.

Instructions

Indicate which balance sheet classification is the most appropriate for reporting each account listed below by selecting the abbreviation of the corresponding section.

CA	Current Assets	CL	Current Liabilities
INV	Long-term Investments	LTL	Long-term Liabilities
PPE	Property, Plant, and Equipment	CS	Capital Shares
ITG	Intangible Assets	CON	Contributed Surplus
OA	Other Assets	RE	Retained Earnings
		STI	Short-term Investments

If the account is a contra account, indicate that fact by putting the abbreviation in parenthesis. If the exact classification depends on facts which are not given, indicate your answer of "depends on" by the abbreviation **DEP** and the possible classifications. If the account is reported on the income statement rather than the balance sheet, indicate that fact with an **IS**. Assume all items are material.

Classification	Account	Classification	Account
_______	1. Accounts Payable.	_______	9. Advances by Customers.
_______	2. Accounts Receivable.	_______	10. Advances to Affiliates.
_______	3. Accrued Interest Receivable on Long-term Investments.	_______	11. Advances to Vendors.
_______	4. Accrued Interest Payable.	_______	12. Advertising Expense.
_______	5. Accrued Taxes Payable.	_______	13. Allowance for Bad Debts.
_______	6. Accumulated Amortization—Building.	_______	14. Allowance for Amortization.
_______	7. Accumulated Amortization—Machinery.	_______	15. Allowance for Doubtful Accounts.
_______	8. Mineral Reserves.	_______	16. Allowance for Excess of Cost Over Market Value of Inventory.
		_______	17. Allowance for Inventory Price Declines.
		_______	18. Allowance for Purchase Discounts.

_______ 19. Allowance for Sales Discounts.
_______ 20. Allowance for Uncollectible Accts.
_______ 21. Appropriation for Bond Sinking Fund.
_______ 22. Appropriation for Contingencies.
_______ 23. Appropriation for Future Plant Expansion.
_______ 24. Work in Process.
_______ 25. Bank Overdraft.
_______ 26. Bond Interest Payable.
_______ 27. Bond Interest Receivable.
_______ 28. Bond Sinking Fund.
_______ 29. Building.
_______ 30. Cash.
_______ 31. Investment in Microsoft shares.
_______ 32. Cash Surrender Value of Life Insurance.
_______ 33. Certificate of Deposit.
_______ 34. Common Shares.
_______ 35. Construction in Process (entity's new plant under construction).
_______ 36. Creditors' accounts with debit balances.
_______ 37. Current Maturities of Bonds Payable (to be paid from Bond Sinking Fund).
_______ 38. Current Maturities of Bonds Payable (to be paid from general cash account).
_______ 39. Current Portion of Mortgage Payable.
_______ 40. Current Portion of Long-term Debt.
_______ 41. Customers' accounts with credit balances.
_______ 42. Customers' Deposits.
_______ 43. Vouchers Payable.
_______ 44. Unexpired Insurance.
_______ 45. Deferred Property Tax Expense.
_______ 46. Deferred Office Supplies.
_______ 47. Deferred Rental Income.
_______ 48. Deferred Subscription Revenue.
_______ 49. Deferred Service Contract Revenue.
_______ 50. Deposits on Equipment Purchases.
_______ 51. Amortization of Equipment.
_______ 52. Discount on Bonds Payable.
_______ 53. Unearned Subscription Income.
_______ 54. Discount on Notes Payable.
_______ 55. Discount on Notes Receivable.
_______ 56. Dishonoured Notes Receivable.
_______ 57. Dividend Payable in Cash.
_______ 58. Dividend Payable in Common Shares.
_______ 59. Earned Rental Revenue.
_______ 60. Accrued Pension Liability.
_______ 61. Estimated Liability for Income Taxes.
_______ 62. Estimated Liability for Warranties.
_______ 63. Estimated Premium Claims Outstanding.
_______ 64. Factory Supplies.
_______ 65. Finished Goods Inventory.
_______ 66. Furniture and Fixtures.
_______ 67. Gain on Sale of Equipment.
_______ 68. General and Administrative Expenses.
_______ 69. Goodwill.
_______ 70. Income Tax Payable.
_______ 71. Income Tax Refund Receivable.

_______ 72. Income Tax Withheld (from employees).
_______ 73. Interest Payable.
_______ 74. Interest Receivable.
_______ 75. Interest Revenue.
_______ 76. Investment in Nortel Shares.
_______ 77. Investment in Canada Savings Bonds.
_______ 78. Investment in Unconsolidated Subsidiary.
_______ 79. Land.
_______ 80. Land Held for Future Plant Site.
_______ 81. Land Used for Parking Lot.
_______ 82. Leasehold Improvements.
_______ 83. Leasehold Costs.
_______ 84. Loss on Sale of Marketable Securities.
_______ 85. Machinery and Equipment.
_______ 86. Machinery and Equip. Sitting Idle.
_______ 87. Marketable Securities.
_______ 88. Merchandise Inventory.
_______ 89. Mortgage Payable.
_______ 90. Notes Payable.
_______ 91. Notes Payable to Banks.
_______ 92. Notes Receivable.
_______ 93. Notes Receivable from Officers.
_______ 94. Office Supplies on Hand.
_______ 95. Office Supplies Prepaid.
_______ 96. Office Supplies Expense.
_______ 97. Office Supplies Used.
_______ 98. Patents.
_______ 99. Petty Cash Fund.
_______ 100. Plant and Equipment.
_______ 101. Preferred Share Redemption Fund.
_______ 102. Premium on Bonds Payable.
_______ 103. Premium on Common Shares.
_______ 104. Prepaid Advertising.
_______ 105. Prepaid Insurance.
_______ 106. Prepaid Insurance Expense.
_______ 107. Prepaid Office Supplies.
_______ 108. Prepaid Royalty Payments.
_______ 109. Prepaid Property Taxes.
_______ 110. Provision for Bad Debts.
_______ 111. Provision for Income Taxes.
_______ 112. Rent Revenue.
_______ 113. Salaries Payable.
_______ 114. Sales Discounts and Allowances.
_______ 115. Selling Expense Control.
_______ 116. Share Dividends Distributable.
_______ 117. Share Dividends Payable.
_______ 118. Store Supplies.
_______ 119. Store Supplies Used.
_______ 120. Tools and Dies (5-year life).
_______ 121. Tools and Dies (6-mos. life).
_______ 122. Unearned Royalties.
_______ 123. Unamortized Bond Issue Costs.
_______ 124. Unamortized Discount on Bonds Payable.
_______ 125. Unearned Rental Income.

Solution to Exercise 5-1

Solution		Explanation and/or Comment
CL	1.	These are trade payables usually due within 30 or 60 days.
CA	2.	These are trade receivables usually due within 30 or 60 days.
CA	3.	Interest is usually due annually or more frequently.
CL	4.	A better title is simply Interest Payable (item 73).
CL	5.	A better title is simply Taxes Payable.
(PPE)	6.	This is a contra account. It is another title for item 14 (item 6 is used more frequently).
(PPE)	7.	This is a contra account and an alternative title for item 14.
PPE	8.	Tracks of natural resources are classified in PPE.
DEP: CL or LTL	9.	These advances refer to revenue amounts received in advance from customers.
DEP: CA or INV or OA	10.	These advances are loans.
DEP: CA or INV or OA	11.	These advances can be prepayments or loans.
IS	12.	This is a selling expense.
(CA)	13.	This is another title for Allowance for Doubtful Accounts (item 15).
(PPE)	14.	This is another title for Accumulated Amortization (items 6 & 7).
(CA)	15.	This is contra to Accounts Receivable.
(CA)	16.	This account arises because of the use of the lower of cost or market rule. It is contra to Inventory.
(CA)	17.	This is contra to Inventory; it is another title for item 16.
(CL)	18.	This account reflects amounts included in Accounts Payable that will not be paid because of purchase discounts to be taken.
(CA)	19.	This account reflects amounts included in Accounts Receivable that will not be collected because of sales discounts allowed.
(CA)	20.	This is another title for Allowance for Doubtful Accounts (item 15).
RE	21.	This is a restriction on retained earnings (portion of total retained earnings).
RE	22.	This is a restriction on retained earnings (portion of total retained earnings).
RE	23.	This is a restriction on retained earnings (portion of total retained earnings).
CA	24.	This is an inventory account for a manufacturer.
CL	25.	When the item exists, it is usually listed as the first item under current liabilities.
CL	26.	Interest is usually payable annually or more frequently.

CA	27.	This is usually receivable annually or more frequently.
INV	28.	A fund can be comprised of restricted cash or securities.
PPE	29.	This is considered under Plant.
CA	30.	This is unrestricted cash.
INV or STI	31.	Depending on management intent, most likely STI. Will require further classification as either held for sale or available for sale.
INV or OA	32.	The assumption is that the entity will continue the insurance coverage rather than take the cash surrender value.
DEP: CA or INV	33.	Some CDs are for 90 days, 180 days, 30 months, or 60 months.
CS	34.	This reflects the par or stated value of issued shares.
PPE	35.	This is one of two exceptions to the general guidelines for items to be included in the PPE classification.
CA	36.	A creditor has been overpaid or items purchased on account have been returned for credit after payment of account has been made.
LTL	37.	This answer assumes that the Bond Sinking Fund is classified under long-term investments.
CL	38.	This item will require current assets to settle the debt.
CL	39.	"Current portion" refers to the portion that is coming due within a year of the balance sheet date.
CL	40.	Some accountants list this item first in the list of current liabilities, others list it last.
CL	41.	This arises when customers overpay or return goods after full payment is made.
DEP: CL or LTL	42.	A deposit may be an advance payment for goods and services or a security deposit.
CL	43.	This is another title for Accounts Payable when a voucher system is in use.
CA	44.	This is another title for items 105 and 106, Prepaid Insurance.
CA	45.	This is another title for item 109, Prepaid Property Taxes.
CA	46.	This is another title for items 94, 95, and 107.
DEP: CL or LTL	47.	This is another title for item 125, Unearned Rental Income.
DEP: CL or LTL	48.	Some subscriptions are for one year, others are for two or more years. This is another title for item 53, Unearned Subscription Revenue.
DEP: CL or LTL	49.	A service contract often covers two or more years; revenue has been collected but not earned.
PPE	50.	This is the second of two exceptions to the general guidelines for items to be included in the PPE classification.

IS	51. This refers to the depreciation charges for the current period.
(LTL)	52. This is another title for item 124. In the rare instance where the bonds payable are classified as current, the discount would be current also.
DEP: (CL) or (LTL)	53. This is another title for item 48.
DEP: (CL) or (LTL)	54. A discount occurs when the effective rate exceeds the stated rate.
DEP: (CA) or (INV)	55. A discount results when the note is issued below par.
CA	56. A dishonoured note receivable is one that has reached its maturity date and remains uncollected.
CL	57. A dividend is usually paid approximately three to four weeks after it is declared.
CS	58. This is a bad title for Share Dividend Distributable. This is the same as items 116 and 117.
IS	59. This is another title for Rent Revenue.
LTL	60. This is payable upon retirement of employees.
CL	61. This is another title for Income Tax Payable.
DEP: CL or LTL	62. Some warranties are for more than one year.
DEP: CL or LTL	63. Premiums in this context are similar to prizes.
CA	64. This item is similar to a prepaid expense; these supplies will be part of factory overhead (hence, work in process inventory) when used.
CA	65. This is one of three inventory accounts for a manufacturer.
PPE	66. This is considered Equipment.
IS	67. This is in the Other Income section of income statement.
IS	68. This is under Generating Expense.
ITG	69. This is referred to as an unidentifiable intangible asset with an indefinite life.
CL	70. This is usually payable annually or more frequently.
CA	71. This is usually receivable annually or more frequently.
CL	72. This is usually payable monthly.
CL	73. This is another title for item 4 (item 73 is the preferable title).
CA	74. This is usually receivable annually or more frequently.
IS	75. This is in the Other Income section of income statement.
STI or INV	76. Depending on management intent—likely STI. It will require further classification as either held for trading or available for sale.
STI or INV	77. This depends on management's intention. It may be classified as held to maturity or available for sale.
INV	78. The fact that the investee is a subsidiary means there is an intention to hold the investee's share for a long-term purpose. A strategic investment.

PPE	79. This is considered Property.
INV	80. This may also be classified under Property.
PPE	81. This is considered Property.
PPE	82. Some textbooks suggest classifying Leasehold Improvements as intangible assets. Most real life companies report them as PPE.
ITG	83. These are costs incurred in obtaining a lease.
IS	84. Classified under Other on income statement.
PPE	85. Considered Equipment.
OA	86. Classified separately from Equipment being used.
CA or INV	87. This is a title often used to refer to short-term investments; it can also refer to securities (shares and/or bonds of other entities) held for long-term purposes.
CA	88. This is another title for Inventory for a retailer.
LTL	89. The portion of this balance due within the next year will be reclassified and reported as a current liability.
DEP: CL or LTL	90. This depends on maturity.
DEP: CL or LTL	91. This depends on maturity.
DEP: CA or INV	92. This depends on maturity.
DEP: CA or INV	93. Separate disclosure must be made of related party transactions.
CA	94. This is another title for items 46, 95, and 107.
IS	95. This is another title for items 46, 94, and 107.
IS	96. This an Operating Expense.
IS	97. This is another title for item 96, Office Supplies Expense.
ITG	98. This is an Intangible Asset.
CA	99. This is usually used up annually or more frequently.
PPE	100. This is self-explanatory.
INV	101. This would require rate disclosures.
LTL	102. This is an adjunct-type valuation account. If the related bonds payable are classified as a current liability, this valuation account will also be in current liabilities.
APC	103. This is an adjunct-type valuation account.
CA	104. This is a prepaid expense.
CA	105. This is another title for items 44 and 106.
IS	106. This is another title for items 44 and 105.
CA	107. This is another title for items 46, 94, and 95.
CA	108. This is a prepaid expense.
CA	109. This is another title for item 45.
IS	110. This is another title for Uncollectible Accounts Expense or Bad Debt Expense.
IS	111. This is another title for Income Tax Expense.
IS	112. This may be considered Other Revenue.
CL	113. This is another title for Accrued Salaries or Accrued Salaries Payable. Salaries Payable is the preferred title.

IS	114.	This is a contra sales revenue item.
IS	115.	A control account is an account in the general ledger for which the details appear in a subsidiary ledger.
CS	116.	This is another title for items 58 and 117. The title in item 116 is the preferred title.
CS	117.	This is another title for items 58 and 116. This is a misleading title because the word "payable" suggests a liability, which a share dividend is not.
CA	118.	This answer assumes the supplies are on hand rather than used.
IS	119.	This item refers to Store Supplies Expense.
PPE	120.	This is considered Equipment.
IS	121.	The service life is so short that the benefits yielded do not extend beyond one year. Therefore, the expenditure is not capitalized.
DEP: CL or LTL	122.	Revenue has been received, but not earned; hence, an obligation exists to provide a service or good or a refund in the future.
OA	123.	This is usually called Bond Issue Costs.
(LTL)	124.	This is another title for item 52. In the rare instance where the bonds payable are classified as a current liability, the discount would be contra current liability.
DEP: CL or LTL	125.	This is another title for item 47.

APPROACH: For each balance sheet classification, write down a definition or description of what is to be reported in that classification. Refer to those notes as you go down the list of items to be classified. Your notes should contain the guidelines summarized in **Illustration 5-1**.

Exercise 5-2

PURPOSE: This exercise will enable you to practice identifying errors and other deficiencies in a balance sheet.

Lee Ward Company has decided to expand its operations. The bookkeeper recently completed the balance sheet presented below to submit to the bank in order to obtain additional funds for expansion.

Lee Ward Company
BALANCE SHEET
For the Year Ended 2008

Current assets	
Cash (net of bank overdraft of $15,000)	$ 180,000
Accounts receivable (net)	380,000
Inventories, at lower of FIFO cost or market	435,000
Marketable securities—at cost (fair value $110,000)	90,000
Property, plant, and equipment	
Building (net)	590,000
Office equipment (net)	180,000
Land held for future use	75,000
Intangible assets	
Franchise	90,000
Cash surrender value of life insurance	80,000
Prepaid insurance	6,000
Current liabilities	
Salaries payable	18,000
Accounts payable	85,000
Note payable, due June 30, 2010	100,000
Pension obligation	92,000
Taxes payable	40,000
Note payable, due October 1, 2009	25,000
Discount on bonds payable	50,000
Long-term liabilities	
Bonds payable, 8%, due May 1, 2012	400,000
Shareholders' equity	
Common shares, authorized 500,000 shares, issued 310,000 shares	310,000
Contributed Surplus	279,000
Retained earnings	?

Instructions

Prepare a revised balance sheet in good form. Correct any errors and weaknesses you find in the presentation above. Assume that the accumulated amortization balance for the building is $150,000 and for the office equipment, $105,000. Marketable securities are classified as available-for-sale securities. Ignore the income tax considerations on the available-for-sale securities. The allowance for doubtful accounts has a balance of $20,000. The pension obligation is considered to be a long-term liability.

Solution to Exercise 5-2

Lee Ward Company
BALANCE SHEET
December 31, 2008

Assets			
Current Assets			
Cash			$ 195,000
Trading securities, at fair value			110,000
Accounts receivable		$ 400,000	
Less allowance for doubtful accounts		20,000	380,000
Inventories, at lower of FIFO cost or market			435,000
Prepaid insurance			6,000
Total current assets			1,126,000
Long-term Investments			
Land held for future use		75,000	
Cash surrender value of life insurance		80,000	
Total long-term investments			155,000
Property, Plant, and Equipment			
Building	$ 740,000		
Less accumulated amortization—building	150,000	590,000	
Office equipment	285,000		
Less accumulated amortization—office equipment	105,000	180,000	
Total property, plant, and equipment			770,000
Intangible Assets			
Franchise			90,000
Total assets			$ 2,141,000
Liabilities and Shareholders' Equity			
Current Liabilities			
Bank overdraft			$ 15,000
Note payable, due October 1, 2009			25,000
Accounts payable			85,000
Taxes payable			40,000
Salaries payable			18,000
Total current liabilities			183,000
Long-term Liabilities			
Note payable, due June 30, 2010		$ 100,000	
8% Bonds payable, due May 1, 2012	$ 400,000		
Less discount on bonds payable	50,000	350,000	
Pension obligation		92,000	
Total long-term liabilities			542,000
Total liabilities			725,000

Shareholders' Equity			
Paid-in capital			
Common shares, 500,000 authorized shares, issued and outstanding 310,000 shares	310,000		
Contributed Surplus	279,000	589,000	
Retained earnings		807,000	
Total shareholders' equity			1,396,000
Total liabilities and shareholders' equity			$ 2,121,000

EXPLANATION:

1. A bank overdraft in one bank account should not be reflected as an offset to positive cash items (such as a positive balance in another account). A bank overdraft must be reported as a current liability. (The one exception to this rule is as follows: if an account with a positive balance exists in the same bank as the overdraft, the overdraft can be reflected as an offset to the extent of that positive balance.)

2. Marketable securities classified as "available-for-sale" are to be reported on the balance sheet at fair value. (This topic will be more fully explained in Chapter 9.) The tax effects of this have been ignored for this exercise.

3. Land held for future use is not to be classified in the property, plant, and equipment section because the land is not currently being used in operations.

4. Cash surrender value of life insurance is an intangible item in a legal sense (because it lacks physical substance), but it is classified as a long-term investment for accounting purposes.

5. Prepaid expenses such as prepaid insurance represent prepayments that relate to benefits that are expected to be consumed within the year that follows the balance sheet date. Hence, they are current assets.

6. A pension obligation is generally not expected to become due in the near future and, therefore, is not expected to require the use of current assets within a year of the balance sheet date. Hence, it is a long-term liability.

7. Discount on Bonds Payable is a contra-type valuation account. A valuation account should always be reported with the account to which it relates.

8. Bonds payable are always assumed to be a long-term liability unless the facts make them appear to meet the definition for a current liability.

9. Accumulated Other Comprehensive Income is for unrealized gains or losses (gains in this case) on available-for-sale securities. It would be shown net of tax, with an increase to Future Tax liability—but taxes were ignored for this example.

10. The balance of retained earnings for this exercise can be derived by determining the amount needed to cause total liabilities and shareholders' equity to equal total assets.

Exercise 5-3

PURPOSE: This exercise will enable you to practice identifying errors and other deficiencies in a balance sheet.

Presented here is a balance sheet for the Gabby Corporation.

Gabby Corporation
BALANCE SHEET
December 31, 2008

Current assets	$ 520,000	Current liabilities	$ 365,000
Investments	700,000	Long-term liabilities	920,000
Property, plant, & equip.	2,185,000	Shareholders' equity	2,690,000
Intangible assets	570,000		
	$ 3,975,000		$ 3,975,000

The following information is available:

1. The current asset section includes: cash $120,000, accounts receivable $190,000 less $10,000 for allowance for doubtful accounts, inventories $230,000, and unearned revenue $10,000 (credit balance). Inventories are stated at their replacement cost; original cost on a FIFO basis is $200,000.

2. The investments section includes the cash surrender value of a life insurance contract $60,000; investments in common shares, short-term $70,000 and long-term $160,000; bond sinking fund $220,000; organizational costs $70,000; and land upon which a new plant is being constructed $120,000. Investments in common shares are all classified as available for sale and have fair values equal to their cost.

3. Property, plant, and equipment includes buildings $1,600,000 less accumulated amortization $375,000; equipment $400,000 less accumulated amortization $240,000; land $500,000; and land held for future use $300,000. The building is stated at a recent appraisal value of $1,600,000; original cost was $1,250,000.

4. Intangible assets include a franchise $140,000, goodwill $80,000, discount on bonds payable $30,000, and construction in process $320,000 (a new plant is under construction and will be ready for operations within nine months).

5. Current liabilities include accounts payable $80,000; notes payable—short-term $110,000, notes payable—long-term $150,000; and salaries payable $25,000. It does not include any amount for loss contingencies. The company's attorney states that it is probable the company will have to pay $60,000 in 2009 due to litigation pending at the balance sheet date.

6. Long-term liabilities are composed of 10% bonds payable (due June 1, 2016) $800,000 and pension obligation $120,000.

7. Shareholders' equity includes preferred shares, 200,000 shares authorized with 70,000 shares issued for $450,000; and common shares, 300,000 shares authorized with 100,000 shares issued at an average price of $10. In addition, the corporation has retained earnings of $1,240,000.

Instructions

Prepare a corrected balance sheet in good form.

Solution to Exercise 5-3

Gabby Corporation
BALANCE SHEET
December 31, 2008

Assets

Current Assets			
Cash			$ 120,000
Available-for-sale securities—at fair value			70,000
Accounts receivable		$ 190,000	
Less allowance for doubtful accounts		10,000	180,000
Inventories, at lower of FIFO cost or market			200,000
Total current assets			570,000
Investments			
Available-for-sale securities—at fair value		160,000	
Bond sinking fund		220,000	
Cash surrender value of life insurance		60,000	
Land held for future use		300,000	
Total long-term investments			740,000
Property, Plant, and Equipment			
Land		620,000	
Buildings	$ 1,250,000		
Less accumulated amortization—building	375,000	875,000	
Construction in process		320,000	
Equipment	400,000		
Less accumulated amortization—equip.	240,000	160,000	
Total property, plant, and equipment			1,975,000
Intangible Assets			
Organization costs		70,000	
Franchise		140,000	
Goodwill		80,000	
Total intangible assets			290,000
Total assets			$ 3,575,000

Gabby Corporation
BALANCE SHEET
December 31, 2008
(Continued)

Liabilities and Shareholders' Equity

Current Liabilities			
Notes payable			$ 110,000
Accounts payable			80,000
Estimated litigation obligation			60,000
Salaries payable			25,000
Unearned revenue			10,000
Total current liabilities			285,000
Long-term Liabilities			
Notes payable		$ 150,000	
10% bonds payable, due June 1, 2016	$ 800,000		
Less discount on bonds payable	30,000	770,000	
Pension obligation		120,000	
Total long-term liabilities			1,040,000
Total liabilities			1,325,000
Shareholders' Equity			
Paid-in capital			
Preferred shares; 200,000 shares authorized, 70,000 issued and outstanding	450,000		
Common shares, $2 par value; 300,000 shares authorized, 100,000 issued and outstanding	200,000		
Contributed Surplus	800,000*	1,450,000	
Retained earnings		800,000**	
Total shareholders' equity			2,250,000
Total Liabilities and Shareholders' Equity			$ 3,575,000

*100,000 shares x ($10 – $2) = $800,000.

**The corrected balance for the Retained Earnings account can be reconciled with the before corrected amount as follows:

Retained Earnings, before corrections	$1,240,000
Overstatement of inventory	(30,000)
Overstatement of buildings	(350,000)
Understatement of litigation liability	(60,000)
Corrected Retained Earnings balance	$ 800,000

The errors that Gabby had on the balance sheet affected some income statement accounts (which were closed to Retained Earnings) or directly affected the Retained Earnings account.

TIP! The $620,000 reported amount for land is comprised of land $500,000 plus land upon which a new plant is being constructed $120,000.

Illustration 5-2

Operating, Investing, and Financing Activities

Definitions

OPERATING ACTIVITIES: Operating activities represent the enterprise's principle revenue-producing activities and all other activities not related to investing and financing. Cash flows from operating activities are generally the cash effects of transactions and other events that enter into the determination of net income.

INVESTING ACTIVITIES: Investing activities represent the acquisitions and disposal of long-term assets and other investments not included in cash equivalents, including (a) making and collecting loans; (b) acquiring and disposing of debt and equity instruments of other entities; and (c) acquiring and disposing of property, plant, and equipment and other productive assets.

FINANCING ACTIVITIES: Financing activities represent activities that result in changes in the size and composition of the enterprise's equity capital and borrowings, including (a) obtaining resources from owners and providing them with a return on and a return of their investment; (b) borrowing money and repaying the amounts borrowed, or otherwise settling the obligation; and (c) obtaining and paying for other resources obtained from creditors. (*CICA Handbook*, Section 1540.06.)

Examples:

OPERATING ACTIVITIES:

CASH INFLOWS:

From sales of goods or services (includes cash sales and collections on account).

From returns on loans (interest received) and on equity securities (dividends received).

From other transactions, such as amounts received to settle lawsuits and refunds from suppliers.

CASH OUTFLOWS:

To suppliers for inventory and other goods and services (includes cash purchases and payments on account).

To employees for services.

To government for taxes.

To lenders for interest.

To others for items such as payments to settle lawsuits, refunds to customers, and contributions to charities.

INVESTING ACTIVITIES:

CASH INFLOWS:

From sale of property, plant, and equipment.
From sale of debt or equity securities of other entities.
From collection of principal on loans to other entities.

CASH OUTFLOWS:

To purchase property, plant, and equipment.[a]
To purchase debt or equity securities of other entities.
To make loans to other entities.

FINANCING ACTIVITIES:

CASH INFLOWS:

From sale of equity securities (company's own shares).
From issuance of debt instruments (bonds and notes).

CASH OUTFLOWS:

To pay dividends to shareholders.
To reacquire capital shares.
To pay debt (both short-term and long-term) other than accounts payable.

[a]The cash outflows included in this category are payments at the time of purchase or soon before or after purchase to acquire property, plant, and equipment and other productive assets. Generally, only advance payments, the down payment, or other amounts paid at the time of purchase or soon before or after purchase of property, plant, and equipment and other productive assets are investing cash outflows. Assets acquired through vendor financing (such as a capital lease) would not be shown on this statement—they would be note disclosed only.

TIP! The statement of cash flows summarizes all of the transactions occurring during a period that have an impact on the cash balance. The activity format is used whereby cash inflows and cash outflows are summarized by the three categories: operating, investing, and financing.

TIP! The difference between net income and net cash provided by operating activities can be substantial.

TIP! As with the income statement, certain information is generally considered to be more important on the balance sheet and statement of cash flows.

TIP! On the balance sheet, working capital is important, as is the amount of debt, especially as it relates to the amount of equity. These elements help focus on the liquidity, solvency, and financial flexibility of the company.

TIP! On the statement of cash flows, cash flow from operating activities is the most important number since it shows whether or not a company is generating cash or using cash in its core operating activities. Companies cannot continue to operate in the longer term if they are not generating cash from their core activities.

Exercise 5-4

PURPOSE: The exercise enables you to practice identifying investing and financing activities.

Instructions

Place the appropriate code in the blanks to identify each of the following transactions as giving rise to an:

Code	
II	inflow of cash due to an investing activity, or
IO	outflow of cash due to an investing activity, or
FI	inflow of cash due to a financing activity, or
FO	outflow of cash due to a financing activity.

_____ 1. Sell common shares to new shareholders.
_____ 2. Purchase treasury shares.
_____ 3. Borrow money from bank by issuance of short-term note.
_____ 4. Repay money borrowed from bank.
_____ 5. Purchase bonds as an investment.
_____ 6. Sell investment in real estate.
_____ 7. Loan money to an affiliate.
_____ 8. Collect on loan to affiliate.
_____ 9. Buy equipment.
_____10. Sell a plant asset.
_____11. Pay cash dividends to shareholders.

Solution to Exercise 5-4

1.	FI	4.	FO	7.	IO	10.	II
2.	FO	5.	IO	8.	II	11.	FO
3.	FI	6.	II	9.	IO		

APPROACH:

1. Reconstruct journal entries for the transactions. Examine each entry to identify if there is an inflow of cash (debit to Cash) or an outflow of cash (credit to Cash).
2. Write down the definitions for investing activities and financing activities (see below). Analyze each transaction to see if it fits one of these definitions.
   a) **Investing activities**—include (1) making and collecting loans, (2) acquiring and disposing of investments in debt and equity instruments, and (3) acquiring and disposing of property, plant, and equipment and other productive assets.
   b) **Financing activities**—include (1) obtaining capital from owners and providing them with a return on and a return of their investment, and (2) borrowing money from creditors and repaying the amounts borrowed, and (3) obtaining and paying for other resources obtained from creditors.
3. Assume purchases and sales of items are for cash, unless otherwise indicated.

TIP! The journal entry to record a transaction that is an investing activity which results in a cash flow will involve: (1) Cash and (2) an asset account other than Cash, such as Investments (short-term or long-term), Land, Building, Equipment, Patent, Franchise, etc.

TIP! The journal entry to record a transaction that is a financing activity which results in cash flow will involve: (1) Cash and (2) a liability account or an owners' equity account, such as Bonds Payable, Note Payable, Dividends Payable, Common Shares, Contributed Surplus, Treasury Shares, etc.

Exercise 5-5

PURPOSE: This exercise will enable you to practice reconciling net income with net cash provided by operating activities.

The following data relate to the L. Heckenmueller Co. for 2008.

Net income	$ 75,000
Increase in accounts receivable	7,000
Decrease in prepaid expenses	3,200
Increase in accounts payable	5,000
Decrease in taxes payable	900
Gain on sale of investment	1,700
Amortization	3,500
Loss on sale of equipment	600

Instructions

Calculate the net cash provided by operating activities for 2008.

Solution to Exercise 5-5

Net income	$ 75,000
Increase in accounts receivable	(7,000)
Decrease in prepaid expenses	3,200
Increase in accounts payable	5,000
Decrease in taxes payable	(900)
Gain on sale of investment	(1,700)
Amortization	3,500
Loss on sale of equipment	600
Net cash provided by operating activities	$ 77,700

EXPLANATION:

1. Net income is a summary of all revenues earned, all expenses incurred, and all gains and losses recognized for a period. Most revenues earned during the year result in a cash inflow during the same period but there may be some cash and/or revenue flows that do not correspond. Most expenses incurred during the year result in a cash outflow during the same period but there may be some cash and/or expense flows that do not correspond.

2. An increase in accounts receivable indicates that revenues earned exceed cash collected from customers and, therefore, net income exceeds net cash provided by operating activities.

3. A decrease in prepaid expenses indicates that expenses incurred exceed cash paid and, therefore, net income is less than net cash provided by operating activities.

4. An increase in accounts payable indicates that expenses incurred exceed cash paid and, therefore, net income is less than net cash provided by operating activities.

5. A decrease in taxes payable indicates expenses incurred are less than the cash paid, and, therefore, net income is greater than net cash provided by operating activities.

6. When an investment is sold, the entire proceeds are to be displayed as an investing activity on the statement of cash flows. The gain included in net income must, therefore, be deducted from net income to arrive at the net cash provided by operating activities. If this adjustment was not made, there would be double counting for the gain amount. For example: An investment with a carrying value of $4,000 is sold for $7,000. The entire $7,000 proceeds is an investing inflow; the $7,000 includes the gain of $3,000 and a recovery of the investment's $4,000 carrying value; the $3,000 gain will be deducted from net income to arrive at the net cash from operating activities figure.

7. Amortization is a non-cash charge (debit) against income. It must be added to net income to arrive at the amount of net cash provided by operating activities.

8. A loss on the sale of equipment does not cause a cash outlay so it is added back to net income to arrive at the amount of net cash provided by operating activities. The cash proceeds from the sale of equipment are shown as a cash inflow from an investing activity.

Exercise 5-6

PURPOSE: This exercise will give you practice in preparing a statement of cash flows.

The comparative balance sheets of Spencer Corporation at the beginning and end of year 2008 appear below.

Spencer Corporation
Balance Sheets

	Dec. 31 2008	Dec. 31 2007	Inc./Dec.	
ASSETS				
Cash	$10,500	$7,100	Inc.	3,400
Accounts receivable	18,000	9,400	Inc.	8,600
Prepaid expenses	2,700	3,200	Dec.	500
Investments	-0-	11,300	Dec.	11,300
Equipment	56,000	42,000	Inc.	14,000
Less: Accumulated amortization	(10,000)	(5,000)	Dec.	5,000
Total	$77,200	$68,000	Inc.	9,200
LIABILITIES AND SHAREHOLDERS' EQUITY				
Accounts payable	$4,900	$4,500	Inc.	400
Unearned revenue	1,700	6,000	Dec.	4,300
Common shares	14,000	10,000	Inc.	4,000
Retained earnings	56,600	47,500	Inc.	9,100
Total	$77,200	$68,000	Inc.	9,200

During the year 2008, Spencer purchased equipment for $14,000 cash, declared and paid cash dividends of $2,500, sold investments for an amount equal to their cost, and reported net income of $11,600.

Instructions

Prepare a statement of cash flows for Spencer Corporation for the year ending December 31, 2008.

Solution to Exercise 5-6

Spencer Corporation
Statement of Cash Flows
For the Year Ending December 31, 2008

Cash flows from operating activities:		
Net income		$11,600
Adjustments to reconcile net income to net cash provided by operating activities:		
Increase in accounts receivable	($8,600)	
Decrease in prepaid expenses	500	
Increase in accounts payable	400	
Decrease in unearned revenue	(4,300)	
Amortization expense	5,000	(7,000)
Net cash provided by operating activities		4,600
Cash flows from investing activities:		
Sale of investments	$11,300	
Purchase of equipment	(14,000)	
Net cash used by investing activities		(2,700)
Cash flows from financing activities:		
Issuance of common shares	$4,000	
Payment of cash dividends	(2,500)	
Net cash provided by financing activities		1,500
Net increase in cash		3,400
Cash at beginning of the year		7,100
Cash at end of the year		$10,500

EXPLANATION: The net change in cash for the year can easily be determined by taking the difference between the cash balance at the end of the year ($10,500) and the cash balance at the beginning of the year ($7,100), which yields a net increase of $3,400. The reasons for that net increase of $3,400 can be found by analyzing all of the transactions that caused changes in all of the balance sheet accounts other than Cash. The changes in Accounts Receivable, Prepaid Expenses, Accounts Payable, and Unearned Revenues are all due to accruals and prepaids, which help to reconcile the net income figure with the amount of net cash provided (used) by operating activities. The changes in Investments and Equipment are due to transactions, which constitute investing activities. The changes in Accumulated Amortization are usually due to the recording of depreciation expense for the current period and disposals of plant assets. The changes in nontrade liability accounts (such as Mortgage Payable, Bonds Payable, Bank Note Payable) and most changes in shareholders' equity accounts are due to transactions, which constitute financing activities.

An increase of $8,600 in Accounts Receivable indicates that sales revenue (on an accrual basis) exceeded cash collections from customers by $8,600. That in turn causes net income to exceed net cash provided by operating activities, so $8,600 is deducted from net income in reconciling net income to a cash basis figure. A decrease of $500 in Prepaid Expenses indicates that expenses incurred on an accrual basis exceeded the cash payments for expenses by $500 which in turn caused net income to be less than net cash provided by operating activities. (Remember that expenses are a negative component of net income so as expenses go up, net income goes down.) An increase in Accounts Payable of $400 results from an excess of expenses incurred over cash payments for expenses, which causes net income to be less than net cash from operations.

Thus, both a decrease in Prepaid Expenses of $500 and an increase in Accounts Payable of $400 are added to net income to calculate a cash basis income amount. A decrease in Unearned Revenue of $4,300 reflects an excess of revenue earned over cash collections from customers this period; this means net income exceeds net cash provided by operations. Thus, the $4,300 decrease in Unearned Revenue is deducted from net income in reconciling net income to net cash provided by operating activities.

It is helpful to reconstruct the journal entry for each transaction that caused a change in the remaining balance sheet accounts. You will be able to see the impact on Cash. Assume the most common transaction caused a change in a particular account. The entries and analyses are as follows:

Cash	11,300	
Investments		11,300
(Sale of investments at book value)		

There was an inflow of cash due to an investing activity—sale of investments.

Equipment	14,000	
Cash		14,000
(Purchase of equipment)		

There was an outflow of cash due to an investing activity—purchase of property, plant, and equipment.

Amortization Expense	5,000	
Accumulated Amortization		5,000
(Recording of amortization for current period)		

Note this is a non-cash item. It is merely allocating the cash cost of purchase to the periods of useful life.

Cash	4,000	
Common Shares		4,000
(Sale of common shares)		

There was an inflow of cash due to a financing activity—issuance of common shares (obtaining resources from owners).

Retained Earnings	2,500	
Cash		2,500
(Declaration and payment of cash dividends)		

There was an outflow of cash due a financing activity—payment of dividends (giving owners a return on their investment).

Income Summary..	11,600	
Retained Earnings		11,600
(Net income amount is closed to Retained Earnings)		

The balance of the Income Summary account before closing is a summarized figure reflecting all revenues and all expenses; it is a summary of all transactions dealing with operations for the period. Most revenues increase cash and most expenses decrease cash so we use net income (a summary of all revenues and all expenses) as our starting point in calculating cash provided by operating activities. The net income figure is then "adjusted" for the following items:

1. revenue transactions that did not bring in cash this period.
2. expense transactions that did not require a cash outlay this period.
3. revenue items of another period that produced a cash inflow this period.
4. expense items of another period that produced a cash outflow this period.

The result is the amount of net cash provided (used) by operating activities (a cash basis income figure).

Illustration 5-3

A Summary of Financial Ratios

Ratio	Formula for Calculation	Purpose or Use
I. Liquidity		
1. Current ratio	Current assets / Current liabilities	Measures short-term debt-paying ability.
2. Quick or acid-test ratio	Cash, marketable securities, and receivables (net) / Current liabilities	Measures immediate short-term liquidity.
3. Current cash debt ratio	Net cash provided by operating activities / Average current liabilities	Measures the company's ability to pay off its current liabilities out of its operations for a given year.
II. Activity		
4. Receivable turnover	Net sales / Average trade receivables (net)	Measures liquidity of receivables
5. Inventory turnover	Cost of goods sold / Average inventory	Measures liquidity of inventory.
6. Asset turnover	Net sales / Average total assets	Measures how efficiently assets are used to generate sales.
III. Profitability		
7. Profit margin on sales	Net income / Net sales	Measures net income generated by each dollar of sales.
8. Rate of return on assets.	Net income / Average total assets	Measures overall profitability of assets.
9. Rate of return on common share equity	Net income minus preferred dividends / Average common shareholders' equity	Measures profitability of owners' investment.

Illustration 5-3 (Continued)

Ratio	Formula for Calculation	Purpose or Use
10. Earnings per share	Net income minus preferred dividends / Weighted shares outstanding	Measures net income earned on each common share.
11. Price earnings ratio	Market price of shares / Earnings per share	Measures the ratio of the market price per share to earnings per share.
12. Payout ratio	Cash dividends / Net income	Measures percentage of earnings distributed in the form of cash dividends.
IV Coverage		
13. Debt to total assets	Total debt / Total assets or equities	Measures the percentage of total assets provided by creditors.
14. Times interest earned	Income before interest charges and taxes / Interest charges	Measures ability to meet interest payments as they come due.
15. Cash debt coverage ratio	Net cash provided by operating activities / Average total liabilities	Measures a company's ability to repay its total liabilities in a given year out of its operations.
16. Book value per share	Common shareholders' equity / Outstanding shares	Measures the amount each common share would receive if the company were liquidated at the amounts reported on the balance sheet.

TIP!

Throughout the remainder of the textbook, ratios are provided to help understand and interpret the information provided. Above, we provide you with the ratios that will be used throughout the text. You should find the chart helpful as you examine these ratios in more detail in the following chapters.

Analysis of Multiple-Choice Questions

Question

1. The amount of time that is expected to elapse until an asset is realized or otherwise converted into cash is referred to as:
   a. solvency.
   b. financial flexibility.
   c. liquidity.
   d. exchangeability.

EXPLANATION: Liquidity describes the amount of time that is expected to elapse until an asset is realized or otherwise converted into cash or until a liability has to be paid; liquidity refers to the "nearness to cash" of assets and liabilities. Current assets are listed in the order of liquidity (with the most liquid items first) on a balance sheet. Solvency refers to the ability of an enterprise to pay its debts as they mature. Liquidity and solvency affect an entity's financial flexibility which measures the ability of an enterprise to take effective actions to alter the amounts and timing of cash flows so it can respond and adapt to financial adversity and unexpected needs and opportunities. (Solution = c.)

Question

2. The Heather Miller Company has the following obligations at December 31, 2008:

I. Accounts payable	$ 72,000
II. Taxes payable	60,000
III. Notes payable issued November 1, 2008, due October 31, 2009	80,000
IV. Bonds payable issued December 1, 1999, due November 30, 2009 (to be paid by use of a sinking fund)	100,000

The amount that should be reported for total current liabilities at December 31, 2008 is:
   a. $312,000.
   b. $212,000.
   c. $132,000.
   d. $72,000.

EXPLANATION: Write down the definition (or key phrases therein) for a current liability. (A **current liability** is an obligation which is coming due within a year of the balance sheet date and is expected to require the use of current assets or the incurrence of another current liability to liquidate it.) Analyze each of the obligations listed to see if it meets the criteria for being classified as current.

Accounts payable and taxes payable will both be due shortly after the balance sheet date and will require cash to liquidate the debts. The notes payable are due within a year of the balance sheet date and there is no evidence to indicate that assets other than current assets will be used for settlement; thus, the notes payable are a current liability. The bonds payable are coming due within a year, but they will not require the use of current assets to liquidate the debt because a sinking fund (restricted cash or securities classified as a long-term investment) is to be used to extinguish that debt: $72,000 + $60,000 + $80,000 = $212,000. (Solution = b.)

Question

3. Land held for a future plant site should be classified in the section for:
   a. current assets.
   b. long-term investments.
   c. property, plant, and equipment.
   d. intangible assets.

EXPLANATION: Review the descriptions of what goes in each of the asset classifications. Then read each answer selection and respond **True** or **False** if the selection answers the question. The land is not being used in operations, so it doesn't belong in property, plant, and equipment. It is not lacking physical existence, so it can't be an intangible asset. The land is not expected to be converted to cash or sold or consumed within the next year, so it is not a current asset. The land properly belongs in long-term investments. (Solution = b.)

Question

4. Working capital is:
   a. current assets less current liabilities.
   b. total assets less total liabilities.
   c. the same as retained earnings.
   d. capital which has been reinvested in the business.

EXPLANATION: The excess of total current assets over total current liabilities is referred to as working capital. Working capital represents the net amount of a company's relatively liquid resources. That is, it is the liquid buffer available to meet the financial demands of the operating cycle. (Solution = a.)

Question

5. Treasury shares are classified as a(n):
   a. current asset.
   b. long-term investment.
   c. other asset.
   d. contra shareholders' equity item.

EXPLANATION: Treasury shares are a company's redemption of their own shares that have been previously issued, but not cancelled. The acquisition of treasury shares represents a contraction of owners' equity; thus it is reported as a reduction of shareholders' equity. (Solution = d.)

Question

6. Which of the following is classified as an intangible asset on a balance sheet?
   a. Long-term receivable
   b. Long-term investment in shares of another enterprise
   c. Licences
   d. Accounts Receivable

EXPLANATION: Intangible assets lack physical substance and usually have a high degree of uncertainty concerning their future benefits. Although receivables and investments in shares lack physical existence, they are properly classifiable elsewhere so they are **not** classified for accounting purposes as intangible assets. Accounts receivable are classified as current assets; long-term receivables and long-term investments in shares are classified as long-term investments; and licences are classified as intangible assets. (Solution = c.)

Question

7. Which of the following should **not** be found in the long-term investment section of the balance sheet?
   a. Land held for speculation
   b. Bond sinking fund
   c. Cash surrender value of life insurance
   d. Patent

EXPLANATION: A patent is classified as an intangible asset. Long-term investments, often referred to simply as investments, normally consist of one of four types:

1. Investments in securities, such as bonds, common shares—depending on management intent.
2. Investments in tangible fixed assets not currently used in operations, such as land held for speculation or future plant site.
3. Investments set aside in special funds such as a sinking fund, pension fund, or plant expansion fund. The cash surrender value of life insurance is included here.
4. Investments in non-consolidated subsidiaries or affiliated companies—"strategic" investments. (Solution = d.)

Question

8. A loss contingency that has a level of likelihood rated as reasonably possible and an amount that can be reasonably estimated should be:

	Accrued	Disclosed
a.	Yes	Yes
b.	Yes	No
c.	No	Yes
d.	No	No

EXPLANATION: Read the stem and write down how you would complete the statement in the stem. Then look at the answer selections one at a time to find the one that corresponds with your anticipated response. A loss contingency that is probable and estimable should be accrued. A loss contingency that is reasonably possible should be disclosed only in the notes (and not be accrued). A loss contingency that is only remotely possible can usually be ignored and not accrued or disclosed. (Solution = c.)

Question

9. Which of the following is a contra account?
   a. Premium on bonds payable
   b. Unearned revenue
   c. Patents
   d. Accumulated amortization

EXPLANATION: After reading the question and before reading the answer selections, write down the description of the term "contra account." (A **contra account** is a valuation account whose normal balance is opposite of the balance of the account to which it relates.) Then take each answer selection and answer **True** or **False** whether it meets that description. Premium on bonds payable is a valuation account, but it is an adjunct type (its normal balance is the same as the normal balance of the account to which it relates). Unearned Revenue and Patents are not valuation accounts. Accumulated Amortization is a valuation account for property, plant, and equipment. The normal balance of the Accumulated Amortization account is a credit and the normal balance of a property, plant, and equipment account is a debit. Hence, Accumulated Amortization is a contra account. (Solution = d.)

Question

10. Which of the following should be classified as an inflow of cash in the investing section of a statement of cash flows?
   a. Cash sale of merchandise inventory.
   b. Sale of delivery equipment at book value.
   c. Proceeds on sale of common shares.
   d. Issuance of a note payable to a bank.

EXPLANATION: Read the question and, before reading the answer selections, write down the items that appear in the definition of investing activities. (**Investing activities** include making and collecting loans to others, acquiring and disposing of stocks and bonds of other entities, acquiring and disposing of property, plant, and equipment and other productive assets.) Think of the items included in that definition that would produce a cash inflow (collecting loans, disposing of investments and property, plant, and equipment). Look for the answer selection that fits that analysis. As you analyze each answer selection, indicate what kind of activity it represents. A cash sale of merchandise inventory is an operating activity. The sale of common shares is a financing activity. The issuance of a note payable is a financing activity. A sale of equipment is an investing activity. (Solution = b.)

Question

11. An example of a cash flow from an operating activity is:
    a. payment to employees for services.
    b. payment of dividends to shareholders.
    c. receipt of proceeds from the sale of an investment.
    d. receipt of proceeds from the sale of common shares to shareholders.

EXPLANATION: Operating activities include the cash effects of transactions that ultimately create revenues and expenses and thus enter into the determination of net income. Operating activities include collections from customers, collections of interest and dividends, payments for merchandise and other goods and services, and payments for interest and taxes. The payment of dividends is a financing activity. The sale of an investment is an investing activity. The sale of common shares is a financing activity. (Solution = a.)

Question

12. In preparing a statement of cash flows, the sale of property, plant, and equipment at an amount greater than its carrying value will be classified as a(n):
    a. operating activity.
    b. investing activity.
    c. financing activity.
    d. extraordinary activity.

EXPLANATION: Think about the nature of each of the three categories on a statement of cash flows and select the one involving disposal of plant assets:
1. **Operating Activities**: Operating activities represent the enterprise's principle revenue-producing activities and all other activities not related to investing and financing. Cash flows from operating activities are generally the cash effects of transactions and other events that enter into the determination of net income.
2. **Investing Activities**: Investing activities represent the acquisitions and disposal of long-term assets and other investments not included in "cash equivalents", including (a) making and collecting loans; (b) acquiring and disposing of debt and

equity instruments of other entities; and (c) acquiring and disposing of property, plant, and equipment and other productive assets.
3. **Financing Activities**: Financing activities represent activities that result in changes in the size and composition of the enterprise's equity capital and borrowings, including (a) obtaining resources from owners and providing them with a return on and a return of their investment; (b) borrowing money and repaying the amounts borrowed, or otherwise settling the obligation; and (c) obtaining and paying for other resources obtained from creditors. (*CICA Handbook*, Section 1540.06.)

There is **no** category called "extraordinary activity" on a statement of cash flows. The fact that the asset was sold for a price exceeding the carrying value does not impact the answer because the entire proceeds from the sale are to be reported in the investing activity section. In the operating activity section, the amount of gain reflected in the net income figure is deducted from net income to arrive at "net cash provided by operating activities". (Solution = b.)

Question

13. In a statement of cash flows, proceeds from the issuance of common shares should be classified as a cash inflow from:
    a. operating activities.
    b. investing activities.
    c. financing activities.
    d. lending activities.

EXPLANATION: The issuance of common shares by a corporation is the company's way of obtaining resources from an owner (i.e., owner investment into the business). Financing activities include obtaining resources from owners. There is no category called "lending activities". (Solution = c.)

Question

14. Which of the following would be classified as an investing activity on a statement of cash flows?
    a. Issuance of bonds payable at a premium.
    b. Purchase of land to be used in operations.
    c. Issuance of common shares at the current market price of $5.
    d. Payment of dividends to shareholders.

EXPLANATION: Think about the types of items to be included in investing activities. Investing activities include making and collecting loans, acquiring and disposing of investments (both debt and equity), and acquiring and disposing of property, plant, and equipment. Take each of the answer choices and identify where it should go on a statement of cash flows. The issuance of bonds and the issuance of shares (regardless of price) are both financing activities that usually bring an inflow of cash. The payment of dividends is a financing outflow. The purchase of land (regardless of use) is an investing outflow. (Solution = b.)

Question

15. In preparing a statement of cash flows, the payment of interest to a creditor should be classified as a cash outflow due to:
    a. operating activities.
    b. investing activities.
    c. financing activities.
    d. borrowing activities.

EXPLANATION: Borrowing money is a financing activity. Repaying amounts (the principal borrowed) is a financing activity. Paying interest on amounts borrowed is an operating activity because it is not included in the definition of financing activities and because the interest paid will be related to the interest incurred (interest expense) which is a transaction that enters into the determination of net income. There is no category called "borrowing activities". (Solution = a.)

Question

16. Alley Cat Corporation had net income for 2008 of $5,000,000. Additional information is as follows:

Amortization of plant assets	$2,000,000
Amortization of intangibles	$400,000
Increase in accounts receivable	$700,000
Increase in accounts payable	$900,000

Alley Cat's net cash provided by operating activities for 2008 was:
a. $2,800,000.
b. $7,200,000.
c. $7,400,000.
d. $7,600,000.

EXPLANATION: The amortization amounts are items that reduce net income but do not cause a decrease in cash during the current period. The increase in accounts receivable indicates that sales revenue earned for the period exceeded the cash collections from customers, and therefore net income exceeded the net cash provided by operating activities. The increase in accounts payable indicates that expenses incurred exceeded cash payments for expense type items which caused net income to be less than net cash provided by operating activities. The solution is as follows:

Net income	$5,000,000
Amortization of plant assets	2,000,000
Amortization of intangibles	400,000
Increase in accounts receivable	(700,000)
Increase in accounts payable	900,000
Net cash provided by operating activities	$7,600,000

(Solution = d.)

Question

17. Net cash flow from operating activities for 2008 for Graham Corporation was $75,000. The following items are reported on the financial statements for 2008:

Amortization	$5,000
Cash dividends paid on common shares	3,000
Increase in accounts receivable	6,000

Based only on the information above, Graham's net income for 2008 was:

a. $64,000.
b. $66,000.
c. $74,000.
d. $76,000.
e. None of the above.

EXPLANATION: Write down the format for the reconciliation of net income to net cash flow from operating activities. Fill in the information given. Solve for the unknown.

Net income	$ X
Amortization	5,000
Increase in accrued receivables	(6,000)
Net cash flow from operating activities	$ 75,000

Solving for X, net income = $76,000. Cash dividends paid on common shares have no effect on this calculation because cash dividends paid is not a component of net income and not an operating activity. Cash dividends paid is classified as a financing activity. (Solution = d.)

Question

18. Free cash flow is:

a. net cash provided by operating activities minus capital expenditures and dividends.
b. net cash provided by operating activities minus retirement of debt and purchases of treasury stock.
c. the amount of cash obtained from donations.
d. the amount of net cash increase during the period.

EXPLANATION: One method of examining a company's financial flexibility is to develop a free cash flow analysis. This analysis starts with net cash provided by operating activities and ends with free cash flow which is calculated as net cash provided by operating activities less capital expenditures and dividends. Free cash flow is the amount of discretionary cash flow a company has for purchasing additional investments, retiring its debt, purchasing treasury stock, or simply adding to its liquidity. This measure indicates a company's level of financial flexibility. (Solution = a.)

Question

19. Net cash provided by operating activities divided by average total liabilities equals the:
    a. current cash debt coverage ratio.
    b. cash debt coverage ratio.
    c. free cash flow.
    d. current ratio.

EXPLANATION: Visualize the calculation of each ratio or calculation referenced in the answer selections. The current cash debt coverage ratio equals net cash provided by operating activities divided by average current liabilities. The cash debt coverage ratio is calculated by taking the net cash provided by operating activities divided by average total liabilities. Free cash flow is calculated as net cash provided by operating activities less capital expenditures and dividends. The current ratio is current assets divided by current liabilities. (Solution = b.)

Question

20. Activity ratios measure the effectiveness of asset usage. One of the activity ratios is the:
    a. inventory turnover ratio.
    b. current ratio.
    c. quick ratio.
    d. rate of return on assets.

EXPLANATION: The activity ratios include the (1) receivable turnover ratio, (2) inventory turnover ratio, and (3) asset turnover ratio. The current ratio and the quick (or acid-test) ratio are both liquidity ratios. The rate of return on assets ratio is a profitability ratio. (Solution = a.)

Question

21. The current ratio is 3:1 for the Hamstock Company at December 31, 2008. What is the impact on that ratio of a collection of accounts receivable?
    a. Current ratio is increased.
    b. Current ratio is decreased.
    c. Current ratio is unaffected.

EXPLANATION: Reconstruct the journal entry for the transaction. Analyze the effect of the debit portion of the entry on each element of the ratio and then analyze the effect of the credit portion of the entry on each element of the ratio. The entry to record the collection of accounts receivable involves a debit to Cash and a credit to Accounts Receivable. There is no change in the total amount of current assets. There is no change in the total amount of current liabilities. Thus, there is no change in the current ratio, which is current assets divided by current liabilities. (Solution = c.)

Question

22. The balance sheet, although providing significant useful information to users, has significant drawbacks including:
    a. valuation, use of estimates, and lack of completeness.
    b. valuation and lack of completeness.
    c. lack of completeness.
    d. use of estimates.

EXPLANATION: There are many limitations relating to the balance sheet, the main ones being the use of historical cost, the fact that accrual accounting requires the use of estimates, such as for bad debts, and the fact that due to inability to measure certain items such as contingencies, many items are left off the balance sheet. (Solution = a.)

Question

23. Albert Limited is being sued by Benny Limited. The lawyers feel that it is likely that Benny will be successful and will likely settle for between $150,000 and $250,000. In this case, the lawyers don't have any insight into the exact amount of the loss within that range. How much should be accrued in the financial statements of Albert?
    a. $150,000
    b. $250,000
    c. $200,000
    d. $0 due to the fact that the range is too large and no estimate is better than another

EXPLANATION: When there is a range of estimates and no one number provides a better estimate than the next, the *CICA Handbook* states that the minimum amount in the range would be accrued (*CICA Handbook* Section 3290.14). This would tend to go against the conservatism principle; however, it provides a measure of consistency between companies. (Solution = a.)

Question

24. Assume the same facts as 23 above. What should Benny accrue?
    a. $150,000
    b. $250,000
    c. $200,000
    d. $0

EXPLANATION: Benny should accrue $0 since this is a contingent gain and contingent gains are not recognized due to the realization and conservatism principles. (Solution = d.)

Chapter 6

Revenue Recognition

Overview

Revenue recognition guidelines generally provide that revenue may be recognized when (1) **performance** is achieved, which means **the risk and rewards** are transferred (2) **measurability** is reasonably assured, and (3) **collectibility** is reasonably assured. These guidelines actually oversimplify revenue recognition since the many methods of marketing products and services make it extremely difficult to apply in certain situations. Although a large percentage of entities find it appropriate to recognize revenue at the point of sale (delivery) of a good or service, other entities find it appropriate to use some other basis of revenue recognition, which may result in recognizing revenue prior to delivery (although very rare, given the specific guidance in EIC 141) or at a point in time after delivery. In this chapter, we discuss accounting guidelines for the recognition of revenue.

Study Steps

Understanding the Business Transaction—Business Content

The earnings process and the timeline

Revenue is defined as an increase in the economic resources of the company from ordinary operations or business of the company. It is, therefore, critical to understand how the entity earns its money. What does the company do to earn revenues and how do they go about doing it? This is called the earnings process.

TIP! When analyzing revenue recognition issues, always begin with an acknowledgement of what the company does to earn money and what the earnings process is. The "business model" approach can be very effective in determining when to recognize revenue.

EIC 141 further clarifies the meaning of **performance**. The standard states that performance is regarded as being achieved when:

- persuasive evidence of an arrangement exists (i.e., the terms of a business deal or contract are agreed upon and finalized),
- delivery has occurred or the service has been rendered, and
- the seller's price to the buyer is fixed and determinable.

Each of these is explained in detail in the standard, allowing for more specific guidance on what can be a very difficult accounting issue.

Sometimes there is one very important step or act in the earnings process that defines a sale. This is called the critical event. For sale of goods, this is often shipment. At this point, possession passes, as does legal title in many cases, and often there is minimal future uncertainty with respect to the sale not going through or the earnings process not being culminated. The presence of uncertainty may affect this point of revenue recognition—particularly if it cannot be measured. Certainly, prior to the shipping point (i.e., when the customer places the order) there is a great deal of uncertainty as to whether the inventory will be in stock or whether the company will be able to deliver the inventory on time and in satisfactory condition, etc. Based on EIC 141, it is clear that delivery **must** occur for a sale to be considered.

The critical event is often evidenced by an outside exchange. In this case, the exchange is the delivery of the inventory to someone outside the company for consideration.

When there is just one critical event, the earnings process is known as a discrete earnings process. Sometimes there is no single defining event; rather, there may be several significant events of equal importance. In this case, the earnings process is known as a continuous earnings process.

TIP!

With a critical event, the revenue is recognized when the critical event has been completed. With a continuous earnings process, the revenue may be recognized gradually as each major step in the earnings process is completed, depending on information available.

An example of a continuous earnings process is the long-term construction of a bridge. The earnings process might look as follows:

Timeline (earnings process) for construction company

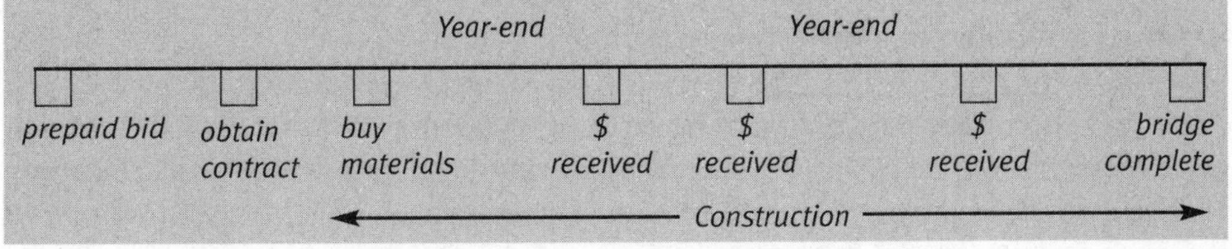

Here, the bridge is effectively sold before it is built. (In a normal manufacturing business, the product is made and then sold, with the outside exchange happening at the end.) Also, the process takes longer, often spanning more than one reporting period. Even though the bridge is pre-sold, the company must still earn the revenue by building it (i.e., performance).

One might argue that the critical event is the completion of the bridge. However, if this is true, then all of the revenue would be recognized in that period, implying that it was earned in that reporting period. Is this truly the case? Furthermore, the completion of the bridge would not signify a sale if there was no pre-signed contract. In this situation, especially since the bridge was sold upfront, the earnings process appears to be made up of several significant events and is, therefore, more like a continuous process. Revenue would be recognized as the significant events are completed, or over time.

TIP!

When analyzing accounting issues such as revenue recognition, it is important to consider the economics of these transactions. For example, is the company economically better off? Is this supported by a valid accounts receivable. When this has been satisfied, it is logical that revenue may be recognized.

Sale of goods—the risks and rewards of ownership concept

For goods, a sale occurs when the risks and rewards of ownership are transferred from the seller to the purchaser and/or when all significant acts in the earnings process are complete. Therefore, it is important to focus on the definition of risks and rewards of ownership and how they affect the earnings process. The earnings process has been discussed above and the risks and rewards will be discussed below.

Sale of goods:

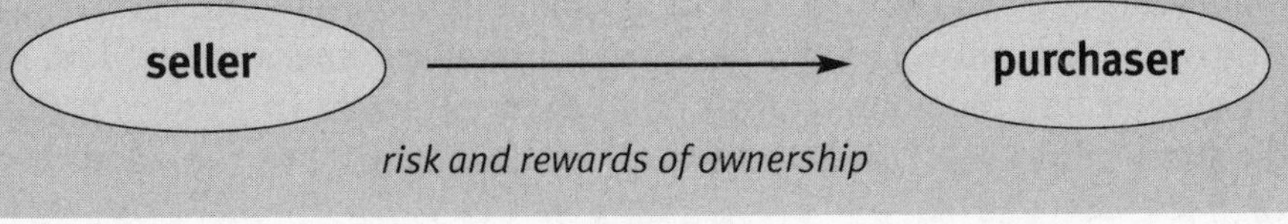

Consider the house that you live in. What are the risks and rewards of owning the house?

Risks:

- loss in value
- loss from vandalism, fire, or other unforeseen circumstances

Rewards:

- increases in value
- use—can live in it or rent it out to someone else for profit
- able to mortgage the property for raising funds

Note that there are many risks and rewards of ownership and that they differ from asset to asset. Ownership is evidenced by having legal title to the asset, but may also be evidenced by possession in certain circumstances. Legal title allows you to live in the house, pledge it to obtain financing, and entitles you to increases in its value. It also means that you are at risk for such things as loss and declines in value. Possession might also signal the existence of some or all of these rights/burdens. Therefore, these two facts are important in determining who has the risks and rewards of ownership and when they pass. Usually the party who is at risk for loss will acknowledge this through insurance.

TIP! When looking at any transaction where an asset is changing hands in terms of legal title or possession, an analysis must be done of who has the risks and rewards of ownership. Many complex transactions involve the transfer of risks and rewards of ownership. Look at who has possession or legal title or who is paying for insurance. These often give hints as to who has the risks and rewards of ownership.

TIP! The concept of risks and rewards is also central to the definition of an asset, i.e., the definition of an asset looks at existence and access to future benefits or rewards.

Dealing with uncertainty

Another major consideration to focus on is the uncertainty factor. Are the goods returnable? Are the funds collectible? Can the transaction be measured? These are a few factors that must also be considered. If there is too much uncertainty, then it is unlikely a sale has occurred.

TIP! Where there is uncertainty, professional judgment must be applied. However, EIC 141 makes it reasonably clear that the presence of uncertainty makes it unlikely a sale has occurred.

Consignment sales

Consignment sales are a special type of arrangement whereby the vendor displays inventory on the premises of another party until a customer buys it. The middle party does not buy the goods upfront and then sell to the customer; rather, the middle party allows the goods to be displayed. Legal title to the goods remains with the company until the customer buys the product even though it is displayed for sale in the showroom/store of the middle party.

Franchise arrangements

A franchise arrangement is when one party (the franchiser) grants another party (the franchisee) the right to use the franchiser's name and sell a product or service. The value to the franchisee is the goodwill associated with the name, e.g., McDonald's, and the expertise and experience of the franchiser who usually assists in the setup of the new business and training of the franchisee.

For these rights, the franchisee pays what is known as an upfront or initial fee (which is often quite substantial) and an ongoing fee. The ongoing fee is normally a percentage of sales and is paid to cover ongoing training and advertising.

The accounting issues usually relate to the initial fee and when to recognize it. Because initial fees are recognized as revenues upfront, there is a tendency or bias to maximize the amount of initial fee in the contract. Care should be taken to ensure that amounts identified as upfront or initial fees are indeed for services, etc. to be provided upfront by the franchiser.

Barter transactions

Barter transactions, also known as non-monetary transactions, will also be discussed in Chapter 10; however, it is worth a brief mention here. A barter transaction is an exchange of goods where there is no monetary consideration. Because there is no monetary consideration, there is a measurement issue, and, more importantly, there is an issue as to whether a real sale took place or whether the transaction was merely an exchange of similar assets.

Becoming Proficient in Using Specific Revenue Recognition Methods

There are methods for recognizing revenues that have become generally accepted in certain industries (e.g., the instalment method in retail sales, franchise accounting in the fast food industry, percentage-of-completion and completed-contract methods in the construction industry, etc.). Furthermore, certain methods make more sense when dealing with sales and uncertainty; e.g., instalment method and cost recovery method.

Not all are dealt with specifically in the *CICA Handbook*. The general principles covered in Section 3400 of the *CICA Handbook* have been enhanced with the more specific guidance given in EIC 141. Franchise fee accounting is dealt with separately in the Accounting Guidelines section in the *CICA Handbook*.

You should develop a proficiency in the mechanics of instalment and cost recovery methods, as well as completed-contract and percentage-of-completion methods.

Tips on Chapter Topics

TIP! All revenues cause an increase in net assets (owners' equity); thus, a revenue item also results in either an increase in assets or a decrease in liabilities. **Revenues** are defined in *CICA Handbook*, Section 1000.37 as: "Revenues are increases in economic resources, either by way of inflows or enhancements of assets or reductions of liabilities, resulting from the ordinary activities of an entity. Revenues of entities normally arise from the sale of goods, the rendering of services or the use by others of entity resources yielding rent, interest, royalties or dividends."

TIP! To **recognize** means to give expression in the accounts. To recognize a revenue means to record an item as revenue in the accounts; thus, the item will get reported as revenue in the financial statements. Likewise, to recognize an asset means to record an increase in an asset account. **Recognition** is "the process of including an item in the financial statements of an entity" (*CICA Handbook*, Section 1000). For an asset or liability, recognition involves recording not only acquisition or incurrence of the item but also later changes in it, including removal from the financial statements.

TIP! It is useful to consider revenue recognition in terms of "defaults"—specifically, when revenue would be recognized in the absence of other information or uncertainties. For example: (a) revenue from selling products is recognized at the date of sale, usually interpreted to mean the date of delivery to customers; (b) revenue from ser-vices rendered is recognized when services have been performed and are billable; (c) revenue from permitting others to use enterprise assets such as interest, rent, and royalties is recognized as time passes or as the assets are used; and, (d) revenue from disposing of assets other than products is recognized at the date of sale.

TIP! **Revenue** is a **gross** amount (an amount before costs are deducted), whereas **gain** is a **net** amount (an amount after costs are subtracted). Gains (as contrasted to revenues) commonly result from transactions and other events that do not involve an earning process. For gain recognition, being earned is generally less significant than being realized or realizable. Gains are commonly recognized at the time of sale of an asset, disposition of a liability, or when prices of certain assets change. The following example illustrates how revenue is a gross concept and gain is a net concept.

A company sells two assets for $1,000 each. The first asset is an inventory item which cost $600. The second asset is a piece of equipment which cost $900 and has been amortized $300 thus far. The first item would cause the following to be reflected in the income statement:

Sales revenue	$1,000
Cost of goods sold	600
Gross profit	400

The second item would cause the following to be reflected in the "other income" section of a multiple-step income statement:

Gain on sale of equipment	$400*

*$900 cost - $300 accumulated amortization = $600 carrying value
$1,000 selling price - $600 carrying value = $400 gain

In the case of the second item, it is not an item held for sale in the main course of business. The proceeds ($1,000) and the related cost (carrying value of $600) are netted off the statement, and only the net amount ($400 gain) appears on the face of the income statement.

TIP! In determining who has the risks and rewards of ownership and hence whether a sale has occurred at the point of delivery, it is important to look at who has the possession of the goods and who has the legal title (e.g. Terms of sale, FOB shipping point means title transfers to the buyer when the goods leave the shipping dock, while FOB destination indicates title does not transfer until the goods arrive at the buyer's location).

TIP! Goods shipped on consignment are **not** considered to be a sale as the revenue recognition criteria are not fully met as full performance by the seller is not complete since ownership (legal title) of the goods are maintained by the seller.

TIP! The revenue recognition bases or methods, the criteria for their use, and the reasons for departing from the sale basis when accounting for the sale of a product are summarized in **Illustration 6-2**. Review those methods and be able to explain when and why they are used.

TIP! The term **income** is sometimes used to refer to a gross amount (such as dividend income, rent income, interest income), which makes its usage synonymous with revenue. The term income is also used to refer to a net amount, such as net income for a period. Thus, if an exam question asks for the calculation of income to be recognized for the current period for a long-term construction contract using the percentage-of completion method, it may be unclear whether the question is using "income" to mean "revenue" or if "income" means "gross profit" (revenue net of related costs). If it is a multiple-choice question, a calculation for both revenue and gross profit may quickly solve the mystery.

TIP! The percentage-of-completion method is used for long-term construction contracts where revenue is appropriately recognized during production (prior to completion and delivery). Justification for recognition of revenue during the construction period is based on the fact that the ultimate sale and the selling price are assured by the contract. The percentage-of-completion method recognizes revenue, costs, and gross profit as progress is made toward completion on a long-term contract. The progress made during a period may be supplied by engineering estimates or determined by the cost-to-cost method (the latter method is used in most textbook situations). The cost-to-cost method is as follows:

$$\left[\frac{\text{Costs incurred to date}}{\text{Estimate of total costs}} \times \text{Estimated total revenue (or gross profit)}\right] - \text{Total revenue (or gross profit) or recognized in prior periods} = \text{Current period revenue (or gross profit)}$$

TIP! In this formula, estimated total revenue is determined by the contract price, and estimated total gross profit is determined by the contract price reduced by an estimate of total costs. The estimate of total costs includes costs incurred to date **plus** an estimate of remaining costs to be incurred to complete the contract. Costs incurred to date include costs incurred in prior periods **plus** costs incurred in the current period.

TIP! Regardless of whether the percentage-of-completion method or the completed-contract method is used, the difference between the balance of the Construction in Process account and the balance of the Billings on Construction in Process account is reported as a current liability (if Billings on Construction in Process has the larger balance) or as a current asset (if Construction in Process has the larger balance). The balance of the Billings on Construction in Process account is offset against the balance of the inventory account (Construction in Process) because the inventory amount should not be double counted (i.e., the inventory account was not removed when the Accounts Receivable account was increased at the date of a billing to a customer).

TIP! The **instalment sales method of revenue recognition** emphasizes collection of the selling price rather than the sale. It recognizes income in the periods of collection rather than in the period of sale. The instalment sales method is **not** a generally accepted method; it is to be used only for situations where uncollectible accounts cannot be reasonably estimated at the time of sale.

TIP! When using the **instalment sales method of accounting**, the amount of gross profit to be recognized for a particular period is determined by multiplying the amount of cash collected during the period on instalment receivables by the appropriate gross profit percentage(s). A rather difficult exam question may give the amount of gross profit recognized along with the gross profit percentage and require the examinee to solve for the amount of cash collected. For example, if gross profit recognized for 2008 is $90,000 and the gross profit percentage is 30%, cash collections during the period amount to $300,000 ($90,000 ÷ 30% = $300,000).

TIP! In a sale and buyback arrangement, professional judgment as to whether a sale has indeed taken place must be used. Legal title has transferred, but the economic substance of the transaction indicates the seller retains the risks of ownership. It is, therefore, unlikely that a sale has taken place. These are often considered financing arrangements.

TIP! Goods on consignment should be reported as inventory by the consignor, not the consignee.

Illustration 6-1

Journal Entries for Long-Term Construction Contracts

ENTRY	PERCENTAGE-OF-COMPLETION METHOD	COMPLETED-CONTRACT METHOD

To record costs of construction	Construction in Process
	    Materials, Cash, Payables, etc.
		Construction in Progress
		    Materials, Cash, Payables, etc.

To record progress billings	Accounts Receivable
	    Billings on Construction in Process
		Accounts Receivable
		    Billings on Construction in Process

To record collections	Cash
	    Accounts Receivable
		Cash
		    Accounts Receivable

To recognize revenue and gross profit	Construction in Process GP** Construction Expenses COSTS Revenue from Long-Term Contracts REV	No Entry*

To record final approval of the contract	Billings on Construction in Process
	    Construction in Process
		Billings on Const. in Process REV
		    Revenue from Long-Term Contracts REV
		
		Construction Expenses*** COSTS
		    Construction in Process COSTS

GP = Gross Profit COSTS = Costs Incurred REV = Revenue

*A loss on an unprofitable contract is recognized, in full, immediately under either method. A loss would be recorded under the completed-contract method by a debit to Loss from Long-Term Contracts and a credit to Construction in Process for the estimated amount of loss.

**When a loss is estimated, this account (Construction in Process) gets credited for the estimated amount of loss. The rest of the entry is the same as what is shown for a profitable situation.

***The account Construction Expenses can be titled Construction Costs or Costs of Construction.

TIP! An estimated loss on a long-term construction contract is to be recognized in the period it is determined there will ultimately be a loss on completion of the contract, regardless of the method being used to account for the contract. The justification for recognizing the loss before completion even under the completed-contract method lies with the conservatism principle—recognize losses when known.

Illustration 6-2

Revenue Recognition Bases Other Than the Sale Basis for Products

Recognition Basis (or Method of Applying a Basis)	Criteria for Use of Basis	Reason(s) for Departing from Sale Basis
Percentage-of-completion method	Long-term construction of property; dependable estimates of extent of progress and cost to complete; reasonable assurance of collectibility of contract price; expectation that both contractor and buyer can meet obligations; and absence of inherent hazards that make estimates doubtful.	Availability of evidence of ultimate proceeds; better measure of periodic income; avoidance of fluctuations in revenues, expenses, and income; performance is a "continuous sale" and therefore not a departure from the sale basis.
Completed-contract method	Use on short-term contracts, and whenever percentage-of-completion criteria are not met for long-term contracts.	Existence of inherent hazards in the contract beyond the normal, recurring business risks; conditions for using the the percentage-of-completion method are absent.
Instalment sales method	Absence of a reasonable basis for estimating degree of collectibility and costs of collection.	Collectibility of the receivable is so uncertain that gross profit is not recognized until cash is actually received.
Cost recovery method	Absence of a reasonable basis for estimating degree of collectibility and cost of collection.	Collectibility of the receivable is so doubtful that no income is recognized until the amount of cash received exceeds the cost of the good sold. Considred more conservative than the instalment sales method.
Deposit method	Cash received before the sales transaction is completed.	No recognition of revenue and income because there is not sufficient transfer of the risks and rewards of ownership.

Exercise 6-1

PURPOSE: This exercise will allow you to compare the results of using the percentage-of-completion method versus the completed-contract method to calculate the amount of gross profit to be recognized in each year of a three-year contract.

At the beginning of 2008, Build-a-lot Construction Company signed a fixed-price contract to construct a sports arena at a price of $26,000,000. Information relating to the costs and billings for this contract is as follows:

	2008	2009	2010
Costs incurred during the period	$ 8,320,000	$11,360,000	$ 3,520,000
Estimated costs to complete, as of December 31	12,480,000	4,320,000	-0-
Billings during the year	3,900,000	15,900,000	6,200,000
Collections during the year	3,120,000	12,000,000	10,880,000

Instructions

(a) Assuming the completed-contract method is used, calculate the gross profit to be recognized in (1) 2008, (2) 2009, and (3) 2010.

(b) Assuming the percentage-of-completion method is used, calculate the gross profit to be recognized in (1) 2008, (2) 2009, and (3) 2010.

(c) Assuming the percentage-of-completion method is used, show how the details related to this construction contract would be disclosed on the balance sheet at December 31, 2010.

Solution to Exercise 6-1

(a) (1) 2008 -0-
(2) 2009 -0-
(3) 2010 $2,800,000*

*Calculations:

Total revenue	$26,000,000
Total costs incurred	23,200,000**
Total gross profit	$ 2,800,000

** Costs incurred in 2008	$ 8,320,000
Costs incurred in 2009	11,360,000
Costs incurred in 2010	3,520,000
Total costs incurred	$23,200,000

EXPLANATION: When the completed-contract method is used, the recognition of all revenue and related costs (and, therefore, resulting gross profit) is deferred until the period of completion (2010 in this case). The only exception to this guideline is in the case where a loss is expected. A loss should be recognized immediately in the period in which it is determined that a loss will result.

(b) (1) 2008 $2,080,000
(2) 2009 $ (440,000)
(3) 2010 $1,160,000

CALCULATIONS:

2008:

Costs incurred to date (12/31/08)	$ 8,320,000
Estimated costs to complete as of 12/31/08	12,480,000
Estimate of total costs as of 12/31/08	$ 20,800,000

Total revenue (contract price)	$ 26,000,000
Estimate of total costs	20,800,000
Estimated total gross profit	$ 5,200,000

$\frac{\$8,320,000}{\$20,800,000} \times \$5,200,000 = \underline{\underline{\$2,080,000}}$ Gross profit to be recognized in 2008

2009:

Costs incurred to date (12/31/09) ($8,320,000 + $11,360,000)	$ 19,680,000
Estimated costs to complete as of 12/31/09	4,320,000
Estimate of total costs as of 12/31/09	$ 24,000,000

Total revenue (contract price)	$26,000,000
Estimate of total costs	24,000,000
Estimated total gross profit	$ 2,000,000

$\frac{\$19,680,000}{\$24,000,000} \times \$2,000,000 - \$2,080,000 = \$(440,000)$ Loss to be recognized in 2009

2010:

Costs incurred in 2008	$ 8,320,000
Costs incurred in 2009	11,360,000
Costs incurred in 2010	3,520,000
Total costs incurred	23,200,000

Total revenue (contract price)	$26,000,000
Total costs incurred	23,200,000
Total gross profit earned on contract	2,800,000
Gross profit recognized in 2008	(2,080,000)
Loss recognized in 2009	440,000
Gross profit to be recognized in 2010	$ 1,160,000

In the calculation for estimated total gross profit, the current (most up-to-date) estimate of total costs is deducted from total revenue (the contract price). The estimate of total costs is likely to change every year, which will cause the estimated total gross profit to change each year. Such is the case in this exercise.

In the second year of the contract, Build-a-lot's cost estimates increased dramatically, which caused the gross profit recognized to date (2008's gross profit of $2,080,000) to exceed the $1,640,000 total gross profit earned to date ($19,680,000 ÷ $24,000,000 x $2,000,000 = $1,640,000). This excess is recognized as a loss of $440,000 in 2009 to bring the total gross profit recognized by the end of 2009 to $1,640,000.

In the last year of the contract, total costs incurred on the contract are deducted from total revenue on the contract to arrive at total gross profit earned on the contract. The amounts reported on prior income statements as gross profit (loss) are deducted from (added to) this amount to arrive at the gross profit to recognize in the last period.

In the situation at hand, the costs incurred in 2010 are less than what was expected, according to the cost estimates at the end of 2009, which results in more total gross profit than was predicted at the end of 2009.

TIP! Notice that **neither** the amount of billings **nor** the amount of cash collections during the year has an impact on the amount of gross profit to be recognized.

TIP! Notice that a loss was recognized in the second year using the percentage-of-completion method but no loss was recognized using the completed-contract method. The reasons for this are that the loss was an interim loss, not an overall loss on the contract. An interim loss refers to the loss that results when the total gross profit to date (at the end of 2009) is less than the amount of gross profit recognized in prior periods (2008). It is a loss in the current period (2009) on a profitable contract. It results from an increase in estimated costs which requires a current period adjustment of excess gross profit recognized on the contract in prior periods. This adjustment is recorded in the current period because it is a change in accounting estimate. If an overall loss is expected on a contract, it must also be recognized immediately even under the completed-contract method.

(c)

Current assets:		
Accounts receivable		$4,680,000
Inventories		
Construction in process	$21,320,000	
Less: Billings on construction in process	19,800,000	
Costs and recognized profit in excess of billings		$1,520,000

EXPLANATION: Draw T-accounts. Mentally think through the journal entries that would be recorded for the facts given. Post these amounts to the T-accounts on paper.

Accounts Receivable

Debit	Credit
2008 3,900,000	2008 3,120,000
2009 15,900,000	2009 12,000,000
12/31/09 Bal. 4,680,000	

Construction in Process

Debit	Credit
2008 8,320,000	2009 440,000
2008 2,080,000	
2009 11,360,000	
12/31/09 Bal. 21,320,000	

Billings on Construction in Process

Debit	Credit
	2008 3,900,000
	2009 15,900,000
	12/31/09 Bal. 19,800,000

TIP! Notice that the amounts reflected in the balance sheet for accounts receivable ($4,680,000) and inventories ($1,520,000) when combined with the increase in cash from collections of billings ($15,120,000 collections to date) equals $21,320,000 (the balance in the Construction in Process account), which also equals the percentage of the total contract revenue earned to date ($19,680,000/ $24,000,000 x $26,000,000 = $21,320,000). The balance of the Billings on Construction in Process account is deducted from the balance in the Construction in Process account so as not to double count assets related to accounting for construction contracts. The total amount billed thus far ($19,800,000) is either collected ($15,120,000 has been collected so the Cash account has increased which is not shown here) or uncollected ($4,680,000 balance in Accounts Receivable).

Exercise 6-2

PURPOSE: This exercise will illustrate the calculations, journal entries, and balance sheet presentations involved in the use of the completed-contract and percentage-of-completion methods of accounting for long-term construction contracts.

The Nifty Construction Company entered into a long-term contract in 2008. The contract price was $1,600,000, and the company initially estimated the total costs of the project to be $1,150,000. The following data pertains to the three years that the contract was in process:

Year	Costs Incurred During the Year	Estimated Costs at End of the Year to Complete Contract	Billings During the Year	Collections During the Year	Operating Expenses
2008	$224,000	$896,000	$ 200,000	$170,000	$80,000
2009	712,000	264,000	1,000,000	900,000	82,000
2010	344,000	-0-	400,000	430,000	74,000

Instructions

(a) Calculate the gross profit to be reported in each of the three years using the completed-contract method.

(b) Calculate the gross profit to be reported in each of the three years using the percentage-of completion method based on the costs incurred to date and the estimated costs to complete the contract. (Also calculate the amount of revenue and cost of sales reflected in each gross profit figure.)

(c) Prepare the related journal entries for all three years using the completed-contract method.

(d) Prepare the related journal entries for all three years using the percentage-of-completion method.

(e) Prepare a partial balance sheet at the end of each of the three years assuming (1) the completed-contract method is used and (2) the percentage-of-completion method is used.

> The use of T-accounts is helpful here to determine the balances of accounts at the balance sheet date.

TIP!

Solution to Exercise 6-2

(a) 2008 -0-
2009 -0-
2010 $1,600,000 – ($224,000 + $712,000 + $344,000) = $320,000

(b) **2008** Estimate of total costs = $224,000 + $896,000 = $1,120,000
Estimate of total gross profit = $1,600,000 – $1,120,000 = $480,000
Gross profit to be recognized in 2008 =

$$\frac{\$224{,}000}{\$1{,}120{,}000} \times \$480{,}000 = \underline{\underline{\$96{,}000}}$$

2009 Costs incurred to date = $224,000 + $712,000 = $936,000
Estimate of total costs = $936,000 + $264,000 = $1,200,000
Estimate of total gross profit = $1,600,000 – $1,200,000 = $400,000
Gross profit to be recognized in 2009 =

$$\left(\frac{\$936{,}000}{\$1{,}200{,}000} \times \$400{,}000\right) - \$96{,}000 = \underline{\underline{\$216{,}000}}$$

2010 Total costs incurred for project = $224,000 + $712,000 + $344,000 = $1,280,000
Contract price of $1,600,000 minus total costs incurred of $1,280,000 equals total gross profit on project of $320,000
Gross profit to be recognized in 2007 = $320,000 – ($96,000 + $216,000) = $8,000

2008 Revenue for 2008 = $\frac{\$224{,}000}{\$1{,}120{,}000} \times \$1{,}600{,}000 = \underline{\underline{\$320{,}000}}$

Costs to match with revenue for 2008 = $224,000

Gross profit for 2008 = $320,000 – $224,000 = $96,000

2009 Revenue for 2009 = $\left(\frac{\$936{,}000}{\$1{,}200{,}000} \times \$1{,}600{,}000\right) - \$320{,}000 = \underline{\underline{\$928{,}000}}$

Costs to match with revenue for 2009 = $712,000

Gross profit for 2009 = $928,000 – $712,000 = $216,000

2010 Revenue for 2010 = \$1,600,000 – (\$320,000 + \$928,000) = \$352,000
Costs to match with revenue for 2007 = \$344,000
Gross profit for 2010 = \$352,000 – \$344,000 = \$8,000

(c) **Journal Entries—Completed-Contract Method**

	2008		2009		2010	
Accounts	**Dr.**	**Cr.**	**Dr.**	**Cr.**	**Dr.**	**Cr.**
Const. in Process	224,000		712,000		344,000	
Operating Expenses	80,000		82,000		74,000	
Materials, Cash,						
Payables, Etc.		304,000		794,000		418,000
Accounts Receivable	200,000		1,000,000		400,000	
Billings on Const.						
in Process		200,000		1,000,000		400,000
Cash	170,000		900,000		430,000	
Accounts Rec.		170,000		900,000		430,000
Billings on Const. in						
Process						
Revenue from					1,600,000	
Long-term						
Contracts						1,600,000
Construction Exp.					1,280,000	1,280,000
Const. in Process						

(d) **Journal Entries—Percentage-of-Completion Method**

	2008		2009		2010	
Accounts	**Dr.**	**Cr.**	**Dr.**	**Cr.**	**Dr.**	**Cr.**
Const. in Process	224,000		712,000		344,000	
Operating Expenses	80,000		82,000		74,000	
Materials, Cash,						
Payables, Etc.		304,000		794,000		418,000
Accounts Receivable	200,000		1,000,000		400,000	
Billings on Const.						
in Process		200,000		1,000,000		400,000
Cash	170,000		900,000		430,000	
Accounts Rec.		170,000		900,000		430,000
Const. Expenses	224,000		712,000		344,000	
Const. in Process	96,000		216,000		8,000	
Revenue from						
Long-term						
Contracts		320,000		928,000		352,000
Billings on Const. in					1,600,000	
Process						
Const. in Process						1,600,000

(e) 1. **Partial Balance Sheet—Completed-Contract Method**

	End of 2008		End of 2009		End of 2010
Current assets:					
Accounts receivable		$30,000		$130,000	$100,000
Inventories					
Construction in process	$224,000				
Less: Billings on const. in process	200,000				
Unbilled contract costs		24,000			
Current liabilities:					
Billings on const. in process			$1,200,000		
Less: Construction in process			936,000		
Billings in excess of costs and recognized profit				$264,000	

APPROACH: Draw T-accounts and post journal entries to determine account balances.

2. **Partial Balance Sheet—Percentage-of-Completion Method**

	End of 2008		End of 2009		End of 2010
Current assets:					
Accounts receivable		$30,000		$130,000	$100,000
Inventories					
Construction in process	$320,000		$1,248,000		
Less: Billings on const. in process	200,000		1,200,000		
Costs and recognized profit in excess of billings		$120,000		$48,000	

APPROACH: Draw T-accounts and post journal entries to determine account balances.

Exercise 6-3

PURPOSE: This exercise will (1) illustrate the calculations involved with the instalment method of accounting, (2) examine the classification of the Deferred Gross Profit account, and (3) apply the cost recovery method.

Arnie Sagar Company has **appropriately** used the instalment method of accounting since it began business in 2007. The following data were obtained for the years 2007 and 2008:

	2007	2008
Instalment sales	$800,000	$900,000
Cost of instalment sales	592,000	684,000
Cash collections on sales of 2007	280,000	320,000
Cash collections on sales of 2008	-0-	400,000

Instructions

(a) Calculate the amount of realized gross profit to report for (1) 2007 and (2) 2008.

(b) Calculate the balance in the deferred gross profit accounts on (1) December 31, 2007, and December 31, 2008.

(c) Explain the classification of the total deferred gross profit on the balance sheet at December 31, 2008.

(d) Prepare the journal entry to record the repossession of merchandise because of a defaulting customer. Assume that at the date of default in 2008, the balance on the related instalment receivable (which originated in 2007) was $14,000 and the fair value of the merchandise was $8,500.

(e) Assume the cost recovery method is used rather than the instalment method. Calculate the amount of realized gross profit that would be recognized (1) on the 2007 income statement, and (2) on the 2008 income statement.

Solution to Exercise 6-3

(a) (1) Gross Profit Ratio—2007:

Instalment sales for 2007	$ 800,000
Cost of instalment sales for 2007	(592,000)
Gross Profit on instalment sales for 2007	$ 208,000

$$\frac{\$208{,}000 \text{ Gross Profit}}{\$800{,}000 \text{ Sales}} = \underline{\underline{26\%}} \text{ Gross Profit ratio on 2007 sales}$$

Cash collections in 2007 on sales of 2007	$ 280,000
Gross Profit ratio for 2007 sales	26%
Gross Profit realized in 2007 on 2007 sales	$ 72,800

(2) Gross Profit Ratio—2008:

Instalment sales for 2008	$ 900,000
Cost of instalment sales for 2008	(684,000)
Gross Profit on instalment sales for 2008	$ 216,000

$$\frac{\$216{,}000 \text{ Gross Profit}}{\$900{,}000 \text{ Sales}} = \underline{\underline{24\%}} \text{ Gross Profit ratio on 2008 sales}$$

Cash collections in 2008 on sales of 2008	$ 400,000
Gross Profit ratio for 2008 sales	24%
Gross Profit realized in 2008 on 2008 sales	$ 96,000

Cash collections in 2008 on sales of 2007	$ 320,000
Gross Profit ratio for 2007 sales	26%
Gross Profit realized in 2008 on 2007 sales	$ 83,200

Gross Profit realized in 2008 on 2008 sales	$ 96,000
Gross Profit realized in 2008 on 2007 sales	83,200
Total gross Profit realized in 2008	$ 179,200

TIP! Always calculate a separate gross profit ratio for each year in which there are instalment sales. Clearly label each ratio so it is ready for use in subsequent calculations. For any given year, the cash collections during the year on Year 1 instalment sales multiplied by the gross profit ratio on Year 1 instalment sales will yield the gross profit realized during that given year on Year 1 instalment sales. The balance of Instalment Accounts Receivable, Year 1, at a balance sheet date, multiplied by the gross profit ratio for Year 1 instalment sales will yield the appropriate adjusted balance for the related Deferred Gross Profit, Year 1 account at the same date.

(b) (1)

Deferred Gross Profit, 2007

2007	72,800[b]	2007	208,000[a]
		12/31/07 Bal.	135,200

(2)

Deferred Gross Profit, 2007

2007	83,200[c]	12/31/07 Bal.	135,200
		12/31/08 Bal.	52,000

Deferred Gross Profit, 2008

2008	96,000[e]	2008	216,000[d]
		12/31/08 Bal.	120,000

[a] Gross profit on 2007 instalment sales = $800,000 – $592,000 = $208,000.
[b] Gross profit realized in 2007 on 2007 sales = $280,000 collections x 26% = $72,800.
[c] Gross profit realized in 2008 on 2007 sales = $320,000 collections x 26% = $83,200.
[d] Gross profit on 2008 instalment sales = $900,000 – $684,000 = $216,000.
[e] Gross profit realized in 2008 on 2008 sales = $400,000 collections x 24% = $96,000.

TIP! The $52,000 balance in the Deferred Gross Profit, 2007 account at December 31, 2008, can be independently verified by multiplying the balance of Instalment Accounts Receivable, 2007 at December 31, 2008 [$800,000 - ($280,000 + $320,000) = $200,000] by the gross profit ratio for 2007 instalment sales (26%).

(c) Per the answers to part (b) (2) above, the total deferred gross profit at December 31, 2008, amounts to $172,000 [$52,000 + $120,000 = $172,000].

(d) **APPROACH:**

Do Second	Deferred Gross Profit (26% x $14,000)	3,640	
Do Third	Repossessed Merchandise	8,500	
Plug	Loss on Repossession	1,860	
Do First	Instalment Accounts Receivable		14,000

EXPLANATION: The amount of the loss is determined by (1) subtracting the deferred gross profit from the amount of the account receivable to determine the unrecovered cost (or book value) of the merchandise repossessed ($14,000 – $3,640 = $10,360), and (2) subtracting the estimated fair value of the merchandise repossessed from the unrecovered cost to get the amount of the loss on repossession ($10,360 – $8,500 = $1,860). As an alternative, the loss on repossession can be charged to the Allowance for Doubtful Accounts account.

(e) (1) Using the cost recovery method, no gross profit would be recognized on the 2007 income statement because the $280,000 cash collections did not exceed the $592,000 cost of the merchandise sold.

(2) Using the cost recovery method of revenue recognition, gross profit of $8,000 would be reported in 2008 due to instalment sales made in 2007. No gross profit would be recognized on 2008 sales because cash collections did not exceed the cost of the merchandise sold.

CALCULATIONS:

Cumulative cash collections on 2007 sales	$ 600,000*
Cost of 2007 instalment sales	(592,000)
Gross profit to be recognized in 2008 using cost recovery method	$ 8,000

*$280,000 + $320,000 = $600,000

EXPLANATION: The cost recovery method provides for gross profit to be recognized only after all costs of related sales have been recovered. All subsequent cash collections are recognized as profit.

Exercise 6-4

PURPOSE: This exercise will examine the treatment for an initial franchise fee under three scenarios.

Ma's Best Cookies Inc. charges an initial franchise fee of $110,000. Upon the signing of the agreement, a payment of $50,000 is due; thereafter, three annual payments of $20,000 are required. The credit rating of the franchisee is such that it would have to pay interest at 10% to borrow money.

Instructions

Prepare the entries to record the initial franchise fee on the books of the franchisor under the following assumptions:

(a) The down payment is not refundable, no future services are required by the franchisor, and collection of the note is reasonably assured.

(b) The franchisor has substantial services to perform, and the collection of the note is very uncertain.

(c) The down payment is not refundable, collection of the note is reasonably certain, the franchisor has yet to perform a substantial amount of services, and the down payment represents a fair measure of the services already performed.

Solution to Exercise 6-4

(a) Cash	50,000	
Notes Receivable	60,000	
Discount on Notes Receivable [\$60,000 – (\$20,000 x 2.48685*)]		10,263
Revenue from Franchise Fees (\$50,000 + \$60,000 – \$10,263)		99,737
(b) Cash	50,000	
Unearned Franchise Fees		50,000
(c) Cash	50,000	
Notes Receivable	60,000	
Discount on Notes Receivable		10,263
Revenue from Franchise Fees		50,000
Unearned Franchise Fees (\$20,000 x 2.48685*)		49,737

*The factor for the present value of an ordinary annuity of 1 for $n = 3$, $i = 10\%$ is 2.48685.

TIP!

The amount of revenue recognized and the carrying value of the note receivable recorded by the franchisor upon the receipt of the franchise agreement and the initial franchise fee depend upon several factors, including: (1) whether or not the fee may be refundable, (2) an estimate of the collectibility of the note, (3) a measure of the future services to be performed by the franchisor, and (4) the incremental borrowing rate of the franchisee.

Exercise 6-5

PURPOSE: This exercise will review calculations involved with consignment sales.

On April 15, 2008, Stayfit Company consigned 70 treadmills, costing $600 each, to Higley Company. The cost of shipping the treadmills amounts to $800 and was paid by Stayfit Company. On December 30, 2008, an account sales was received from the consignee, reporting that 35 treadmills had been sold for $700 each. Remittance was made by the consignee for the amount due, after deducting a commission of 6%, advertising of $200, and total delivery costs of $300 on the treadmills sold.

Instructions

(a) Calculate the inventory value of the units unsold in the hands of the consignee.
(b) Calculate the profit for the consignor for the units sold.
(c) Calculate the amount of cash that will be remitted by the consignee.

Solution to Exercise 6-5

(a) Inventoriable Costs:

70 units shipped at cost of $600 each		$ 42,000
Freight to consignee		800
Total inventoriable cost		$ 42,800
35 units on hand (1/2 x $42,800)		$ 21,400

(b) Calculation of Consignment Profit:

Consignment sales (35 x $700)		$ 24,500
Cost of units sold (1/2 x $42,800)		(21,400)
Commission charged by consignee (6% x $24,500)		(1,470)
Advertising costs		(200)
Delivery costs to customers		(300)
Profit on consignment sales		$ 1,130

(c) Remittance of Consignee:

Consignment sales		$ 24,500
Less: Commissions	$ 1,470	
Advertising	200	
Delivery	300	1,970
Remittance from consignee		$ 22,530

Analysis of Multiple-Choice Questions

Question

1. The process of formally including an item in the financial statements of an entity is:
   a. presentation.
   b. measurement.
   c. realization.
   d. recognition.

EXPLANATION: Write down a brief definition of each term listed. Select the one that matches the description in the question. **Presentation** is the process of determining where an item will be presented on the financial statements. **Measurement** refers to the amount recorded for the item in the financial statements. **Realization** means the process of converting non-cash resources and rights into money (such as the sale of assets for cash or claims to cash). **Recognition** is defined in *CICA Handbook*, Section 1000 as the process of including an item in the financial statements of an entity. (Solution = d.)

Question

2. Dot Point, Inc. is a retailer of washers and dryers and offers a three-year service contract on each appliance sold. Although Dot Point sells the appliances on an instalment basis, all service contracts are cash sales at the time of purchase by the buyer. Collections received for service contracts should be recorded as:
   a. service revenue.
   b. unearned service revenue.
   c. a reduction in instalment accounts receivable.
   d. a direct addition to retained earnings.

EXPLANATION: Recall the fundamentals of revenue recognition and think about how it would apply to this situation. Revenue is to be recognized when performance is substantially complete and when collection is reasonably assured. The service contract revenue is realized at the date the cash is received; however, it is earned over the three-year period to which the contract pertains. Therefore, at the point of collection, the cash should be recorded by a credit to an Unearned (Deferred) Service Revenue account. The revenue will be earned over the three-year period as the company performs the services it promises by the contract. (Solution = b.)

Question

3. On December 31, 2008, Mahoney sold a piece of equipment to C. Bailey for $30,000 with the following terms: 2% cash discount if paid within 30 days, 1% discount if paid between 31 and 60 days of purchase, or payable in full within 90 days if not paid within a discount period. Bailey had the right to return this equipment to Mahoney if Bailey could not resell it before the end of the 90 day payment period, in which case Bailey would no longer be obligated to Mahoney. How much should be included in Mahoney's net sales for 2008 because of the sale of this machine?
   a. $30,000
   b. $29,700
   c. $29,400
   d. $0

EXPLANATION: Per the terms of the sale/purchase, Bailey has the right to return the equipment to the seller if Bailey is not able to resell the equipment before expiration of the 90-day payment period. If the right to return the product exists, there are three alternatives available: (1) not recording the sale until all return privileges have expired; (2) recording the sale, but reducing the sales by an estimate of future returns; and (3) recording the sale and accounting for the returns as they occur. Since this situation involves a specific return provision (vs. a general right of return) EIC 141 would not allow any revenue to be recognized until the uncertainty had been removed. (Solution = d.)

Question

4. Bella Construction Co. uses the percentage-of-completion method. In 2008, Bella began work on a contract for $2,200,000; it was completed in 2009. The following cost data pertain to this contract:

	Year Ended December 31	
	2008	2009
Costs incurred during the year	$780,000	$560,000
Estimated costs to complete at end of year	520,000	—

   The amount of gross profit to be recognized on the income statement for the year ended December 31, 2008 is:
   a. $0.
   b. $516,000.
   c. $540,000.
   d. $900,000.

EXPLANATION: Write down the formula used to calculate the gross profit recognized to date at the end of 2008. Use the data given to calculate the gross profit.

$$\left[\frac{\text{Costs incurred to date}}{\text{Estimate of total Costs}} \times \text{Estimated total gross profit}\right] - \text{Total gross profit recognized in prior periods} = \text{Current period gross profit}$$

$$\left[\frac{\$780{,}000}{\$520{,}000 + \$780{,}000} \times [\$2{,}200{,}000 - (\$780{,}000 + \$520{,}000)]\right] - \$0 =$$

$$\left[\frac{\$780{,}000}{\$1{,}300{,}000} \times (\$2{,}200{,}000 - \$1{,}300{,}000)\right] - \$0 =$$

$$[.60 \times \$900{,}000] - \$0 = \underline{\underline{\$540{,}000}} \qquad \text{(Solution = c.)}$$

Question

5. Refer to the facts for Question 4 above. The amount of gross profit to be recognized on the income statement for the year ended December 31, 2009 is:
   a. $860,000.
   b. $360,000.
   c. $344,000.
   d. $320,000.

EXPLANATION: Use the formula shown for Question 4 and plug in the data for 2009.

$$\left[\frac{\$780{,}000 + \$560{,}000}{\$780{,}000 + \$560{,}000 + \$0} \times [\$2{,}200{,}000 - (\$780{,}000 + \$560{,}000)]\right] - \$540{,}000 =$$

$$\left[\frac{\$1{,}340{,}000}{\$1{,}340{,}000} \times (\$2{,}200{,}000 - \$1{,}340{,}000)\right] - \$540{,}000 =$$

$$\$860{,}000 - \$540{,}000 = \underline{\underline{\$320{,}000}} \qquad \text{(Solution = d.)}$$

Question

6. Refer to the data for Question 4 above. If the completed-contract method of accounting were used, the amount of gross profit to be reported for years 2008 and 2009 would be:

	2008	**2009**
a.	$0	$ 860,000
b.	$0	$ 900,000
c.	$900,000	$(40,000)
d.	$860,000	$ 0

EXPLANATION: The completed-contract method calls for deferral of all revenue and costs related to a contract (project) until the period of completion. Thus, the entire gross profit ($2,200,000 total revenue – $1,340,000 total costs = $860,000 total gross profit) is recognized in the period the contract is completed. (Solution = a.)

Question

7. Designer Homes Construction Company uses the percentage-of-completion method. The costs incurred to date as a proportion of the estimated total costs to be incurred on a project are used as a measure of the extent of progress made toward completion of the project. During 2008, the company entered into a fixed-price contract to construct a mansion for Donald Trumper for $24,000,000. The following details pertain to that contract:

	At Dec. 31, 2008	At Dec. 31, 2009
Percentage of completion	25%	60%
Estimated total costs of contract	$18,000,000	$20,000,000
Gross profit recognized to date	1,500,000	2,400,000

The amount of construction costs incurred during 2009 was:
a. $2,000,000.
b. $4,500,000.
c. $7,500,000.
d. $12,000,000.

EXPLANATION: Write down the formula used to calculate the gross profit recognized to date at the end of 2009. Look at the components of the fraction.

$$\frac{\text{Costs incurred to date}}{\text{Estimate of total costs}} \times \text{Estimated total gross profit} = \text{Total gross profit earned to date}$$

According to the facts given, the fraction at December 31, 2009 is equal to 60%. Therefore, the costs incurred by the end of 2009 = 60% x $20,000,000 = $12,000,000. According to the facts given, the fraction for the same formula at the end of 2008 is equal to 25%. Therefore, the costs incurred by the end of 2008 = 25% x $18,000,000 = $4,500,000. The difference between the cumulative costs at the end of 2009 ($12,000,000) and the cumulative costs at the end of 2008 ($4,500,000) equals the costs incurred during 2009 of $7,500,000. (Solution = c.)

Question

8. A manufacturer of large equipment sells on an instalment basis to customers with questionable credit ratings. Which of the following methods of revenue recognition is least likely to overstate the amount of gross profit reported?
a. at the time of completion of the equipment (completion of production method)
b. at the date of delivery (sale method)
c. the instalment sales method
d. the cost recovery method

EXPLANATION: Recognition of income at the time the equipment is completed would be the method most likely to overstate gross profit. The recognition of gross profit at the time the equipment is completed or at the date the equipment is delivered would provide for the recognition of profits before any or much of the cash has been received; thus, these methods are not appropriate for situations where there is doubt about the collectibility of the selling price. The use of the instalment sales method would allow for the recognition of profits in proportion to the amount of the revenue collected in cash. The cost recovery method defers the recognition of all gross profit until cash collections of revenue are equal to the cost of the item sold; all remaining cash collections are reported as profit. Therefore, the cost recovery method is least likely to overstate the amount of gross profit reported. (Solution = d.)

Question

9. Eazy-Pay Sales Company has appropriately used the instalment method of accounting since it began operations at the beginning of 2008. The following information pertains to its operations for 2008:

Instalment sales	$ 600,000
Cost of instalment sales	420,000
Collections on instalment sales	240,000
General and administrative expenses	60,000

The amount to be reported on the December 31, 2008 balance sheet as Deferred Gross Profit should be:

a. $360,000.
b. $144,000.
c. $108,000.
d. $72,000.

EXPLANATION: The $360,000 balance of Instalment Accounts Receivable, 2008 ($600,000 – $240,000 = $360,000) is multiplied by the 2008 gross profit ratio of 30% ($600,000 – $420,000 = $180,000; $180,000 ÷ $600,000 = 30%) to arrive at deferred gross profit of $108,000 ($360,000 x 30% = $108,000) at the balance sheet date. (Solution = c.)

General and administrative expenses have no effect on the calculations of realized gross profit or deferred gross profit. They are to be classified as operating expenses on the income statement of the period in which they are incurred.

TIP!

Question

10. Kayla Inc. appropriately uses the instalment method of accounting to recognize income in its financial statements. Some pertinent data relating to this method of accounting include:

	2008	2009
Instalment sales	$ 300,000	$ 360,000
Cost of sales	180,000	252,000
Gross profit	$120,000	$108,000
Collections during year:		
On 2008 sales	100,000	100,000
On 2009 sales		120,000

What amount of realized gross profit should be reported on Kayla's income statement for 2009?

a. $108,000
b. $88,000
c. $76,000
d. $66,000
e. None of the above

EXPLANATION: (1) Calculate the gross profit percentages for 2008 and 2009. (2) Apply the appropriate gross profit percentage to the amount of collections of instalment receivables during 2009.

CALCULATIONS:

(1) $120,000 / $300,000 = 40% gross profit percentage for 2008 instalment sales
$108,000 / $360,000 = 30% gross profit percentage for 2009 instalment sales

(2)

Collections in 2009 on 2008 instalment sales	$ 100,000
Gross profit percentage for 2008 instalment sales	40%
Gross profit realized in 2009 on 2008 instalment sales	$ 40,000
Collections in 2009 on 2009 instalment sales	$ 120,000
Gross profit percentage for 2009 instalments sales	30%
Gross profit realized in 2009 on 2009 instalment sales	$ 36,000
Gross profit realized in 2009 on 2008 instalment sales	$ 40,000
Gross profit realized in 2009 on 2009 instalment sales	36,000
Total gross profit realized in 2009	$ 76,000

(Solution = c.)

Question

11. Marvel Mart sells large-screen televisions on an instalment basis and appropriately uses the instalment sales method of accounting. A customer with an account balance of $4,000 refuses to make any more payments and the merchandise is repossessed. The gross profit rate on the original sale is 40%. Marvel estimates that the television can be sold as is for $1,250, or for $1,500 if 100 is spent to refurbish the cabinet. The loss on repossession is:

a. $1,000.
b. $1,150.

c. $1,600.
d. $2,750.

EXPLANATION: Prepare the journal entry to record the repossession; it is as follows:

Deferred Gross Profit ($4,000 x 40%)	1,600	
Repossessed Merchandise ($1,500 – $100)	1,400	
Loss on Repossession [($4,000 – $1,600) – ($1,500 – $100)]	1,000	
Instalment Accounts Receivable		4,000

The book value of the receivable is removed from the accounts ($4,000 – $1,600), the repossessed merchandise is recorded at its fair value (or net realizable value of $1,400 in this case), and a loss ($1,000) is recorded for the excess of the receivable's book value ($4,000 – $1,600 = $2,400) over its net realizable value ($1,400) (a measure of fair value). (Solution = a.)

Question

12. Revenue is generally recognized when:
    a. performance is complete and the money is collected.
    b. performance is substantially complete and collection is reasonably assured.
    c. performance is complete and collection is reasonably assured.
    d. performance is substantially complete and the money is collected.

EXPLANATION: Recognizing revenue when cash is collected is not accrual accounting. It is used only when there is great uncertainty as to whether it will be collected at all. GAAP, therefore, requires substantial completion and reasonable assurance of collecting the cash. (Solution = b.)

Question

13. For consignment sales, the critical event is:
    a. shipment of goods to the consignee, i.e., when the goods leave the consignor's loading dock.
    b. sale of goods to a third party other than the consignee.
    c. when the goods are received by the consignee.
    d. when the goods are received by the consignor.

EXPLANATION: Because the risks and rewards of ownership do not pass until a third party buys the goods, the earnings process is not complete until then. Prior to that, the consignor still has legal title and is exposed to the risks of ownership. (Solution = b.)

TIP!

> Be careful in applying a "default" point of recognition of revenue (e.g., the shipping point). It may that the goods have been "shipped" on a consignment basis only and, therefore, is not yet a valid sale.

Question

14. Chang Corp. recently mounted a new campaign whereby their salespeople aggressively marketed the company's products. As part of the campaign, the company offered the products for sale at deep discounts and allowed unlimited returns. The transactions were recognized as revenues and as of year-end there was a significant increase in sales.
    a. The revenue recognition policy is acceptable since the legal title and possession to the goods has passed.
    b. Revenue should not be recognized, as these goods will likely be returned.
    c. Revenue may be recognized as long as a significantly increased allowance for returns is accrued at the same time.
    d. Revenues may be recognized and no allowance is needed.

EXPLANATION: The issue here is one of measurement. Specifically, revenue cannot be measured accurately since there is a generous return policy. Another way to express this is that the risk of ownership has not been passed, due to the return policy. However, although this is aggressive, as long as an accrual is measurable and booked for the returns, recognition would be acceptable. (Solution = c.)

TIP!

> Since revenue recognition criteria as provided in the *CICA Handbook* are necessarily general, there is often a motivation to stretch the interpretation of those criteria in order to meet an objective. There have been many cases in where companies (especially public companies) have aggressively interpreted the *Handbook* to meet an objective. It is important to remember that the preparation of financial statements should not be done with any particular bias or objective in mind—but rather that economic reality be properly reflected. The presence of a particular bias or objective should not be a factor in the accounting decision.

Case Study

Investico Limited

Investico Limited (IL) is a small real estate development company that was started up by two investors. Adam Adams, one of the investors, runs the company and makes the key decisions, whereas Brent Boudreau, the other investor, put up half of the initial capital required, and is basically a silent partner. The main objective of the company, initially agreed upon by the two men, was to invest in low-risk real estate properties and sell them for profit once the real estate appreciated to a certain point.

The first project that IL invested in was some vacation property. Adam found the property, and made the decision to buy it without consulting Brent. Adam planned to subdivide and service the resulting lots and to sell them as vacation properties. Even though the purchase did not quite fit in with IL's objectives, Adam figured that he could sell the lots at a better-than-average profit before Brent could have a chance to object.

Adam subdivided the lots and was able to sell all of them on the following terms:

- $2,500 downpayment (5% of the sale price).
- IL would take back a note receivable from the purchaser under an agreement of sale. The note is interest free and title to the land remains with IL until the note is fully repaid (five-year term).
- The purchaser would take immediate possession.
- IL would service the lot with electricity within a year of the purchase date.

Most of the lots were sold at the beginning of 2008; however, by the end of 2008, about 30% of the purchasers were behind in their loan payments. Adam was not anxious to repossess the properties and had worked out a deal with the owners that they would allow him to cut down the wood on the properties for resale. The owners felt that the resale value on the wood would more than cover the overdue payments.

Meanwhile, Brent found out about the property and that it had all been sold and was considering taking some of his investment out of the company. He wished to see the financial statements for the year ended December 31, 2008. Adam has hired you, a chartered accountant, to advise him as to how he should prepare the financial statements. He is considering selling the notes receivable connected with the sales of property in order to have some cash on hand, should Brent want his money back.

Required

Assume the role of the chartered accountant and prepare a memo to Adam analyzing the accounting and reporting issues. Your memo should consider users and constraints and provide recommendations.

Suggested Approach to Case Study

Memo: Re Investico
To: Adam
From: CA

(Overview: It is very important to set a framework for your analysis. GAAP does not occur in a "vacuum". It is affected directly by the motivations of the preparers and the needs of the users. This is especially true when GAAP provides only guidance, as opposed to strict rules.)

Brent is a key user and needs information to determine (1) whether to divest himself of the interest in the company, (2) whether Adam is looking after the company (stewardship function); and (3) to assess risk since the objective of the company is to invest in low-risk properties. Therefore, he needs realistic financial statements that focus on the real value of the asset.

The potential purchasers of the notes receivable need conservative financial statements to determine whether to purchase the notes.

GAAP will be a constraint in providing reliable statements to the users. Even though the users may want financial statements that are conservative and realistic, Adam will want to portray the company and himself in the most favourable light to show Brent that he is looking after Brent's best interests and to induce someone to purchase the notes. Adam will want to downplay risk due to the intended nature of the company.

Analysis and Recommendations

The issues are as follows: (Where possible, issues should be ranked in order of importance. A more important issue would be one that will have a major impact on users. There will likely be a choice under GAAP as well.)

1. When to recognize revenues.
2. How to value the notes receivable given the collectibility problem.
3. How to value the wood.

Revenue recognition

Revenue could be recognized when the contract is signed (customer found upfront) or when possession occurs, since it could be argued that the risks and rewards of ownership have passed (i.e., possession has passed and consideration has been received indicating a reasonable amount of certainty that the deal will go through as planned). At this point, there has been an exchange with an outside party. Also, the sales price is measurable, since fixed by agreement.

However, legal title has not yet passed and it could be argued that the earnings process is not substantially complete as the lots have not yet been serviced (it may also be difficult to estimate costs). Collectibility is also a problem as evidenced by the tardy payments.

This position is aggressive and would support Adam's financial reporting objective, but there is uncertainty with respect to measuring the profit on the sale and collectibility.

Another alternative would be to wait until the end of the earnings process. At this point, legal title would have passed and there is no question as to collectibility. All revenues and costs are measurable at this point.

This position is very conservative, however, and does not meet Adam's needs.

Recommendation

(May attempt to reflect the objectives of the major user, provided that it is in accordance with GAAP. However—never contravene GAAP to meet an objective.)

Even though Adam wants aggressive financial statements, revenue should probably not be recognized until the lots are at least serviced. At this point, the uncertainty will be cleared up regarding costs and IL will have a better idea of collectibility. This might be considered aggressive since legal title has not yet passed; however, the intent is that the payments will be made and that the title will pass and, therefore, the substance is that a sale has been made. (Other arguments are possible—it is important to integrate the economics of the transaction into the accounting analysis—i.e., accounting should reflect the economic reality of the situation).

Asset Valuation (Note receivable)
GAAP requires that a provision for bad debts be estimated if there are collections problems. However, in this case, payments are still being made—although in a "non-monetary" fashion.

One alternative is to set up a provision as required under GAAP. This would provide a more realistic value for the potential purchasers of the notes. As a chartered accountant, knowing that potential purchasers will rely on the value in the financial statements, you will want to ensure that they are properly valued in order to reflect accurately the economic reality of the situation. Even though the payments are being made (in kind) at the present, there is uncertainty as to whether the note holders will be able to make future payments if they are in trouble now. Another alternative is to make no provision since payments in kind are just as good as monetary payments since they have value. Also, the payments are up to date.

Recommendation
It is best that a provision be set up due to the high exposure to legal action if the potential purchasers rely on the value and subsequently suffer a loss.

Value of the Wood
(A relatively minor issue on its own—it should be considered with the issue above.)

This issue is tied in with the one above. How should the value of the wood be determined? It must be valued to assess whether the wood covers the overdue payments. The value must be net of any additional costs to sell the wood. This would directly affect the amount, if any, of any provision for the note receivable.

Cash and Receivables

Chapter 7

Overview

In previous chapters, you learned the basic formats for general purpose financial statements. In this chapter you begin your in-depth study of accounting for items appearing on the balance sheet: (1) what is to be included in an item classification, (2) related internal control procedures, (3) rules for determining the dollar amount to be reported, (4) disclosure requirements, and (5) special accounting procedures which may be required. In this chapter, you will learn what is to be included under the cash caption on the balance sheet and the definition of financial assets. Also key internal controls which should be employed for business activities involving cash. Finally, the methods of accounting for accounts receivable and notes receivable are discussed.

Many businesses grant credit to customers. They know that, when making sales "on account," a risk exists because some accounts will never be collected. However, the cost of these bad debts is more than offset by the profit from the extra sales made due to the attraction of granting credit. The collections department may make many attempts to collect an account before "writing off" a bad debtor. Frequently, an account is deemed to be uncollectible a year or more after the date of the credit sale. In this chapter, we will discuss the allowance method of accounting for bad debts. The allowance method permits the accountant to estimate the amount of bad debt expense that should be matched with current revenues rather than waiting to book expense at the time of an actual write-off.

Study Steps

Understanding the Definition of Financial Assets

Financial assets are defined by *CICA Handbook* Section 3855 as any asset that is:

- Cash;
- A contractual right to receive cash or another financial asset from another party;
- A contractual right to exchange financial instruments with another party under conditions that are potentially favourable to the entity; or
- An equity instrument of another entity.

Financial assets are covered in various chapters of the textbook. This chapter covers cash, cash equivalents, accounts, notes and loans receivable. Chapter 9 covers other major categories of financial assets—mainly investments in debt and equity securities of other companies.

Cash and liquid assets are crucial to any business since a company needs to keep a certain amount of liquid assets in order to pay off operating expenses and short-term payables. Users of financial statements, therefore, often focus on liquid assets and short-term liabilities to assess the liquidity of a company.

Understanding the basics of receivables

Receivables are claims held against customers and others for money, goods, or services. When receivables represent contractual rights to receive cash or other financial assets from another party, they are termed financial assets. Receivables are classified as either current or non-current, depending on expected collection dates. They are further classified in the balance sheet as either trade or nontrade receivables.

Understanding the transfer of receivables to generate cash

Sometimes a company will experience a cash shortage because it has a significant amount of working capital tied up in accounts receivable; therefore, some companies will use receivables to generate cash. One way of doing this is to pledge or assign the receivables to a lender. Another method of using receivables to generate cash is to sell or dispose of them. This is sometimes called factoring, discounting, or securitization. It is important to understand this business transaction prior to understanding the accounting issues. Generally, the company will give up rights to the future stream of cash receipts that will be collected from the receivables for immediate receipt of cash.

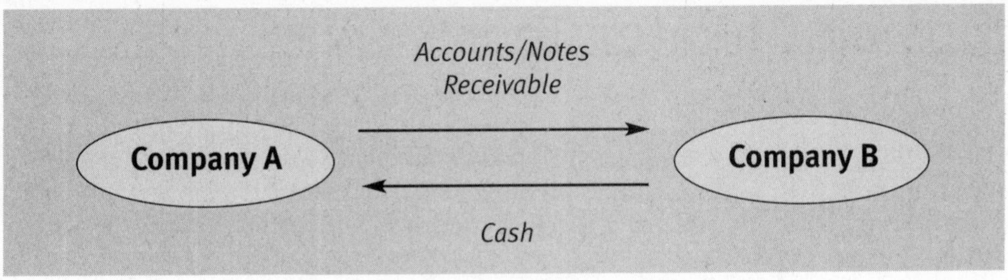

Company B has possession of and legal title to the receivables after the transaction. The arrangement may be such that Company B in the above situation has no recourse to Company A if the receivables prove to be uncollectible in future periods. Conversely, the arrangement may allow Company B to seek compensation from Company A if they cannot collect the full amount of the receivables from the customers. In the latter case, Company B has recourse to Company A.

Generally, the amount of cash received by Company A would be less than the net book value (NBV) of the receivables. This discount is to compensate Company B for their collection efforts and for any potential losses from uncollected amounts. Company B would probably rather have recourse to Company A for uncollectible amounts, although, it may be willing to give this right up for a lower cash payment.

Pledging or assigning receivables is a method of generating cash from receivables up front, usually in the form of a loan. The legal right to the cash from collecting the receivables remains with the company unless the company defaults on the loan. **TIP!**

Factoring or discounting is another method of generating cash from receivables upfront. In this case, however, the legal right to collect the receivables is transferred to the other party. **TIP!**

The sale of receivables may be with or without recourse. **TIP!**

Recourse signals that the risks and rewards of ownership may still rest, at least partially, with the company. **TIP!**

Becoming Proficient in the Related Calculations

The key calculations required in this area are as follows:

- Bank reconciliations
- Estimation of bad debts

Tips on Chapter Topics

TIP! Cash is the most liquid of assets, and is the standard medium of exchange and the basis for measuring and accounting for most items. It is also the most susceptible to theft and improper use. Internal controls are imperative to safeguard and ensure accuracy of accounting records.

TIP! Restricted cash is classified as either current or long-term assets, depending upon the date of availability or disbursement.

TIP! Cash and cash equivalents are short-term, highly liquid investments that are both readily convertible to known amounts of cash, and so near to their maturity that they present insignificant risk of change in value. Generally, only investments with maturities of three months or less qualify as cash and cash equivalents.

TIP! Bank overdrafts occur when cheques are written for more than the balance in the cash account. These are recorded as current liabilities and are normally included with accounts payable.

TIP! Trade accounts receivable result from the sale of products or services to customers. Nontrade accounts receivable (amounts that are due from nontrade customers who do not buy goods or services in the normal course of the company's main business activity) should be listed separately on the balance sheet from the trade accounts receivable with debit balances.

TIP! In the event that a customer's account has a credit balance on the balance sheet date, it should be classified as a current liability and not offset against other accounts receivable expected to be ultimately converted to cash.

TIP! Whenever you want to analyze the effect of (1) recording bad debt expense, (2) writing off an individual customer's account receivable, and/or (3) the collection of an account receivable that was previously written off, write down the related journal entry(ies) and analyze each debit and credit separately. (See **Illustration 7-1** for examples.)

TIP! There are two methods of accounting for bad debts; they are:

1. **Direct Write-Off Method:** No entry is made until a specific account has definitely been established as uncollectible. Then the loss is recorded by crediting Accounts Receivable and debiting Bad Debt Expense.
2. **Allowance Method:** An estimate is made of the expected uncollectible accounts from all sales made on account or from the total of outstanding receivables. This estimate is entered as an expense and an indirect reduction in accounts receivable (via an increase in the allowance account) in the period in which the sale is recorded.

TIP! The direct write-off method is not a generally accepted method for an entity having a material amount of bad debts because it fails to properly match bad debt expense with the related revenue (in the period the credit sale was recognized) and it overstates accounts receivable as to their net realizable value.

TIP! Short-term notes receivables are generally recorded at face value (less allowances) because the interest implicit in the maturity value is immaterial, while long-term notes receivables should be recorded at the present value of the cash expected to be collected.

A note receivable is considered to be impaired when it is probable that the creditor will be unable to collect all amounts due (both principal and interest) according to the contractual terms of the loan. In that case, the present value of the expected future cash flows is determined by discounting those flows at the historical effective rate. This present value amount is deducted from the carrying amount of the receivable to measure the loss. **TIP!**

The objective of a bank reconciliation is to explain all reasons why the bank balance differs from the book balance and to identify errors and omissions in the bank's records and in the book records. In the context of a bank reconciliation, "per bank" refers to the records of the bank pertaining to the depositor's account and "per books" refers to the depositor's records of the same bank account. **TIP!**

Total receipts per bank for a month include all deposits made by the depositor during the month plus any bank credit memos (such as for interest credited by the bank or a customer's noted receivable collected by the bank). **TIP!**

Total disbursements per bank for a month include all the depositor's cheques which cleared the banking system during the month plus any bank debit memos originating during the month (such as for bank service charges or a customer's NSF cheque). **TIP!**

Beginning cash balance per bank plus total receipts for the month per bank minus total disbursements for the month per bank equals ending cash balance per bank. **TIP!**

Beginning cash balance per books plus total receipts for the month per books minus total disbursements for the month per books equals ending cash balance per books. **TIP!**

Exercise 7-1

PURPOSE: This exercise will review the items which are included in the "Cash" caption on a balance sheet.

In auditing the balance sheet at December 31, 2008, for the Show-me-the-Money Company, you find the following:

(a) Coins and currency for change funds.
(b) Coins and currency which are from the current day's receipts which have not yet been deposited in the bank.
(c) Petty cash.
(d) General chequing account at First Union Bank.
(e) General chequing account at Sun Trust Bank.
(f) Unused stamps.
(g) Deposit in transit.
(h) Customer's NSF cheque (returned with bank statement).
(i) Postdated cheques from customers.
(j) Certificate of deposit—60 day CD purchased on December 1, 2008.
(k) Certificate of deposit—5 year CD purchased 2 years ago.

(l) 100 shares of a public company (intention is to sell in one year or less).
(m) Cash to be used to retire long-term debt.
(n) Travel advances made to executives for business purposes.

Instructions

Select the items from the list above that should be included in the "Cash" caption on the balance sheet as of December 31, 2008. For any item not included in "Cash", indicate the proper classification.

Solution to Exercise 7-1

Items to be **included** as "Cash" on the balance sheet include:

(a) Coins and currency for change funds.
(b) Coins and currency which are from the current day's receipts which have not yet been deposited in the bank—this is said to be "cash on hand" or could be considered a "deposit in transit."
(c) Petty cash.
(d) General chequing account at First Union Bank—the amount included should be the "adjusted cash balance" per a bank reconciliation.
(e) General chequing account at Sun Trust Bank—the amount included should be the "adjusted cash balance" per a bank reconciliation.
(f) Unused stamps—report as prepaid expense.
(g) Deposit in transit—this amount is already reflected in the "balance per books" and will be reflected in the "adjusted cash balance" per the bank reconciliation.

Items **not included** as "Cash" on the balance sheet include:

(h) Customer's NSF cheque—classify as a receivable.
(i) Postdated cheques from customers—accounts receivable.
(j) Certificate of deposit—60 day original maturity date was 3 months or less—cash equivalent. Some entities include cash equivalents with cash; others report them as short-term (temporary) investments.
(k) Certificate of deposit—original maturity date not 3 months or less—long-term, held-to-maturity investment.
(l) 100 public company shares—short-term investment because there is a lack of intent to hold for a long-term purpose and is readily marketable.
(m) Cash to be used to retire long-term debt—long-term investment (assuming the related debt is classified as long-term).
(n) Travel advances made to executives for business purposes—prepaid expense.

Illustration 7-1

Entries for the Allowance Method

Journal Entry			Effect on Net Income	Effect on Working Capital	Effect on Allowance Account	Effect on Net Receivables
Entry to record bad debt expense, $1,000						
Bad Debt Expense	1,000		Decrease $1,000	No effect	No effect	No effect
Allowance for Doubtful Accounts		1,000	No effect	Decrease $1,000	Increase $1,000	Decrease $1,000
Net effect of entry			Decrease $1,000	Decrease $1,000	Increase $1,000	Decrease $1,000
Entry to write-off a customer's account, $200						
Allowance for Doubtful Accounts	200		No effect	Increase $200	Decrease $200	Increase $200
Accounts Receivable		200	No effect	Decrease $200	No effect	Decrease $200
Net effect of entry			No effect	No effect	Decrease $200	No effect
Entries to record collection of account receivable previously written off, $120						
Accounts Receivable	120		No effect	Increase 120	No effect	Increase 120
Allowance for Doubtful Accounts		120	No effect	Decrease $120	Increase $120	Decrease $120
Cash	120		No effect	Increase $120	No effect	No effect
Accounts Receivable		120	No effect	Decrease $120	No effect	Decrease $120
Net effect of entries			No effect	No effect	Increase $120	Decrease $120

TIP! Be careful to distinguish the entry to write-off a customer account from the entry to record the bad debt expense. The journal to record the estimated bad debt expense for a period and to adjust the corresponding allowance for doubtful accounts involves a debit to Bad Debt Expense and a credit to Allowance for Doubtful Accounts. The entry to write-off an individual customer's account (an actual bad debt) involves a debit to Allowance for Doubtful Accounts and a credit to Accounts Receivable.

TIP! Two entries are necessary to record the recovery of an account that was previously written off:

1. An entry to record the reinstatement of the account receivable (debit Accounts Receivable and credit Allowance for Doubtful Accounts). This is simply a reverse of the write-off entry.
2. An entry to record the collection of the receivable (debit Cash and credit Accounts Receivable).

TIP! Allowance for Doubtful Accounts is often called Allowance for Uncollectible Accounts. Bad Debt Expense is often called Uncollectible Accounts Expense or Doubtful Accounts Expense. Provision for Bad Debts is another name for the Bad Debt Expense account; Reserve for Bad Debts is a frequently used but objectionable title for the allowance account.

TIP! Notice that the entry to record a bad debt reduces current assets and reduces net income. The entry to record the write-off of an individual account has **no** net effect on the amount of current assets nor does it affect income. It merely reduces Accounts Receivable and the Allowance for Doubtful Accounts account (which is a contra item) so the entry has no **net** effect on the net realizable value of accounts receivable. Thus, it is the entry to record the bad debt expense that impacts both the income statement and the balance sheet.

TIP! The normal balance of the Allowance for Doubtful Accounts is a credit. Therefore, a debit balance in this account indicates an abnormal balance. It is not uncommon to have a debit balance in the allowance account before adjusting entries are prepared because individual accounts may be written off at various times during a period and the entry to adjust the allowance account is prepared at the end of the period before financial statements are prepared. After adjustment, the allowance account should have a credit balance.

TIP! When using the allowance method of accounting for bad debts, there are two methods available for determining the amount of the adjusting entry to record bad debt expense and to adjust the allowance account. Each method has adaptations.

1. Percentage-of-Sales (Income Statement) approach:

   a. The average percentage relationship between actual debt losses and net credit sales is ascertained from prior experience. This percentage, adjusted for current conditions, is then applied to the actual net credit sales of the period to determine the amount of the expense for the period.

   b. Use of the same procedure as in "a" above, except the percentage of bad debts to total sales is used. This method is not as logical as "a" because cash sales will not result in bad debts, and, if the relationship between cash sales and credit sales shifts, that change will necessitate revision of the percentage being used to estimate bad debts.

2. Percentage-of-Receivables (Balance Sheet) approach:

   a. From experience, the average percentage relationship between uncollectible accounts receivable and outstanding accounts receivable is determined. This percentage, adjusted for current conditions, is applied each period to the ending balance in accounts receivable to determine the desired balance of the allowance account.

   b. Total uncollectible accounts at the end of an accounting period is determined by an aging analysis. The balance in the allowance account is then adjusted so that it equals the total amount of the estimated uncollectible accounts. This aging method is preferable to "2a" because it takes into consideration the age of a receivable. (The older the age, the lower the probability of collection.)

Both methods (and their variations) listed above are acceptable. The first method discussed, estimation of bad debt expense based on credit sales, focuses on matching current bad debt expense with revenues of the current period and thus emphasizes the income statement. The second method, estimation of the net realizable value of existing receivables, focuses on an evaluation of the net realizable value of all accounts receivable and thus emphasizes the balance sheet. It only incidentally measures bad debt expense; the expense reported may not be directly related to the credit sales of the current period, thus violating the matching principle. If this method is to be used, the aging technique is preferable to the use of a simple percentage times total accounts receivable.

TIP! Very often, an entity may use the percentage-of-sales method to account for bad debts for interim periods and then the aging method to adjust the allowance account at year-end for annual reporting purposes.

TIP! When it is time to prepare the adjusting entry for bad debts (at the end of an accounting period), the existing balance in the Allowance for Doubtful Accounts account (that is, the balance before adjustment) is **NOT** considered in determining the amount of the adjusting entry IF the percentage-of-sales approach is used. However, the balance in the allowance account before adjustment IS used in determining the amount of the adjusting entry when the aging analysis approach (one method of estimating the net realizable value of existing receivables) is used to implement the allowance method of accounting for bad debts. The application of these two guidelines is illustrated by the **Solution to Exercise 7-2** (entries 1 and 2).

TIP! When using the allowance method and estimating bad debt expense as a percentage of credit sales for the period, the amount of bad debt expense is simply calculated and recorded; a by-product of this approach is the increasing of the allowance account. When using the allowance method and estimating the net realizable value of accounts receivable (such as by an aging analysis), the amount of uncollectible accounts calculated represents the new ending balance of the allowance account. The adjusting entry records the amount necessary to increase (or decrease) the current allowance account balance to equal the newly calculated one. A by-product of this approach is the increasing of bad debt expense for the period.

Exercise 7-2

PURPOSE: This exercise will require you to record: (1) the adjusting entry to recognize bad debt expense and adjust the Allowance for Doubtful Accounts account, and (2) the transfer of accounts receivable without recourse.

The trial balance before adjustment at December 31, 2008, for the Liz Company shows the following balances:

	Dr.	Cr.
Accounts Receivable	$ 90,000	
Allowance for Doubtful Accounts	2,120	
Sales (all on credit)		$ 500,000
Sales Returns and Allowances	7,600	

Instructions

Using the data above, give the journal entries required to record each of the following cases (each situation is **independent**):

1. The company estimates bad debts to be 1.5% of net credit sales.
2. Liz performs an aging analysis at December 31, 2008, which indicates an estimate of $6,000 of uncollectible accounts.
3. The company wants to maintain the Allowance for Doubtful Accounts at 4% of gross accounts receivable.
4. To obtain additional cash, Liz factors, without recourse, $20,000 of accounts receivable with Fleetwood Finance. The finance charge is 10% of the amount factored.

Solution to Exercise 7-2

	Dr.	Cr.
1. Bad Debt Expense [($500,000 – $7,600) x 1.5%]...............	7,386	
Allowance for Doubtful Accounts		7,386

EXPLANATION: The percentage of net credit sales approach to applying the allowance method of accounting for bad debts focuses on determining an appropriate expense figure. The existing balance in the allowance account is **not** relevant in the calculation.

	Dr.	Cr.
2. Bad Debt Expense	8,120	
Allowance for Doubtful Accounts ($6,000 + $2,120)....		8,120

EXPLANATION: An aging analysis provides the best estimate of the net realizable value of accounts receivable. By using the results of the aging to adjust the allowance account, the amount reported for net receivables on the balance sheet is the net realizable value of accounts receivable. It is important to notice that the balance of the allowance account before adjustment is a determinant in the adjustment required. The following T-account reflects the facts used to determine the necessary adjustment:

Allowance for Doubtful Accounts			
Unadjusted balance	2,120	Adjustment needed	8,120
		Desired balance at 12/31/05	6,000

3. Bad Debt Expense	5,720	
Allowance for Doubtful Accounts [($90,000 x 4%) + $2,120]		5,720

EXPLANATION: This entry is to adjust the allowance account. A by-product of the entry is the recognition of uncollectible accounts expense. Because an appropriate balance for the valuation account is determined to be a percentage of the receivable balance at the balance sheet date, the existing balance ($2,120 debit) in the allowance account **must** be considered in calculating the necessary adjustment.

4. Cash	18,000	
Loss on Sale of Receivables ($20,000 x 10%)	2,000	
Accounts Receivable		20,000

EXPLANATION: The factoring of accounts receivable without recourse is accounted for as a sale of accounts receivable; hence, the receivables are removed from the accounts, cash is recorded, and a loss is recognized for the excess of the face value of the receivables over the proceeds received.

Illustration 7-2

Accounting for Transfers of Receivables

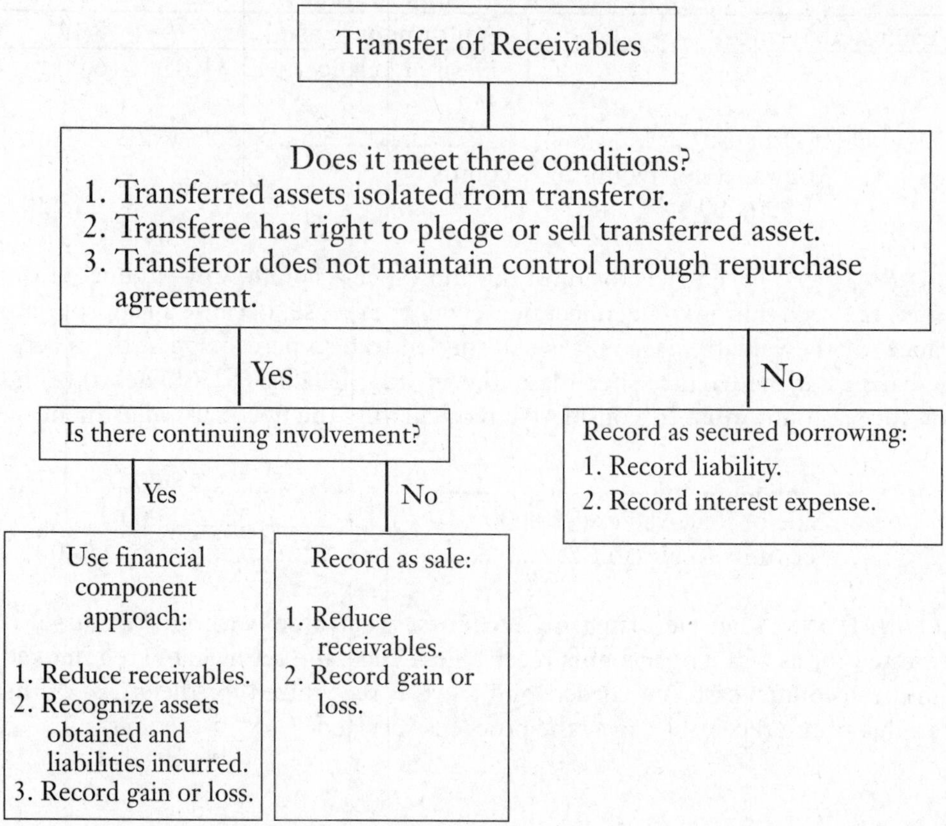

TIP! If there is continuing involvement in a sale transaction, the assets obtained and liabilities incurred must be recorded at fair value.

Exercise 7-3

PURPOSE: This exercise will help you to compare two possible ways of structuring a sale of accounts receivable (1) without recourse, or (2) with recourse.

Raytech Corporation factors $90,000 of accounts receivable with NL Financing, Inc. NL Financing will collect the receivables. The receivable records are transferred to NL Financing on August 15, 2008. NL Financing assesses a finance charge of 4% of the amount of accounts receivable and also retains an amount equal to 6% of accounts receivable to cover probable adjustments.

Instructions

(a) Explain the conditions that must be met for a transfer of receivables with recourse to be accounted for as a sale.
(b) Explain when the financial components approach is used in accounting for a transfer of accounts receivable.
(c) Prepare the journal entry for both Raytech Corporation and NL Financing to record the transfer of accounts receivable on August 15, 2008, assuming the receivables are sold without recourse.
(d) Prepare the journal entry for both Raytech Corporation and NL Financing to record the transfer of accounts receivable on August 15, 2008, assuming the receivables are sold with recourse and the conditions required for sale accounting are met. Further, assume the recourse obligation has a fair value of $2,000.

Solution to Exercise 7-3

(a) The CICA Accounting Standards Board concluded that a sale occurs only if the seller surrenders control of the receivables to the buyer and receives in exchange consideration other than a beneficial interest in the transferred asset. The following three conditions must be met before a sale can be recorded:

1. The transferred asset has been isolated from the transferor (put beyond reach of the transferor and its creditors).
2. The transferees have obtained the right to pledge or exchange either the transferred assets or beneficial interests in the transferred assets.
3. The transferor does not maintain effective control over the transferred assets through an agreement to repurchase or redeem them before their maturity.

If the three conditions are met, a sale occurs. Otherwise, the transferor should record the transfer as a secured borrowing. If sale accounting is appropriate, it is still necessary to consider assets obtained and liabilities incurred in the trans-action. If there is continuing involvement in a sale transaction, the assets obtained and liabilities incurred must be recorded at fair value.

(b) A **financial components approach** is used to account for a transfer of accounts receivable with recourse whenever the transfer arrangement meets the conditions necessary for the transfer to be accounted for as a sale (see answer (a) above). If receivables are sold (factored) with recourse, the seller guarantees payment to the purchaser in the event the debtor fails to pay. Under the financial components approach, each party to the sale recognizes the assets and liabilities that it controls after the sale and no longer recognizes the assets and liabilities that were sold or extinguished.

(c) Sale of receivables without recourse:

Raytech Corp.

Cash	81,000	
Due from Factor	5,400 *	
Loss on Sale of Receivables	3,600**	
Accounts Receivable		90,000

NL Financing

Accounts Receivable	90,000	
Due to Raytech		5,400
Financing Revenue		3,600
Cash		81,000

* $90,000 x 6% = $5,400
**$90,000 x 4% = $3,600

TIP! The factor's profit will be the difference between the financing revenue of $3,600 and the amount of any uncollectible receivables.

(d) Sale of receivables with recourse:

Raytech Corp.

Cash	81,000	
Due from Factor	5,400 *	
Loss on Sale of Receivables	5,600	
Accounts Receivable		90,000
Recource Liability		2,000

NL Financing

Accounts Receivable	90,000	
Due to Raytech		5,400
Financing Revenue		3,600
Cash		81,000

*Cash received	$81,000
Due from factor	5,400
Subtotal	86,400
Resource obligation	(2,000)
Net proceeds expected	$84,400

Carrying (book) value	$90,000
Net proceeds	(84,400)
Loss on sale of receivables	$ 5,600

TIP! In this case, a liability of $2,000 is recorded by Raytech to indicate the probable payment to NL Financing for uncollectible receivables. If all the receivables are collected, Raytech would eliminate its recourse liability and increase net income. NL Financing's profit is the financing revenue of $3,600 because it will have no bad debts related to these receivables.

Exercise 7-4

PURPOSE: This exercise will illustrate the calculations and entries involved in accounting for the transfer of receivables that is treated as a secured borrowing transaction.

Banff Winery transfers $350,000 of its accounts receivable to Calgary International Financial (CIF) as collateral for a $250,000 note on September 1, 2008. Ashton will continue to collect the accounts receivable; the account debtors are not notified of the arrangement. CIF assesses a finance charge of 1% of the accounts receivable and interest on the note of 12%. Settlement by Banff Winery to CIF is made monthly for all cash collected on the receivables.

Instructions

Prepare the journal entries for both Banff Winery and Calgary International Financial to record the following:

(a) Transfer of accounts receivable and issuance of the note on September 1, 2008.

(b) Collection in September of $220,000 of the transferred accounts receivable less cash discounts of $3,000. In addition, sales returns of $7,000 were processed.

(c) Remittance by Banff of September collections plus accrued interest to the bank on October 1.

(d) Collection in October of the balance of the transferred accounts receivable less $1,000 written off as uncollectible.

(e) Remittance by Banff of the balance due of $33,000 ($250,000 – $217,000) on the note plus interest on November 1.

Solution to Exercise 7-4

(a)

Banff Winery			**Calgary International Financial**		
Cash	246,500		Notes Receivable	250,000	
Finance Charge	3,500 *		Finance Revenue		3,500*
Notes Payable		250,000	Cash		246,500

*1% x $350,000 = $3,500

(b)

Banff Winery			**Calgary International Financial**
Cash	217,000		(No Entry)
Sales Discounts	3,000		
Sales Returns	7,000		
Accounts Receivable		227,000*	

*$220,000 + $7,000 = $227,000

(c)

Banff Winery			Calgary International Financial		
Interest Expense	2,500*		Cash	219,500	
Notes Payable	217,000		Interest Revenue		2,500*
Cash		219,500	Notes Receivable		217,000

*$250,000 x 12% x 1/12 = $2,500

(d)

Cash	122,000		(No Entry)
Allowance for Doubtful Accounts	1,000		
Accounts Receivable		123,000*	

*$350,000 – $227,000 = $123,000

(e)

Interest Expense	330 *		Cash	33,330	
Notes Payable	33,000		Interest Revenue		330*
Cash		33,330	Notes Receivable		33,000

*$33,000 x 12% x 1/12 = 330

TIP! Receivables are often used as collateral in a borrowing transaction. A creditor often requires that the debtor designate or pledge receivables as security for the loan. If the loan is not paid when due, the creditor has the right to convert the collateral to cash—that is, to collect the receivables. (If the receivables are transferred to the transferee for custodial purposes, the custodial arrangement is often referred to as a **pledge.**) **Factors** are finance companies or banks that buy receivables from businesses for a fee and then collect remittances directly from the customers. This exercise (**Exercise 7-4**) illustrates a borrowing transaction whereas **Exercise 7-3** illustrates a sales transaction.

TIP! If you have a chequing account, look at the back of your bank statement. A bank often includes a form to assist you in reconciling your bank account. Very often that form reconciles the cash balance and the book cash balance to the correct (adjusted) cash balance.

TIP! The "Balance per bank" caption on a bank reconciliation is often replaced with "Balance per bank statement," and "Balance per books" is often titled "Balance per ledger."

TIP! The "Correct cash balance" caption on a bank reconciliation is often replaced with "Adjusted cash balance." The adjusted cash balance as determined by the bank reconciliation will be the amount used to report for cash on the balance sheet. (The Cash account in the general ledger often includes cash on hand and cash in the bank, although separate ledger accounts and any other unrestricted cash accounts, such as the Petty Cash account, are added together to report cash on the balance sheet.)

TIP! Some items in a bank reconciliation will require adjustments either on the depositor's books or in the bank's records, while the others will not. When the balance per bank to correct cash balance format is used in preparing a single-column bank reconciliation, balance per books to correct cash balance requires adjustment on the depositor's books. All of the reconciling items appearing in the upper half of the reconciliation, except for deposits in transit and outstanding cheques, require adjustment on the bank's books.

TIP! Unless otherwise indicated, an NSF cheque is assumed to be a customer's NSF cheque; that is, an NSF cheque is considered to be from a customer of the depositor, rather than a depositor's NSF cheque.

TIP! A depositor's chequing account is a liability on the bank's books, so a bank debit memo decreases the depositor's cash balance and a bank credit memo increases the depositor's cash balance. On the bank statement, debits appear as a result of cheques that have cleared during the month or bank debit memos for items such as bank service charges (BSC). Credits on the bank statement represent deposits or bank credit memos.

Exercise 7-5

PURPOSE: This exercise will help you review situations that give rise to reconciling items on a bank reconciliation and identify those which require adjusting entries on the depositor's books.

A sketch of the bank reconciliation at July 31, 2008, for the Ace Electric Company and a list of possible reconciling items appear below.

Ace Electric Co.
BANK RECONCILIATION
July 31, 2008

Balance per bank statement, July 31		$X,XXX
A. Add:	$XXX	
	XXX	X,XXX
		X,XXX
B. Deduct:		X,XXX
Correct cash balance, July 31		$X,XXX
Balance per books, July 31		$ X,XXX
C. Add:	$XXX	
	XXX	X,XXX
D. Deduct:	XXX	X,XXX
	XXX	
	XXX	X,XXX
Correct cash balance, July 31	XXX	$X,XXX

_____ 1. Deposits of July 30 amounting to $1,482 have not reached the bank as of July 31.

_____ 2. A customer's cheque for $40 that was deposited on July 20 was returned NSF by the bank; return has not been recorded by Ace.

_____ 3. Bank service charge for July amounts to $3.

_____ 4. Included with the bank statement was cheque No. 422 for $702 as payment of an account payable. In comparing the cheque with the cash disbursement records, it was discovered that the cheque was incorrectly entered in the cash disbursements journal for $720.

_____ 5. Outstanding cheques at July 31 amount to $1,927.

_____ 6. The bank improperly charged a cheque of the Ace Plumbing Co. for $25 to Ace Electric Co.'s account.

_____ 7. The bank charged $8 during July for printing cheques.

_____ 8. During July, the bank collected a customer's note receivable for the Ace Electric Co.; face amount $1,000, interest $20, and the bank charged a $2 collection fee. This transaction has not been recorded by Ace.

_____ 9. A cheque written by Ace in June for $180 cleared the bank during July.

_____ 10. Deposits of June 30 for $1,200 were recorded by the company on June 30 but were not recorded by the bank until July 2.

Instructions

(a) Indicate how each of the 10 items listed above would be handled on the bank reconciliation by placing the proper code letter in the space provided. The applicable code letters appear in the sketch of the bank reconciliation. Use the code "NR" for any item which is not a reconciling item on July 31.

(b) Assume that the July 31 balance per bank statement was $4,332. Complete the bank reconciliation using the items given and answer the questions that follow:

1. What is the adjusted (correct) cash balance at July 31? $_____________
2. What is the balance per books **before** adjustment at July 31? $_________
3. What reconciling items require an adjusting entry on Ace Electric Company's books? (Identify by item numbers.) ____________________
4. What item(s) requires a special entry on the bank's records to correct an error(s)?________________________________

Solution to Exercise 7-5

(a)

1.	A	6.	A
2.	D	7.	D
3.	D	8.	C, D
4.	C	9.	NR
5.	B	10.	NR

(b)

1. \$3,912* (\$4,332 + \$1,482 + \$25 – \$1,927 = \$3,912)
2. \$2,927* [X + \$18 + \$1,020 – \$40 – \$3 – \$8 – \$2 = \$3,912 (answer to question 1)] X = \$2,927
3. 2; 3; 4; 7; 8
4. 6

*See the completed bank reconciliation below.

TIP! Items 9 and 10 would have been reconciling items of cash balances on the June 30 bank reconciliation (the prior month).

APPROACH: You can calculate the correct cash balance by completing the top half of the bank reconciliation (balance per bank to correct cash balance). The correct cash balance can then be entered on the last line of the bottom half of the reconciliation and used along with certain reconciling items to "work backwards" to calculate the \$2,927 cash balance per books before adjustment.

Ace Electric Co.
BANK RECONCILIATION
July 31, 2008

Balance per bank statement, July 31		\$ 4,332
Add: Deposits in transit on July 31	\$1,482	
Cheque improperly charged by bank	25	1,507
		5,839
Deduct: Cheques outstanding as of July 31		1,927
Correct cash balance at July 31		\$3,912
Balance per books, July 31		\$2,927
Add: Error in recording cheque No. 422	\$ 18	
Collection of customer's note receivable and interest by bank	1,020	1,038
		3,965
Deduct: Customer's NSF cheque	40	
Bank service charge for July	3	
Cost of printing cheques	8	
Bank collection fee	2	53
Correct cash balance at July 31		\$3,912

TIP! The required adjusting entries on the depositor's books would be:

Cash	18	
Accounts Payable		18
(To correct error in recording cheque No. 422)		
Cash	1,020	
Note Receivable		1,000
Interest Revenue		20
(To record collection of note receivable by bank)		

Accounts Receivable	40	
Cash		40
(To record customer's NSF cheque)		
Miscellaneous Expense	13	
Cash		13
(To record bank service charges: [$3 + $8 + $2 = $13])		

TIP! The above entries can be combined into one compound entry.

Exercise 7-6

PURPOSE: This exercise will illustrate how to determine deposits in transit and outstanding cheques.

Shown below for Molly's Folly are the:

(1) bank reconciliation at September 30, 2008.
(2) listing of deposits for October per the bank statement.
(3) listing of deposits for October per the books.
(4) listing of cheques paid by the bank during October.
(5) listing of cheques written by the depositor during October.

Molly's Folly
BANK RECONCILIATION
September 30, 2008

Balance per bank statement		$ 15,000
Add: Deposits in transit		
September 29	$ 2,000	
September 30	1,600	3,600
		18,600
Deduct: Outstanding cheques		
No. 514	650	
No. 516	410	
No. 520	560	
No. 521	740	
No. 522	1,000	3,360
Correct cash balance		$ 15,240
Balance per books		$ 15,690
Deduct: Customer's NSF cheque	$ 400	
Bank service charge	50	450
Correct cash balance		$ 15,240

Bank Statement for October—Deposits

Date	Amount	Date	Amount	Date	Amount
10/1	$ 2,000	10/11	$ 1,200	10/25	$ 100
10/2	1,600	10/15	200	10/27	600
10/3	500	10/18	400	10/28	800
10/5	300	10/21	700	10/29	1,300
10/11	1,100	10/22	900	Total	$ 11,700

Cash Receipts Journal

Date	Amount	Date	Amount	Date	Amount
10/1	$ 500	10/20	$ 700	10/29	$ 1,400
10/4	300	10/21	900	10/30	1,500
10/8	1,100	10/23	100	10/31	550
10/10	1,200	10/25	600	Total	$ 11,550
10/13	200	10/27	800		
10/16	400	10/28	1,300		

Bank Statement for October—Cheques Paid and Debit Memos

Date	Cheque #	Amount	Date	Cheque #	Amount
10/1	514	$650	10/13	534	$ 220
10/1	520	560	10/14	535	240
10/4	521	740	10/18	538	380
10/4	522	1,000	10/18	536	250
10/5	525	120	10/18	537	320
10/5	526	140	10/18	539	430
10/6	528	230	10/19	540	510
10/8	529	310	10/23	541	330
10/8	527	210	10/25	542	340
10/8	530	420	10/29	545	540
10/11	532	160	10/29	546	470
10/11	531	130	10/31	DM	30
10/12	533	190	Total		$ 8,920

Cash Payments Journal—Cheques Issued

Date	Cheque #	Amount	Date	Cheque #	Amount
10/1	525	$ 120	10/5	530	420
10/1	526	140	10/7	531	130
10/3	527	210	10/7	532	106
10/4	528	230	10/7	533	190
10/5	529	310	10/11	534	220

Date	Cheque #	Amount	Date	Cheque #	Amount
10/11	535	240	10/25	543	110
10/12	536	250	10/26	544	160
10/14	537	320	10/27	545	540
10/14	538	380	10/28	546	470
10/15	539	430	10/31	547	590
10/17	540	330	10/31	548	640
10/20	541	340	Total		$ 7,386
10/23	542	510			

Instructions

(a) Prepare a list of deposits in transit at October 31, 2008.
(b) Prepare a list of outstanding cheques at October 31, 2008.
(c) Locate any errors per books, assuming that the information recorded in the bank's records is correct.
(d) Locate any bank memoranda that will need to be recorded on the books.

Solution to Exercise 7-6

(a) Deposits in transit at October 31, 2008:

October 29	$1,400
October 30	1,500
October 31	550
Total	$3,450

(b) Outstanding cheques at October 31, 2008:

No.	Amount
516	$410
543	110
544	160
547	590
548	640
	$1,910

(c) Cheque No. 532 was recorded on the depositor's books for $106 when it should have been recorded for the correct amount of $160.
(d) The DM for $30 on October 31 will need to be recorded on the depositor's books. (The DM is likely for bank service charges for October.)

EXPLANATION:
(a) To identify the deposits in transit at October 31:
(1) Compare the deposits in transit at September 30 (per the company's bank reconciliation at that date) with the October bank statement. If the

deposit did not get recorded by the bank during October it is to be considered a deposit in transit at October 31. (It would be extremely rare for a particular deposit to be listed as a deposit in transit on **two** successive bank reconciliations because it would indicate the deposit was lost in the mail or lost in the bank's facilities or a victim of some strange fate.)

For Molly's Folly, the $2,000 and $1,600 items deposited at the end of September (deposits in transit at September 30, 2008) both were recorded by the bank in early October as expected.

(2) Compare the deposits made during October per company records with the October deposits per the bank's records. Deposits not recorded by the bank represent **deposits in transit**. As can be expected, the receipts recorded on the books at the very end of October have not had enough time to be processed by the bank by the end of the day on October 31. These include the deposits made by Molly's Folly on October 29 ($1,400), October 30 ($1,500), and October 31 ($550).

(b) To identify the outstanding cheques at October 31, 2008:

(1) Compare the cheques outstanding at September 30, 2008 (per the September 30 bank reconciliation) with the cheques clearing the bank as shown on the October bank statement. If September cheque remains unpaid at the end of October, it is an outstanding cheque at October 31.

For Molly's Folly, cheque numbers 514, 520, 521, and 522 all cleared the bank during October, but cheque number 516 ($410) remains unpaid at October 31, 2008. (The cheque could be lost in the mail or lost in the banking system. More likely, the cheque is still in the hands of the payee, who for some reason has not yet deposited it to his account.)

(2) Compare the cheques written by Molly's Folly during October with the cheques paid by the bank. Issued cheques that have not been paid by the bank represent **outstanding cheques**.

For Molly's Folly, October cheque numbers 543 ($110), 544 ($160), 547 ($590), and 548 ($640) were written during October and are outstanding at October 31.

(c) To identify errors on either the bank's records or the depositor's books, compare all of the figures on the October bank statement with their source on the depositor's records. If there are any discrepancies, determine which is in error. For Molly's Folly, cheque number 532 correctly cleared the bank for $160 but was entered in the cash payments journal as $106. (The facts of the problem state that the bank's records are correct.) This transposition-type error caused the depositor's bank balance per ledger to be overstated by $54 ($160 – $106 = $54).

TIP!

Note that a transposition error (reversing the order of numbers) will cause a difference that is divisible by 9.

Exercise 7-7

PURPOSE: This exercise will allow you to practice preparing a bank reconciliation.

A bank reconciliation should be prepared by a depositor every month.

The cash balance per bank at October 31 is $17,780, and the cash balance per Molly's Folly's books at October 31 is $19,404.

Instructions

(a) Using the data in **Exercise 7-6** and the solution to that exercise, prepare a bank reconciliation for Molly's Folly at October 31, 2008.
(b) Prepare the adjusting entries at October 31 for the depositor's books. Assume cheque No. 532 was issued to the power company for utilities.

Solution to Exercise 7-7

(a)

Molly's Folly
BANK RECONCILIATION
October 31, 2008

Balance per bank statement		$ 17,780 *
Add: Deposits in transit [Answer (a) Exercise 7-6]		3,450
		21,230
Deduct: Outstanding cheques [Answer (b) Exercise 7-6]		1,910
Correct cash balance		$ 19,320
Balance per books		$ 19,404 **
Deduct: Bank service charge	$30	
Error in recording cheque No. 532	54	84
Correct cash balance		$ 19,320

* To add to the complexity of this exercise, you could be asked to solve for the $17,780 cash balance per bank statement. The calculation would be as follows:

Balance per bank statement at September 30, 2008	$15,000
Add: Deposits recorded during October and credit memoranda	11,700
Deduct: Cheques paid during October and debit memoranda	8,920
Balance per bank statement at October 31, 2008	$17,780

** To add to the complexity of this exercise, you could be asked to solve for the $19,404 cash balance per books at October 31, 2008. The calculation would be as follows:

Balance per books at September 30, 2008 before adjustment	$ 15,690
Deduct: NSF cheque recorded by an adjusting entry	400
Deduct: Bank service charge for September recorded by an adjusting entry	50
Correct cash balance at September 30	15,240
Add: Deposits made during October	11,550
Deduct: Cheques written (issued) during October	7,386
Balance per books at October 31, 2008	$ 19,404

An alternate approach to solving for the balance per books before adjustment is illustrated in the **Solution to Exercise 7-5** part (b) 2.

Keep in mind that deposits in transit and outstanding cheques are reconciling items but do not require adjusting entries on either the bank's books or the depositor's books.

TIP!

(b)	Oct. 31	Miscellaneous Expense	30	
		Cash		30
		(To record the bank service charges for Oct.)		
	Oct. 31	Utilities Expense	54	
		Cash		54
		(To correct error in recording cheque no. 532)		

Exercise 7-8

PURPOSE: This exercise reviews the journal entries involved with establishing and maintaining a petty cash fund.

The Montreal Smoked Meat Corporation makes most expenditures by cheque. The following transactions relate to an imprest fund established by the Montreal Smoked Meat Corporation to handle small expenditures on an expedient basis.

Transactions

May	4	Wrote a $100 cheque to establish the petty cash fund.
	6	Paid taxi $2 to deliver papers to a branch office.
	6	Purchased stamps, $13.
	8	Paid $15 for advertising posters.
	12	Paid $6 for mail received with "postage due."
	12	Paid $8 for coffee supplies.
	13	Paid $17 for office supplies.

14 Paid bus charges of $18 to ship goods to a customer.
15 Counted the remaining coins and currency in the fund, $20
15 Wrote a cheque to replenish the fund.

Instructions

(a) Record the transactions in general journal form.
(b) Answer the questions that follow:
1. How much coin and currency should have been in the petty cash box at the end of the day on May 12? $______
2. How much coin and currency should have been in the petty cash box on May 15 before replenishment? $______
3. What was the balance in the Petty Cash ledger account on May 12? $______
4. What was the balance in the Petty Cash ledger account at the end of the day, May 15? $______

TIP! In order to answer the last two questions, it would be helpful to post the journal entries to a T-account for Petty Cash.

Solution to Exercise 7-8

(a) May 4	Petty Cash	100	
	Cash		100
	(To establish a petty cash fund)		
May 15	Miscellaneous Expense ($2 + $8)	10	
	Postage Expense ($13 + $6)	19	
	Advertising Expense	15	
	Office Supplies	17	
	Transportation-out	18	
	Cash Over and Short	1	
	Cash		80
	(To replenish the petty cash fund)		

(b) 1. There should have been $56 in coin and currency in the fund at the end of the day on May 12. ($100 – $2 – $13 – $15 – $6 – $8 = $56)
2. There should have been $21 in coin and currency in the fund on May 15 before replenishment. ($100 – $2 – $13 – $15 – $6 – $8 – $17 – $18 = $21)
3. $100
4. $100

TIP! Because only $20 was found in the fund at that date, there was a shortage of $1 which must be recorded by a debit to the Cash Over and Short account.

TIP! The balance of the Petty Cash account changes only when the fund is established or the size of the fund is increased or decreased. The Petty Cash account balance is not affected by expenditures from the fund nor replenishments. (No journal entry is made at the time the expenditure is made. Expenditures from the fund are accounted for at the date of replenishment.)

Petty cash is not normally reported separately on the balance sheet. The balance of the Petty Cash account is generally lumped together with all other cash items when a balance sheet is prepared.

TIP!

Exercise 7-9

PURPOSE: This exercise will allow you to practice preparing a proof of cash. The following data pertain to the Burghard Company for 2008:

1. Per the bank statement for February: January 31 balance, $20,000; February receipts, $22,000; February disbursements, $24,000; February 28 balance, $18,000.
2. Per the books: January 31 unadjusted balance, $16,020; February receipts, $19,410; February disbursements, $21,505, February 28 balance, $13,925.
3. Bank service charge of $20 for January is included in book disbursements for February.
4. Bank service charge of $35 for February is included on the bank statement for February.
5. The first deposit shown on the February bank statement was $5,000 and was included in January's cash receipts per books.
6. $7,000 of cheques written in February have not cleared the bank by February 28.
7. A cheque written for office supplies in February for $970 was incorrectly recorded in the cash disbursements journal and in the cheque register as $790. This cheque cleared the bank in February for $970. Office supplies are charged to Office Supplies Expense when purchased.
8. The bank credited the firm's account in error for $500 in February for another firm's deposit.
9. The bank collected a $1,000 note receivable for the company in February plus $90 interest. The company has not yet recorded this transaction.
10. Cash receipts for February 28 of $4,000 did not reach the bank until March 2.
11. All $9,000 of cheques outstanding at January 31 cleared the banking system during February.
12. A customer's NSF cheque in the amount of $300 was returned with the February bank statement. This cheque was redeposited in March. As of the end of February, Burghard has not yet made an entry for the return of this cheque by the bank.

Instructions

(a) Prepare a bank reconciliation for the Burghard Co. for February.
(b) Prepare any adjusting entry(ies) required for the books.

Solution to Exercise 7-9

(a)

Burghard Company
BANK RECONCILIATION
For February, 2008

Balance per bank statement		$18,000*
Add: Outstanding deposit (February 28)		4,000
		22,000
Deduct: Outstanding cheques	$7,000	
Bank error	500	7,500
Correct cash balance		$ 14,500
Balance per books		$ 13,925 *
Add: cash collection on Note (including $90 interest)**	$1,090	1,090
		15,015
Deduct: Bank service charge	35	
Error in recording cheque (office supplies)	180	
N.S.F. cheque	300	515
Correct cash balance		$14,500

* The starting point is the ending balances for both the bank and company books. The only reconciliation which needs to be performed are for items that the other party does not know about (ex. Bank Service Charge recorded in February is already included in the opening balance of the company's books and does not need to be reconciled).

** The note collected by the bank and associated interest can be recorded individually or lumped together, however, the associated journal entry (see below) must record the two types of revenues individually.

(b)

Office Expenses—Bank Charges	35	
Cash		35
Office Supplies Expense	180	
Cash		180
Cash	1,090	
Note Receivable		1,000
Interest Revenue		90
Accounts Receivable	300	
Cash		300

Analysis of Multiple-Choice Questions

Question

1. Which of the following items should **not** be included in the Cash caption on the balance sheet?
   a. Coins and currency in the cash register.
   b. Cheques, from other parties, presently in the cash register.
   c. Amounts on deposit in chequing account at the bank.
   d. Postage stamps on hand.

EXPLANATION: Cash on hand, cash in banks, and petty cash are often combined and reported simply as Cash. Undeposited cheques from other parties is a component of cash on hand. Postage stamps on hand are classified as a prepaid expense. (Solution = d.)

Question

2. Legally restricted deposits held at a bank as compensating balances against long-term borrowing arrangements should be:
   a. used to reduce the amount reported as long-term debt on the balance sheet.
   b. reported separately among the "cash and cash equivalent items" in Current Assets on the balance sheet.
   c. separately classified as noncurrent assets in either the Investments or Other Assets sections of the balance sheet.
   d. used to reduce the amount reported as short-term debt on the balance sheet.

EXPLANATION: Restricted deposits held as compensating balances against long-term borrowing arrangements should be separately classified as non-current assets in either the Investments or Other Assets sections, using a caption such as "Cash on deposit maintained as compensating balance". To use the asset balance to directly reduce a debt (answer selections "a" and "d") would be "offsetting assets against liabilities" which violates a rule against offsetting or setoff. Only in rare circumstances is it permissable to offset assets and liabilities. (Solution = c.)

Question

3. Gatorland recorded uncollectible accounts expense of $30,000 and wrote off accounts receivable of $25,000 during the year. The net effect of these two transactions on working capital was a decrease of:
   a. $55,000.
   b. $30,000.

c. $25,000.
d. $5,000.

EXPLANATION:

			Effect on Working Capital
Uncollectible Accounts Expense	30,000		None
Allow. for Uncollectible Accounts		30,000	Decrease 30,000
Allowance for Uncollectible Accounts	25,000		Increase 25,000
Accounts Receivable		25,000	Decrease 25,000
Net Effect			Decrease 30,000

(Solution = b.)

Question

4. Chelser Corporation performed an analysis and an aging of its accounts receivable at December 31, 2008, which disclosed the following:

Accounts receivable balance	$ 100,000
Allowance for uncollectible accounts balance	5,000
Accounts deemed uncollectible	7,400

The net realizable value of the accounts receivable at December 31 is:
a. $87,600.
b. $92,600.
c. $95,000.
d. $97,600

EXPLANATION: Read the last sentence of the question: "The net realizable value of the accounts receivable at December 31 is ...." Underline "net realizable value of accounts receivable." Write down the definition of net realizable value of accounts receivable—amount of accounts receivable ultimately expected to be converted into cash. Read the details of the question. If an aging shows $7,400 of the $100,000 accounts are deemed uncollectible, then the remaining $92,600 are expected to be converted into cash. (Because the balance of the allowance account does not agree with the amount of uncollectibles per the aging, the allowance for uncollectible accounts balance must be the unadjusted balance, or the percentage-of-sales method is being used to determine the amount to record as bad debt expense.) (Solution = b.)

Question

5. The following data are available for 2008:

Sales, cash	$200,000
Sales, credit	500,000
Accounts Receivable, January 1	80,000

Accounts Receivable, December 31	72,000
Allowance for Doubtful Accounts, January 1	4,000
Accounts written off during 2008	4,600

The journal entry to record bad debt expense for the period and to adjust the allowance account is to be based on an estimate of 1% of credit sales. The entry to record the uncollectible accounts expense for 2008 would include a debit to the Bad Debt Expense account for:

a. $7,200.
b. $5,600.
c. $4,400.
d. $5,000.

EXPLANATION: Think about the emphasis of the entry when the percentage-of-sales basis is used. This method emphasizes the income statement. Therefore, 1% times credit sales equals bad debt expense ($500,000 x 1% = $5,000). The balance of the allowance account before adjustment does not affect this calculation or entry. (Solution = d.)

Question

6. The following data are available for 2008:

Sales, cash	$200,000
Sales, credit	500,000
Accounts Receivable, January 1	80,000
Accounts Receivable, December 31	72,000
Allowance for Doubtful Accounts, January 1	4,000
Accounts written off during 2008	4,600

The journal entry to record bad debt expense for the period and to adjust the allowance account is to be based on an aging analysis of accounts receivable. The aging analysis of accounts receivable at December 31, 2008, reveals that $5,200 of existing accounts receivable are estimated to be uncollectible. The entry to record the uncollectible accounts expense for 2008 will involve a debit to the Bad Debt Expense account for:

a. $9,800.
b. $5,800.
c. $5,200.
d. $4,600.

EXPLANATION: An aging analysis is performed to determine the best figure to represent the cash (net) realizable value of the accounts receivable in the balance sheet. Thus, $5,200 is the desired balance for the allowance account at the reporting date. Determine the existing balance in the allowance account and the adjusting entry needed to arrive at the desired ending balance.

Allowance for Doubtful Accounts.

Write-offs, 2008	4,600	Balance, 1/1/08	4,000	**Entry**
Balance before adjustment	600	Adjustment needed	X ←	**Needed**
		Desired balance at 12/31/08	5,200	

Solving for X: X – $600 = $5,200

X = $5,200 + $600

X = $5,800 (Solution = b.)

Question

7. The following data are available for 2008:

Allowance for Doubtful Accounts, January 1	$ 41,000
Write-offs of accounts receivable during the year	35,000
Net credit sales for the year	1,300,000

Bad debts are estimated to be 3% of net credit sales. The balance of the allowance account after adjustment should be:
a. $4,000.
b. $39,000.
c. $45,000.
d. $80,000.

EXPLANATION: Draw a T-account. Enter the data given and solve for the amount requested.

Allowance for Doubtful Accounts

		41,000	Beginning Balance
Write-offs	35,000	39,000	Expense = 3% x $1,300,000
		45,000	Ending Balance

(Solution = c.)

Question

8. An adjusting entry is made whereby there is a debit to Sales Returns and Allowances and a credit to Allowance for Sales Returns and Allowances. The effect of this entry is to:
a. reduce assets and net sales.
b. increase assets and net sales.
c. reduce net sales and liabilities.
d. increase net sales and liabilities.

EXPLANATION: The debit to Sales Returns and Allowances reduces net sales (and owners' equity) because of an increase in a contra sales account. The credit to Allowance for Sales Returns and Allowances increases a contra account to

Accounts Receivable and thereby reduces total assets. The entry is necessary to properly match sales returns and allowances with the period in which the related sales revenue was reported. At the end of a period, an estimate is made regarding the sales made during the last few weeks of that period that may yet be subject to refunds (by way of reductions of the balances of accounts receivable) during the beginning weeks of the subsequent accounting period. (Solution = a.)

Question

9. A company has a large amount of accounts receivable and a ready need for cash. The company may accelerate the receipt of cash from customers' accounts receivable through:

	Factoring	Assignment
a.	Yes	Yes
b.	Yes	No
c.	No	Yes
d.	No	No

EXPLANATION: The company can transfer accounts receivable to a third party for cash by the assignment or factoring (sale) of the accounts receivable. (Solution = a.)

Question

10. The accounts receivable turnover ratio measures the:
   a. number of times the average balance of accounts receivable is collected during the period.
   b. percentage of accounts receivable turnover over to a collection agency during the period.
   c. percentage of accounts receivable arising during certain seasons.
   d. number of times the average balance of inventory is sold during the period.

EXPLANATION: Write down the components of the accounts receivable turnover ratio. Think about why it is calculated. The calculation is as follows:

$$\text{Accounts Receivable Turnover Ratio} = \frac{\text{Net Sales}}{\text{Average trade receivables (net)}}$$

Because cash sales do not go through the Accounts Receivable account, only net credit sales belong in the numerator; however, very often that information is not available. The accounts receivable ratio measures the number of times, on average, the accounts receivable balance was collected during the period. This ratio is used to assess the liquidity of the receivables. This ratio can be divided into 365 days to obtain the average days to collect accounts receivable. (Solution = a.)

Question

11. The term "outstanding cheques" refers to:
    a. cheques that have been lost in the mail or for some other reason have been misplaced.
    b. depositor cheques which have been processed by the bank but have not yet been recorded by the depositor.
    c. customer cheques which have been returned by the bank because the customer's bank would not honour them.
    d. depositor cheques which have not yet cleared the banking system.

EXPLANATION: There is a time lag between the date a cheque is issued and the date the cheque clears the banking system. During the time between these two dates, the cheques are referred to as "outstanding cheques". Cheques written by the enterprise but not mailed until **after** the balance sheet date should not be included with outstanding cheques. Rather, they should be added back to the cash balance and reported as accounts payable. (Solution = d.)

Question

12. The following information pertains to Cruiser Co. at December 31, 2008:

Bank statement balance	$20,000
Chequebook balance	28,200
Deposit in transit	10,000
Outstanding cheques	2,000
Bank service charges for December	200

In Cruiser's balance sheet at December 31, 2008, cash should be reported as:
    a. $18,000.
    b. $20,000.
    c. $28,000.
    d. $30,000.

EXPLANATION: When a question relates to data used in a bank reconciliation, you should sketch out the format for a bank reconciliation, put in the information given, and solve for the unknown piece.

Balance per bank statement	$ 20,000
Deposit in transit	10,000
Outstanding cheques	(2,000)
Correct cash balance	$ 28,000
Balance per books	$ 28,200
Bank service charges	(200)
Correct cash balance	$ 28,000

In this particular question, the completion of either the top half or the bottom half of the reconciliation using the bank-to-correct balance method would be enough to solve for the answer requested. (Solution = c.)

Question

13. The following data relate to the bank account of Springfield Cleaners:

Cash balance, September 30, 2008 per bank	$ 10,000
Cash balance, October 31, 2008 per bank	21,500
Cheques paid during October by bank	5,900
Cheques written during October per books	800
Cash balance, October 31, 2008 per books	22,200
Bank service charges for October, not recorded on books	100
Deposits per books for October	19,000

The amount of deposits recorded by the bank in October is:

a. $19,000.
b. $17,500.
c. $11,500.
d. $5,700.

EXPLANATION: Think about how deposits recorded by the bank affect the cash balance per bank and other items that cause that balance to change. Plug in the figures given to solve for the unknown.

Balance per bank, September 30	$ 10,000
Deposits per bank during October	X
Bank credit memoranda	0
Cheques paid by bank during October	(5,900)
Bank service charge for October and other bank debit memoranda	(100)
Balance per bank, October 31	$ 21,500

Solving for X:

$10,000 + X – $5,900 – $100 = $21,500
X = $21,500 – $10,000 + $5,900 + $100
X = $17,500 (Solution = b.)

Question

14. The following information pertains to Kimbell Corporation at December 31, 2008:

Balance per bank	$ 10,000
Deposit in transit	3,000
Outstanding cheques	8,000
Bank service charges for December	200
Bank erroneously charged Kimbell account for Franklin Co. cheque written for $700. As of Dec. 31, the bank had not corrected this error	700

Kimbell's cash balance per ledger (books) before adjustment at December 31, 2008 is:
a. $14,100.
b. $5,900.
c. $5,500.
d. $4,100.

EXPLANATION: The balance per books (before adjustment) can easily be calculated by putting the data into the format for a bank reconciliation. Either format (balance per bank to balance per books or balance per bank to correct balance) can be used. Each approach is illustrated.

Balance per bank statement	$ 10,000
Deposit in transit	3,000
Outstanding cheques	(8,000)
Bank service charges	200
Bank error in charge for cheque	700
Balance per ledger	$ 5,900

Balance per bank statement	$ 10,000
Deposit in transit	3,000
Outstanding cheques	(8,000)
Bank error in charge for cheque	700
Correct cash balance	$ 5,700

Balance per books (ledger)	$ X
Bank service charge	(200)
Correct cash balance	$ 5,700

X = $5,900 (Solution = b.)

Case Study

Dundee Developments

Dixie Dundee, the V.P. of Finance of Dundee Developments (DD) stared at the draft financial statements for the November month-end. The financial statements looked as though the company was facing a liquidity crisis. There were current liabilities that had to be paid, as well as a large repayment of principal on one of the loans. Unless there were some drastic changes, the year-end financial statements would look even worse.

Dixie was not worried about getting the funds. They were already negotiating to renew the loan in question, although the bank was nowhere near finalizing the deal and would not be before the year-end statements were issued. However, unless something very disastrous happened, the loan would go through and DD would get the funds.

Dixie's prime concern was how the market would react to the perceived liquidity problem as presented in the financial statements and whether the reaction would cause the stock prices to tumble. DD was also in the process of making a new share offering in order to finance an expansion of the company into the United States. The deal was not worth doing unless a certain share price could be obtained.

In this regard, DD was considering entering a deal to transfer certain notes receivable to EE Ltd. (EE). The notes were long-term and had always provided DD with a much needed steady stream of cash from the interest. The terms were as follows:

- DD would transfer the notes to EE on a non-recourse basis for the fair value of the notes less a small discount since the notes were considered fully collectible.
- DD guaranteed a rate of return of 12% on the notes to EE. That is, if market rates went down, DD would pay to EE the difference between the variable interest rate paid to EE under the note and 12%. Conversely, if market rates went up, EE would pay the difference to DD.
- DD also retained the right to repurchase the notes at the book value plus a small premium.
- The debtor owing the money will make payments directly to EE.

The deal was consummated within a few days, resulting in DD obtaining a significant inflow of cash. At year-end, market interest rates had declined significantly.

REQUIRED:
Discuss the accounting and reporting issues, and advise Dixie as to how they affect the year-end financial statements.

Suggested Approach to Case Study

Overview

The V.P. of Finance is concerned that the financial statements portray the company in a negative light. This is troubling since this could cause stock prices to fall at a time when the company needs higher stock prices to maximize proceeds from an impending stock issue. Stakeholders of the statements would include the bank, especially due to the loan renewal, and potential investors. Both would want information that is realistic and perhaps even conservative. GAAP is a constraint since the shares are publicly traded.

Assuming that you work for DD, the financial reporting objective would be to downplay the apparent liquidity problem as it appears in the financial statements. If your role is that of the auditors, the needs of the users would play a more important role. Since the company plans to use the statements for refinancing, the engagement would be high risk and you would advise Dixie along more conservative lines. That is, if there are liquidity problems, this is information that would affect the users and, therefore, it should be apparent in the financial statements, regardless of what Dixie wants. Full disclosure of complex transactions would also be important.

Analysis and Recommendations

The issues are as follows:

- How to account for the transfer of the notes.
- How to present the loan that is currently due.

Notes Receivable

- Should the transfer of the notes be treated as a disposition or merely a financing?

The resolution would appear to revolve around whether the risks and rewards of owning the notes have passed to EE, as well as whether control has been surrendered.

Firstly, the financial reporting implications will be reviewed. If it is seen as a bona fide transfer, the long-term receivables will be removed from the financial statements at a small loss, and replaced with cash. This would greatly enhance the perceived liquidity position.

Cash
Loss
        Notes receivable

If it is perceived as a financing, the transaction would increase liabilities (questionable whether this would be current or long-term) and cash. The discount would be deferred and amortized. If it was booked as long-term liabilities, this would also improve the appearance of the statements; although if booked as current liabilities, it would be of no help.

Cash
Deferred discount
        Current or non-current liability

In order to determine whether this is a sale or borrowing, Accounting Guideline 12 (*CICA Handbook*) looks at three criteria:

1. Are the assets isolated from the transferor?
   In this case EE is a separate legal entity and is also an arm's-length party. Therefore the criterion is met.

2. Does EE have the right to pledge or sell the receivables?
   Yes, since legal title to the receivables has passed.

3. Does DD maintain control through any repurchase agreements?
   In this case, there is a repurchase agreement in place; i.e., DD has the right to repurchase. On the one hand, the agreement does not obligate the transferor to reacquire the assets and therefore it may be concluded

that DD has transferred the risks of ownership. However, the right to reacquire means that they have retained some of the rewards of ownership.

DD notes that it values the "steady stream of income." This might be an inducement for DD to exercise this right. Also, DD does not really need the cash if the loan and equity financing go through, as they likely will. It should be acknowledged that the transaction appears to have been entered into for its short-term, window-dressing value only.

DD has guaranteed a certain rate of return to EE and, therefore, is at risk for fluctuations in interest rates.

It might be acceptable to argue that the arrangement is a financing arrangement but that the intent is not to repurchase the notes until after the upcoming year. This would result in a long-term liability and would still enhance the financial statement picture. However, declining interest rates will be an inducement to repurchase in the shorter run.

Given the intent, treat the transaction as financing, especially since it is not clearly evident that the risk and rewards have passed. Treat it as a long-term liability since this is justifiable under GAAP. It also helps to achieve the (likely) financial reporting objective (although this is secondary to GAAP compliance). Full disclosure of the arrangement will be required due to the significance of the transaction and due to the interest guarantee which will affect cash flows.

Loan Refinancing

The loan will have to be classified as current even though there is intent to refinance, since the refinancing is not in place by the financial statement issue date. Consider disclosing the intent to refinance in the notes to the financial statements since the negotiations are in progress, and since this will affect future cash flows.

Inventory

Chapter 8

Overview

In accounting, the term inventory refers to a stock of goods held for sale in the ordinary course of business or goods that will be used or consumed in the production of goods to be sold. A number of questions regarding inventory are addressed in this chapter; these include: (1) What goods should be included in inventory? (2) What costs should be included in inventory cost? (3) What cost flow assumption should be used? (4) How will the selection of a particular cost flow assumption affect the income statement and balance sheet? (5) How do inventory errors affect the financial statements?

Sometimes a business is faced with the situation where impairments in the value of its inventory are so great relative to selling prices that items cannot be sold at a normal profit. In compliance with conservatism, any impairments in value should be recognized in the current period and the inventory should be reported at the lower of cost and net realizable value on the balance sheet. By following this rule, the impairment is recognized in the period in which it occurs, rather than in the later period of disposal of the inventory. Accounting for declines in inventory value, presentation, and valuation of inventories are also discussed in this chapter.

Finally, there are times when a business may need to estimate the cost of inventory on hand at a certain date. Two estimation techniques—the gross profit and the retail method of inventory estimation—are discussed in this chapter. Although the conventional retail method yields results which are to approximate a lower of average cost and market valuation for the inventory, the retail method also can be used to approximate FIFO cost or weighted-average cost. Markups and markdowns are also discussed in relation to the retail method in this chapter.

Study Steps

Understanding the Importance of Inventory in Business and Inventory Related Transactions

Inventory defined

Inventory is defined in S. 3031.06 as: "assets held for sale in the ordinary course of business; in the process of production for such sale; or in the form of materials or supplies to be consumed in the production process or in the rendering of services". Therefore, it is comprised of either goods held for resale or materials that will be used to produce goods for sale, i.e., raw materials. It also includes partially completed goods that will eventually be sold, i.e., work in process. The business objective is that the finished product will be sold, hopefully at a profit. Inventory differs from fixed assets in that fixed assets are used to produce profits whereas inventory is sold to produce profits.

It can be difficult at times to distinguish between inventory and fixed assets, professional judgement may be required. This is discussed further in Chapter 10.

TIP! Inventory includes items that will eventually be sold for profits and/or to recover costs.

Inventory is one of the **essential assets** in many businesses since the manufacture and sale of inventory is often the primary source of income. Inventory has a dual use. Not only will it be sold to generate profits, it may also be used as collateral to secure bank loans.

TIP! Because inventory affects the calculation of the current ratio, and because it is often used to secure loans, the amount of inventory included and the value are very important.

Ownership

Shipping terms

As previously mentioned, inventory in a manufacturing company consists of raw materials, work in process, and finished goods. Sometimes the raw materials may not have actually made it into the warehouse (i.e., they may be sitting on the loading dock, in a railway car, or even in a truck **in transit**). Are these goods part of the company's inventory? Analysis of this issue revolves around whether the **risks and rewards** of ownership have passed to the company buying the inventory. Sometimes this may be determined by looking at the **shipping terms**. The same applies to finished goods being shipped by the company.

If the goods are sent **f.o.b. shipping point** (free on board), the company selling the goods takes responsibility and retains the ownership only until the goods are shipped. After that, the purchaser obtains ownership. Likewise, if the terms are **f.o.b. destination**, the company selling the goods retains ownership until the

Shipping terms

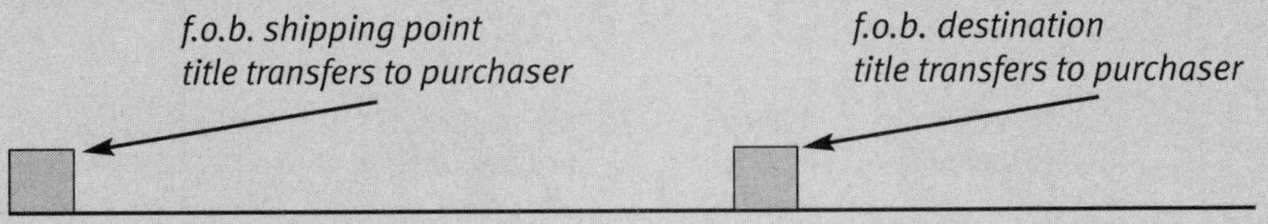

goods reach the destination. For this reason, the goods should be insured by the company selling them, up until they reach their destination.

TIP!

Shipping terms are very important in identifying whether an asset should be recorded on the balance sheet since risks and rewards stay with the seller up to the point designated in the shipping terms.

Inventory on consignment

See discussion of business arrangements under consignment sales in Chapter 6 of the Study Guide.

Parking transactions/product financing arrangements

These arrangements are usually characterized by a sale of inventory plus an agreement to buy the inventory back over a future period of time. This may be seen as two separate transactions, i.e., a sale and then a future purchase, or as one transaction, i.e., a financing transaction.

Professional judgment should be used to determine whether a real sale has occurred or whether the inventory still, in substance, belongs to the company.

Sales involving uncertainty

See also the comments under revenue recognition in Chapter 6 of the Study Guide. Inventory remains on the books of the company when there is major uncertainty as to collection or measurement.

Understanding How Inventory Issues Fit into the Financial Reporting Model and Conceptual Framework—Analysis and Critical Thinking

The key issues in this area are:

- **which items** to include in inventory (e.g., goods in transit, consignment items)—**recognition**
- **which costs** to include (e.g., freight, factory overhead, labour)—**measurement/classification costing**

Valuation of inventories: cost flow methods, relevant criteria, definitions, and issues

TIP! Business perspective: Inventory is an essential asset since it is included in current assets, it is essential that it is properly reported and valued.

	How it relates to inventory	**Relevant criteria/ definitions**	**Topic specific analysis—how it should be**	**What makes the analysis challenging—how it is**
Recognition	when to recognize or de-recognize inventory	• overall, when **R&R** have passed • consider shipping terms **fob shipping point vs fob destination**	• normally when received/shipped **(possession)** and **legal title**	• complicated by complex selling terms where company may have either legal title or possession but not both
		• for complex transactions **economic substance**	• is it a real sale/purchase or a financing type of transaction?	• complex transactions, such as parking transactions where buy back—difficult to determine who has R&R of inventory
Measurement	what to include as inventory cost (partly classification issue)	• **laid down cost** plus **direct costs** and **applicable share of overhead—based on normal production levels**	• include any cost incurred to get the inventory to the company and any further costs to get it ready for sale	• **standard costs** may be used if not significantly different from actual cost • PJ needed in deciding how much overhead to allocate • costs from abnormal situations generally not included
	what cost flow method to use	• **FIFO, LIFO, weighted average, specific ID** • fairest **matching of** costs with revenues	• the key is to match costs with revenues (actual inventory flow need not be the determining factor	• the method chosen may have a significant impact on net income and, therefore, potential for a bias exists
Presentation/ Disclosure	note disclosure	• **full disclosure**	• disclose basis of valuation and cost flow method since choice	

Becoming Proficient in Using Inventory Costing and Valuation Methods

Determining the **cost of inventory** would be easy if there were only a few high-priced items. However, inventory often consists of a multitude of different products of varying values which were purchased at different times and at different prices. Even identical products that were purchased at different times may have different prices.

If all the items were purchased at different prices but are identical and only half were sold, which items are left? Is it the ones that were purchased first, or the most recent purchases? An assumption must be made about the inventory flow (i.e., which items were sold first). The most common assumption is **FIFO (first-in, first-out)**. FIFO probably reflects reality, since most people would want to sell the oldest inventory first.

The LIFO method is no longer acceptable in Canadian GAAP.

Keeping track of quantities—periodic versus perpetual inventory methods

The **perpetual method** of inventory involves keeping track of each inventory item and noting individual purchases and sales when they are made. Perpetual inventory records are like a subledger that gives details about the balance of inventory in the general ledger (like the accounts receivable subledger). It requires extra bookkeeping but allows the company to see the exact number of items on hand for each inventory item at any point in time. Also, like the accounts receivable subledger, it allows the company to verify the control account for inventory in the general ledger.

Under the **periodic method**, no such subledger is kept. The inventory account in the general ledger is verified only when an inventory count is performed (usually annually).

Under both methods, physical inventory must be taken. With a perpetual system, specific types of inventory can be spot checked and compared to the individual perpetual inventory amounts. Whereas with a periodic inventory, a full count must be performed. The perpetual system offers more control over inventory; however, it may be time consuming and costly. With more businesses using computers, this factor is becoming less and less of an issue.

The inventory equation

Cost of goods sold is often determined by the following equation:

Cost of goods sold = opening inventory + purchases – closing inventory

Cost of goods sold is a residual figure since opening inventory and purchases are known in a periodic system, and since closing inventory is usually determined by a physical count. It is important to acknowledge the relationship between these components and realize that an error in one will affect another of the components.

Becoming Proficient in Applying the Retail Method and Gross Profit Methods

Gross profit method

The **gross profit method** of determining ending inventory is used to **estimate** inventory where perpetual records are not kept and where a count is not practical. Inventory must be counted at least annually. However, if inventory values are needed more frequently, as they usually are (e.g., for interim reporting), the gross profit method may be used to estimate the number. Ending inventory would be calculated as follows under the gross profit method.

Ending Inventory = beginning inventory + purchases – cost of sales

(+ sales X gross profit %) → cost of sales

The **gross profit percentage** must be determined. This is done by looking at gross profit divided by sales from **prior periods** or from budgets. Many companies use this to estimate cost of sales and ending inventory for interim reporting.

TIP! The gross profit method is used to estimate CGS and ending inventory where no inventory count is taken.

TIP! It often uses a normalized historic gross profit to estimate CGS and ending inventory and, therefore, it tends to smooth seasonal and quarterly fluctuations and to emphasize past trends rather than existing and future trends.

Retail sales method

The **retail inventory method** is often used by retailers to value inventory where there is high volume/low unit cost. The method uses the same calculation as the gross profit method; however, it uses retail value (i.e., sales price) instead of cost to track and value inventory. Where the gross profit method is used to get an estimate of CGS and inventory when no inventory count is performed, the retail method is used for this and to estimate year-end inventory **dollar** values even when a count is performed.

The inventory count is valued using retail value, not cost, as is usually the norm. Retail value or sales price is easier to obtain. The ending inventory is then **converted back to cost** by applying a percentage that represents cost of sales divided by sales. Normally the following method is used:

Retail Method

	@ retail		@cost		
Opening inventory	actual		actual		
plus: purchases	actual		actual		
Goods available for sale	total		total		calculate
Less: sales	actual (1)				ratio of cost to retail
Ending inventory	total	X	ratio	=	ending inventory at cost

(1) from cash/sales register

TIP! The retail method is a way of tracking costs using retail or sales prices. Where a company has a more sophisticated computerized system, the need for the retail method diminishes.

TIP! Both the gross method and the retail method are estimation techniques that are used in the absence of better information. (i.e., cost /benefit)

Tips on Chapter Topics

TIP! The cost of an inventory item includes all costs necessary to acquire the item and bring it to the location and condition for its intended use. This cost would include the item's purchase price, transportation-in, and any special handling charges. However, transportation-out is **not** included in the cost of inventory; it is classified as a selling expense on the income statement for the period in which the expense was incurred.

TIP! The transportation terms designate the point at which title passes. F.o.b. shipping point (or seller) means the title passes to the buyer when it leaves the seller's dock. F.o.b. destination (or buyer) means the title passes to the buyer when it arrives at the buyer's dock. Assuming that Palmer Company in Richmond Hill, Ontario, sells to Woods in St. Catharines, Ontario, the following shows synonymous terms:

f.o.b. shipping point	**f.o.b. destination**
or f.o.b. seller	or f.o.b. buyer
or f.o.b. Richmond Hill, Ontario	or f.o.b. St. Catharines, Ontario

TIP! FIFO (first-in, first-out) means the cost of the first items put into inventory are used to price the first items out to cost of goods sold. Thus, the earliest acquisition prices are used to price cost of goods sold for the period, and the latest (most current) acquisition prices are used to price items on the ending inventory.

TIP! When working a problem which requires the calculation of either ending inventory or cost of goods sold, remember that the total of the ending inventory (EI) and the cost of goods sold (COGS) should equal the total cost of goods available for sale

(COGAS) during the period (beginning inventory [BI] plus the net cost of purchases), i.e., BI + Purchases = COGAS - EI = COGS.

TIP! Sales revenue represents the **selling prices** of goods sold, whereas cost of goods sold expense represents the **cost price** of items sold.

TIP! An understatement in ending inventory of year 1 will cause an understatement in net income for year 1 and an overstatement in net income for year 2. Thus, retained earnings and working capital at the end of year 1 are understated. However, assuming no more errors are committed at the end of year 2, retained earnings and working capital are not affected at the end of year 2.

TIP! The **net realizable value of inventory** is the net amount of cash to ultimately be received from the sale of the inventory. Thus, the net realizable value of inventory is the estimated selling price in the ordinary course of business, less reasonably predictable future costs of completion and disposal. This is the term most commonly used in Canada. **Net realizable value less a normal** profit margin is determined by subtracting the normal profit margin from the net realizable value of inventory.

Ex.	Inventory–Sales Value	$ 1, 000
	Less: estimated cost of completion and disposal	225
	Net Realizable Value	$ 775
	Less: allowance for normal profit margin (10%)	100
	Net Realizable Value less normal profit margin	$ 675

TIP! The historical cost principle is abandoned when the asset's future utility (revenue producing ability) is no longer greater than its original cost.

TIP! To apply the lower cost and market rule:

(a) determine the cost using an acceptable historical cost flow
(b) determine the net realizable value to be used
(c) compare the cost with the net realizable value

The lower of cost and net realizable value figure is then used for inventory valuation.

TIP! If the utility of an inventory item declines prior to the period of sale (disposal), that loss of utility should be recognized in the period of decline rather than the period of disposal. Thus, if an inventory item has become obsolete, the amount of write down determined by the above rule should be recognized as a loss in the period of the decline in utility.

TIP! The lower of cost and net realizable value rule can be applied on an item-by-item basis, a category basis, or a total inventory basis.

TIP! **Gross profit** is synonymous with **gross margin**.

TIP! The gross profit percentage (expressed as a percentage of selling price) and the cost of goods sold percentage (also expressed as a percentage of selling price) are complements; that is, their sum is 100%. When the gross profit method of inventory estimation is used and the gross profit is expressed in terms of cost, the gross profit must first be expressed in terms of selling price before you can proceed with the calculations. One method of conversion is to memorize and use the following formula:

$$\text{Gross margin on selling price} = \frac{\text{Percentage markup on cost}}{100\% + \text{Percentage markup on cost}}$$

Another approach to deriving this formula is shown below. It uses the familiar formula:

Sales (S) - Cost of Goods Sold (CGS) = Gross Profit (GP).

Example: If GP = 25% of cost, then cost of goods sold is 100%.
Putting this much information into our formula above: S - 100% = 25%.
Therefore S = 125%.
Expressing GP as a percentage of S we get: 25% ÷ 125% = 20%.
Thus, gross profit = 20% sales.

Exercise 8-1

PURPOSE: This exercise will enable you to practice identifying the effects of inventory errors on the financial statements.

The net income per books of Wacky Wicks Company was determined without knowledge of the errors indicated.

Year	Net Income Per Books	Error in Ending Inventory	
2007	$ 150,000	Overstated	$ 9,000
2008	156,000	Overstated	21,000
2009	162,000	Understated	33,000
2010	168,000	No error	

Instructions

Calculate the correct net income figure for each of the four years after taking into account the inventory errors.

Solution to Exercise 8-1

Year	Net Income Per Books	Add Over-statement Jan. 1	Deduct Under-statement Jan. 1	Deduct Over-statement Dec. 31	Add Under-statement Dec. 31	Corrected Net Income
2007	$ 150,000			$ 9,000		$ 141,000
2008	156,000	$ 9,000		21,000		144,000
2009	162,000	21,000			$ 33,000	216,000
2010	168,000		$ 33,000			135,000

EXPLANATION: When more than one error affects a given year (such as in 2008), analyze each error separately then combine the effects of each analysis to get the net impact of the errors. The beginning inventory for 2008 (ending inventory for 2007) was overstated by $9,000. Therefore, cost of goods sold was overstated by $9,000, and net income for 2008 was understated by $9,000. The ending inventory for 2008 was overstated by $21,000. Therefore, cost of goods sold was understated, and net income for 2008 was overstated by $21,000. An understatement in net income of $9,000 and an overstatement of $21,000 in 2008 led to an overstatement of $12,000 for the net income figure reported for 2008. This overstatement of $12,000, combined with the $156,000 amount reported, yields a corrected net income figure of $144,000 for 2008.

Another way of analyzing the effects of an individual error is illustrated below for the $21,000 overstatement of inventory at the end of 2008.

		Effect on 2008		Effect on 2009	
	Beginning inventory			Overstated	$21,000
+	Cost of goods purchased				
=	Cost of goods available for sale			Overstated	21,000
–	Ending inventory	Overstated	$21,000		
=	Cost of goods sold	Understated	21,000	Overstated	21,000
	Sales				
–	Cost of goods sold	Understated	21,000	Overstated	21,000
=	Gross profit	Overstated	21,000	Understated	21,000
–	Operating expenses				
=	Net income	Overstated	21,000	Understated	21,000

Thus, the previously calculated net income figure for 2008 must be reduced by $21,000 to correct for this error. Also, the net income figure for 2009 must be increased by $21,000 to correct for the same error.

TIP! The ending inventory for year 1 is the beginning inventory for year 2. Thus, when the ending inventory for year 1 is overstated, it will cause an overstatement in the net income for year 1 and an understatement in net income for year 2 for the same amount. This error will cause retained earnings at the end of year 1 to be overstated because net income for year 1 (which is overstated) is closed into retained earnings. The balance of retained earnings at the end of year 2 will be unaffected by this error because the net income for year 2 (which is understated by the same amount as the overstatement in retained earnings at the end of year 1) is closed into retained earnings; the error at this point counterbalances. Working capital at the end of year 1 is overstated (because inventory is a current asset), but working capital at the end of year 2 is unaffected because the inventory figure at the end of year 2 is determined by a physical inventory counting and pricing procedure. No new error in this process is assumed unless otherwise indicated.

Exercise 8-2

PURPOSE: This exercise reviews the characteristics and the effects of using various pricing methods to determine inventory costs.

Instructions

Answer each of the following questions by inserting one of these abbreviations in the space provided:

SI (specific identification) FIFO (first-in, first-out)
WA (weighted average)

_________ 1. Which inventory cost method yields the most realistic amount for inventory, compared to replacement cost, on the balance sheet?

_________ 2. Which method results in the most exact ending inventory valuation when inventory items of the same type are not homogenous?

_________ 3. Which method is based on the assumption that inventory flow is "mixed" and therefore "mixes" all acquisition prices?

_________ 4. During a period of **rising prices**, which method yields the lowest cost of goods sold figure?

During a period of **declining prices**, which method yields the:

_________ 5. lowest net income figure?

_________ 6. lowest amount for inventory on the balance sheet?

_________ 7. lowest owners' equity figure?

_________ 8. best cash flow?

Solution to Exercise 8-2

1. FIFO	4. FIFO	7. FIFO
2. SI	5. FIFO	8. FIFO
3. WA	6. FIFO	

APPROACH: Write down a description of specific identification, weighted average and FIFO cost flow assumptions. Note the relative effects of these methods on the income statement and the balance sheet in a period of rising prices.

TIP! **Inventory pricing method** is a synonymous term for **inventory costing method.**

TIP! **FIFO (first-in, first-out)** means the cost of the first items put into inventory are used to price the first items out to cost of goods sold. Thus, the earliest acquisition prices are used to price cost of goods sold for the period, and the latest (most current) acquisition prices are used to price items in the ending inventory.

TIP!

In a period of rising prices:

Method	COGS	Net Income	Ending Inventory
FIFO	Low	High	High
W/A	Always	In	Between

Illustration 8-1

Perpetual vs. Periodic Inventory Systems

Features of a Perpetual System	Features of a Periodic System
1. Purchases of merchandise for resale are debited to Inventory rather than to Purchases.	1. Purchases of merchandise for resale are debited to Purchases.
2. The Freight-in, Purchase Returns and Allowances, and Purchase Discounts are recorded in Inventory rather than in separate accounts.	2. Freight-in, Purchase Returns and Allowances, and Purchase Discounts accounts are separate accounts which are used to record information about inventory acquisitions during the accounting period.
3. Cost of goods sold is recognized for each sale by debiting the account, Cost of Goods Sold, and crediting Inventory.	3. Cost of goods sold is recognized only at the end of the accounting period when the (1) ending inventory amount (determined by physical count, pricing, and extensions) is recorded in the Inventory account, (2) the Purchases, Freight-in, Purchase Returns and Allowances, and Purchase Discounts account balances are closed to the Income Summary account, and (3) the beginning inventory amount is transferred from the Inventory account to the Income Summary account.
4. Inventory is a control account that is supported by a subsidiary ledger of individual inventory records. The subsidiary records show the quantity and cost of each type of inventory on hand. At any point during the accounting period (assuming all postings are up to date), the balance of the Inventory account reflects the cost of the items that should be on hand at that point in time.	4. There is no subsidiary ledger for inventory. All during the accounting period, the Inventory account reflects the cost of the inventory items on hand at the beginning of the period (beginning inventory). The Inventory account is **not** updated for acquisitions and withdrawals of inventory during the period; it is updated only at the end of the period to reflect the cost of the items on hand at the balance sheet date.

Illustration 8-1 (Continued)
Perpetual vs. Periodic Inventory Systems

EXAMPLE					
PERPETUAL SYSTEM			**PERIODIC SYSTEM**		
1. There are 8 units in beginning inventory at a cost of $2,000 each.					
The Inventory account shows the inventory on hand at $16,000.			The Inventory account shows the inventory on hand at $16,000.		
2. Purchase 12 items on account at $2,000 each.					
Inventory	24,000		Purchases	24,000	
Accounts Payable		24,000	Accounts Payable		24,000
3. Return one defective item for $2,000 credit.					
Accounts Payable	2,000		Accounts Payable	2,000	
Inventory		2,000	Purchase Returns & Allowances		2,000
4. Sell 15 items on account for $3,000 each.					
Accounts Receivable	45,000		Accounts Receivable	45,000	
Sales		45,000	Sales		45,000
Cost of Goods Sold	30,000				
Inventory		30,000			
5. End of period entries for inventory-related accounts (4 units on hand at $2,000 each).					
No entries are necessary:			Inventory (ending by physical count)	8,000	
The Inventory account shows the ending balance as $8,000 ($16,000 + $24,000 - $2,000 - $30,000)			Purchase Returns & Allowances	2,000	
			Cost of Goods Sold	30,000	
			Purchases		24,000
			Inventory (beginning)		16,000

Exercise 8-3

PURPOSE: This exercise will allow you to practice performing calculations to determine inventory cost under two costing (pricing) methods, using both the periodic and the perpetual systems.

The New Brunswick Toy Company is a multi-product firm. Presented below is information concerning one of their products, Infusion-39:

Date	Transaction	Quantity	Cost
1/1	Beginning inventory	1,000	$12
2/4	Purchase	2,000	18
2/20	Sale	2,500	
4/2	Purchase	3,000	22
11/4	Sale	2,000	

Instructions

Calculate the cost of the ending inventory, assuming New Brunswick Toy uses:
(a) Periodic system, FIFO cost method.
(b) Perpetual system, FIFO cost method.
(c) Periodic system, average cost method.
(d) Perpetual system, moving-average cost method.

Solution to Exercise 8-3

(a) **Periodic-FIFO:**

	Units	
Beginning inventory	1,000	
Purchases (2,000 + 3,000)	5,000	
Units available for sale	6,000	
Sold (2,500 + 2,000)	4,500	
Goods on hand (assumed)	1,500	1,500 units x $22 = $33,000

(b) **Perpetual-FIFO:** Same as periodic: $33,000

TIP! The use of FIFO with a perpetual system always yields the same results as the use of FIFO with a periodic system.

(c) **Periodic-average:**

1,000 x $12	=	$ 12,000			
2,000 x $18	=	36,000			
3,000 x $22	=	66,000			1,500 Units
6,000		$114,000	÷	6,000 = $19 each	x $19
					$28,500

(d) **Perpetual-average:**

Date	Purchased	Sold	Balance
1/1			1,000 x $12 = $12,000
2/4	2,000 x $18 = $36,000		3,000 x $16[a] = $48,000
2/20		2,500 x $16 = $40,000	500 x $16 = $ 8,000
4/2	3,000 x $22 = $66,000		3,500 x $21.14[b] = $73,990
11/4		2,000 x $21.14 = $42,280	1,500 x $21.14 = $31,710

a	1,000 x $12 =	$12,000	b 500 x $16 =	$ 8,000
	2,000 x $18 =	36,000	3,000 x $22 =	66,000
	3,000	$48,000	3,500	$74,000

$48,000 ÷ 3,000 = $16.00 $74,000 ÷ 3,500 = $21.14

TIP!

When using the average method and a perpetual system, a new average unit cost must be calculated only after each new purchase; a sale will **not** affect the average unit cost. The average method applied to a perpetual system is often called the **moving-average** method.

Exercise 8-4

PURPOSE: This exercise will enable you to practice determining how to handle goods in transit and other items necessary for proper inventory valuation.

Jennifer Laudermilch Company, a supplier of artworks, provided the following information from its account records for the year ended December 31, 2008.

Inventory at December 31, 2008 (at cost, based on a physical count of goods in Laudermilch's warehouse on 12/31/08)	$ 820,000
Accounts payable at December 31, 2008	460,000
Net sales (sales less sales returns)	7,000,000

Additional information is as follows:

1. Laudermilch received goods costing $32,000 on January 2, 2009. The goods had been shipped f.o.b. shipping point on December 27, 2008, by Geoffrey Harrill Company.
2. Laudermilch received goods costing $41,000 on January 4, 2009. The goods had been shipped f.o.b. destination on December 28, 2008 by Nanula Company.
3. Laudermilch sold goods costing $18,000 to O'Toole Company on December 29, 2008. The goods were picked up by the common carrier on that same date and shipped f.o.b. shipping point. They were expected to arrive at the buyer's business as early as January 3, 2009. An invoice for $29,000 was recorded and mailed on December 29.

4. Laudermilch sold goods costing $30,000 to Matheson Company on December 31, 2008. The goods were picked up by the common carrier on that same date and shipped f.o.b. destination. They were expected to arrive at the buyer's store as early as January 2, 2009. These goods were billed to the customer for $45,000 on December 31 and were not included in the physical count at December 31, 2008.
5. Laudermilch is the consignor for a collection of prints. The prints are hanging in the showroom of The Dizzy Decorator. They cost Laudermilch $62,000 and are priced to sell at $95,000. They were not included in the physical count.
6. Laudermilch is the consignee for some goods from Asian Collectibles. They cost the consignor $50,000 and are priced to sell for $76,000 with Laudermilch to get a commission of 10%. They were included in the ending inventory at the selling price.
7. Included in the physical count were goods billed to a customer f.o.b. shipping point on December 31, 2008. These items had a cost of $24,000 and were billed at $38,000. The shipment was on Laudermilch's loading dock waiting to be picked up by the common carrier and was included in the physical count at December 31, 2008.
8. Goods received from a vendor on December 26, 2008 were included in the physical count. However, the related $44,000 vendor invoice was not included in accounts payable at December 31, 2008 because the accounts payable copy of the receiving report was lost. These goods are marked to sell for $65,000.

Instructions

Using the format shown below, prepare a schedule of adjustments as of December 31, 2008 (the company's year end and physical inventory count date), to the initial amounts per Laudermilch's accounting records. Show separately the effect, if any, of each of the eight transactions on the December 31, 2008 amounts. If the transactions would have no effect on the initial amount shown, state NONE.

Adjustments increase (or decrease)	**Inventory**	**Accounts Payable**	**Net Sales**
Initial Amounts	$ 820,000	$ 460,000	$ 7,000,000
1.			
2.			
3.			
4.			
5.			
6.			
7.			
8.			
Total Adjustments	$	$	$
Adjusted Amounts	$	$	$

Solution to Exercise 8-4

Adjustments increase (or decrease)	Inventory	Accounts Payable	Net Sales
Initial Amounts	$ 820,000	$ 460,000	$ 7,000,000
1.	32,000	32,000	None
2.	None	None	None
3.	None	None	None
4.	30,000	None	(45,000)
5.	62,000	None	None
6.	(76,000)	None	None
7.	None	None	(38,000)
8.	None	44,000	None
Total Adjustments	48,000	76,000	(83,000)
Adjusted Amounts	$ 868,000	$ 536,000	$6,917,000

EXPLANATION:

1. When the terms of the purchase are f.o.b. shipping point, ownership of the goods passes to the buyer when the public carrier accepts the goods from the seller. Therefore, title passed to Laudermilch on December 27, 2008 but the goods were not physically present to be included in the physical count at December 31, 2008.
2. These goods would not have been included in the physical count at December 31, 2008 and are not to be included in the inventory at that date. Title did not pass to Laudermilch until the goods were received on January 4, 2009.
3. With shipping terms of f.o.b. shipping point, title passed to the customer (O'Toole) when the goods were picked up by the common carrier on December 29, 2008. Therefore, the goods are properly excluded from the ending inventory, and the sale has been properly recorded in 2008.
4. With shipping terms of f.o.b. destination, title did not pass to Matheson (the buyer) until the goods were received by the buyer, which had to be sometime in 2009. Therefore, the sale was improperly recorded in 2008. The goods were not on the premises late December 31, 2008 so were excluded from the physical count. However, their cost should be included in ending inventory to be reported on the balance sheet.
5. Under a consignment arrangement, the holder of the goods (called the **consignee**) does not own the goods. Ownership remains with the shipper of the goods (called the **consignor**) until the goods are sold to a customer. Laudermilch, the consignor, should include merchandise held by the consignee as part of its inventory. The goods were not in Laudermilch's warehouse when the physical count was taken; however, they should be included as part of the inventory balance at December 31, 2008.
6. Laudermilch does not own the goods which it holds on consignment. Therefore, these goods should be excluded from its inventory; they should be included in the inventory of Asian Collectibles.

7. The $24,000 of goods on the loading dock were properly included in the physical count because they had not been released to the common carrier by the end of the day, December 31, 2008. However, the sale was improperly recorded; therefore, an adjustment is needed to reduce sales by the billing price of $38,000.
8. The $44,000 of goods received on December 26, 2008 were properly included in the physical count of inventory; $44,000 must be added to accounts payable since the invoice was not included in the December 31, 2008 accounts payable balance.

Exercise 8-5

PURPOSE: The following exercise will help you in determining what items are inventoriable costs.

Rebelde Corporation manufactures a single product. Assume the following data for the 2009 year:

Variable Cost per unit:	
Selling and administrative	$3
Production cost	$5
Fixed Cost in total:	
Selling and administrative	$16,000
Production cost	$32,000

During the period, 8,000 units were produced and 7,800 units were sold (assume beginning inventory is zero). Normal capacity is 8,000 units.

Instructions

(a) Determine the inventoriable cost per unit.
(b) Determine the ending inventory value.
(c) Determine the cost of goods sold.

Solution to Exercise 8-5

(a) Cost per unit	
Variable production cost	$3
Fixed production cost	$4 ($32,000/8,000 units)
Total inventoriable cost	$7

Manufacturing overhead is allocated based on normal production levels. The selling and administration are not inventoriable costs. They would be expensed in the period.

(b) Ending inventory
200 units x inventory cost $1,400

The ending inventory is 200 units (8,000 produced – 7,800 units sold)

(c) Cost of Goods Sold	
Beginning Inventory	$ 0
Add: current production	$56,000
Cost of Goods Available for Sale	$56,000
Less: Ending Inventory (from b)	1,400
Cost of Goods Sold	$54,600

Proof: COGS = 7,800 units sold x $7 = 54,600

Exercise 8-6

PURPOSE: This exercise reviews the steps involved in the determination of the lower of cost and net realizable value for inventory.

The Richard G. Long Company handles 10 different inventory items. The normal profit on each item is 25% of the selling price.

Instructions

From the information below, complete the blanks to calculate the value to be used for the inventory figure for financial statements if the lower of cost and net realizable value rule is applied to individual items. (Use the lowest value in each separate case to determine net realizable value.)

		Per Unit								
Item	No. of Units on Hand	Cost	Replacement Cost	Expected Selling Price	Expected Cost to Sell	NRV	NRV less profit margin	Market	LCM	Item Total
1	100	$7.00	$ 7.50	$ 10.00	$ 1.00					
2	10	6.00	6.25	10.00	1.00					
3	50	5.75	9.25	10.00	1.00					
4	10	9.50	9.25	10.00	1.00					
5	20	5.00	6.25	10.00	1.00					
6	100	8.00	7.25	10.00	1.00					
7	30	12.00	11.50	16.00	1.00					
8	10	10.00	15.50	16.00	1.00					
9	20	14.00	11.00	20.00	2.00					
10	10	12.00	16.00	20.00	2.00					
					Grand Total					

Solution to Exercise 8-6

	Per Unit				# of Units	Item Total
Item	NRV	NRV less profit margin	Market	LCM		
1	$ 9.00	$ 6.50	$ 6.50	$ 6.50	100	$ 650.00
2	9.00	6.50	6.25	6.00	10	60.00
3	9.00	6.50	6.50	5.75	50	287.50
4	9.00	6.50	6.50	6.50	10	65.00
5	9.00	6.50	6.25	5.00	20	100.00
6	9.00	6.50	6.50	6.50	100	650.00
7	15.00	11.00	11.00	11.00	30	330.00
8	15.00	11.00	11.00	10.00	10	100.00
9	18.00	13.00	11.00	11.00	20	220.00
10	18.00	13.00	13.00	12.00	10	120.00
				Grand	Total	$2,582.50

EXPLANATION: Write down the two steps involved in determining the lower of cost and net realizable value and perform the steps in order for each of the items:

Step 1: Determine the net realizable value and net realizable value less normal profit margin.

	Item 1	Item 2	Item 3	Item 4
Estimated selling price	$10.00	$10.00	$10.00	$10.00
- Cost to complete and dispose	1.00	1.00	1.00	1.00
= Net realizable value	9.00	9.00	9.00	9.00
- Normal profit margin	2.50 *	2.50	2.50	2.50
= Net realizable value less normal profit margin	$ 6.50	$ 6.50	$ 6.50	$ 6.50

*$10.00 x 25% = $2.50.

Net realizable value	$ 9.00	$ 9.00	$ 9.00	$ 9.00
Net realizable value less normal profit margin	6.50	6.50	6.50	6.50
Replacement cost	7.50	6.25	9.25	9.25
Lowest of these (NRV)	6.50	6.25	6.50	6.50

Step 2: Compare cost with NRV and choose the lower.

Cost	$ 7.00	$ 6.00	$ 5.75	$ 9.50
NRV (from Step 1)	6.50	6.25	6.50	6.50
Lower of cost and NRV	7.00	6.00	5.75	6.50

Net realizable value can be subjective. However, it is considered a more acceptable term than the also somewhat subjective "market".

Exercise 8-7

PURPOSE: This exercise will illustrate the use of the gross profit method of inventory estimation when: (1) gross profit is expressed as a percentage of cost and (2) gross profit is expressed as a percentage of selling price.

Tim McInnes requires an estimate of the cost of goods lost by fire on April 2. Merchandise on hand on January 1 was $38,000. Purchases since January 1 were $72,000; freight-in, $3,400; and purchase returns and allowances, $2,400. Sales totalled $100,000 to April 2. Goods costing $7,700 were left undamaged by the fire; all other goods were destroyed.

Instructions

(a) Calculate the cost of goods destroyed, assuming that the gross profit is 25% of cost.

(b) Calculate the cost of goods destroyed, assuming that the gross profit is 25% of sales.

Solution to Exercise 8-7

(a)

Merchandise on hand, January 1		$ 38,000
Purchases	$ 72,000	
Purchase returns and allowances	(2,400)	
Net purchases	69,600	
Freight-in	3,400	73,000
Total merchandise available for sale		111,000
Estimated cost of goods sold*		(80,000)
Estimated ending inventory on April 2		31,000
Undamaged goods		(7,700)
Estimated fire loss		23,300

*Gross profit = 25% ÷ (100% + 25%) = 20% of sales.
Therefore, cost of goods sold = 80% of sales of $100,000 = $80,000.

(b) Gross profit is 25% of sales.
Therefore, cost of goods sold = 75% of sales of $100,000 = $75,000.

Total merchandise available for sale (as calculated above)	$ 111,000
Estimated cost of goods sold	(75,000)
Estimated ending inventory at April 2	36,000
Undamaged goods	(7,700)
Estimated fire loss	$ 28,300

TIP! It is important to understand that inventory is accounted for in terms of the cost of goods acquired, and the Sales account reflects the **selling prices** of goods that have been sold during the period. Therefore, the profit element must be removed from the sales amount to arrive at the cost of the goods sold.

APPROACH: Use these steps to perform the calculations:

(1) **Calculate the cost of goods available for sale** for the period January 1 through April 2. This is done by combining the cost of inventory on hand at the beginning of the year (January 1) and the net cost of purchases during the period (net purchases plus freight-in).
(2) **Determine the estimated cost of goods sold** during the period. This is done by multiplying the sales figure for the period by the cost of goods sold percentage. The cost of goods sold percentage is 100% minus the gross margin percentage. **Caution**: *The gross margin percentage used here must be stated in terms of selling price*. In part (b) of this exercise, gross profit is given in terms of sales. In part (a), however, you must convert the "25% of cost" to "20% of sales" before the cost of goods sold percentage of 80% can be applied to the sales amount.
(3) **Calculate the estimated inventory on hand at the end of the period** (April 2, date of fire) by subtracting the estimated cost of goods sold (Step 2) from the cost of goods available for sale (Step 1).
(4) **Determine the estimated** loss from fire by deducting the cost of the undamaged goods from the estimated cost of inventory on hand at April 2 (Step 3).

Exercise 8-8

PURPOSE: This exercise illustrates the use of the retail inventory method to value inventory.

The records of Nancy Klintworth's Baubles report the following data for the month of May.

Sales	$ 79,000
Sales returns	1,000
Markups	10,000
Markup cancellations	1,500
Markdowns	9,300
Markdown cancellations	2,800
Freight on purchases	2,400
Purchases (at cost)	48,000
Purchases (at sales price)	88,000
Purchase returns (at cost)	2,000
Purchase returns (at sales price)	3,000
Beginning inventory (at cost)	30,000
Beginning inventory (at sales price)	46,500

Instructions

Calculate the ending inventory by the conventional retail inventory method.

Solution to Exercise 8-8

	Cost		Retail
Beginning inventory	$ 30,000		$ 46,500
Purchases	48,000		88,000
Purchase returns	(2,000)		(3,000)
Freight on purchase	2,400		
Goods available for sale	78,400		131,500
Net markups:			
Markups		$ 10,000	
Markup cancellations		(1,500)	8,500
	78,400		140,000
Net markdowns:			
Markdowns		9,300	
Markdown cancellations		(2,800)	(6,500)
	78,400		133,500
Net sales ($79,000 – $1,000)			(78,000)
Ending inventory, at retail			55,500

Cost-to-retail ratio = $78,400 ÷ $140,000 = 56%
Ending inventory at lower of average cost and market
= 56% x $55,500 = $31,080

EXPLANATION:

Step 1: **Calculate the ending inventory at retail.** This is done by determining the retail value of goods available for sale, adjusting that figure for net markups and net markdowns, and deducting the retail value of goods no longer on hand (sales, estimated theft, etc.).

Step 2: **Calculate the cost-to-retail ratio.** The conventional retail method approximates an average cost amount so both beginning inventory and net purchases information is used in the ratio. The conventional retail method is to approximate a lower of cost and market value so the net markups are included but the net markdowns are excluded from the ratio calculation.

Step 3: **Determine the ending inventory at an approximate lower of average cost and market value.** Apply the appropriate cost-to-retail ratio (Step 2) to the total ending inventory at retail (Step 1).

TIP!

If prices had not been stable, additional procedures would have been required to eliminate the effects of price-level changes in order to measure the real increases in inventory, not the dollar increase.

Analysis of Multiple-Choice Questions

Question

1. At December 31, 2008, a physical count of merchandise inventory belonging to Rhoda Corp. showed $1,000,000 to be on hand. The $1,000,000 was calculated before any potential necessary adjustments related to the following:
   - Excluded from the $1,000,000 was $80,000 of goods shipped f.o.b. shipping point by a vendor to Rhoda on December 30, 2008 and received on January 3, 2009.
   - Excluded from the $1,000,000 was $72,000 of goods shipped f.o.b. destination to Rhoda on December 30, 2008 and received on January 3, 2009.
   - Excluded from the $1,000,000 was $95,000 of goods shipped f.o.b. destination by Rhoda to a customer on December 28, 2008. The customer received the goods on January 4, 2009.

The correct amount to report for inventory on Rhoda's balance sheet at December 31, 2008 is:

a. $1,072,000
b. $1,095,000
c. $1,175,000
d. $1,247,000

EXPLANATION:

(1) The $80,000 should be added to the $1,000,000 because f.o.b. shipping point means the title transferred to Rhoda when the goods left the seller's dock on December 30, 2008.
(2) The $72,000 is properly excluded from the ending inventory because title did not pass to Rhoda until Rhoda received the goods on January 3, 2009.
(3) The $95,000 should be added to the $1,000,000 because the goods belong to Rhoda until they are received by the customer (in 2009).

$ 1,000,000	
+ 80,000	
+ 95,000	
$ 1,175,000	Amount to report for ending inventory at December 31, 2008.

(Solution = c.)

Question

2. The following amounts relate to the current year for the Rod Buckley Company:

Beginning inventory	$ 40,000
Ending inventory	56,000
Purchases	332,000
Purchase returns	9,600
Freight-out	12,000

The amount of cost of goods sold for the period is:

a. $338,400
b. $325,600
c. $306,400
d. $374,400

EXPLANATION: Write down the calculation model for cost of goods sold. Enter the amounts given and solve for the unknown.

	$ 40,000		Beginning Inventory	
+	332,000	+	Purchases	
-	9,600	-	Purchase Returns and Allowances	
	0	-	Purchase Discounts	
	0	+	Freight-in	
	362,400	=	Cost of Goods Available for Sale	
-	56,000	-	Ending Inventory	
	$306,400	=	Cost of Goods Sold	(Solution = c.)

TIP! Freight-out is classified as a selling expense, not a component of cost of goods sold. Freight-out is not a cost necessary to get the inventory item to the place and condition for sale; it is a cost incurred in the selling function.

Question

3. The accountant for the Orion Sales Company is preparing the income statement for 2008 and the balance sheet at December 31, 2008. Orion uses the periodic inventory system. The January 1, 2008 merchandise inventory balance will appear:
   a. only as an asset on the balance sheet.
   b. only in the cost of goods sold section of the income statement.
   c. as a deduction in the cost of goods sold section of the income statement and as a current asset on the balance sheet.
   d. as an addition in the cost of goods sold section of the income statement and as a current asset on the balance sheet.

EXPLANATION: The January 1, 2008 inventory amount is the beginning inventory figure. Beginning inventory is a component of the cost of goods available for sale for the period which is a component of cost of goods sold. (Solution = b.)

Question

4. If the beginning inventory for 2007 is overstated, the effects of this error on cost of goods sold for 2007, net income for 2007, and assets at December 31, 2008, respectively are:
   a. overstatement, understatement, overstatement
   b. overstatement, understatement, no effect
   c. understatement, overstatement, overstatement
   d. understatement, overstatement, no effect

EXPLANATION: For questions dealing with inventory errors, assume a periodic system unless otherwise indicated. Write down the components of the cost of goods sold calculation and analyze the resulting effects on net income.

		2007	2008
	Beginning inventory	Overstated	No effect
+	Cost of goods purchased		
=	Cost of goods available for sale	Overstated	
-	Ending inventory		
=	Cost of goods sold	Overstated	
	Net income	Understated	

The inventory at the end of 2007 and the inventory at the end of 2008 are both apparently free of error because the inventory at a balance sheet date is determined by a physical count and pricing process. Assume there are no errors in this process unless otherwise indicated. (Solution = b.)

TIP! The fact that the inventory at the beginning of 2007 was in error indicates that the inventory at the end of 2006 was in error because the ending inventory of one period is the beginning inventory of the next period.

TIP! When analyzing a question like this one, it is often helpful to create an example with numbers.

Question

5. If beginning inventory is understated by $7,000, and ending inventory is overstated by $3,000, net income for the period will be:
   a. overstated by $10,000
   b. overstated by $4,000
   c understated by $4,000
   d. understated by $10,000

EXPLANATION: Each error's effect on net income should be determined separately. The effect on net income is dependent on the effect on the calculation of cost of goods sold (which is an expense affecting net income). The effects are then combined to calculate the total effect on net income for the period. (Solution = a.)

		First Error	Second Error	Total Effect
	Beg. Inventory	Understated $7,000		Understated $7,000
+	Purchases			
=	Goods Available	Understated $7,000		Understated $7,000
-	Ending Inventory		Overstated $3,000	Overstated $3,000
=	Cost of Goods Sold	Understated $7,000	Understated $3,000	Understated $10,000
	Net Income	Overstated $7,000	Overstated $3,000	Overstated $10,000

Question

6. The Windsor Salt Company purchased goods with a list price of $50,000, subject to trade discounts of 20% and 10%, with a 2% cash discount allowed if payment is made within 10 days of receipt. Windsor uses the gross method of recording purchases. Windsor should record the cost of this merchandise as:
   a. $34,000
   b. $35,000
   c. $36,000
   d. $50,000
   e. None of the above

EXPLANATION: Trade discounts are not recorded in the accounts; they are means of calculating a sales (purchase) price. Using the gross method of recording purchases, the cash discount allowed does not affect the amount recorded in the Purchases account; the cash discount allowed will be recorded if it is taken and will be recorded as a credit to Purchase Discounts. (Solution = c.)

CALCULATIONS:

List price	$ 50,000
First trade discount ($50,000 x 20%)	(10,000)
Subtotal	40,000
Second trade discount ($40,000 x 10%)	(4,000)
Purchase price	$ 36,000

TIP!

A chain discount occurs when a list price is subject to several trade discounts. When a chain discount is offered, the amount of each trade discount is determined by multiplying (1) the list price of the merchandise **less** the amount prior trade discounts by (2) the trade discount percentage.

Question

7. Grennan Retail Company incurred the following costs in 2008:
   Freight-in on purchases
   Interest on loan to acquire inventory
   Selling costs

   Should the above items be included or excluded in determining Grennan's inventory valuation for its balance sheet?

	Freight-in	Interest	Selling Costs
a.	Include	Include	Include
b.	Include	Include	Exclude
c.	Include	Exclude	Exclude
d.	Exclude	Exclude	Exclude

EXPLANATION: Freight-in is a product cost. The cost of inventory should include all costs necessary to get the inventory in the place and condition for its intended purpose (resale). Freight-in is necessary to get the merchandise to the location for resale. Interest costs should not be capitalized for inventories that are acquired by a merchandiser (because the goods do not require a period of time to ready them for sale) or inventories that are routinely manufactured or otherwise produced in large quantities on a repetitive basis. Therefore, the interest on this inventory is a period cost. Selling expenses are treated as a period cost. (Solution = c.)

Question

8. The following facts pertain to the cost of one product carried in the merchandise inventory of the Herara Store:

Inventory on hand, January 1	200 units @ $20 =	$ 4,000
Purchase, March 18	600 units @ $24 =	14,400
Purchase, July 20	800 units @ $26 =	20,800
Purchase, October 31	400 units @ $30 =	12,000

A physical count of the inventory on December 31 reveals that 500 units are on hand. If the FIFO cost method is used with a periodic inventory system, the inventory should be reported on the balance sheet at:
a. $40,000
b. $36,600
c. $14,600
d. $11,200
e. None of the above

EXPLANATION: Think about what FIFO stands for: the first cost in is the first out to cost of goods sold. Therefore, ending inventory is comprised of the latest costs experienced. (Solution = c.)

400 units @ $30 =	$ 12,000
100 units @ $26 =	2,600
Ending inventory at FIFO	$ 14,600

Question

9. Refer to the data in question 8 above. If the average costing method is used, the cost of goods sold for the year amounts to:
a. $38,400
b. $37,500
c. $12,800
d. $12,500

EXPLANATION: Read the question carefully. Notice it asks for the cost of goods sold and not for the ending inventory as you might expect.

Total cost of all units available for sale:

Beginning inventory	$ 4,000
Purchases ($14,400 + $20,800 + $12,000)	47,200
Cost of goods available for sale	$ 51,200

\$51,200	Cost of goods available for sale
÷ 2,000[1]	Units available for sale
= \$25.60	Average unit cost

\$25.60 Average unit cost x 500 units = \$12,800 Ending inventory
\$25.60 Average unit cost x 1,500[2] units = \$38,400 Cost of goods sold

[1]200 + 600 + 800 + 400 = 2,000 units available for sale.
[2]2,000 units available - 500 units in ending inventory = 1,500 units sold.
(Solution = a.)

Question

10. Which of the following items would not likely be classified as inventory on a balance sheet?
    a. cleaning supplies held by a janitorial firm
    b. lots of land held by a land developer
    c. laying hens held by a farmer
    d. work-in-process held by an equipment manufacturer

EXPLANATION: The laying hens would not be considered to be inventory since they are not held for resale at a profit; rather, they are held to produce inventory and are therefore more like fixed assets. (Solution = c.)

Question

11. In applying the lower of cost or net realizable value rule to inventories at December 31, 2008, Xavier Corporation wrote the inventory down from \$500,000 to \$420,000. This writedown should be reported:
    a. as a prior period adjustment of \$80,000.
    b. as an operating expense in 2008.
    c. as an extraordinary item on the 2008 income statement.
    d. as a part of Cost of Goods Sold Expense.
    e. immediately after cost of goods sold or immediately after gross profit on the 2008 income statement.

EXPLANATION: The \$80,000 loss should be shown separately from cost of goods sold in the income statement; it is not an extraordinary item. (Solution = e.)

Question

12. In 2008, Lucas Manufacturing signed a contract with a supplier to purchase raw materials in 2009 for \$700,000. Before the December 31, 2008 balance sheet date, the market price for these materials dropped to \$510,000. This will be treated in the following manner on the 2008 financials:

a. as a valuation account to Inventory on the balance sheet.
b. as a current liability.
c. as an appropriation of retained earnings.
d. note disclosure only.

EXPLANATION: Normally, the commitment is a disclosure issue only. It is an executory contract since neither party has fulfilled their part of the arrangement. GAAP would require this commitment to be disclosed at 2008. However, since the value of the goods has declined in the period, contingency accounting would require a current liability (with an offsetting loss) to be recorded in 2008. (Solution = b.)

Question

13. The following information pertains to the Godfrey Company for the six months ended June 30 of the current year:

Merchandise inventory, January 1	$ 700,000
Purchases	5,000,000
Freight-in	400,000
Sales	6,000,000

Gross profit is normally 25% of sales. What is the estimated amount of inventory on hand at June 30?
a. $100,000
b. $1,600,000
c. $2,100,000
d. $4,600,000

EXPLANATION: Use the following steps to solve a gross profit inventory method question:

(1) Calculate the cost of goods available for sale during the period:

Beginning inventory	$ 700,000
Purchases	5,000,000
Freight-in	400,000
Cost of goods available for sale	$ 6,100,000

(2) Determine the estimated cost of goods sold during the period:

Sales	$ 6,000,000
Cost of goods sold percentage (100% – 25%)	x 75%
Estimated cost of goods sold	$ 4,500,000

TIP! This problem was simple because the gross profit percentage given in the problem is stated in terms of sales. When the gross margin percentage is expressed in terms of cost, that percentage must first be converted to the equivalent percentage of selling price before the other calculations can be preformed.

(3) Calculate the estimated inventory on hand at the end of the period:

Cost of goods available for sale	$ 6,100,000
Estimated cost of goods sold	(4,500,000)
Estimated ending inventory	$ 1,600,000

(Solution = b.)

Question

14. The cost of goods available for sale for 2008 for Storey Corporation was $2,700,000. The gross profit rate was 20% of sales. Sales for the year amounted to $2,400,000. The ending inventory is estimated to be:
    a. $0
    b. $480,000
    c. $540,000
    d. $780,000

EXPLANATION: Step 1: Calculate the cost of goods available for sale during the period. Cost of goods available is given at $2,700,000.

Step 2: Determine the estimated cost of goods sold during the period:

Sales	$2,400,000
Cost of goods sold percentage (100% – 20%)	x 80%
Estimated cost of goods sold	$ 1,920,000

Step 3: Calculate the estimated inventory on hand at the end of the period:

Cost of goods available for sale	$2,700,000
Estimated cost of goods sold	(1,920,000)
Estimated ending inventory (at cost)	$ 780,000

(Solution = d.)

Question

15. If gross profit is 25% of cost, then gross profit as a percentage of sales equals:
    a. 80%
    b. 75%
    c. 33.66%
    d. 20%

EXPLANATION: Sales (S) – Cost of Goods Sold (CGS) = Gross Profit (GP)
If GP = 25% of cost, then cost of goods sold = 100%.
S – 100% = 25%.
S = 125%.
Expressing gross profit (GP) as a percentage of sales (S) we get:
25% ÷ 125% = 20%.
Thus, gross profit = 20% of sales.

(Solution = d.)

Question

16. A company uses the retail method to estimate ending inventory for interim reporting purposes. If the retail method is used to approximate a lower of average cost or market valuation, which of the following alternatives describe the proper treatment of net markups and net markdowns in the cost-to-retail ratio calculation?

	Net Markups	Net Markdowns
a.	Include	Include
b.	Include	Exclude
c.	Exclude	Include
d.	Exclude	Exclude

EXPLANATION: First notice that the lower-of-average-cost-and-market approach to the retail method is often referred to as the conventional retail method. Recall that using a lower-of-cost-and-market figure is an application of the principle of conservatism. Also recall that the retail method involves multiplying the ending inventory at retail by a ratio. The lower the ratio, the lower the calculated inventory value. Including the net markups (increases in retail prices) but excluding the net markdowns (decreases in retail prices) gives the highest denominator possible for the ratio calculation which yields the lowest ratio possible. (Note: Net markups are often called net additional markups.) (Solution = b.)

Question

17. The following data relate to the merchandise inventory of the Hofma Company:

Beginning inventory at cost	$ 13,800
Beginning inventory at selling price	20,000
Purchases at cost	31,000
Purchases at selling price	50,000

Using the information, determine the cost to retail ratio for Hofma Company:

a. 156%
b. 145%
c. 69%
d. 64%

EXPLANATION:

Ratio = Cost ÷ Retail
Ratio = ($13,800 + $31,000) ÷ ($20,000 + $50,000)
Ratio = $44,800 ÷ $70,000
Ratio = 64%

(Solution = d.)

Question

18. The Ruffier Department Store uses the conventional retail inventory method. The following information is available at December 31, 2008:

	Cost	Retail
Beginning inventory	\$ 37,800	\$ 60,000
Purchases	200,000	290,000
Freight-in	7,200	
Sales		275,000

What is the estimated cost of the ending inventory?

a. \$47,250
b. \$52,500
c. \$53,586
d. \$192,500

CALCULATIONS:

	Cost	Retail
Beginning inventory	\$ 37,800	\$ 60,000
Purchases	200,000	290,000
Freight-in	7,200	
Cost of goods available for sale	\$ 245,000	350,000
Sales		(275,000)
		\$ 75,000

Step 1: Ending inventory at retail
Step 2: Cost-to-retail ratio = \$245,000 ÷ \$350,000 = 70%
Step 3: Estimated cost of ending inventory = \$75,000 x 70% = \$ 52,500

EXPLANATION: Think about how the conventional retail method of inventory estimation works. An estimate of the ending inventory at retail is made by deducting sales from the retail value of goods available for sale, and the ending inventory at retail is converted to a cost value by applying an appropriate ratio, which is an expression of the relationship between inventory cost and its retail value. Apply the following steps to calculate the amount required:

Step 1: **Calculate the ending inventory at retail.** Deduct net sales from the retail price of all of the goods available for sale during the period. Arrive at \$75,000.

Step 2: **Calculate the cost-to-retail ratio.** Divide the cost of the goods available for sale (\$245,000) by the retail value of those same goods (\$350,000). Arrive at 70%.

Step 3: **Determine the estimated cost of the ending inventory**. Apply the cost-to-retail ratio (70%) to the ending inventory at retail (\$75,000). Arrive at \$52,500. (Solution = b.)

Question

19. The Billy Dial Department Store uses a calendar year and the conventional retail inventory method.

The following information is available at December 31, 2008:

	Cost	Retail
Beginning inventory	$ 37,200	$ 60,000
Purchases	200,000	290,000
Freight-in	4,000	
Net markups		30,000
Net markdowns		20,000
Sales		285,000

What is the ending inventory at cost (round to the nearest dollar)?
a. $46,763
b. $47,400
c. $47,603
d. $50,250

CALCULATIONS:

	Cost	Retail
Beginning inventory	$ 37,200	$ 60,000
Purchases	200,000	290,000
Freight-in	4,000	
Goods available for sale	241,200	350,000
Net markups		30,000
Subtotals	$ 241,200	380,000
Net markdowns		(20,000)
		360,000
Sales		(285,000)
Ending inventory at retail		$ 75,000

Cost-to-retail ratio = $\frac{\$241,200}{\$380,000}$ = 63.47%

Ending inventory = 63.47% x $75,000 = $47,603

EXPLANATION: Think about how the retail method of inventory estimation works. An estimate of the ending inventory at retail is made by deducting sales from the retail value of goods available for sale and the ending inventory at retail is converted to a cost or to a lower of cost and market value by applying an appropriate ratio which is an expression of the relationship between inventory cost and its retail value. Apply the following steps to calculate the amount required:

Step 1: **Calculate the ending inventory at retail.** Arrive at $75,000.

Step 2: **Calculate the cost-to-retail ratio.** The ratio should include net markups but not net markdowns.

Step 3: **Determine the ending inventory at cost.** Multiply the cost-to-retail ratio by the ending inventory at retail (including markdowns) = $47,603. (Solution = c.)

Question

20. The inventory turnover ratio is a measure of the liquidity of the inventory. This ratio is calculated by dividing:

a. the cost of goods sold by 365 days.
b. the cost of goods sold by the average amount of inventory on hand.
c. net credit sales by the average amount of inventory on hand.
d. 365 days by the cost of goods sold.

EXPLANATION: Write down the formula to calculate the inventory turnover ratio. Think about the logic of each of the calculation's components. The formula is as follows:

$$\text{Inventory Turnover ratio} = \frac{\text{Cost of Goods Sold}}{\text{Average Inventory}}$$

The cost of goods sold figure is a cost figure whereas net credit sales is a figure reflecting the selling prices of items sold. The cost of an inventory item is reflected in the Inventory account until such time when the item is sold; then, the cost is transferred to the Cost of Goods Sold account. If an item is sold on credit, the selling price of the item is recorded in the Accounts Receivable account. Hence, the accounts receivable turnover ratio uses net credit sales and average accounts receivable balance; whereas, the inventory turnover ratio uses cost of goods sold and the average inventory balance for its calculation. A variant of the inventory turnover ratio is the **average days to sell inventory**. (Solution = b.)

Question

21. The average days to sell inventory is calculated by dividing:
    a. 365 days by the inventory turnover ratio.
    b. the inventory turnover ratio by 365 days.
    c. net sales by the inventory turnover ratio.
    d. 365 days by cost of goods sold.

EXPLANATION: The **average days to sell inventory** is a variant of the inventory turnover ratio. It is calculated by dividing 365 days by the inventory turnover ratio. It measures the average number of days an item remains in inventory before it is sold. (Solution = a.)

Question

22. The gross profit method is often used to calculate inventory and cost of goods sold. Under which of the following scenarios would it not be acceptable?
    a. where ending inventory numbers are not available due to fire
    b. for interim reporting purposes
    c. for year-end reporting purposes
    d. for projection purposes

EXPLANATION: The gross profit method is an estimation technique only, and should not be used for the official, audited financial statements at year-end. Having said this, the method may be used where the numbers are otherwise not available, (theft, fire, etc.), or where an estimate is acceptable (for internal decision making or interim financial reporting). (Solution = c.)

Question

23. Standard costs are another option for costing inventory. Standard costing is allowable for year-end financial statement purposes under GAAP under the following circumstances:
    a. where it does not differ materially from actual cost
    b. where actual cost is not available
    c. where management uses it for internal decision making
    d. where the company is a manufacturing company and needs the information in order to track variances.

EXPLANATION: Standard costing systems are put in place by management to control operations and to monitor costs. While this function is critical to a manufacturing company, the most relevant information for users of the financial statements is actual cost, and therefore, both must be tracked. (Solution = a.)

Question

24. Dino Corporation agreed with a supplier to buy 10 tons of raw materials at a fixed price over the next year. The amount is material and the contract non-cancellable. Which of the following statements is true?
    a. The transaction should be recorded on the balance sheet as it represents a liability to the company.
    b. The transaction should be recorded since it is material.
    c. The transaction should not be recorded on the balance sheet since it represents an executory contract.
    d. The transaction should be recorded since it is non-cancellable.

EXPLANATION: The contract would generally not be recorded as it represents a promise by both parties to do something in the future (an executory contract). The future commitments are recorded. They would have to be disclosed. If the value of the raw material declines, a loss would likely be accrued under contingency accounting. (Solution = c.)

Case Study # 1

Acme Limited

Acme Limited (AL) is a manufacturing company that produces various synthetic construction materials. The shares trade on the local stock exchange. In 2008, the company was able to negotiate an extremely low price on raw materials. As part of the deal, AL had to buy more material than was needed. However, since they had the excess cash, and since the production manager, Owen, was able to assure the purchasing manager, Enid, that the material would all be used up within the year, the deal was consummated.

Unfortunately, the following year, Acme found demand for its products had fallen dramatically because new housing starts were down significantly. As a result, cash was short and AL was considering going to the bank for financing.

After preliminary discussions with the bank, Warren, the V.P. of Finance, found out that AL was considered to be a high-risk company. The bank was reluctant to lend AL the funds and would do so only at a significant premium. Warren felt that the interest rate was excessive and was looking for alternative means of financing. He called a meeting with his managers to discuss the problem.

Warren:
We are short of cash and we need some operating capital. Our customers are taking longer to pay than usual due to the state of the housing markets and demand is down. Any suggestions?

Hiroko (controller):
I guess we've tried the usual sources, like the bank?

Warren:
Of course! The bank, however, is not willing to loan us funds unless we pay them some exorbitant interest rate. Owen, what are we doing with all this raw material? Can't we sell it off? That would generate the money that we need. Or do we need the inventory for production?

Owen:
Well, we don't really need it in the short run since demand has fallen off. However, I'm not sure that we can find a buyer. Besides, I don't really want to let too much of it go since I feel that demand will pick up again within the next few months. Prices have already started to rise.

Warren:
Well it seems to me that we have too much capital tied up in that darn inventory. Whose decision was it to buy that much?

Enid:
It was mine. At the time, we felt that the price was too good to pass up, but we had to buy a large quantity to get the price. I think that I might have a solution to our problem, however. Recently, I had lunch with the controller of Warehouses Unlimited. He was dismayed over the fact that they had excess warehouse space they couldn't "give away". I know that they have excess cash as well. Perhaps something can be worked out.

Warren:
I have another meeting to run to now. Enid, will you please follow up on your idea and report back to me as soon as possible?

Enid contacted Warehouses Unlimited (WU) and was able to strike the following deal:

WU agreed to:
- Buy the excess raw material from AL for $700,000 cash. AL's cost was $600,000.
- Store the inventory and insure it.
- Sell it back to AL over the next year as AL needed it with the proviso that it all had to be repurchased within the year.

AL agreed to:
- Buy back the inventory over the year at a total cost of $800,000, sufficient to cover the inventory costs (including the carrying costs on the inventory) and provide a reasonable return on WU's money.

Enid called Warren immediately to tell him of the deal.

Enid:
Warren, I think that I've solved our problem. I've negotiated a deal that will get us $700,000 cash, ensure a steady supply of raw materials at not much more than market rates, and boost our net income before tax by $100,000!

REQUIRED:
Assume the role of an independent advisor to the company and comment on how the proposed transaction should be accounted for.

Suggested approach to case study # 1

Acme Limited

Overview

Since AL is a public company, GAAP is a constraint. Stakeholders of the information will be WU, which may want the statements to determine the solvency of AL, and shareholders, who will want to determine stewardship and the value of their investment.

Management of AL (i.e., Enid and Owen) will want the financial statements to show that they are making good business decisions (stewardship). Since the first inventory transaction has turned out to be less than ideal, they will want to ensure that the second transaction shows good management.

As an independent advisor, however, you will have to ensure that the financial statements are not misleading and that the needs of the users are met.

Analysis and Recommendations

The issue is how to account for the deal that Enid has set up with a transaction:
1. Either the transaction may be treated like a sale, in which case, the inventory

would be removed from the balance sheet and perhaps a profit recognized since the price is greater than the book value; or

2. The arrangement may be treated like a financing arrangement with the inventory being put up as collateral for a loan (i.e., the $700,000).

Sale of the Inventory

The journal entry to record this as a sale would be as follows:

Cash	700,000	
Sales		700,000
Cost of sales	600,000	
Inventory		600,000

This would result in a profit of $100,000 being recorded and would result in AL not having to record any liability on the balance sheet. If they had borrowed the money from the bank, they would have had to record a liability. Possession of the inventory is with WU, as is legal title. This would seem to imply that the inventory should be removed from the books of AL.

Financing Arrangement

The underlying substance of the transaction must be reviewed. In essence, this could be viewed as off-balance-sheet financing. Has a sale really taken place? In reality, it could be argued that the risks and rewards of ownership still rest with AL. The inventory is still theirs since they will end up buying it all back. They are also effectively covering the costs, albeit indirectly (they are paying more for the inventory when they buy it back, thus covering storage, insurance costs, and interest costs on the money). The return to WU is $800,000 ÷ $700,000 = 14.3%. EIC #121 (Accounting for Wash Sales) seems to support this treatment since control over the inventory is retained through the buy-back agreement.

Recommendation

Since the substance of the transaction is that the risks and rewards of ownership have not really passed to WU, the transaction should probably be treated as a financing arrangement with the inventory staying on the books and the $700,000 being recorded as a loan. Adequate note disclosure should also be made of the transaction since legal title to the inventory temporarily rests with WU.

TIP!

This case is a good example of how the motivations of managers to achieve a desired accounting result (not successful in this case), may lead them to make poor economic decisions.

Case Study # 2

Sheung Steel Limited

Sheung Steel Limited (SSL) manufactures steel. The market for its raw materials is fairly volatile and the prices are a function of supply and demand. In the past, SSL has often purchased more than necessary in order to get a good price. Chuck Chung, the general manager, was in the process of reviewing current raw material prices and inventory levels in order to determine how much he should buy. Samantha Tse, a recently hired employee, stopped by his office.

Samantha:
Free for lunch today Chuck?

Chuck:
Maybe a bit later, Samantha. I have to make a decision today on how much raw material to purchase. The price is at an all-time low and I'm not sure that it will get any better. The problem is that we don't really need all this inventory now, not to mention the fact that the boss is worried about cash flows.

Samantha:
You know that there are other costs involved besides the purchase price. Have you considered the storage costs and the cost of tying up cash in assets that are not in use?

Chuck:
I guess not. I always make my decision based on the purchase price alone. I guess that I should factor in those other costs as well. But the purchase price is so low that it's probably still a good deal.

Samantha:
Why don't you see if you can lock into the price now but not take delivery of the product until we need it? That way, we wouldn't incur storage costs and we wouldn't have to pay until we take delivery. You might have to lock in at a higher price but, considering the other benefits, it might be worth it.

Chuck:
Sounds good. I'll call the supplier right away. We've got a pretty good working relationship. Maybe he'll join us for lunch. I have to get this finalized today so that I can work on the year-end financial statements. It's already mid-December and before you know it, year-end and the auditors will descend on us. I'll have to think about how this would be accounted for.

It is now January 15, 2009 and Chuck has negotiated a deal with the supplier to purchase the raw materials at a very good price. SSL must take delivery of a fixed amount within the next six months and pay a fixed total price even if they do not take delivery of the full amount. The deal was signed December 15, 2008 and SSL has not yet taken delivery of the first shipment.

On December 31, 2008, the price of the raw material dropped even further. Chuck was annoyed since he could have saved $200,000 had he waited. Prices have since begun to move (slowly) upwards, however.

Required

Assume the role of Chuck and consider how the raw material deal should be presented in the financial statements.

Suggested approach to Case Study # 2

Sheung Steel Limited

Overview

Favourable presentation of the deal will be important to Chuck. He might not be very keen on showing the fact that, had he delayed the signing of the deal, he could have saved the company $200,000. GAAP is a constraint since it is mentioned that the auditors will be coming in soon. Stakeholders of the statements will include shareholders who will want information in order to assess their investment in the company.

Analysis and Recommendations

The issue is how the raw material purchase commitment should be accounted for. The arrangement for the undelivered material is called an executory contract since both parties have agreed to do something but neither has fulfilled their part of the deal. SSL has agreed to take delivery of the material and to pay the supplier for the goods and the supplier has agreed to sell the goods to SSL at an agreed upon price. There is, as yet, no liability for the goods, that is, until they are delivered.

The commitment should be disclosed in the notes to the financial statements since it will help users predict cash flows of the company. Furthermore, there is the question of whether Chuck should accrue the difference between the contract price and the market price of the raw material at year-end.

Accrue the Loss

Since the market price is below the committed purchase price at the financial statement date, the loss should be accrued. Otherwise when the inventory is delivered and recorded on the books it will be overvalued. And since it must be carried at the lower of cost and market, it will be written down to market. Since the decline in value occurred in the current year, it would make sense for the loss to be booked in 2008.

However, accrual would reduce net income and highlight the fact that the company could have saved money had they waited.

Should the loss be presented as part of cost of goods sold? Since it relates to inventory this would make sense. If booked to cost of goods sold, gross profit and gross profit ratio would decline.

Do Not Accrue the Loss

Contingency accounting would require that the loss be accrued when it is estimable (which it is) and when it is likely that a future event will confirm the fact that the inventory value has been impaired. The latter is arguable. The fact that the market price is below market at the balance sheet date is surely relevant. However, if the market price increases after year-end and before the financial statements are issued, it is hard to argue that it is likely that a loss will be incurred. In fact, if the price keeps rising prior to the delivery dates, there will be no loss. In this case, the price is rising.

It might also be argued that since the price is volatile, it is not easy to estimate the potential loss, if any, and, therefore, the first criterion is not met either.

Recommendation

Since the price is volatile and since it is rising, no loss should be accrued in the financial statements. The notes to the statements should describe the deal but not necessarily that market is below cost. It is not likely that a loss will occur.

Chapter 9

Investments

Overview

This chapter emphasizes the nature of, and accounting for, primary financial asset investments: long-term loans and receivables; investment in debt securities, and investments in equity securities. This latter category includes those investments where there is little or no influence over the investee company as well as those where there is significant influence or control.

Accounting for investments is a function of both the type of instrument (debt or equity) and management's intent, which may be quite different from security to security.

Study Steps

Understanding the Fundamental Differences in Different Types of Non-Strategic Investments

According to *CICA Handbook* Section 3855, financial assets that are non-strategic investments are grouped into four separate categories for accounting and reporting purposes

- Loans and receivables
- Held-to-maturity investments
- Held-for-trading investments
- Available-for-sale securities

Each of these is subject to different measurement and income recognition rules. Loans and receivables and held-to-maturity investments will not recognize any unrealized gains or losses and will be measured at amortized cost. Held-for-trading investments will be measured at fair value with unrealized gains and losses being recognized in income. Available-for-sale securities' unrealized gains or losses will be included in comprehensive income.

Specifically, loans and receivables (long term) will be recorded at their amortized amount, using the effective interest method. The discount rate used will be the market rate. Therefore, if the stated rate equals the market rate (sometimes called the effective rate) then it will be carried at face value. Any differences will be recorded as premiums or discounts as appropriate. There are no adjustments to fair value for this category of investments.

Held-to-maturity investments will include only debt securities since equity securities have no maturity date. It is classified as such only if there is an **intention** and an **ability** to hold the investment to maturity. These are fairly difficult criteria to meet since they require an organization to assess not only their intention (i.e., to hold it to maturity) but also whether they will be able to do so. Planned expansions or normal business cycles may be reasons not to include an investment in this category. Amortized cost is also the measurement basis for this category. There are no adjustments to fair value.

A financial asset **held for trading** is one that is acquired for the purpose of selling in the near term, specifically for profit taking. Near term is defined as not exceeding one year from the date of the financial statements.

When acquired, held-for-trading investments are recorded at fair value of the consideration given. Income (dividends and interest primarily) is recorded as it is received or receivable.

At each balance sheet date, held-for-trading securities are reported at fair value, with unrealized gains and losses reported as part of net income.

Available-for-sale securities are reported at fair value. However, changes from initial cost to fair value are included as a component of comprehensive income (Other Comprehensive Income or OCI), and a separate component of shareholder's equity (Accumulated Other Comprehensive Income or AOCI). Therefore, any changes in fair value are not shown in net income until actually realized through a sale—but the fair value is reflected on the balance sheet. Other comprehensive income will be used to capture the changes in fair value, net of tax effects. If there is more than one available-for-sale security, a company may elect to use the portfolio method. This method involves comparing the total fair value of the portfolio in the previous period to the total fair value of the portfolio in the current period.

Becoming Proficient in Accounting for Strategic Investments

Investments in Common Shares

Little or no influence

Similar to above, the first decision to be made is whether the investment is available for sale or held for trading. If either of these conditions apply, the investment is subject to essentially the same rules noted above for debt securities either available for sale or held for trading. Generally, if the investment allows for little or no influence on the acquired company, then it will be classified under one of these two.

Significant influence

If there exists what is called significant influence, then the equity method of accounting would be employed.

Factors indicating significant influence begin with, but are not limited to, the percentage of voting shares held. For example, with less than 20% shareholdings it is assumed, in the absence of any other information, that the investor company does not have significant influence. However, other factors to consider include:

- Representation on the Board of Directors of the investee
- Material inter-company transactions
- Interchange of management

TIP!

Be careful in applying the 20% rule in determining whether significant influence exists. It may be that an investment of 25% does not represent significant influence while a 10% investment does.

The equity method recognizes that the investor has influence over the dividend decision and, therefore, the critical event in the earnings process (i.e., for the investor to recognize earnings from the investee) is the point when the investee earns the income. The declaration of the dividend is secondary. Theoretically, revenue could be recognized by the investor as each dollar is earned by the investee; however, practically speaking, it is only booked monthly or even annually (dr. investment and cr. equity pickup or investment income). If the investor owns 25% of the shares of the investee, then it would record 25% of the profits of the investee, or 25% of the losses.

When the dividends are actually received, income is not recognized, but rather the journal entry appears as follows: dr. cash and cr. investment (B/S). This is because the income has already been accrued when the investee earns the income.

Under the equity method, pro rata income is accrued by the investor and dividends are treated as a decrease in the investment account on the balance sheet.

The investment is booked at cost originally, and is increased as earnings are accrued and decreased as dividends are received. This makes intuitive sense since the value of the investment/company increases as the investee earns profits, and as the investee pays out cash the value of the investment/company decreases.

In addition, an assessment of whether there has been a decline in value that is other than temporary should be made at every reporting date. The criteria used to assess this are the same as used for assessing cost investments.

The income recognized by the investee under the equity method must be adjusted for amortization of the purchase price discrepancy (PPD). The PPD is the difference between what the investor paid for the shares and the value of the company.

The purchase price discrepancy must be calculated when an investor invests in common shares of a company and obtains significant influence or control of that company through the purchase.

For instance, Beakman Limited (BL) might pay $4 million for 25% of World Limited (WL) as follows:

- Paid $4 million for 25%.
- Net Book Value (NBV) = $12 million.
- Fair Market Value (FMV) of underlying net assets $15 million.

The purchase price equation (PPE) shows what the investor paid and what they received. For BL, the PPE is as follows:

Amount paid for 25% interest	$4,000,000
NBV of 25% interest	
($12,000,000 x 25%)	3,000,000
Difference	1,000,000

Why would BL pay more for the shares than the recorded NBV? There are two reasons: one being that the recorded values of assets seldom reflect the FMV of the underlying assets due to the historical cost principle. The other reason is that there are often unrecorded assets such as goodwill. Goodwill is the extra value attributable to a going concern company and results from the reputation of the company: the company having established suppliers, steady customers, etc. Goodwill is not recorded on the balance sheet of a company unless it is purchased. Therefore, in this case, BL could have paid more for the shares because the assets have FMV > NBV, or because of goodwill, or both.

TIP! PPDs arise due to perceived excess value inherent in a company purchased. PPD arises either because the underlying tangible assets are seen to have a greater worth than the NBV or that there are unrecorded assets such as goodwill.

TIP! In most cases, there is at least some amount of PPD that is attributable to the perceived excess value of tangible assets since the historical cost principle dictates that assets cannot be written up in the financial statements to reflect increases in value.

Finally, we must adjust the equity pickup or investment income booked by BL for amortization of these differences. The FMV>NBV is amortized over the life of the underlying assets (e.g., if the asset is a building with a 20-year life with 15 years remaining, then the amortization would be as follows: $750,000 ÷ 15 = $50,000). This amount would be booked each year by BL as a reduction of the investment income. Goodwill is not amortized.

Control

If control is evident through the acquisition of common shares, the investment will be accounted for using the consolidation method. This involves adding all assets, liabilities, revenues, and expenses of the subsidiary to the parent's financial statements. Care must be taken to eliminate any inter-company transactions.

Tips on Chapter Topics

Long-term loans and receivables and **held-to-maturity** investments will be reported as long-term assets at **amortized** cost. **TIP!**

Amortized cost is the amount recognized when an asset is acquired, reduced by principal payments received, and adjusted for amortization of discount or premium (if appropriate) and writedowns for impairment or uncollectibility. **TIP!**

Available-for-sale securities are reported at fair value, with unrealized gains or losses reported as other comprehensive income and as a separate component of shareholder's equity. Available-for-sale securities may be classified as long-term or short term. Income from Available-for-sale securities is recognized as earned in net income. **TIP!**

Held-for-trading securities will be reported as current assets at fair value. Unrealized gains or losses are included in net income. **TIP!**

Fair value is the amount that would be agreed upon in an arm's length transaction between knowledgeable, willing parties who are under no compulsion to act. **TIP!**

Discounts or premiums on long-term loans and receivables should be amortized using the **effective interest method**. **TIP!**

Equity securities are classified first by management intent. For example, if it is considered a **held-for-trading** security, meaning it is the intention that it be sold in a short period of time, it is classified as a current asset and measured at fair value. Unrealized gains or losses are reported in net income. **TIP!**

Long-term investments in equity instruments are next classified by level of influence. An investment exercising no significant influence is classified as available for sale. It is valued at fair value, with unrealized losses being reported in other comprehensive income. A significant influence investment is reported using the equity method. If control exists, the consolidation method is used. **TIP!**

Illustration 9-1

Summary of Investments in Debt and Equity Securities

The major categories for investments in debt and equity securities and their reporting treatments are summarized below.

Non-Strategic Investments

Category	Valuation	Unrealized Holding Gains or Losses
Loans and receivables	Amortized cost	Not recognized
Held to maturity	Amortized cost	Not recognized
Held for trading	Fair value	Recognized in net income
Available for sale	Fair value	Recognized as other comprehensive income (OCI) and as separate component of shareholders' equity (AOCI)

Equity Securities (Non-Strategic and Strategic)

Category	Valuation	Unrealized Holding Gains or Losses
Non-Strategic		
1. Available for sale	Fair value	Recognized as other comprehensive income and as separate component of shareholders' equity
2. Held for trading	Fair value	Recognized in net income
Strategic		
Significant influence	Equity	Not recognized
Control	Consolidation	Not recognized

Exercise 9-1

PURPOSE: This exercise will review the process of determining the required year-end entry to adjust the valuation account for an investment in equity securities that have been classified as held for trading.

Nevercrash Airlines has a portfolio of temporary marketable equity securities, the first of which was acquired in 2007. The aggregate cost is $142,000. The fair value of the securities contained in that investment portfolio for five balance sheet dates are as follows:

Date	Fair value
12/31/07	$138,000
12/31/08	$143,000
12/31/09	$163,000
12/31/10	$203,000
12/31/11	$184,000

Instructions

At each balance sheet date, determine the unrealized gain or loss to be recorded for the year. Ignore tax effects.

Solution to Exercise 9-1

Date	Unrealized (gain) loss to be recorded
12/31/07	$4,000
12/31/08	$(5,000)
12/31/09	$(20,000)
12/31/10	$(40,000)
12/31/11	$19,000

The total unrealized gain at the end of 2011 is $42,000. This is confirmed by comparing the initial cost of $142,000 with the fair value at the end of 2011, which is $184,000.

EXPLANATION: Investments in equity securities which are classified as held for trading are initially recorded at cost, but they are subsequently reported at fair value. Since there is more than one security, the determination of the adjustment is done on a portfolio basis. The total carrying value of the portfolio is compared to the market value at each balance sheet date and the adjustment is made accordingly. These unrealized gains or losses are included in net income for the respective periods.

TIP! In the above example, it was assumed to be the same portfolio of securities. This is a simplifying assumption to show the impact of the unrealized gains or losses. Realistically, the securities in the portfolio would be sold in the coming year, which is the intention required in order to be classified as held-for-trading securities initially.

TIP! In the above exercise, it would also be effective to use an allowance account to track unrealized gains or losses. See **Exercise 9-2** for an example.

Exercise 9-2

PURPOSE: This exercise will review the accounting for investments in equity securities classified as available for sale.

At December 31, 2008, Ed & Kay Hastings Company had no investments. One equity security is purchased for $34,680 on November 15, 2007; commission costs on the purchase amount to $320. At December 31, 2007, a balance sheet date, the fair value of that security is $32,000. At December 31, 2008, the security is still held and the fair value is $34,000. The security is classified as available for sale, and Ed & Kay Hastings Company follows the policy of adding the transaction costs to the initial cost of the investment. On January 15, 2009, the security is sold for a price of $42,800.

Instructions

Prepare all relevant journal entries for the acquisition, subsequent measurement, and disposition of this security. Ignore income tax.

Solution to Exercise 9-2

November 15, 2007		
Available-for-sale security	35,000	
Cash		35,000
December 31, 2007		
Unrealized loss on available-for-sale security—OCI	3,000	
AFS security		3,000

This loss will be included in other comprehensive income (OCI) and as a separate component of shareholders' equity (AOCI). The allowance will be a "contra" account on the balance sheet—it may be shown separately or "netted" against the investment itself.

December 31, 2008

Available-for-sale security	2,000	
Unrealized gain on available-for-sale security—OCI		2,000

This gain will be included in other comprehensive income (OCI) and as a separate component of shareholders' equity (AOCI). Note that the AOCI amount is cumulative and will reflect the total unrealized gain or loss, while OCI reflects the change in the year.

January 15, 2009

Entry #1

Available-for-sale investment	8,800	
Unrealized gain on available-for-sale investment—OCI		8,800

This entry adjusts the AFS investment to its fair value on the date of disposal and records it in OCI

Entry #2

Cash	42,800	
Available-for-sale investment		42,800

This entry removes the carrying amount of the asset from the investment account and records the proceeds of disposal

Entry #3

Unrealized gain on available-for-sale investment—OCI	7,800	
Realized gain on available-for-sale security		7,800

This entry is a reclassification adjustment that removes the now realized holding gain from OCI and recognizes it in net income.

The fair value allowance account must be closed since there are no other securities held. This may be done by a separate entry. This will be offset to the amount in the AOCI. Essentially, the amount of the gain that had "stored" in the AOCI account is transferred to net income since it is now "realized".

EXPLANATION: The loss incurred in the first period is charged to an allowance account for investment decline. In the subsequent year, the market value increases and the allowance is reduced. When the security is sold in 2009, the allowance account is first reduced to zero, with the subsequent gain being classified as realized.

Exercise 9-3

PURPOSE: This exercise will review the accounting procedures appropriate for an investment in debt securities held to maturity.

A five-year $100,000 bond with a 7% stated interest rate and a 5% yield rate is purchased on December 31, 2007, for $108,660. The bond matures on December 31, 2012. Interest is to be received at the end of each year. The following amortization schedule reflects interest to be received, interest revenue, amortization of bond premium, and amortized cost of the bond investment at year end. It is the intention of management to hold this security until maturity.

Date	Cash Received	Interest Revenue	Premium Amortization	Carrying Amount
12/31/07				$108,660
12/31/08	$ 7,000	$ 5,433	$1,567	107,093
12/31/09	7,000	5,354	1,646	105,447
12/31/10	7,000	5,272	1,728	103,719
12/31/11	7,000	5,186	1,814	101,905
12/31/12	7,000	5,095	1,905	100,000
Totals	$35,000	$26,340	$8,660	

The following presents a comparison of the amortized cost and market value (given) of the bond at year end.

Date	Amortized Cost	Market Value	Difference
12/31/07	$108,660	$108,660	$0
12/31/08	107,093	106,000	(1,093)
12/31/09	105,447	107,500	2,053
12/31/10	103,719	105,500	1,781
12/31/11	101,905	103,000	1,095
12/31/12	100,000	100,000	0

Instructions

(a) Record the journal entries at December 31, 2007, December 31, 2008, and December 31, 2009.

(b) Describe what will be reflected in the income statement and balance sheet prepared at December 31, 2008, and December 31, 2009, with regard to this investment.

(c) Prepare the journal entry to record the sale of the investment if it is sold on January 2, 2010, for $107,250.

Solution to Exercise 9-3

(a)

December 31, 2007

Held-to-maturity Investment	108,660	
Cash		108,660

TIP! Although the issuer of the bonds sets up a separate account for premium or discount on bonds, an investor typically does not set up a separate account; rather, any discount or premium is reflected in the investment account.

December 31, 2008

Cash	7,000	
Interest Income		5,433
Held-to-maturity Investment		1,567

December 31, 2009

Cash	7,000	
Interest Income		5,354
Held-to-maturity Investment		1,646

(b) The bond investment would be reported in the long-term investment section of the balance sheet at amortized cost of $107,093 at December 31, 2008, and $105,447 at December 31, 2009. Interest revenue of $5,433 would be reported in the income statement for the year ending December 31, 2009, and interest revenue of $5,354 would be reported in the income statement for the year ending December 31, 2009. Interest revenue is classified as "other revenue" on a multiple-step income statement.

(c)

January 2, 2010

Cash	107,250	
Held-to-maturity Investment		105,447 [a]
Gain on Sale of Held-to-maturity Investment		1,803

[a] $108,660 - ($1,567 + $1,646) = $105,447 balance

Exercise 9-4

PURPOSE: This exercise will illustrate (1) the calculations and journal entries for a bond investment purchased at a discount and (2) the accounting procedures required when the bond investment is sold prior to the bond's maturity date.

John and Martha Hitt Company purchased bonds to be held to maturity. The following details pertain:

Face value	$100,000.00
Coupon interest rate	7%
Yield rate	10%
Maturity date	January 1, 2011
Date of purchase	January 1, 2008
Interest receipts due	Annually on January 1
Method of amortization	Effective interest
Purchase price	$92,539.95

Instructions

(a) Calculate the amount of purchase premium or discount.
(b) Prepare the journal entry for the purchase of the bonds. Do not record the premium or discount separately in the accounts.
(c) Prepare the amortization schedule for these bonds.
(d) Prepare all of the journal entries (subsequent to the purchase date) for 2008 and 2009 that relate to these bonds. Assume the accounting period coincides with the calendar year. Assume reversing entries are not used.
(e) Prepare the journal entry to record the sale of the bonds, assuming they are sold on January 1, 2010, for $102,000. Assume the sale occurs immediately after the annual interest receipt.

Solution to Exercise 9-4

(a)

Face value	$100,000.00
Purchase price	92,539.95
Discount on investment in held-to-maturity bonds	$ 7,460.05

(b)

January 1, 2008

Held-to-maturity Investments	92,539.95	
Cash..		92,539.95

EXPLANATION: The discount of $7,460.05 is reflected in the investment account because the instructions indicate the discount is not to be shown separately in the accounts.

(c)

Date	7% Cash Received	10% Interest Revenue	Discount Amortization	Carrying Value
1/1/08				$ 92,539.95
1/1/09	$ 7,000.00	$ 9,254.00	$ 2,254.00	94,793.95
1/1/10	7,000.00	9,479.40	2,479.40	97,273.35
1/1/11	7,000.00	9,726.65 [a]	2,726.65	100,000.00
	$ 21,000.00	$ 28,460.05	$ 7,460.05	

[a] Includes rounding error of $.69.

EXPLANATION: Cash received is determined by multiplying the par value ($100,000) by the contract rate of interest (7%). Interest revenue is calculated by multiplying the carrying value at the beginning of the interest period by the effective interest rate (10%). The amount of discount amortization for the period is the excess of the interest revenue over the stated interest (cash interest) amount. The carrying value at an interest receipt date is the carrying value at the beginning of the interest period plus the discount amortization for the interest period.

TIP! The amount of interest revenue of $9,479.40 appearing on the "1/1/10" receipt line is the amount of interest revenue for the interest period ending on that date. Thus, in this case, $9,479.40 is the interest revenue for the twelve months preceding the date 1/1/10, which would be the calendar year 2009.

TIP! Any rounding error should be plugged to (included in) the interest revenue amount for the last period. Otherwise, there would be a small balance left in the Investment in Held-to-maturity Bonds account after the bonds are extinguished.

TIP! Notice that the total interest revenue ($28,460.05) over the three-year period equals the total cash interest ($21,000.00) plus the total purchase discount ($7,460.05). Thus, you can see that the purchase discount represents an additional amount of interest to be recognized over the time the bonds are held.

(d)	12/31/08	Held-to-maturity investments	2,254.00	
		Interest Receivable	7,000.00	
		Interest Revenue		9,254.00

EXPLANATION: This entry records (1) the accrual of interest for twelve months, and (2) the amortization of discount for the first twelve months the bonds are held. This compound entry could be replaced with two single entries to accomplish the same objectives. The first entry would include a debit to Interest Receivable and a credit to Interest Revenue for $7,000.00. The second entry would include a debit to Held-to-maturity Investments and a credit to Interest Revenue for $2,254.00. The two entry approach is sometimes easier to employ when reversing entries are used because the first of the two single entries can be reversed, but the second of the two single entries (the one to record the amortization of discount or premium) should **never** be reversed.

	1/1/09	Cash	7,000.00	
		Interest Receivable		7,000.00
	12/31/09	Held-to-maturity Investments	2,479.40	
		Interest Receivable	7,000.00	
		Interest Revenue		9,479.40
(e)	1/1/10	Cash	7,000.00	
		Interest Receivable		7,000.00
		Cash	102,000.00	
		Held-to-maturity Investments		97,273.35[a]
		Gain on Sale of Securities		4,726.65[b]

[a] ($92,539.95 + $2,254.00 + $2,479.40 = $97,273.35 carrying amount)
[b] ($102,000.00 - $97,273.35 = $4,726.65 gain)

TIP! Gain or losses on the sale of investments are to be classified in the "other revenues, gains, expenses, and losses" section of a multiple-step income statement. They very rarely meet the criteria to be classified as an extraordinary item.

Exercise 9-5

PURPOSE: This exercise will allow you to compare the results of using the fair value and equity methods of accounting for an investment in shares.

On January 1, 2008, Rocky Mountain Corporation acquired 100,000 of the 400,000 outstanding common shares of Great Plains Corporation as a long-term investment at a cost of $50 per share. The fair value and the book value of the investee's net assets were both $20,000,000 at January 1, 2008. Great Plains Corporation paid a cash dividend of $2.00 per common share on September 5, 2008 and reported net income of $1,400,000 for the year ending December 31, 2008. The market value of the Great Plains shares was $47 at December 31, 2008.

Instructions

(a) Assuming Rocky Mountain does **not** exercise significant influence over the investee, determine the following:
  (1) Amount to report as investment (dividend) revenue for the year ending December 31, 2008.
  (2) Amount to report as the carrying value of the investment at December 31, 2008.

(b) Assuming Rocky Mountain **does** exercise significant influence over the investee, determine the following:
  (1) Amount to report as investment revenue for the year ending December 31, 2008.
  (2) Amount to report as the carrying value of the investment at December 31, 2008.

Solution to Exercise 9-5

EXPLANATION: If there is no significant influence, the company must classify the investment as either available for sale or held for trading. Both require valuing the investment at fair value each period. The available-for-sale classification treats unrealized gains or losses as part of comprehensive income, whereas a trading classification treats them as part of net income. For this example we will assume classification as available for sale.

(a) (1) $200,000.
  100,000 shares times $ 2 per share dividend
  (2) $4,700,000.

EXPLANATION: Because the investor does not exert significant influence over the investee, the investor must measure the investment at fair value. At December 31, 2008, the fair value is ($47 x 100,000 = $4,700,000), thus the available-for-sale investment account will be reduced by $300,000.

(b) (1) $350,000.
(2) $5,150,000.

Investment in Great Plains Shares

Debit		Credit	
1/1/08	5,000,000	9/5/08	200,000[3]
12/31/08	350,000[4]		
12/31/08 Bal.	5,150,000		

Revenue From Investment

Debit		Credit	
		12/31/08	350,000[4]
		12/31/08 Bal.	350,000

[3] 100,000 shares x $2 = $200,000.
[4] 100,000 ÷ 400,000 = 25% ownership; 25% x $1,400,000 = $350,000.

EXPLANATION: The investor should use the equity method when the investment allows the investor to exercise significant influence over the investee. The investor recognizes its proportionate share of the investee's earnings by a debit to the investment account and a credit to investment revenue. When the investee distributes earnings, the investor records an increase in cash and a decrease in the carrying value of the investment. Because the cost of the investment was equal to the carrying value of the investee's underlying net assets, there is no amortization to be considered (which would affect investment revenue and the investment account balance) in this case. The market value of the shares at the balance sheet date is not relevant when the equity method is used.

TIP!

Under the **equity method**, the investment is originally recorded at cost and then subsequently adjusted by the investor's **proportionate share** of the investee's earnings and dividend payments. Income earned by the investee results in investment revenue and an increase in the investment account on the books of the investor. An investee's net loss or dividend payments reduce the investment account. When the investor acquires the shares at a price unequal to the book value of the investee's underlying net assets, the investor must amortize the difference between the investor's cost and the investor's proportionate share of the underlying book value of the investee at the date of acquisition. This amortization affects investment revenue and the investment account balance.

Exercise 9-6

PURPOSE: This exercise will illustrate how to use the equity method of accounting for an investment in shares.

Delight Corporation acquired 30% of the 1,000,000 outstanding shares of Touch Corporation on January 1, 2008, for $3,240,000 when the book value of the net assets of Touch totalled $9,600,000. At January 1, 2008, Touch's plant assets, having a remaining life of ten years, had a fair value which exceeded book value by $700,000.

Touch Corporation reported net income of $1,600,000 for 2008 and $2,000,000 for 2009. Touch paid dividends of $400,000 on December 6, 2008, and $500,000 on December 5, 2009.

Instructions

(a) Prepare all journal entries for Delight Corporation for 2008 and 2009 that relate to this investment.
(b) Indicate the amount that should appear as investment income on Delight's income statement for (1) the year ending December 31, 2008, and (2) the year ending December 31, 2009.
(c) Indicate the amount that should appear as the balance of Delight's investment on: (1) the balance sheet at December 31, 2008, and (2) the balance sheet at December 31, 2009.

Solution to Exercise 9-6

(a) 1/1/08	Investment in Touch Company Shares.........	3,240,000	
	Cash		3,240,000
12/6/08	Cash	120,000	
	Investment in Touch Company Shares...		120,000
	(30% x $400,000 = $120,000)		
12/31/08	Investment in Touch Company Shares.........	480,000	
	Revenue from Investment......................		480,000
	(30% x $1,600,000 = $480,000)		
	Revenue from Investment............................	21,000	
	Investment in Touch Company Shares...		21,000
	(30% x $700,000 = $210,000; $210,000 ÷ 10 years = $21,000) To amortize the fair value of investment		

***Calculations:**

Total book value of net assets of investee at 1/1/08	$9,600,000
Investor's percentage	30%
Book value of investor's share of investee's net assets	2,880,000
Cost of investment	3,240,000
Excess cost over book value of underlying net assets	360,000
Portion attributable to excess fair value over book value of net identifiable assets ($700,000 x 30% = $210,000)	(210,000)

Portion attributable to an unidentifiable asset			
Represents goodwill—not amortized			150,000
12/5/09	Cash	150,000	
	Investment in Touch Company Shares...		150,000
	(30% x $500,000 = $150,000)		
12/31/09	Investment in Touch Company Shares.........	600,000	
	Revenue from Investment......................		600,000
	(30% x $2,000,000 = $600,000)		
	Revenue from Investment...........................	21,000	
	Investment in Touch Company Shares...		21,000
	(30% x $700,000 = $210,000; $210,000 ÷ 10 years = $21,000)		

EXPLANATION: The equity method is an accrual method of accounting for an investment in shares. A portion of the investee's earnings is recorded as income by the investor in the same time period the investee earns it. Dividends received are recorded as a recovery of investment, not as income. (To record dividends as income would "double count" the amount already recorded as a share of the investee's earnings.)

The excess of the investor's cost over the carrying value of the underlying net assets on the investee's books must be determined and amortized. In this exercise, a portion ($210,000) of that excess is due to the fact that the investee has identifiable assets whose fair values are in excess of their carrying values; this portion should be amortized by the investor over the remaining life of the underlying assets (10 years in this case). The remaining excess cost over book value ($150,000) is attributed to an unidentifiable and unrecorded asset—goodwill. Goodwill is not amortized. It is not subject to an impairment test but rather is considered in the overall fair value of the investment compared to the carrying value. Any impairment in this value, other than temporary, is recorded as a charge to net income.

(b) (1) $459,000 for the year ending December 31, 2008.
(2) $579,000 for the year ending December 31, 2009.

APPROACH: Post the amounts from the entries in part (a) to a T-account to solve.

Revenue from Investment

12/31/08	21,000	12/31/08	480,000
		12/31/08 Balance	459,000
12/31/09	21,000	12/31/09	600,000
		12/31/09 Balance	579,000

(c) (1) $3,579,000 at December 31, 2008.
(2) $4,008,000 at December 31, 2009.

APPROACH: Post the amounts from the entries in part (a) to a T-account to solve. Investment in Touch Company

Investment in Touch Company

1/1/08	3,240,000	12/6/08	120,000
		12/31/08	21,000
12/31/08	480,000		
12/31/08 Balance	3,579,000		
12/31/09	600,000	12/5/09	150,000
		12/31/09	21,000
12/31/09 Balance	4,008,000		

Analysis of Multiple-Choice Questions

Question

1. An investor purchased bonds as a held to maturity investment with a face amount of $100,000 between interest payment dates. The investor purchased the bonds at $102,000 paid incidental costs of $1,500, and paid accrued interest for three months of $2,500. The investor follows the policy of adding any transaction costs to the initial carrying amount of the investment. The amount to record as the cost of this long-term investment in bonds is:
   a. $100,000.
   b. $102,000.
   c. $103,500.
   d. $106,000.

EXPLANATION: The cost is determined as follows:

Purchase price (102% x $100,000 par)	$102,000
Incidental costs to acquire	1,500
Total acquisition cost of investment	103,500

The cost of an investment includes its purchase price and all incidental costs to acquire the item, such as brokerage commissions and taxes. Any accrued interest is to be recorded by a debit to Interest Receivable or by a debit to Interest Revenue; it is **not** an element of the investment's cost. Accrued interest increases the cash outlay to acquire an investment but does not increase the investment's cost. (Solution = c.)

Question

2. Refer to the facts in **Question 1** above. The amount of cash outlay required to acquire the investment is:
   a. $100,000.
   b. $102,000.
   c. $103,500.
   d. $106,000.

EXPLANATION: The amount of cash required to acquire the investment is determined as follows:

Purchase price (102% x $100,000 par)	$ 102,000
Incidental costs to acquire	1,500
Total acquisition cost of investment	103,500
Accrued interest for three months	2,500
Total cash required to acquire investment	$ 106,000

(Solution = d.)

Question

3. When an investor's accounting period ends on a date that does not coincide with an interest receipt date for bonds held as an investment, the investor must:
   a. make an adjusting entry to debit Interest Receivable and to credit Interest Revenue for the amount of interest accrued since the last interest receipt date.
   b. notify the issuer and request that a special payment be made for the appropriate portion of the interest period.
   c. make an adjusting entry to debit Interest Receivable and to credit Interest Revenue for the total amount of interest to be received at the next interest receipt date.
   d. do nothing special and ignore the fact that the accounting period does not coincide with the bond's interest period.

APPROACH: Think of the requirements of the accrual basis of accounting: revenues are to be recognized when they are earned and expenses are to be recognized (recorded and reported) when they are incurred. Interest is earned by the passage of time and is usually collected after the time period for which it pertains. Thus, to comply with the revenue recognition principle, an adjusting entry is necessary to record the accrued revenue (revenue earned but not yet received). (Solution = a.)

Question

4. The market value of Security A exceeds its cost, and the market value of Security B is less than its cost at a balance sheet date. Both securities are classified as held-for-trading securities. How should each of these assets be reported on the balance sheet?

	Security A	Security B
a.	Market value	Market value
b.	Cost	Cost
c.	Cost	Market value
d.	Market value	Cost

EXPLANATION: Mentally review the accounting requirements for held-for-trading securities. Held-for-trading securities are acquired with the intention of being sold in a short period of time. They are required to be measured at fair (or market) value, with unrealized gains or losses being included in net income. (Solution = a.)

Question

5. ABC Entertainment holds four equity securities at December 31, 2008. They are all classified as available for sale. All securities were purchased in 2008. The portfolio of securities appears as follows at December 31, 2008:

	Cost	Market Value	Difference
McKinnet Corp.	$100,000	$ 80,000	$(20,000)
Hip Corp.	220,000	230,000	10,000
Big Sea Corp.	210,000	150,000	(60,000)
Adams Corp.	140,000	145,000	5,000
Totals	$670,000	$605,000	$(65,000)

What is the amount of unrealized gain or loss to be recognized in 2008?

a. $60,000
b. $20,000
c. $65,000
d. $15,000

EXPLANATION: A security classified as available for sale is remeasured to fair value at each reporting period. Unrealized gains or losses are reported in other comprehensive income and a separate component of shareholder's equity (accumulated other comprehesive income). The value of the total portfolio is considered in making this measurement. (Solution = c.)

Question

6. During 2007, Colquitt Company purchased 4,000 shares of Welshner Corp. common shares for $63,000 as a held-for-trading security. The fair value of these shares was $60,000 at December 31, 2007. Colquitt sold all of the

Welshner shares for $17 per share on December 3, 2008, incurring $2,800 in brokerage commissions. Colquitt Company should report a realized gain on the sale of shares in 2008 of:

a. $8,000.
b. $5,200.
c. $5,000.
d. $2,200.

EXPLANATION: The gain is calculated as follows:

Selling price ($17 x 4,000 shares)	$ 68,000
Cost of sale—commissions	(2,800)
Net proceeds (or net selling price)	65,200
Fair value at Dec. 31/07	60,000
Realized gain on sale	$ 5,200
	(Solution = b.)

TIP! The held-for-trading investment would have been adjusted on December 31, 2007, to $60,000.

Question

7. On its December 31, 2008 balance sheet, Simpson Company appropriately reported a $4,000 debit balance in its Investment Fair Value allowance account. There was no change during 2009 in the composition of Simpson's portfolio of available-for-sale equity securities. The following information pertains to that portfolio:

Security	Cost	Fair value at 12/31/08	Fair value at 12/31/09
A	$ 50,000	$58,000	$65,000
B	40,000	39,000	38,000
C	70,000	67,000	50,000
	$160,000	$164,000	$153,000

What is the adjustment required to the portfolio of available-for-sale investments in 2009?

a. $11,000 (credit)
b. $22,000 (credit)
c. $18,000 (credit)
d. $7,000 (credit)

EXPLANATION: At the end of 2008, the fair value of the portfolio showed a balance of $164,000. At the end of 2009, the fair value of the portfolio has dropped by $11,000 to $153,000. Therefore, the fair investment portfolio must be reduced by $11,000. (Solution = a.)

Question

8. An investor has a long-term investment in shares. Regular cash dividends received by the investor are recorded as:

No significant influence	Significant influence
a. Income	Income
b. A reduction of the investment	A reduction of the investment
c. Income	A reduction of the investment
d. A reduction of the investment	Income

EXPLANATION: If an equity investment does not represent significant influence, it is classified as either available for sale or held for trading. In any event, the investment is carried at fair value and income is recorded as dividends are received. If significant influence exists, the equity method would be employed. Since the investor corporation picks up their share of income (or loss) from the investee corporation each reporting period, the actual dividends received are recorded as a reduction in the investment account. (Solution = c.)

TIP! Note that income will also be affected by unrealized gains or losses for securities classified as held for trading and available for sale.

Question

9. The Higgins Corporation purchased 6,000 shares of common shares of the Barnett Corporation for $40 per share on January 2, 2008. The Barnett Corporation had 60,000 common shares outstanding during 2008, paid cash dividends of $30,000 during 2008, and reported net income of $120,000 for 2008. The Higgins Corporation should report revenue from investment for 2008 in the amount of:
   a. $3,000.
   b. $9,000
   c. $12,000.
   d. $15,000.

EXPLANATION: Because the Higgins Corporation owns only 10% of the outstanding common shares of the investee, it is assumed that Higgins Corporation cannot exercise significant influence over the financing and operating policies of the investee. Therefore, the investment would be classified as available for sale or held for trading. The investor will report dividend revenue equal to the amount of cash dividends received during the period. ($30,000 x 10% = $3,000). (Solution = a.)

TIP! In addition to dividend revenue, income will be affected by the change in fair value of the security from one period to the next.

Question

10. When the equity method is used to account for an investment in common shares of another corporation, the journal entry on the investor's books to record the receipt of cash dividends from the investee will:
    a. include a debit to Cash and a credit to Dividend Revenue.
    b. reduce the carrying value of the investment.
    c. increase the carrying value of the investment.
    d. be the same journal entry that would be recorded if the cost method were used to account for the investment.

EXPLANATION: The journal entry will be a debit to Cash and a credit to Investment in Shares. The credit portion of this entry reduces the balance of the investment account and, therefore, it reduces the carrying value of the investment. (Solution = b.)

Question

11. Which of the following investments would appropriately be accounted for under the equity method?
    a. A 30% investment in preferred shares of a company.
    b. A 20% investment in common shares of a company where there is no significant influence.
    c. A 25% investment in subordinated non-voting shares of a company.
    d. A 15% investment in the common shares of a company where significant influence exists.

EXPLANATION: The existence of significance influence is the key factor here, regardless of the percent ownership. Note also that the shares must be voting. (Solution = d.)

Question

12. On January 1, A Company Limited purchased 30% of the common shares of B Company Limited for $3 million. B's shares trade on a public stock exchange. The book value of B at the time was $9 million. The excess paid was due to intangible assets, which will be amortized over 20 years. During the year, B Company Limited had profits of $400,000 and dividends of $300,000 were paid out. Market value of the shares at year-end was $2.7 million. Assume significant influence. What is the amount that should be recorded as investment income for the year?
    a. $120,000
    b. $127,500
    c. $105,000
    d. $0

EXPLANATION:

• Paid	=	$3,000,000
30% x 9,000,000	=	2,700,000
		300,000
		÷ 20 years
	=	15,000 amortization
• Income:	=	400,000
		x 30%
		120,000
• 120,000 - 15,000	=	105,000

(Solution = c.)

Question

13. Assuming the same information as **12** above, what would the investment income be, assuming no significant influence?
    a. no change
    b. $90,000
    c. $82,500
    d. $0

EXPLANATION: The investment would be classified as held for trading or available for sale. Both recognize income from the investment as dividends are received only. The investment income would be based on the dividends as follows: $300,000 x 30% = $90,000.
The purchase price discrepancy is ignored as is the earnings of B. (Solution = b.)

TIP! The investment would also be adjusted by the drop in market value. If classified as held for trading , the unrealized loss would be recorded in net income, if available for sale it would be recorded in other comprehensive income.

Acquisition of Property, Plant, and Equipment

Chapter 10

Overview

Assets that have physical existence and that are expected to be used in revenue-generating operations for more than one year or operating cycle, whichever is longer, are classified as long-term tangible assets, or more specifically as Property, Plant, and Equipment. Some problems may arise in determining the acquisition cost of a fixed asset: the initial acquisition may be the result of several expenditures, one fixed asset may be exchanged for another fixed asset, a plant asset may be obtained on a deferred payment plan, a plant asset may be constructed internally by the company, or additional expenditures may be involved subsequent to acquisition. These and other issues, and their related accounting procedures, are examined in this chapter.

Study Steps

Understanding Property, Plant, and Equipment within a Business Context

Property, plant, and equipment (PP&E) are **tangible assets** that are **used to generate income**. This latter factor differentiates property, plant, and equipment from inventory, which is **held for resale in the ordinary course of business**. Generally, PP&E are used up or wear out over time and must be replaced, except for land, which presumably retains its value over time.

TIP! PP&E are used to generate income while inventory is held for resale in the ordinary course of business. This is a key distinction as PP&E are amortized, while inventory is not.

From time to time, money must be spent on maintaining the revenue-generating capacity of the assets, and they must be safeguarded to reduce risk of loss from fire, theft, etc. Even though certain assets may last a specific period of time (**economic life**), the company might choose only to use the asset for a shorter period (**useful life**). At the end of the asset's useful life, there may be a **residual value**, i.e., an amount that the company will realize through sale or disposition. This residual value is normally net of any additional costs that the company would have to incur to dispose of the asset.

TIP! An asset's life may be defined as either useful or economic. Economic life is the life of the asset, whereas useful life represents the period over which the company intends to use the asset. This will be equal to or less than the economic life.

TIP! Residual value is the value of the asset at the end of its useful life. Therefore, there is a residual value at the end of the useful life and a salvage value at the end of the economic life.

Barter transactions relating to PP&E

PP&E are considered to be non-monetary assets since their value is not fixed in terms of dollars; i.e., the values will change over time. If a company trades another non-monetary asset for some PP&E, a barter transaction occurs and the company faces the challenge of assigning a transaction cost to the transaction.

Becoming Proficient in Calculations Relating to PP&E

There are few complex calculations or methods specific to this topic. One possible area relates to the potential capitalization of interest costs on self-constructed assets. There are several different ways to approach this and, in Canada, there are no set methods that are more acceptable than any others. Furthermore, the decision whether to capitalize interest or not is open to judgment.

Tips on Chapter Topics

TIP! **Tangible capital assets** are also referred to as **property, plant**, and **equipment, fixed assets**, or **plant assets**. Included in this section should be long-lived tangible assets that are currently being used in operations to generate goods and services for customers. Two exceptions to this guideline are: (1) Construction of Plant in Process, and (2) Deposits on Machinery. In each of these cases, the asset is not yet being used in operations but an expenditure has been made which is to be classified in the property, plant, and equipment section of the balance sheet. Idle fixed assets are to be classified as other assets, and plant assets no longer used and held for sale are to be classified either as current assets or other assets, depending on whether they are expected to be sold within the next year or not.

TIP! In determining the cost of a plant asset, the same basic guideline that is used for inventory is used here as well. Specifically, the cost (initial carrying value) includes all costs necessary to get the item to the location and condition for its intended use.

TIP! In the past, amortization of capital tangible assets was called depreciation, and amortization referred to intangible assets.

TIP! Additions, improvements, and replacements, which add to the assets future service potential, are capitalized after the acquisition.

TIP! In determining the cost of a plant asset, it is useful to remember the historical cost principle. Cost is measured by the cash or the fair market value of the non-cash consideration given or the fair market value of the consideration received, whichever is the more clearly evident. Fair market value refers to cash equivalent value. When cash is given to acquire an asset, it is a relatively simple matter to determine the asset's cost. However, when a non-cash asset is given in exchange or when a deferred payment plan is involved, more thought is required to determine the asset's cost.

TIP! The potential amount of interest to capitalize is the lesser of the actual amount of interest paid and the amount determined by multiplying the weighted-average accumulated expenditures by the weighted-average interest rate.

TIP! When one non-cash asset is exchanged for another non-cash asset, it is recorded at fair value. Carrying value would only be used if (1) the transaction lacks commercial substance, (2) fair values are not determinable, or (3) the exchange transaction was merely to facilitate a sale to customers.

TIP! When a deferred payment plan is involved in the acquisition of a non-cash asset, pay careful attention to whether a fair rate is stated in the agreement. When an unreasonably low stated interest rate is present, interest must be imputed so that the effective amount of interest reported reflects the market rate of interest.

TIP! In the context of accounting for property, plant, and equipment, the term "capitalize" means to record and carry forward into one or more periods expenditures from which benefits or proceeds will be realized; thus, a balance sheet account is debited.

TIP! In accounting for the many expenditures related to the operation and maintenance of property, plant, and equipment, the accountant must keep in mind that expenditures benefiting the company for more than the current accounting period should be capitalized in order to properly match expenses with revenues over successive accounting periods; expenditures for items that do not yield benefits beyond the current accounting period should be expensed.

TIP! In the context of the topic of tangible capital assets, the term **carrying value** refers to the amount derived by deducting the balance in the Accumulated Amortization account from the balance in the related asset account. Synonymous terms are **book value**, net asset value, unamortized value, and **carrying amount**. Book value may be very different from fair value. Fair value is often referred to as fair market value or market value. The calculation of book value is **not** affected by the estimated residual value or salvage value.

TIP! The net cost (cost less scrap proceeds) of tearing down an old building should be charged (debited) to the Land account if the building was an existing structure and recently acquired along with the land as a site to be used for another structure. (The cost is charged to Land because it was necessary to get the land in the condition for its intended purpose—to provide space upon which to erect a new building.)

TIP! There are several areas in accounting that utilize the formula to allocate a single sum between two or more items based on the relative fair market values of the items involved. That formula is as follows:

$$\frac{\text{Market Value of One Item in Group}}{\text{Market Value of ALL Items in Group}} \times = \text{Amount to be Allocated} = \text{Amount to be Assigned to Item Designated in the Numerator}$$

TIP! This formula is used in Chapter 9 to allocate one lump-sum amount of cost to the individual assets acquired in a **lump sum purchase** (often called a **basket purchase**). The formula will also be used to allocate the proceeds from the issuance of several classes of securities, to allocate the proceeds from the issuance of bonds with detachable warrants, to allocate the cost of certain inventory items to units based on their relative sales values, and to allocate the cost of an investment. The formula is also useful in the managerial accounting arena such as in the case where there are joint costs to be allocated to joint products.

TIP! An investment tax credit received should be treated as a reduction in the cost of the qualified property (similar to a purchase discount) and accounted for over the same period as the related asset (cost reduction or deferral method).

Case 10-1

PURPOSE: This case will review the costs to be capitalized for property, plant, and equipment.

Property, plant, and equipment generally represent a large portion of the total assets of a company. Accounting for the acquisition and usage of such assets is, therefore, an important part of the financial reporting process.

Instructions

(a) Distinguish between a revenue expenditure and a capital expenditure. Explain why the distinction is important.
(b) Identify at least six costs that should be capitalized as the cost of land. Assume that land with an existing building is acquired for cash and that the existing building is to be removed immediately in order to provide space for a new building on that site.
(c) Identify at least five costs that should be capitalized as the cost of a building.
(d) Identify at least six costs that should be capitalized when equipment is acquired for cash.
(e) Describe the factors that determine whether expenditures relating to property, plant, and equipment already in use should be capitalized.

Solution to Case 10-1

(a) A **capital expenditure** is expected to yield benefits either in all future accounting periods (acquisition of land) or in a limited number of accounting periods (acquisition of buildings and equipment). Capital expenditures are capitalized (that is, recorded as assets) and, if related to assets of limited life, amortized over the periods which will be benefited. A **revenue expenditure** is an expenditure for which the benefits are **not** expected to extend beyond the current period. Hence, they benefit only the current period (recorded as an expense) or they benefit no period at all (recorded as a loss).

The distinction between capital and revenue expenditures is of significance because it involves the timing of the recognition of expense and, consequently, the determination of periodic earnings. This distinction also affects the costs reflected in the asset accounts which will be recovered from future periods' revenues.

If a revenue expenditure is improperly capitalized, net income of the current period is overstated, assets are overstated, and future earnings are understated for all the periods to which the improperly capitalized cost is amortized. If the cost is not amortized, future earnings will not be affected, but assets and retained earnings will continue to be overstated for as long as the cost remains on the books. If a non-amortizable capital expenditure is improperly expensed, current earnings are understated and assets and retained earnings are understated for all foreseeable periods in the future. If an amortizable capital expenditure is improperly expensed, net income of the current period is understated, assets and retained earnings are understated, and net income is overstated for all future periods to which the cost should have been amortized.

(b) The cost of land may include:
(1) purchase price.
(2) title search fees.
(3) delinquent property taxes assumed by buyer.
(4) legal fees.
(5) recording fee.

(6) unpaid interest assumed by buyer.
(7) cost of clearing, grading, and landscaping.
(8) cost of removing old building (less salvage).
(9) special assessments such as lighting or sewers if they are permanent in nature.
(10) landscaping of permanent nature.
(11) any other cost necessary to acquire the land and get it in the condition necessary for its intended purpose.

(c) The cost of a building may include:
(1) purchase price or construction costs (including an allocation of overhead if self-constructed).
(2) excavation fees.
(3) architectural fees.
(4) building permit fee.
(5) interest during construction (only interest actually incurred).
(6) any other cost necessary to acquire the building and get it in the location and condition for its intended purpose.

(d) The cost of equipment may include:
(1) purchase price (less discounts allowed).
(2) sales tax.
(3) installation charges.
(4) freight charges during transit.
(5) insurance during transit.
(6) cost of labour and materials for test runs.
(7) cost of special foundations.
(8) other costs necessary to acquire the equipment and get it to the location and condition for its intended use.

(e) The factors that determine whether expenditures relating to property, plant, and equipment already in use should be capitalized are as follows:
(1) The asset's useful life is increased.
(2) The quantity of units produced from the asset is increased.
(3) The quality of the units produced from the asset is enhanced.
(4) The associated operating costs are reduced.
Only one factor must be met.

TIP! Typically, the cost of land includes the cost of elements that occur prior to excavation for a new building. Costs related to the foundation of the building are elements of building cost.

Exercise 10-1

PURPOSE: This exercise will help you identify which expenditures related to property, plant, and equipment should be capitalized and which should be expensed.

TIP!

Remember that expenditures which benefit the company for more than the current accounting period should be capitalized in order to properly match expenses with revenues over successive accounting periods. Expenditures for items that do not yield benefits beyond the current accounting period should be expensed.

Instructions

Assume all amounts are material. For each of the following independent items, indicate by use of the appropriate letter if it should be:

C = Capitalized or E = Expensed

_____ 1. Invoice price of drill press.
_____ 2. Sales tax on computer.
_____ 3. Costs of permanent partitions constructed in an existing office building.
_____ 4. Installation charges for new conveyer system.
_____ 5. Costs of trees and shrubs planted in front of office building.
_____ 6. Costs of surveying new land site.
_____ 7. Costs of major overhaul of delivery truck.
_____ 8. Costs of building new counters for show room.
_____ 9. Costs of powders, soaps, and wax for office floors.
_____ 10. Cost of janitorial services for office and show room.
_____ 11. Costs of carpets in a new office building.
_____ 12. Costs of annual termite inspection of warehouse.
_____ 13. Insurance charged for new equipment while in transit.
_____ 14. Property taxes on land used for parking lot.
_____ 15. Cost of a fan installed to help cool old factory machine.
_____ 16. Cost of exterminator's services.
_____ 17. Costs of major redecorating of executives' offices.
_____ 18. Cost of fertilizers for shrubs and trees.
_____ 19. Cost of labour services for self-constructed machine.
_____ 20. Costs of materials used and labour services expended during trial runs of new machine.

Solution to Exercise 10-1

1. C	4. C	7. C	10. E
2. C	5. C	8. C	11. C
3. C	6. C	9. E*	12. E

13. C	15. C	17. C	19. C
14. E	16. E	18. E*	20. C

*This answer assumes the products were consumed during the current period. Material amounts of unused supplies on hand at the balance sheet date should be reported as a prepaid expense (supplies inventory).

TIP! As used in this chapter, the term **capital expenditure** refers to an expenditure that is expected to benefit more than one period; hence, it is initially recorded as an asset and should be expensed over the periods benefited. A **revenue expenditure** is an expenditure which is expected **not** to be of benefit to any period beyond the current period; hence, it is recorded by a debit to either an expense account or to a loss account in the period incurred.

Exercise 10-2

PURPOSE: This exercise will give you practice in identifying capital versus revenue expenditures.

Hughes Supply Company, a newly formed corporation, incurred the following expenditures related to Land, to Buildings, and to Machinery and Equipment.

Cash paid for land and dilapidated building thereon		$ 300,000
Removal of old building	$ 60,000	
Less salvage	16,500	43,500
Surveying before construction to determine best position for building		1,110
Interest on short-term loans during construction		22,200
Excavation before construction for basement		57,000
Fee for title search charged by abstract company		1,560
Architect's fees		8,400
Machinery purchased (subject to 2% cash discount, which was not taken)		165,000
Freight on machinery purchased		4,020
Storage charges on machinery, necessitated by non-completion of building when machinery was delivered on schedule		6,540
New building constructed (building construction took 8 months from date of purchase of land and old building)		1,500,000
Assessment by city for sewers (a one-time assessment)		4,800

Transportation charges for delivery of machinery from storage to new building	1,860
Installation of machinery	6,000
Trees, shrubs, and other landscaping after completion of building (permanent in nature)	16,200

Instructions

(a) Identify the amounts that should be debited to Land.
(b) Identify the amounts that should be debited to Buildings.
(c) Identify the amounts that should be debited to Machinery and Equipment.
(d) Indicate how the costs above **not** debited to Land, Buildings, or Machinery and Equipment should be recorded.

Solution to Exercise 10-2

	(a) Land	(b) Bldgs.	(c) M&E	(d) Other	
Cash paid for land & old bldg.	$300,000				
Removal of old building ($60,000 – $16,500)	43,500				
Surveying before construction		$ 1,110			
Interest on loans during construction		22,200			
Excavation before construction		57,000			
Abstract fees for title search	1,560				
Architect's fees		8,400			
Machinery purchased			$161,700	$ 3,300	Misc. Exp. (Int. Exp.)
Freight on machinery			4,020		
Storage charges caused by non-completion of building				6,540	Misc. Exp. (Loss)
New building construction		1,500,000			
Assessment by city	4,800				
Transportation charges—machinery				1,860	Misc. Exp. (Loss)
Installation—machinery			6,000		
Landscaping	16,200				
Totals	$366,060	$1,588,710	$171,720	$11,700	

TIP!

The purchase price of the machine is the **cash equivalent price** at the date of acquisition which is the $165,000 reduced by the 2% cash discount allowed ($3,300), whether or not the discount is taken. The additional outlay of $3,300 is due to extending the time for payment, which is equivalent to interest (time value of money). The cost of the machine does **not** include the $6,540 storage charges and $1,860 transportation charges out of storage because these costs were not planned costs necessary to get the equipment to the location intended for use; rather they were caused by the lack of completing the building on schedule (hence, a loss or miscellaneous expense).

Case 10-2

PURPOSE: This case will review the rules for determining a plant asset's cost when the asset is acquired on a deferred payment plan or in a non-monetary exchange.

A company often acquires property, plant, and equipment by means other than immediate cash payment.

Instructions

(a) Explain how to determine a plant asset's cost if it is acquired on a deferred payment plan.
(b) Explain how to determine a plant asset's cost if it is acquired in exchange for another non-monetary asset.

Solution to Case 10-2

(a) A plant asset acquired on a deferred-payment plan should be recorded at an equivalent cash price excluding interest. If a fair rate of interest is not stated in the sales contract, an imputed interest rate should be determined. The asset should then be recorded at the contract's present value, which is calculated by discounting the payments at the stated or imputed interest rate. The interest portion (stated or imputed) of the contract price should be charged to interest expense over the life of the contract.
(b) A plant asset acquired in exchange for another non-monetary asset should be recorded at the fair value (cash equivalent value) of the consideration given up or the fair value of the consideration received, whichever is more clearly evident. Any gain or loss on the exchange should be recognized because the earning process is considered complete on the old asset and the earnings process is commencing on the new asset.

TIP! The general measurement rule for non-monetary transactions is fair value, unless:

- the transaction lacks commercial substance;
- fair values are not determinable;
- the exchange transaction was merely to facilitate a sale to customers.

Exercise 10-3

PURPOSE: This exercise will provide an example of the capitalization of interest cost incurred during construction.

Marvel Company engaged Invention Company to construct a special purpose machine to be used in its factory. The following data pertain:

1. The contract was signed by Marvel on August 30, 2008. Construction began immediately and was completed on December 1, 2008.
2. To aid in the financing of this construction, Marvel borrowed $600,000 from Bank of X-Men on August 30, 2008, by signing a $600,000 note due in 3 years. The note bears an interest rate of 12% and interest is payable each August 30.
3. Marvel paid Invention $200,000 on August 30, 2008, and invested the remainder of the note's proceeds ($400,000) in 5% government securities until December 1.
4. On December 1, Marvel made the final $400,000 payment to Invention.
5. Aside from the note payable to the Bank of X-Men, Marvel's only outstanding liability at December 31, 2008, is a $60,000, 9%, 5-year note payable dated January 1, 2005, on which interest is payable each December 31.

Instructions

(a) Calculate the weighted-average accumulated expenditures, interest revenue, avoidable interest, total interest incurred, and interest cost to be capitalized during 2008. Round all calculations to the nearest dollar.

(b) Prepare the journal entries needed on the books of Marvel Company at each of the following dates: August 30, 2008; December 1, 2008; and December 31, 2008.

Solution to Exercise 10-3

(a) **Calculation of Weighted-Average Accumulated Expenditures:**

Expenditures Date	Expenditures Amount	x	Capitalization Period	=	Weighted-Average Accumulated Expenditures
August 30	$200,000		3/12		$50,000
December 1	400,000		0		0
					$50,000

Interest Revenue: $400,000 x 5% x 3/12 = $5,000

Avoidable Interest:

Weighted-Average Accumulated Expenditures	x	Interest Rate	=	Avoidable Interest
$50,000		12%		$6,000

Total Interest Incurred:	\$600,000 x 12% x 4/12	=	\$ 24,000
	\$60,000 x 9%	=	5,400
			\$ 29,400

Interest to be capitalized: \$6,000 (lesser of avoidable interest and total interest incurred)

Examples of assets that qualify for interest capitalization are (1) assets that an enterprise constructs for its own use (such as facilities), and (2) assets intended for sale or lease that are constructed as discrete projects (such as ships or real estate projects). Interest cannot be capitalized for inventories that are routinely manufactured or otherwise produced in large quantities on a repetitive basis. Marvel's machine is a qualifying asset.

(b) 8/30	Cash	600,000	
	Notes Payable		600,000
	Machine	200,000	
	Short-term Investments	400,000	
	Cash.		600,000
12/1	Cash	405,000	
	Interest Revenue (\$400,000 x 5% x 3/12)		5,000
	Short-term Investments		400,000
	Machine	400,000	
	Cash.		400,000
12/31	Machine [calculated in part (a)]	6,000	
	Interest Expense (\$29,400 – \$6,000)	23,400	
	Cash (\$60,000 x 9%)		5,400
	Interest Payable (\$600,000 x 12% x 4/12)		24,000

EXPLANATION:

The amount to be capitalized is that portion of the interest cost incurred during the asset's acquisition period that theoretically could have been avoided (for example, by avoiding additional borrowings or by using the funds expended for the asset to repay existing borrowings) if expenditures for the asset had not been made.

Avoidable interest is determined by applying an appropriate interest rate(s) to the weighted-average amount of accumulated expenditures for the asset during the period. The appropriate rate is that rate associated with a specific new borrowing, if any. If average accumulated expenditures for the asset exceed the amount of a specific new borrowing associated with the asset, the capitalization rate to be applied to such excess shall be a weighted average of the rates applicable to other borrowings of the enterprise.

The weighted-average amount of accumulated expenditures for the asset represents the average investment tied up in the qualifying asset during the period. For Marvel, a $200,000 balance in Machine for the three-month capitalization period (date of expenditures to the date the asset is ready for use) means an equivalent (average) investment of $50,000 on an annual basis. Marvel uses only the 12% rate applicable to the specific new borrowing to calculate the avoidable interest because the specific borrowing ($600,000) exceeds the weighted-average accumulated expenditures.

The amount of interest to be capitalized is not to exceed the actual interest costs incurred. Thus, Marvel compares its avoidable interest of $6,000 and its actual interest incurred of $29,400 and chooses the lower amount to capitalize. Any interest amounts earned on funds borrowed that are temporarily in excess of the company's needs are to be reported as interest revenue rather than be used to offset the amount of interest to be capitalized. Thus, Marvel will report $5,000 as interest revenue and that $5,000 will not affect the amount of interest to be capitalized.

Exercise 10-4

PURPOSE: This exercise will give you practice in accounting for the acquisition of a plant asset on a deferred payment plan.

St. John's Fishing Inc. purchased a computer network on December 31, 2008, for $200,000, paying $50,000 down and agreeing to pay the balance in five equal instalments of $30,000 payable each December 31 beginning in 2009. An assumed interest rate of 10% is implicit in the purchase price.

INSTRUCTIONS (Round to the nearest cent)

(a) Prepare the journal entry(ies) at the date of purchase.
(b) Prepare an amortization schedule for the instalment agreement.
(c) Prepare the journal entry(ies) at December 31, 2009, to record the cash payment and the applicable interest expense (assume the effective interest method is employed).
(d) Prepare the journal entry(ies) at December 31, 2010, to record the cash payment and the applicable interest expense (assume the effective interest method is employed).

Solution to Exercise 10-4

(a) Time diagram:

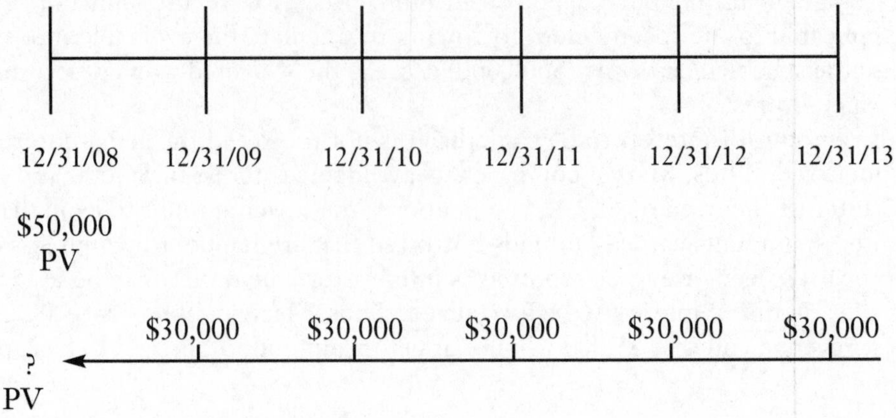

Entry:

Equipment	163,723.70*	
Discount on Notes Payable	36,276.30	
Cash		50,000.00
Notes Payable ($30,000 x 5)		150,000.00

*PV of a $30,000 ordinary annuity @ 10% for 5 years ($30,000 x 3.79079)	$ 113,723.70
Down payment	50,000.00
Capitalized value of equipment	$ 163,723.70

(b)

Date	Cash Payment	10% Interest Expense	Reduction of Principal	Liability Balance
12/31/08				$113,723.70
12/31/09	$ 30,000.00	$ 11,372.37	$ 18,627.63	95,096.07
12/31/10	$ 30,000.00	9,509.61	20,490.39	74,605.68
12/31/11	$ 30,000.00	7,460.57	22,539.43	52,066.25
12/31/12	$ 30,000.00	5,206.63	24,793.37	27,272.88
12/31/13	$ 30,000.00	2,727.12 *	27,272.88	-0-
Totals	$ 150,000.00	$ 36,276.30	$113,723.70	

*This is a plug figure, which includes a rounding error of $0.17.

(c) **December 31, 2009**

Notes Payable	30,000.00	
Interest Expense (see schedule)	11,372.37	
Cash		30,000.00
Discount on Notes Payable		11,372.37

(d)

December 31, 2010

Notes Payable	30,000.00	
Interest Expense (see schedule)	9,509.61	
Cash		30,000.00
Discount on Notes Payable		9,509.61

TIP!

For each entry in (c) and (d), two entries could replace the one compound entry. For example, the two equivalent entries for (c) would be:

Notes Payable	30,000.00	
Cash		30,000.00
Interest Expense	11,372.37	
Discount on Notes Payable		11,372.37

Exercise 10-5

PURPOSE: This exercise reviews the calculations involved in a lump-sum purchase of plant assets.

The Eliason Company paid $750,000 cash for a package of plant assets. The package consisted of the following:

	Seller's Book Value	Market Value
Land	$ 60,000	$ 300,000
Building	120,000	400,000
Equipment	220,000	250,000
Tools	100,000	50,000
Total	$ 500,000	$ 1,000,000

Instructions

(a) Prepare the journal entry for Eliason to record the acquisition of these assets on the company's books.

(b) Why must you allocate the total cost to separate accounts for the individual assets? Why can't you simply use "Plant Assets" as an account and record the total cost to that account? Explain.

Solution to Exercise 10-5

(a) Land	225,000	
Building	300,000	
Equipment	187,500	

Tools	37,500	
Cash		750,000

EXPLANATION: The total cost ($750,000) is to be allocated to the individual assets based on the relative market values of these assets. The formula that can be used to accomplish this objective is as follows:

$$\frac{\text{Market Value of One Item in Group}}{\text{Market Value of All Items in Group}} \times \text{Amount to be Allocated} = \text{Amount to be Assigned to Item designated in the Numerator}$$

Land:	($300,000 ÷ $1,000,000) x $750,000 =	$225,000
Building:	($400,000 ÷ $1,000,000) x $750,000 =	$300,000
Equipment:	($250,000 ÷ $1,000,000) x $750,000 =	$187,500
Tools:	($50,000 ÷ $1,000,000) x $750,000 =	$ 37,500
		$750,000

TIP! Sum the four answers obtained by using the formula. They should total to the amount you set out to allocate ($750,000, in this case).

(b) The total cost must be allocated to the individual assets because land is not subject to the process of amortization, and the amortizable assets normally are subject to different service lives and maybe even different amortization methods.

Illustration 10-1

Accounting for Asset Exchange

Type of Exchange	Accounting Guidance	Rationale
Monetary exchange 	New asset(s) at FV of asset(s) given up Recognize gains and losses immediately	Company's economic situation has changed, and earnings process is complete
Nonmonetary exchange —general rule 	New asset(s) at FV of asset(s) given up Recognize gains and losses immediately	Company's economic situation has changed, and earnings process is complete
Nonmonetary exchange to facilitate sale, fair values not available, or lacking commercial substance 	New asset(s) at BV of asset(s) given up No gains recognized; losses recognized immediately	Company's economic situation has not changed (or is not measurable) or earnings process is not complete

Exercise 10-6

PURPOSE: This exercise will allow you to practice recording the exchange of assets.

Soon Yoon Company exchanged equipment used in its manufacturing operations for equipment used in the operations of Peggy Gunshanan Company. The following information pertains to the exchange:

	Soon Yoon Co.	Peggy Gunshanan Co.
Equipment (cost)	$ 84,000	$ 84,000
Accumulated amortization	66,000	30,000
Fair value of equipment	41,500	46,500
Cash given up	1,000	

Instructions

Prepare the journal entries to record the exchange on the books of both companies.

Solution to Exercise 10-6

Soon Yoon Company:

Equipment (New)	42,500	
Accumulated Amortization	66,000	
Equipment (Old)		84,000
Cash.		1,000
Gain on disposition		23,500

Fair value of asset given up:

Fair value of equipment	$ 41,500
Cash	1,000
	$ 42,500

Peggy Gunshanan Company:

Cash	1,000	
Equipment (New)	46,500	
Accumulated Amortization	30,000	
Equipment (Old)		84,000
Loss on disposition	6,500	

EXPLANATION: Refer to **Illustration 10-1** which summarizes the rules for asset exchanges. Fair value of what is given up is used unless certain criteria are met, in which case carrying value is used. There is no indication of these criteria being met and, therefore, Soon Yoon Company will recognize a gain and Peggy Gunshanan Company will recognize a loss.

TIP! It is important to note that Peggy Gunshanan had an asset that was carried in excess of its fair value. Had this transaction not occurred (and a loss recognized), it would be subject to impairment testing.

TIP! Further, it may still be subject to an impairment test, since it has been exchanged for an asset that has a fair value of $41,500, which is less than the $46,500 fair value estimated for the asset given up. Care must be taken when recording fair values on non-monetary exchanges to ensure the asset is not over valued.

Illustration 10-2

Expenditures Subsequent to Acquisition

A plant asset often requires expenditures subsequent to acquisition. Generally, four major types of expenditures may be incurred relative to existing plant assets; they are as follows:

- **Additions**. Increase or extension of existing assets.
- **Improvements and Replacements**. Substitution of an improved asset for an existing one.
- **Rearrangement and Reinstallation**. Movement of assets from one location to another.
- **Repairs**. Expenditures that maintain assets in condition for operation.

Costs that are incurred subsequent to acquisition are to be capitalized (by a debit to an asset account or to an accumulated amortization account, depending on the circumstances) if they are material, non-recurring in nature, and benefit future periods in some manner such as by doing one or more of the following:

a. They extend the useful life of a plant asset.
b. They enhance the quality of existing services.
c. They add new asset services.
d. They reduce future operating costs of existing assets.
e. They are required to meet governmental regulations (such as for environmental reasons).
f. They increase the number of units produced.

The accounting treatment appropriate for various costs incurred subsequent to the acquisition of capitalized assets is summarized as follows:

Type of Expenditure	Normal Accounting Treatment
Additions	Capitalize cost of addition to asset account.
Improvements and Replacements	(a) **Carrying value of old asset known:** Remove cost of and accumulated amortization on old asset, recognizing any gain or loss. Capitalize cost of improvement/replacement. (b) **Carrying value of old asset unknown:** 1. If the asset's useful life is extended, debit accumulated amortization for cost of improvement/replacement. 2. If the quantity or quality of the asset's productivity is increased, capitalize cost of improvement/replacement to asset account.
Rearrangement and Reinstallation	(a) If original installation cost is **known**, account for cost of rearrangement/reinstallation as a replacement (carrying value known). (b) If original installation cost is **unknown** and rearrangement/reinstallation cost is **material** in amount and benefits future periods, capitalize as an asset. (c) If original installation cost is **unknown** and rearrangement/reinstallation cost is **not material or future benefit is questionable**, expense the cost when incurred.
Repairs	(a) **Ordinary**: Expense cost of repairs when incurred. (b) **Major**: As appropriate, treat as an addition, improvement, or replacement.

Case 10-3

PURPOSE: This case will provide a few examples of the accounting for costs subsequent to the acquisition of fixed assets.

Hardent Resources Group has been in its plant facility for 20 years. Although the plant is quite functional, numerous repair costs are incurred to maintain it in sound working order. The company's plant asset book value is currently $750,000, as indicated below:

Original cost	$ 1,350,000
Accumulated amortization	600,000
Book value	$ 750,000

During the current year, the following expenditures were made involving the plant facility:

(a) The entire plant was repainted at a cost of $26,000.

(b) The roof was an asbestos cement slate; for safety purposes, it was removed and replaced with a new and better quality roof at a cost of $62,000. Book value of the old roof was $31,000.

(c) Because of increased demands for its product, the company increased its plant capacity by building a new addition at a cost of $315,000.

(d) The plumbing system was completely updated at a cost of $53,000. The cost of the old plumbing system was not known. It is estimated that the useful life of the building will not change as a result of this updating.
(e) A series of major repairs were made at a cost of $50,000, because parts of the wood structure were rotting. The cost of the old wood structure was not known. These extensive repairs are estimated to increase the useful life of the building.

Instructions

Indicate how each of these transactions would be recorded in the accounting records.

Solution to Case 10-3

(a) Expenditures that do not increase the service benefits of the asset are expensed. Painting costs are considered ordinary repairs because they maintain the existing condition of the asset or restore it to normal operating efficiency.
(b) The approach to follow is to remove the old book value of the roof and substitute the cost of the new roof. It is assumed that the expenditure increases the future service potential of the asset. Recognize a loss equal to the book value of the old roof removed.
(c) Any addition to plant assets is capitalized because a new asset has been created. This addition increases the service potential of the plant.
(d) Conceptually the book value of the old plumbing system should be removed. However, in practice, it is often difficult if not impossible to determine this amount. In this case, one of two approaches is followed. One approach is to capitalize the cost of the replacement on the theory that sufficient depreciation was taken on the item to reduce the carrying amount to almost zero. A second approach is to debit accumulated depreciation on the theory that the replacement extends the useful life of the asset and thereby recaptures some or all of the past depreciation. In our present situation, the problem specifically states that the useful life is not extended, and, therefore, debiting accumulated depreciation is inappropriate. Thus, this expenditure should be added to the cost of the plant facility.
(e) See discussion in (d) above. In this case, because the useful life of the asset has increased, a debit to accumulated depreciation would appear to be the most appropriate treatment.

Exercise 10-7

PURPOSE: This exercise will (1) illustrate several different ways in which you may dispose of property, and (2) discuss the appropriate accounting procedures for each.

Presented below is a schedule of property dispositions for Friedlander Co.

Schedule of Property Dispositions

	Cost	Accumulated Amortization	Cash Proceeds	Fair Market Value	Nature of Disposition
Land	$ 80,000	—	$ 64,000	$ 64,000	Condemnation
Building	30,000	—	7,200	—	Demolition
Warehouse	130,000	$22,000	148,000	148,000	Destruction by fire
Machine	16,000	6,400	3,600	14,400	Trade-in
Furniture	20,000	15,700	—	5,600	Contribution
Automobile	16,000	6,920	5,920	5,920	Sale

The following additional information is available:

- **Land.** On January 7, a condemnation award was received as consideration for unimproved land held primarily as an investment, and on April 7 another parcel of unimproved land to be held as an investment was purchased at a cost of $70,000.
- **Building.** On May 4, land and building were purchased at a total cost of $150,000, of which 20% was allocated to the building on the corporate books. The real estate was acquired with the intention of demolishing the building, and this was accomplished during the month of August. Cash proceeds received in August represent the net proceeds from demolition of the building.
- **Warehouse.** On January 2, the warehouse was destroyed by fire. The warehouse had an accumulated amortization of $22,000. On June 15, part of the insurance proceeds was used to purchase a replacement warehouse at a cost of $130,000.
- **Machine.** On October 31, the machine was exchanged for another similar machine having a fair market value of $10,800 and cash of $3,600 was received.
- **Furniture.** On July 2, furniture was contributed to a qualified charitable organization. No other contributions were made or pledged during the year.
- **Automobile.** On December 31, the automobile was sold to Dee Dee Burgess, a shareholder.

Instructions

Indicate how these items would be reported on the income statement of Friedlander Co.

Solution to Exercise 10-7

The following accounting treatment appears appropriate for these items:

- **Land**. The loss on the condemnation of the land of $16,000 ($80,000 – $64,000) should be reported as an extraordinary item on the income statement. A condemnation comes about from a government unit exercising its right of eminent domain. Eminent domain is defined as "expropriation of assets by a government." The $70,000 land purchase has no income statement effect.
- **Building**. There is no recognized gain or loss on the demolition of the building. The entire purchase cost ($30,000), decreased by the demolition proceeds ($7,200), is allocated to land.
- **Warehouse**. The gain on the destruction of the warehouse should be reported in the "other revenues and gains" section of the income statement. A fire can happen in any environment; therefore, it is not an extraordinary item. The gain is calculated as follows:

Insurance proceeds		$148,000
Cost	$130,000	
Accumulated amortization	(22,000)	(108,000)
Realized gain		$ 40,000

Fair market value of old machine		$14,400
Cash received		3,600
Cost	$16,000	
Accumulated amortization	(6,400)	(9,600)
Total gain experienced		$8,400

  This gain would probably be reported in the "other revenues and gains" section. It might be considered an unusual item, but it would usually not be infrequent. The cost of the new machine would be capitalized at $14,400.
- **Furniture.** The contribution of the furniture to a charitable organization would be reported as a contribution expense of $5,600 with a related gain on disposition of furniture of $1,300 [$5,600 – ($20,000 – $15,700)]. The contribution expense and the related gain may be netted, if desired, for reporting purposes.
- **Automobile.** The loss on sale of the automobile of $3,160 [$5,920 – ($16,000 – $6,920)] should probably be reported in the "other expenses and losses" section. This is a related party transaction; such transactions require special disclosure.

TIP! The receipt of the condemnation award (January 7) represents an **involuntary conversion of non-monetary assets to monetary assets**. Any gain or loss related to the transaction shall be recognized even though the enterprise reinvests or is obligated to reinvest the monetary assets in replacement non-monetary assets. The receipt of insurance proceeds due to the destruction of the warehouse is also an involuntary conversion of non-monetary assets to monetary assets.

TIP!

The sale of property, plant, and equipment for cash should be accounted for as follows:
(1) The carrying value at the date of the sale (cost of the property, plant, and equipment less the accumulated depreciation) should be removed from the accounts.
(2) The excess of cash from the sale over the carrying value removed is accounted for as a gain on the sale, while the excess of carrying value removed over cash from the sale is accounted for as a loss on the sale.

TIP!

When a plant asset is disposed of, the accumulated amortization must be updated before the gain or loss can be calculated. The discussions above assume that updating has taken place.

Exercise 10-8

PURPOSE: This exercise is designed to give you additional practice in analyzing changes in property, plant, and equipment accounts during a period. Problems of this type frequently appear on professional exams.

At December 31, 2007, certain accounts included in the property, plant, and equipment section of the Busch Company's balance sheet had the following balances:

Land	$ 100,000
Buildings	800,000
Leasehold improvements	500,000
Machinery and equipment	700,000

During 2008 the following transactions occurred:

- Land site number 52 was acquired for $1,000,000. Additionally, to acquire the land Busch paid a $60,000 commission to a real estate agent. Costs of $15,000 were incurred to clear the land. During the course of clearing the land, timber and gravel were recovered and sold for $5,000.

- A second tract of land (site number 53) with a building was acquired for $300,000. The closing statement indicated that the land value was $200,000 and the building value was $100,000. Shortly after acquisition, the building was demolished at a cost of $30,000. A new building was constructed for $150,000 plus the following costs:

Excavation fees	$ 11,000
Architectural design fees	8,000
Building permit fee	1,000
Imputed interest on equity funds used during construction (The company had no debt outstanding and no actual interest cost incurred.)	6,000

The building was completed and occupied on September 30, 2008.

- A third tract of land (site number 54) was acquired for $600,000 and was put on the market for resale.

- Extensive work was done to a building occupied by Busch under a lease agreement that expires on December 31, 2017. The total cost of the work was $125,000, which consisted of the following:

Painting of ceilings	$ 10,000	estimated useful life is 1 year
Electrical work	35,000	estimated useful life is 10 years
Construction of extension to current working area	80,000	estimated useful life is 30 years
	$ 125,000	

The lessor paid one-half of the costs incurred in connection with the extension to the current working area.

- During December 2008, costs of $65,000 were incurred to improve leased office space. The related lease will terminate on December 31, 2010, and is not expected to be renewed.
- A group of new machines were purchased under a royalty agreement which provides for payment of royalties based on units of production for the machines. The invoice price of the machines was $75,000, freight costs were $2,000, unloading charges were $1,500, and royalty payments for 2008 were $13,000.

Instructions

(a) Prepare a detailed analysis of the changes in each of the following balance sheet accounts for 2008:

Land	Leasehold improvements
Buildings	Machinery and equipment

Disregard the related accumulated amortization accounts.

(b) List the items in the situation which were not used to determine the answer to (a) above, and indicate **where, or if**, these items should be included in Busch's financial statements.

Solution to Exercise 10-8

(a)

Busch Company
ANALYSIS OF LAND ACCOUNT
for 2008

Balance at January 1, 2008			$ 100,000
Land site number 52			
Acquisition cost		$ 1,000,000	
Commission to real estate agent		60,000	
Clearing costs	$ 15,000		
Less amounts recovered	5,000	10,000	
Total land site number 52			1,070,000

Land site number 53		
Land value	200,000	
Building value	100,000	
Demolition cost	30,000	
Total land site number 53		330,000
Balance at December 31, 2008		$ 1,500,000

Busch Company
ANALYSIS OF BUILDING ACCOUNT
for 2008

Balance at January 1, 2008		$ 800,000
Cost of new building constructed on land site number 53		
Construction costs	$ 150,000	
Excavation fees	11,000	
Architectural design fees	8,000	
Building permit fee	1,000	170,000
Balance at December 31, 2008		$ 970,000

Busch Company
ANALYSIS OF LEASEHOLD IMPROVEMENTS ACCOUNT
for 2008

Balance at January 1, 2008	$500,000
Electrical work	35,000
Construction of extension to current work area ($80,000 x 1/2)	40,000
Office space improvements	65,000
Balance at December 31, 2008	$640,000

Busch Company
ANALYSIS OF MACHINERY AND EQUIPMENT ACCOUNT
for 2008

Balance at January 1, 2008		$ 700,000
Cost of new machines acquired		
Invoice price	$ 75,000	
Freight costs	2,000	
Unloading charges	1,500	78,500
Balance at December 31, 2008		$ 778,500

(b) Items in the situation which were not used to determine the answer to (a) above are:

- Imputed interest of $6,000 on equity funds used during construction should not be included anywhere in Busch's financial statements. Only interest actually incurred should be capitalized during construction.
- Land site number 54, which was acquired for $600,000 and held for resale, should be included in Busch's balance sheet in the investment classification.
- Painting of ceilings for $10,000 should be included as a normal operating expense in Busch's income statement.
- Royalty payments of $13,000 should be included as a normal operating expense in Busch's income statement.

Analysis of Multiple-Choice Questions

Question

1. Jacobson Manufacturing Company purchased a machine for $65,000 on January 2, 2008. At the date of purchase, Jacobson incurred the following additional costs:

Loss on sale of old machine	$2,000
Freight-in	900
Installation cost	1,500
Breaking-in costs	650

The amount to record for the acquisition cost of the new machine is:

a. $65,000.
b. $67,400.
c. $68,050.
d. $69,400.

EXPLANATION: Apply the guideline that the cost of a plant asset includes all costs required to get the item to the location and condition for its intended purpose.

Purchase price	$ 65,000
Freight-in	900
Installation cost	1,500
Breaking-in costs	650
Total acquisition cost	$ 68,050

The loss on sale of the old machine should be charged to an income statement account so it will not impact the new asset's value. (Solution = c.)

Question

2. Buena Vista Hotel purchases Embassy Hotel with the intention of demolishing the Embassy Hotel and building a new high-rise hotel on the site. The cost of the Embassy Hotel should be:

a. capitalized as part of the cost of the land.
b. capitalized as part of the cost of the new hotel.
c. written off as a loss when it is torn down.
d. amortized over the life of the new hotel structure.

EXPLANATION: The cost of the land should include all costs necessary to acquire it and prepare it for its intended use by the buyer—to provide a site for a new building. (Solution = a.)

Question

3. The Jupiter Company purchased a parcel of land to be used as the site of a new office complex. The following data pertains to the purchase of the land and the beginning of construction for the new building:

Purchase price of land	$200,000
Attorney's fees for land transaction	1,000
Title insurance cost	2,000
Survey fees to determine the boundaries of the lot	800
Excavation costs for the building's foundation	8,000
Costs of clearing and grading the land	1,400

The total acquisition cost of the land is:

a. $213,200.
b. $205,200.
c. $203,800.
d. $202,400.
e. $200,000.

EXPLANATION: Think about how the cost of land is determined: an asset's cost includes all costs necessary to acquire the asset and get it to the location and condition for its intended purpose. When land has been purchased for the purpose of constructing a building, all costs incurred up to the excavation for the new building are considered land costs. Think of the common components of land cost (refer to the listing in the **Solution to Case 10-1**). The cost is calculated as follows:

Purchase price	$200,000
Attorney's fees	1,000
Title insurance	2,000
Survey fees	800
Costs of clearing and grading	1,400
Total cost of land	$205,200

The $8,000 excavation costs for the building's foundation should be charged (debited) to the Building account. (Solution = b.)

Question

4. The Venus Company hired an architect to design plans and a construction firm to build a new office building on a parcel of land it owns. The following data relates to the building:

Price paid to the construction firm	$320,000
Architect fees	18,000
Permit fees	1,200
Property taxes during the construction period	800
Insurance premium for first year of operations	3,000
Property taxes during the first year of operations	6,000

The total acquisition cost of the new building is:
a. $349,000.
b. $340,000.
c. $338,000.
d. $320,000.

EXPLANATION: Think about how the cost of a building is determined: an asset's cost includes all costs necessary to acquire the asset and get it to the location and condition for its intended purpose. Think of the common components of building cost (refer to the listing in the **Solution to Case 10-1**). The cost is calculated as follows:

Price paid to construction firm	$320,000	
Architect's fees	18,000	
Permit fees	1,200	
Property taxes during construction	800	
Total cost of building	$340,000	(Solution = b.)

Question

5. The Patty Company purchased a piece of office equipment to be used in operations. The following expenditures and other data relate to the equipment:

Invoice price excluding sales tax	$12,000
Sales tax	600
Delivery charges	200
Installation costs	300
Cost of a special platform	400
Cost of supplies used in testing	80
Insurance premium for first year of use	60

The total acquisition cost of this piece of equipment is:
a. $13,640.
b. $13,580.
c. $13,100.
d. $12,700.

EXPLANATION: Apply the cost principle: the cost of equipment includes all costs necessary to acquire the equipment, transport it to the place where it will be used, and prepare it for use. Thus, all costs related to equipment incurred prior to use in regular operations are charged to the Equipment account. Recurring costs (such as for insurance and maintenance) incurred after the equipment is ready for use should be expensed in the period incurred. Refer to the list of common elements of equipment cost in the **Solution to Case 10-1**. The cost of the equipment is determined as follows:

Invoice price	$12,000
Sales tax	600
Delivery charges	200
Installation costs	300

Costs of special platform	400
Costs of supplies used in testing	80
	$13,580 (Solution = b.)

Question

6. A manufacturing company decides to build its own factory equipment. The cost of self-constructed plant assets may include which of the following:

	Materials	Labour	Mfg. Overhead
a.	Yes	Yes	Yes
b.	Yes	Yes	No
c.	Yes	No	No
d.	No	Yes	No

EXPLANATION: In addition to the materials and labour used to build a plant asset, the manufacturer should assign a pro rata portion of the manufacturing overhead to obtain the asset's cost. However, the asset should not be recorded for more than its fair value (the total amount that would be charged by an outside independent producer). (Solution = a.)

Question

7. Herndon Inc. has a fiscal year ending October 31. On November 1, 2007, Herndon borrowed $20,000,000 at 15% to finance construction of a new plant. Repayments of the loan are to commence the month following completion of the plant. During the year ending October 31, 2008, expenditures for the partially completed structure totalled $12,000,000. These expenditures were incurred evenly through the year. Interest earned on the unexpended portion of the loan amounted to $800,000 for the year. What amount of interest should be capitalized as of October 31, 2008?
   a. $0
   b. $100,000
   c. $900,000
   d. $2,200,000
   e. $3,000,000

EXPLANATION: The situation is one which qualifies for the capitalization of interest. The following steps should help to calculate the amount:

(1) **Find the weighted-average accumulated expenditures** for the period:

Total expenditures at beginning of the period	$ 0
Total expenditures at end of the period	12,000,000
Sum	$ 12,000,000

$12,000,000 ÷ 2 = average of $6,000,000

(2) **Determine the interest rate to use.** Because the amount of a specific borrowing ($20,000,000) exceeds the weighted-average accumulated expenditures ($6,000,000), use the interest rate for that specific borrowing (15%).

(3) **Calculate the avoidable interest** by multiplying the appropriate interest rate (15% from Step 2) by the weighted-average accumulated expenditures ($6,000,000 from Step 1).

$6,000,000 x 15% = $900,000 avoidable interest

(4) **Determine the amount of interest to capitalize** by selecting the lower of the actual interest incurred (15% x $20,000,000 = $3,000,000) or the amount of avoidable interest ($900,000 from Step 3). The lower in this case is the $900,000 avoidable interest. (Solution = c.)

TIP! The interest earned ($800,000) is to be reported as revenue on the income statement and should not be used to offset the interest to be capitalized.

Question

8. A building was donated by a local entrepreneur to the Dupont Corporation to allow the company to expand and provide new jobs in the community. The building should be recorded on Dupont's books at:
   a. the cost of the lawyer's fees involved in handling the transaction.
   b. the value assigned by Dupont's board of directors.
   c. the building market value.
   d. no more than one dollar because the building was obtained for no cost.

EXPLANATION: A donation (contribution) is a non-reciprocal transfer (value goes in only one direction rather than in both directions as happens in an exchange transaction). A non-reciprocal transfer is to be recorded at the fair value of the property, goods, or services involved. (Solution = c.)

TIP! The credit side to the above transaction would be recorded in other comprehensive income.

Question

9. The Holstrum Corporation intends to acquire some plant assets from Bailey Corporation by issuing common shares in exchange. The cost of the assets should be measured by:
   a. the par value of the shares.
   b. the market value of the shares.
   c. the book value of the shares.
   d. bailey's carrying value of the assets.

EXPLANATION: Cost is measured by the fair market value (cash equivalent) of the consideration given (the shares in this case), or the fair market value of the consideration received (the plant assets in this case), whichever is the more clearly evident. If the market value of the common shares is not determinable, the fair market value of the plant assets should be used. (Solution = b.)

TIP! If treasury shares are used to acquire a new asset, the same rule applies: record the asset at the fair value (market value) of the treasury shares or at the fair value of the asset, whichever is the more clearly evident.

Question

10. In January 2008, Barbie Company entered into a contract to acquire a new machine for its factory. The machine, which had a cash price of $300,000, was acquired in exchange for the following:

Down payment	$ 30,000
Note payable in 24 equal monthly instalments	240,000
500 shares of Barbie common shares, with an agreed value of $100 per share	50,000
Total	$ 320,000

Prior to the machine's use, installation costs of $8,000 were incurred. The amount to record for the acquisition cost of the machine is:
a. $300,000.
b. $308,000.
c. $320,000.
d. $328,000.

EXPLANATION: Any time you have a question regarding the acquisition cost of a plant asset, write down (or mentally review) the two rules regarding asset cost: (1) cost is measured by the fair market value (cash equivalent) of the consideration given or the fair market value of the consideration received, whichever is the more clearly evident; and (2) an asset's cost includes all costs necessary to get it to the location and condition for its intended purpose. Then apply the rules to the situation given.

The cash equivalent of the machine acquired is $300,000 (cash price). The cash equivalent of the consideration given is the cash down payment of $30,000 plus the fair value of the shares ($50,000) plus the present value of the note payable (something less than $240,000). Because no information is given about the market value of the note or the appropriate interest rate for the note, but the cash equivalent price is given for the asset received, the more clearly evident figure is the $300,000. The $8,000 installation cost must be added to get the total acquisition cost. (Solution = b.)

Question

11. Two home builders agree to exchange tracts of land that each holds for purposes of development. An appraiser was hired and the following information is available:

	Batson	Beamer
Book value of land	$ 50,000	$ 72,000
Fair value of land	90,000	100,000
Cash paid	5,000	

In recording this exchange should a gain be recognized by Batson, Beamer, or both parties?

	Batson	Beamer
a.	Yes	Yes
b.	Yes	No
c.	No	Yes
d.	No	No

EXPLANATION: The general measurement rule for non-monetary transactions is that they are accounted for on the same basis as monetary transactions—fair value.

Carrying value is only used if:

- the transaction lacks commercial substance.
- fair values are not determinable.
- the exchange was merely to facilitate a sale to customers.

There is no indication of these conditions therefore fair value is appropriate. (Solution = d.)

Question

12. Refer to the facts of question 11. The amount to be recorded by Batson for the acquisition cost of the new tract of land is:
    a. $55,000.
    b. $95,000.
    c. $85,000.
    d. $90,000.
    e. $100,000.

EXPLANATION: The cost of the new asset is based on the fair value of what was given up, unless the fair value of what was received is more clearly evident. Therefore, the fair value of what was given up equals $90,000 plus $5,000 in cash: $95,000. (Solution = b.)

Question

13. The King-Kong Corporation exchanges a plant asset for another plant asset and gives a small amount of cash in the exchange. The gain on the disposal of the old asset will:
    a. be reported in the other revenues and gains section of the income statement.
    b. effectively reduce the amount to be recorded as the cost of the new asset.
    c. be recorded as an extraordinary item.
    d. be credited directly to the owner's capital account.

EXPLANATION: Non-monetary exchanges are recorded at fair value of the asset(s) given up, including any cash component. Any gains or losses are recognized in income immediately under "Other". It does not meet the criteria for extraordinary item treatment. (Solution = a.)

Question

14. A van has an original cost of $42,000 and accumulated amortization of $11,000. It is sold for $27,000 cash. The journal entry to record the sale will include a:
    a. debit to Loss on Disposal of Plant Assets for $4,000.
    b. credit to Gain on Disposal of Plant Assets for $4,000.
    c. credit to Vans for $27,000.
    d. debit to Loss on Disposal of Plant Assets for $15,000.

EXPLANATION: Prepare the journal entry to record the sale. Begin with the cash received and debit Cash. Remove the old asset from the books: credit Vans for $42,000 and debit Accumulated Amortization for $11,000. Examine the entry and determine what is needed to balance the entry; a debit balancing figure represents a loss or a credit balancing figure represents a gain.

In this case, a debit of $4,000 is needed to balance; hence, a loss of $4,000 is recorded.

Cash	27,000	
Accumulated Amortization—Vans	11,000	
Loss on Disposal of Plant Assets	4,000	
Vans		42,000

(Solution = a.)

Question

15. In accounting for plant assets, which of the following outlays made subsequent to acquisition should be fully expensed in the period the expenditure is made?
    a. Expenditure made to increase the efficiency or effectiveness of an existing asset.
    b. Expenditure made to extend the useful life of an existing asset beyond the time frame originally anticipated.
    c. Expenditure made to maintain an existing asset so that it can function in the manner intended.
    d. Expenditure made to add new asset services.

EXPLANATION: If an expenditure benefits future periods, it should be capitalized (debited to a balance sheet account); if the expenditure does not yield benefits to a future period, it should be recorded by a debit to an income statement account. An expenditure made to maintain an existing asset in good working condition does not provide any benefits other than those that were in potential when the original asset was acquired; hence, it should be expensed. Answer selections "a," "b," and "d" all represent future economic benefits; hence, they should be debited to an asset account or to an accumulated amortization account, depending on whether or not an asset's life is increased by the expenditure subsequent to acquisition. (Solution = c.)

Question

16. Which of the following would not be charged to a fixed asset account?
    a. A cost which prolongs the service life of the asset.
    b. The cost of maintaining the normal operating condition of the assets.
    c. A cost which improves the quality of the asset's service.
    d. A cost which increases the useful life of the asset.

EXPLANATION: The cost of maintaining the normal operating conditions are treated as repairs and maintenance expense since they do not contribute to any increase in value of the asset beyond its original life. (Solution = b.)

Case Study

Laidle Disposal Limited (Part 1)

Laidle Disposal Limited (LDL) is a small company that collects household garbage and disposes of it in a manner that is acceptable to the communities involved. The company has a fleet of trucks that pick up the garbage weekly. The garbage is then trucked to a local disposal site where it is dumped and then covered with topsoil. The disposal site is usually owned by LDL, having been purchased after the required permits for zoning have been obtained from government authorities.

This is the first year that LDL will be up and running and L.L. Laidle (L.L.), the president of the company, is deliberating on how he should account for the landfill sites (i.e., as inventory or fixed assets). The sites are purchased, filled with garbage, and ultimately sold as industrial land. The resale will be accompanied by a guarantee that no toxic materials are buried in the landfill.

Financial statements are used to obtain new contracts. Obtaining new contracts, as well as keeping old contracts, depends on competitive bidding, profile in the community, past work performance, financial stability, and adherence to strict environmental standards.

REQUIRED:

As an independent consultant to L.L., discuss the financial reporting issues and provide recommendations.

Suggested Approach to Case Study

Overview

The financial statements will be used to obtain new contracts, and users will focus on financial stability and adherence to environmental standards. Management will want the financial statements to show the company in the most favourable light (i.e., maximize profits and assets and minimize negative disclosures). The statements will likely be constrained by GAAP since the government will want reliable statements.

Analysis

ISSUE: Are the landfill sites inventory (in which case they do not have to be amortized) or are they fixed assets (in which case they must be amortized)?

Inventory vs. Fixed Assets

To the extent that the land is purchased and always resold, likely at a profit, it could be deemed as inventory. On the other hand, the resale is incidental to the real reason for buying the land, and that is to fill it up with waste. The process of filling it up with waste generates income, and, therefore, the land is purchased primarily to generate revenues. The resale is secondary. Many fixed assets are resold once their usefulness has ended.

Recommendation

It would, therefore, seem reasonable to treat the landfill sites as fixed assets.

TIP!

The inventory vs. fixed assets issue can be very difficult at times. Consider an organization that has returnable containers (such as brewery or a water cooler company)—are these containers inventory or fixed assets? It is likely they are fixed assets, but consider the impact that decision can have on the financials—current vs. long term, depreciable vs. non-depreciable, lower of cost or market vs. net recoverable amount. It is important to consider the impact decisions like this have on the external financial statements.

Amortization, Impairment, and Disposition

Chapter 11

Overview

Expenses arise from the cost of goods or services that are consumed in the process of generating revenue. When a long-term tangible asset is acquired, it actually represents a bundle of future asset services. The total cost of these services equals the acquisition cost of the asset **minus** the asset's expected (estimated) market value at the end of its useful life. As a productive asset is used, services (benefits) are consumed to generate revenues; therefore, a portion of the original asset cost should be charged to expense in order to comply with the matching principle. The process of allocating (expensing) the cost of long-term tangible assets over the accounting periods during which the asset is used is called **amortization**. The process of allocating the costs of natural resources to inventory (and later to cost of goods sold) is called **depletion**. Amortization, impairment of property, plant, and equipment, and depletion are discussed in this chapter. Finally, the disposal of long-lived assets is also covered in this chapter.

Study Steps

Understanding the Concept of Amortization Within a Business Context

Amortization is a **cost allocation**, which is arbitrary at best. There is no cash flow impact of amortization. Having stated this, allocating the cost of the asset to the product that it is used to produce or the period in which the product will be produced or sold is very important from a business sense. It helps management get an idea of the **full cost** to produce a product or run the business. This is important for pricing and for deciding whether or not to stay in business.

TIP! Even though amortization has no cash flow impact, it is important in pricing and profitability decisions.

Where amortizable assets are a significant portion of the balance sheet, the amortization expense can have a material impact on net income. Net income is a key number for management and users in decision making. Therefore, the choice of amortization method is very important.

TIP! The choice of amortization can impact significantly on net income and, hence, is very relevant to the decision-making process.

Capital cost allowance (CCA) is tax amortization according to the Income Tax Act. It is the amount that may be deducted for tax purposes in arriving at taxable income. CCA is calculated in a completely different manner than GAAP amortization since financial reporting objectives and Income Tax Act objectives are different. GAAP strives to match costs with revenues, whereas the Income Tax Act has different objectives and may be attempting, for instance, to encourage spending on certain types of assets in order to promote job creation. To that end, the government might allow assets to be charged to taxable income over a shorter period of time, thereby giving the company a greater tax break.

TIP! GAAP amortization allocates costs to revenues under the matching principle, whereas tax amortization is usually designed by the government to motivate certain types of behaviour.

Becoming Proficient in Calculating Amortization under the Various Generally Accepted Methods

Any asset that has a limited life should be amortized in order to **match** the cost of the asset with the revenue that it helps to generate. The amount to be amortized should be the cost less any expected net residual value. For all methods, the residual value is deducted first, and then the remaining amount is amortized. The exception to this rule is the declining-balance method. Under this method, the residual value is not deducted first.

Focus on the impact on net income of the various methods, i.e., does it increase net income or decrease it? What is the pattern over time?

Understand the accounting issues related to asset impairment

Impairment is a condition that exists when the carrying amount of a long-lived asset exceeds its fair value. Some examples where there may be an impairment include (*CICA*, 3063):

- A significant decrease in an asset's market value.
- A significant change in the extent or manner in which an asset is used.

If any of the factors exist, a recoverability test is used to determine whether an impairment has occurred. This involves estimating the future net cash flows from the asset's use and eventual disposition. This sum (undiscounted) is then compared to the asset's carrying value. If it is less, then an impairment has occurred.

However, the measurement of the impairment is the difference between the carrying value and the fair value of the related asset. Fair value may involve a calculation of the asset's net cash flows on a **discounted** basis.

Understand the accounting issues related to the disposition of long-lived assets by sale or otherwise

If a long-lived asset is to be disposed of by sale, then it is reclassified as **held for sale**, and remeasured at the lower of carrying amount and fair value less costs to sell. There are strict criteria for classifying an asset as held for sale. These were discussed in Chapter 4 in conjunction with the discussion on discontinued operations.

If a long-lived asset is to be disposed of other than by sale, it is not subject to reclassification. It will, however, be subject to the impairment test noted above.

Tips on Chapter Topics

Amortization is also called depreciation or depletion, although amortization will be used here. It is more common in the U.S. to refer to depreciation, with amortization referring to intangible assets and depletion to wasting assets such as oil and gas or forestry industries. **TIP!**

Residual value is often referred to as **salvage value**, and sometimes it is called estimated scrap value. **TIP!**

Residual value, used in the calculation of amortization for the early years of life of an asset, is defined as the estimated net realizable value of a capital asset at the end of its **useful life** to an enterprise (Assets are usually retired for either physical—casualty or economic factors—technology, supersession, or obsolescence). Salvage value is **not** a factor in determining amortization for the early years **TIP!**

of life, and is defined as the asset's estimated net realizable value at the end of its life and is normally negligible; however, salvage value can affect the amount calculated for amortization in the last year(s) of an asset's life. An asset should **not** be amortized below its salvage value. (*CICA Handbook*, Section 3060, pars. 14 and 31)

TIP! Three basic questions in amortization are: What is the amount to be amortized? What is the asset's useful life? What pattern and method of cost apportionment is best for this asset?

TIP! The **activity method** is often called the **variable charge** approach or the **units of output** or the **units of production method**. This is most useful when the use of the asset in producing revenue streams differs from one period to another.

TIP! The **declining-balance amortization** method applies a constant rate to a declining book value to calculate amortization. The rate used is often twice the straight-line rate, in which case the method is then referred to as the **200% declining-balance method** or the **double-declining-balance method**. Another declining-balance method is the sum-of-the-years'-digits, whereby the amortizable amount is multiplied by a decreasing fraction each period. This method is rarely used in practice in Canada.

TIP! The **book value** of a plant asset is determined by deducting the balance of accumulated amortization from the balance of the related asset account. The balance in the related asset account is generally the asset's original cost. Thus, the estimated residual value does not directly affect the book value calculation. Book value is often called **carrying value**, **carrying amount**, **net asset value**, or **unamortized value**. An asset's book value at a given date may be far different than its market (fair) value at the same date.

TIP! **Amortizable cost** or **amortization base** is a term that refers to the total amount to be amortized over the life of the asset. It is determined by deducting the estimated residual value from the cost of the asset.

TIP! When an asset being amortized by a group or composite amortization method is disposed of, no gain or loss is recorded; the difference between the original cost of the asset and the proceeds from disposal is charged to Accumulated Amortization. The group method is used when assets are fairly homogeneous, while the composite method is employed when assets are heterogeneous in nature.

TIP! It is not uncommon for companies to have "two different sets of books" as financial reporting to shareholders can employ any acceptable method under GAAP, while tax reporting requires companies to use the prescribed government method of Capital Cost Allowance (CCA) which is a form of a declining-balance method.

TIP! Amortization should be recognized for only the time an asset is in a "ready to use" form. If an asset is purchased on July 1, only six month's amortization should be recognized. Similarly, if an asset is sold on March 1, two months amortization should be recognized prior to disposal.

TIP! Revisions of amortization rates, due to management decisions to change estimated lives, residual values, or due to capitalization of costs, is done on a **prospective** basis.

TIP! Canadian standards for impairment require that when the net carrying amount of the asset, less any amount for restoration or future site removal and future income taxes, are greater than the net recoverable amount, a charge to income should occur in the period. Once an impairment has been written down, it is not subsequently increased if conditions change.

When disposing of assets for taxation purposes, it is important to determine if it is the ultimate asset in the class. Upon disposal, there is the possibility of a **recapture** into income of CCA if a negative balance occurs in the asset class. Regardless, if the asset is sold for more than the original cost, a capital gain is recognized into income.

TIP!

Case 11-1

PURPOSE: This case examines the process of matching the cost of fixed assets with the revenues which the assets help to generate.

Plant assets provide services for two or more periods. There is a cost to the services consumed; this cost should be matched with the periods benefited.

Instructions

(a) Briefly define amortization as used in accounting.
(b) Identify the factors that are relevant in determining the annual amortization and explain whether these factors are determined objectively or whether they are based on judgment.

Solution to Case 11-1

(a) Amortization is the accounting process of allocating an asset's historical cost (recorded amount) to the accounting periods benefited by the use of the asset. It is a process of cost allocation, not valuation. Amortization is not intended to provide funds for an asset's replacement; it is merely an application of the matching principle.
(b) The factors relevant in determining the annual amortization for an amortizable asset are the initial recorded amount (acquisition cost and any subsequent capitalized costs), estimated salvage value, estimated useful life, and amortization method.

Assets are typically recorded at their acquisition cost, which is in most cases objectively determinable. But cost assignments in other cases—"basket purchases" and selection of an implicit interest rate in asset acquisition under deferred-payment plans—may be quite subjective and involve considerable judgment.

The salvage value is an estimate of an amount potentially realizable when the asset is retired from service. It is initially a judgment factor and is affected by the length of the asset's useful life to the enterprise.

The useful life is also a judgment factor. It involves selecting the "unit" of measure of service life and estimating the number of such units embodied in the asset. Such units may be measured in terms of time periods or in terms of activity (for example, years or machine hours). When selecting the life, one should select the lower (shorter) of the physical life or the economic life to the user. Physical life involves wear and tear and casualties; economic life involves such things as technological obsolescence and inadequacy.

Selecting the amortization method is generally a judgment decision; but, a method may be inherent in the definition adopted for the units of service life, as discussed earlier. For example, if such units are machine hours, the method is a function of the number of machine hours used during each period. A method should be selected that will best measure the portion of services expiring each period. Once a method is selected, it may be applied by using a predetermined, objectively derived formula.

Exercise 11-1

PURPOSE: This exercise will give you practice in calculating amortization for three successive periods for two commonly used methods.

Red River Company purchases equipment on January 1, Year 1, at a cost of $645,000. The asset is expected to have a service life of 12 years and a salvage value of $60,000.

Instructions

(a) Calculate the amount of amortization for each of Years 1 through 3 using the straight-line amortization method.
(b) Calculate the amount of amortization for each of Years 1 through 3 using the double-declining-balance method. (In performing your calculations, round the constant percentage to the nearest one-hundredth of a percentage point and round final answers to the nearest dollar.)

Solution to Exercise 11-1

(a) $\frac{\$645,000 - \$60,000}{12} = \underline{\underline{\$48,750}}$ Amortization for each of years 1 through 3

(b) $\frac{100\%}{12} \times 2 = 16.67\%$

$645,000 x 16.67% =	$107,522	amortization Year 1
($645,000 – $107,522) x 16.67% =	$ 89,598	amortization Year 2
($645,000 – $107,522 - $89,598) x 16.67% =	$ 74,662	amortization Year 3

Exercise 11-2

PURPOSE: This exercise will provide an illustration of the calculations for amortization of partial periods.

Koehn Company purchased a new plant asset on April 1, 2008, at a cost of $345,000. It was estimated to have a service life of 20 years and a salvage value of $30,000. Koehn's accounting period is the calendar year.

Instructions (Round all final answers to the nearest dollar.)

(a) Calculate the amount of amortization for this asset for 2008 and 2009 using the straight-line method.
(b) Calculate the amount of depreciation for this asset for 2008 and 2009 using the double-declining-balance method.

Solution to Exercise 11-2

(a) $\frac{\$345{,}000 - \$30{,}000 \times 9/12}{20 \text{ years}} = \$11{,}813$ amortization for 2008

$\frac{\$345{,}000 - \$30{,}000}{20 \text{ years}} = \$15{,}750$ amortization for 2009

EXPLANATION: Write down and apply the formula for straight-line amortization. Multiply the annual amortization amount by the portion of the asset's first year of service that falls in the given accounting period.

$$\frac{\text{Cost – Salvage Value}}{\text{Estimated Service Life}} \times \frac{\text{Cost – Salvage Value}}{\text{12 months}} = \text{Amortization Charge}$$

(b) Straight-line rate $= \frac{100\%}{20} = 5\%$; $5\% \times 2 = 10\%$

10% x $345,000 = $34,500 amortization for asset's first year
10% x ($345,000 – $34,500) = $31,050 amortization for asset's second year

9/12 x $34,500 = $25,875 amortization for 2008

3/12 x $34,500 =	$ 8,625
+ 9/12 x $31,050 =	23,288
	$ 31,913 amortization for 2009

EXPLANATION: Write down and apply the formula for the declining balance method. Apportion the amortization for a given **asset year** between the two accounting periods involved.

Constant Percentage x Book Value at Beginning of Asset Year = Amortization for Asset Year

An alternative approach is as follows:

After the first partial year, calculate amortization for a full **accounting year** by multiplying the constant percentage by the book value of the asset at the beginning of the accounting period.

Thus, the calculation for 2009 would be as follows:

10% x ($345,000 – $25,875) = $31,913.

TIP! Companies use many methods to deal with partial year amortization as long as it is applied consistently, i.e., charging a full year's amortization in the year of purchase and no amortization in the year of disposal, or a half-year in the year of acquisition and a half-year in the year of disposal.

TIP! Taxation reporting requires the use of the half-year rule in which a company is deemed to make purchases half way through their fiscal year, regardless of the actual date of purchase. This is why many companies will make purchases in the later part of the year and receive a half-years worth of CCA.

Exercise 11-3

PURPOSE: This exercise is designed to test your ability to solve for missing data by applying your knowledge regarding amortization calculations.

Dunlap Company acquired a plant asset at the beginning of Year 1. The asset has an estimated service life of 5 years. An employee has prepared amortization schedules for this asset using three different methods to compare the results of using one method with the results of using other methods. You are to assume that the following schedules have been correctly prepared for this asset using (1) the straight-line (SL) method, (2) Activity (AM) method, and (3) the double-declining-balance (DDB) method (switching to the straight-line method after the mid-life of the asset).

Year	Straight-line	Activity	Double-declining balance
1	$ 6,000	$ 10,000	$ 14,400
2	6,000	8,000	8,640
3	6,000	6,000	5,184
4	6,000	4,000	888
5	6,000	2,000	888
Total	$ 30,000	$ 30,000	$ 30,000

Instructions

Answer the following questions:

(a) What is the cost of the asset being amortized?

(b) What amount, if any, was used in the amortization calculations for the salvage value of this asset?

(c) Which method will produce the highest charge to income in Year 1?

(d) Which method will produce the highest charge to income in Year 4?

(e) Which method will produce the highest book value for the asset at the end of Year 3?

(f) If the asset is sold at the end of Year 3, which method would yield the highest gain (or lowest loss) on disposal of the asset?

Solution to Exercise 11-3

(a) If there is any salvage value and the amount is unknown (as is the case here), the cost would have to be determined by looking at the data for the double-declining-balance method.
100% ÷ 5 = 20%; 20% x 2 = 40%
Cost x 40% = $14,400; $14,400 ÷ 0.40 = $36,000 cost of asset

APPROACH: Write down the formula for each of the amortization methods mentioned. Fill in the data given for Year 1. Examine what remains to be solved.

(Cost – Salvage Value) ÷ Estimated Service Life = SL Amortization
(Cost – Salvage Value) ÷ 5 = $6,000

(Cost – Salvage Value) = Amortization rate
Total estimated base
Amortization rate x # units per year = AM Amortization

Constant Percentage x Cost = DDB Amortization
40% x Cost = $14,400

There are two variables (cost and salvage value) unknown for each of the first two methods, and there is no way to solve for either of them. However, cost can easily be determined for the third method (DDB). Once you solve for cost, it is a simple matter to solve for salvage value.

(b) $36,000 cost (answer a) – $30,000 total amortization = $6,000 salvage value

APPROACH: The difference between the answer to part (a) and the total amortization per the schedule ($30,000) is the salvage value used.

(c) The highest charge to income for Year 1 will be yielded by the double-declining-balance method.

APPROACH: Examine the amortization schedules. Notice the method that results in the highest amortization amount for Year 1.

(d) The highest charge to income for Year 4 will be yielded by the straight-line method.

APPROACH: Examine the amortization schedules given. Notice the method that results in the highest amortization amount for Year 4.

(e) The method to yield the highest book value at the end of Year 3 would be the method that yields the lowest accumulated amortization at the end of Year 3 which is the straight-line method. Calculations:

SL	= \$36,000 – (\$6,000 + \$6,000 + \$6,000)
	= \$18,000 book value at the end of Year 3.
AM	= \$36,000 – (\$10,000 + \$8,000 + \$6,000)
	= \$12,000 book value at the end of Year 3.
DDB	= \$36,000 – (\$14,400 + \$8,640 + \$5,184)
	= \$7,776 book value at the end of Year 3.

APPROACH: Write down the formula to calculate book value: Cost – Accumulated Amortization = Book Value. To obtain a high book value, you need a low accumulated amortization. Examine the amortization schedules to determine the method that would yield the lowest total amortization for the first three years.

(f) The method that will yield the highest gain (or lowest loss) if the asset is sold at the end of Year 3 is the method which will yield the lowest book value at the end of Year 3. In this case, it is the double-declining-balance method.

APPROACH: Write down the formula to calculate gain or loss on disposal: Selling Price – Book Value = Gain (Loss). To obtain a high gain, you need a low book value. Examine the formula for book value. To get a low book value, you need high amortization charges. Use the amortization schedules to determine the method that would yield the highest accumulated amortization balance at the end of three years.

Exercise 11-4

PURPOSE: This exercise will enable you to practice working with the composite method for calculating amortization.

Presented below is information related to the Arctic Wolf Corporation (all assets are acquired at the beginning of Year 1):

Asset	Cost	Estimated Scrap	Estimated Life (in years)
A	$60,750	$8,250	10
B	50,400	7,200	9
C	54,000	4,800	8
D	28,500	2,250	7
E	35,250	3,750	6

Instructions

(a) Calculate the rate of amortization per year to be applied to the plant assets under the composite method.
(b) Calculate the composite life.
(c) Prepare the adjusting entry necessary at the end of the year to record amortization for Year 1.
(d) Prepare the entry at the end of Year 6 to record the sale of fixed asset D for cash of $7,500. It was used for 6 years, and amortization was recorded under the composite method.

Solution to Exercise 11-4

(a)

Asset	Cost	Estimated Scrap	Amortizable Cost	Estimated Life	Amortization Per Year
A	$ 60,750	$ 8,250	$ 52,500	10	$ 5,250
B	50,400	7,200	43,200	9	4,800
C	54,000	4,800	49,200	8	6,150
D	28,500	2,250	26,250	7	3,750
E	35,250	3,750	31,500	6	5,250
	$228,900	$26,250	$202,650		$25,200

Composite rate = $25,200 ÷ $228,900; or 11.009%

EXPLANATION: Steps to calculate the composite rate:

1. Calculate what would be the amount of annual straight-line amortization for each asset by dividing each asset's amortizable cost by its estimated service life. Sum these amounts ($25,200).
2. Calculate the composite rate by dividing the total amortization per year (results of Step 1—$25,200) by the amount of original cost ($228,900).

(b) Composite life = $202,650 ÷ $25,200; or 8.04 years

EXPLANATION: Calculate the composite life by dividing the total amortizable cost ($202,650) by the total annual amortization charge ($25,200).

(c) **End of Year 1**

Amortization Expense on Plant Assets	25,200	
Accumulated Amortization on Plant Assets		25,200
($228,900 x 11.009% = $25,200)		

EXPLANATION: Calculate the amortization for any given year by multiplying the balance in the asset account by the composite rate (results of Step 2). The balance in the asset account will change over time due to the acquisition of new assets and the disposal of old assets.

(d) **End of Year 6**

Cash	7,500	
Accumulated Amortization on Plant Assets	21,000	
Plant Assets		28,500

EXPLANATION: When using the group or composite method, no gain or loss on disposition is recorded. The difference between the proceeds (if any) on disposal and the original cost of the asset is debited (or credited) to the Accumulated Amortization account. Thus, if an asset is retired before, or after, the average service of the group is reached, the resulting gain or loss is buried in the Accumulated Amortization account.

Exercise 11-5

PURPOSE: This exercise will provide you with an illustration of how to account for a change in the estimated service life and salvage value of a plant asset due to an expenditure subsequent to acquisition.

The Russell Company purchased a machine on January 1, 1998, for $105,000. The machine was being amortized using the straight-line method over an estimated life span of 20 years, with a $15,000 salvage value. At the beginning of 2008, when the machine had been in use for 10 years, the company paid $25,000 to overhaul the machine. As a result of this improvement, the company estimated that the useful life of the machine would be extended an additional 5 years and the salvage value would be reduced to $10,000.

Instructions

Calculate the amortization charge for 2008.

Solution to Exercise 11-5

Cost	$ 105,000
Accumulated amortization at 1/1/08	45,000 [a]
Book value at 1/1/08	60,000
Additional expenditure capitalized	25,000
Revised book value	85,000
Current estimate of salvage value	10,000
Remaining amortizable cost at 1/1/08	75,000
Remaining years of useful life at 1/1/08	÷ 15 [b]
Amortization expense for 2008	$ 5,000

[a] Cost	$105,000
Original estimate of salvage value	15,000
Original amortizable cost	90,000
Original service life in years	÷ 20
Original amortization per year	4,500
Number of years used	x 10
Accumulated Amortization at 1/1/08	$ 45,000

[b] Original estimate of life in years	20
Number of years used	(10)
Additional years	5
Remaining years of useful life at 1/1/08	15

TIP! A change in the estimated useful life and/or salvage value of an existing amortizable asset is to be accounted for prospectively (in current and/or future periods). Therefore, the book value at the beginning of the period of change, less the current estimate of salvage value, is to be allocated over the remaining periods of life using the appropriate amortization method. The book value at the beginning of the period of change is calculated using the original estimates of service life and salvage value.

TIP! The $25,000 cost of overhaul is capitalized in this case because the cost will benefit future periods by extending the useful life of the machine.

EXPLANATION: Whenever you have a situation that involves a change in the estimated service life and/or salvage value of an amortizable asset, use the format shown above to calculate the remaining amortizable cost and allocate that amount over the remaining useful life using the given amortization method.

Exercise 11-6

PURPOSE: This exercise will allow you to practice using various amortization methods and it will also give you the opportunity to compare the results of using one method to the results of using another method.

On January 1, 2008, Irish Company, a machine-tool manufacturer, acquires a piece of new industrial equipment for $1,000,000. The new equipment has a useful life of 5 years and the salvage value is estimated to be $100,000. Irish estimates that the new equipment can produce a total of 40,000 units and expects it to produce 10,000 units in its first year. Production is then estimated to decline by 1,000 units per year over the remaining useful life of the equipment.

The following depreciation methods may be used:

- Double-declining-balance
- Straight-line
- Units-of-output

Instructions

(a) Identify which amortization method would result in the maximization of profits for financial statement reporting for the **three-year** period ending December 31, 2010. Prepare a schedule showing the amount of accumulated amortization at December 31, 2010, under the method selected (show supporting calculations in good form). Ignore present value and income tax considerations in your answer.

(b) Identify which amortization method would result in the minimization of profits for the **three-year** period ending December 31, 2010. Prepare a schedule showing the amount of accumulated amortization at December 31, 2010, under the method selected (show supporting calculations in good form). Ignore present value and income tax considerations in your answer.

Solution to Exercise 11-6

(a) The straight-line method of amortization would result in the maximization of profits for financial statement reporting for the three-year period ending December 31, 2010.

Irish Company
ACCUMULATED AMORTIZATION USING STRAIGHT-LINE METHOD
December 31, 2010

(Cost – Salvage Value) ÷ Estimated Service Life

($1,000,000 – $100,000) ÷ 5 years = $180,000

Year	Amortization Expense	Accumulated Amortization
2008	$ 180,000	$ 180,000
2009	180,000	360,000
2010	180,000	540,000
	$ 540,000	

(b) The double-declining-balance method of amortization would result in the minimization of profits for the three-year period ending December 31, 2010.

Irish Company
ACCUMULATED AMORTIZATION USING DOUBLE-DECLINING-BALANCE METHOD
December 31, 2010

Straight-line rate is 5 years, or 20%. Double-declining-balance rate is 40% (20% x 2). Ignore salvage value.

Year	Book Value at Beginning of Year	Amortization Expense	Accumulated Amortization
2008	$1,000,000	$400,000	$400,000
2009	600,000	240,000	640,000
2010	360,000	144,000	784,000
		$784,000	

Other supporting calculations:

Irish Company
ACCUMULATED AMORTIZATION USING UNITS-OF-OUTPUT METHOD
December 31, 2010

(Cost – Salvage Value) ÷ Total Units of Output =
($1,000,000 – $100,000) ÷ 40,000 =
$22.50 Amortization per Unit

10,000 x $22.50 = $225,000
9,000 x $22.50 = $202,500
8,000 x $22.50 = $180,000

Year	Amortization Expense	Accumulated Amortization
2008	$225,000	$225,000
2009	202,500	427,500
2010	180,000	607,500
	$ 607,500	

Exercise 11-7

PURPOSE: This exercise will give you practice in calculating depletion.

During 2008, Big Rock Corporation acquired a mineral mine for $2,700,000, of which $450,000 is attributable to the land value after the mineral has been removed. Engineers estimate that 15 million units of mineral can be recovered from this mine. During 2008, 1,200,000 units were extracted and 800,000 units were sold.

Instructions

Calculate the depletion for 2008.

Solution to Exercise 11-7

($2,700,000 – $450,000) ÷ 15,000,000 = $.15

$.15 x 1,200,000 = $180,000 Depletion for 2008

EXPLANATION: Write down the formula to calculate depletion, enter the data given, and solve.

$$\frac{\text{Acquisition Cost} + \text{Costs to Explore and Develop} - \text{Residual Value of Land} + \text{Costs to Restore Land to Alternative Use}}{\text{Number of Units to be Extracted}} = \text{Depletion Cost Per Recoverable Unit}$$

$$\text{Depletion Cost Per Recoverable Unit} \times \text{Units Extracted During Period} = \text{Depletion for the Period}$$

TIP! The depletion charge for the period is the amount to be removed from the property, plant, and equipment classification ($180,000 in this case). It is based on the units extracted from the earth during the period. The portion of this $180,000 that gets to the income statement is dependent upon the number of units sold. When the number of units extracted exceeds the number sold, as in this exercise, a portion of the depletion costs goes into the Inventory account on the balance sheet.

Exercise 11-8

PURPOSE: This exercise will give you practice in calculating CCA.

Westcoast Fishing purchased equipment for their boat (class 8-20%), valued at \$60,000 in March of 2008. The Unamortized Capital Cost at the beginning of 2008 was \$240,000. In 2009, the company sold a boat for \$25,000 for which they had originally paid \$40,000. In 2010, the company sold an asset for \$150,000, which had originally cost \$325,000. This was the last asset in the class.

Instructions

Calculate the CCA for each of years 2008, 2009, and 2010. Determine if there was any recapture, terminal losses, or capital gains for the company.

Solution to Exercise 11-8

Draw up a chart to recognize the CCA and UCC for the year. Remember the half-year rule is in effect for equipment purchases. Since there is already an opening balance in the UCC, two separate calculations will need to be done to recognize the CCA in the period.

Class 8-20%		CCA	UCC
December 31, 2007			\$240,000
Additions less disposals, 2008			
Equipment (\$60,000)			\$60,000
			\$300,000
CCA, 2008			
\$240,000 x 20% =	\$48,000		
\$60,000 x 1/2 x 20% =	6,000	\$54,000	(54,000)
December 31, 2008			\$246,000
Additions less disposals, 2009			
Equipment (lesser of original cost \$40,000 and proceeds of disposal \$25,000)			(25,000)
			\$221,000
CCA, 2009			
\$221,000 x 20%		\$44,200	(44,200)
December 31, 2009			\$176,800
Additions less disposals, 2010			
Equipment (lesser of original cost \$325,000 and proceeds of disposal \$150,000)			150,000
			\$26,800

Terminal Loss, 2010	$26,800	(26,800)
		$0

The company experienced a terminal loss in 2010 as the disposal of this asset represented the last asset in the class. Once disposed of, there was a positive balance left in the account which would be written off against current income. (In essence, the company did not amortize enough during the life of the asset.)

Illustration 11-1

Accounting for Impairments

A **recoverability test** is used to determine whether an impairment has occurred: If the sum of the expected future net undiscounted cash flows (from the use of the asset and its eventual disposition) is less than the carrying amount of the asset, the asset has been impaired.

If the recoverability test indicates that an impairment has occurred, a loss is calculated. The impairment loss is the amount by which the carrying amount of the asset exceeds its fair value. The fair value of an asset is measured by its market value (if an active market exists) or by the present value of expected future net cash flows (if an active market does not exist). If an asset is to be disposed of by sale instead of held for use, the asset's net realizable value (fair value less cost to sell) is used as a measure of the net cash flows that will be received from this asset. The asset is also reclassified as "held-for-sale." If the asset is to be disposed of other than by sale, it is not reclassified, but will be subject to the impairment test described above. The criteria to consider for held for sale were discussed in Chapter 4, but are repeated here:

To be classified as **held for sale**, all of the following criteria must be met:

- an authorized plan to sell assets
- the asset is available for immediate sale in its current state
- an active program to find a buyer exists
- sale is probable within one year
- the asset is reasonably priced and actively marketed
- changes to the plan are unlikely

TIP!

Losses or gains related to impaired assets should be reported as part of income from continuing operations. Thus, they are **not** classified as extraordinary items.

As discussed in Chapter 4, the disposal of an asset may be considered the disposal of a component, if it can generate its own cash flows and is considered a separate business. In that case, gains or losses are shown net of tax, below income from continuing operations.

Analysis of Multiple-Choice Questions

Question

1. The term "amortizable cost" or "amortizable base," as it is used in accounting, refers to:
   a. the total amount to be charged (debited) to expense over an asset's useful life.
   b. cost of the asset less the related amortization recorded to date.
   c. the estimated market value of the asset at the end of its useful life.
   d. the acquisition cost of the asset.

EXPLANATION: Write down a definition of amortizable cost **before** you read any of the answer selections. **Amortizable cost** or **amortizable base** is the total amount of asset cost that can be expensed over the life of the asset; thus, it is original cost less estimated residual (salvage) value. Answer selection "b" describes the term book value. Answer selection "c" describes salvage value or residual value. Selection "d" represents the total cost of the asset. (Solution = a.)

Question

2. A machine is purchased by the Dunnagin Company for $18,000. Dunnagin pays $6,000 in cash and gives a note payable for $12,000 that is payable in instalments over a four-year period. Dunnagin estimates that the machine could physically last for 12 years, even though Dunnagin expects to use it in its business for only 9 years. The period of time to be used by Dunnagin for amortization purposes is:
   a. 4 years
   b. 5 years
   c. 9 years
   d. 12 years

EXPLANATION: Think about the objective of the amortization process—to allocate an asset's cost to the periods benefited. The asset should be amortized over its useful life, which is the length of time the asset will be of service to the entity using it. (Solution = c.)

Question

3. A machine with an estimated service life of 5 years and an expected salvage value of $5,000 was purchased on January 1, 2008, for $50,000. The amount to be recorded for amortization for years 2008, 2009, and 2010, respectively, using the 200% declining-balance method will be:
   a. $20,000; $12,000; $7,200.

b. $18,000; $10,800; $6,480.
c. $16,667; $13,333; $10,000.
d. $10,000; $8,000; $6,400.

EXPLANATION: Write down the formula for the declining-balance method. Enter the data given and solve.

Book Value at Beginning of Year x Constant Percentage = Amortization

Constant Percentage = 2 x (100% ÷ Life) = 2 x (100% ÷ 5) = 40%

2008: $50,000 x 40% =	$20,000
2009: ($50,000 – $20,000) x 40% =	$12,000
2010: ($50,000 – $20,000 – $12,000) x 40% =	$7,200

(Solution = a.)

Question

4. Salvage (residual) value may or may not be used in calculating amortization expense in the early years of an asset's life. Net income is understated if, in the first year, estimated salvage value is excluded from the amortization calculation when using the:

	Units of Output Method	Double-Declining-Balance Method
a.	Yes	Yes
b.	No	No
c.	No	Yes
d.	Yes	No

EXPLANATION: Before looking at the methods addressed directly in the question, think about how salvage value affects the amortization calculation under various methods. In considering the common amortization methods such as straight-line, activity methods, and declining-balance methods, the declining-balance methods are the only methods that do not use the residual value in calculating amortization in the early years of the asset's life. However, the residual value may affect the calculations with the declining-balance method in the latter years of the asset's life because the asset should not be amortized below its residual value. The units-of-output method is an activity method. (Solution = d.)

Question

5. A machine was purchased for $8,000,000 on January 1, 2008. It has an estimated useful life of 8 years and a residual value of $800,000. Amortization is being calculated using the double-declining method. What amount should be shown for this machine, net of accumulated amortization, in the company's December 31, 2009 balance sheet?

a. $4,000,000
b. $4,500,000
c. $6,000,000
d. $6,125,000

EXPLANATION: Write down the formula to calculate book value and the formula to calculate amortization using the double-declining-balance method. Fill in the data from the scenario at hand and solve. Be careful that you don't get so involved with the calculation for amortization that you lose sight of the question—which is to calculate the book value of the equipment. It would be helpful to underline the middle of the last sentence of the stem of the question in order to keep your focus on what is being asked.

Cost – Accumulated Depreciation = Book Value

Constant Percentage x Book Value at Beginning of the Year = Amortization
100% / 8 x 2 = 25%

Year	BV beginning	Rate	Amortization Expense	Balance of Accumulated Amortization	NBV (End of year)
1	$8,000,000	25%	$2,000,000	$2,000,000	$6,000,000
2	$6,000,000	25%	$1,500,000	$3,500,000	$4,500,000

(Solution = b.)

Question

6. Tammy Corporation purchased a machine on July 1, 2008 for $900,000. The machine has an estimated life of 5 years and a salvage value of $120,000. The machine is being amortized by the 150% declining-balance method. What amount of amortization should be recorded for the year ended December 31, 2009?
   a. $229,500
   b. $198,900
   c. $189,000
   d. $163,800

EXPLANATION: Write down the formula to use for the declining-balance approach. (Notice the facts indicate there is a partial period for the first year (2008) and the question asks for the amortization for the 2009 reporting period.) Calculate the rate that is 150% of the straight-line rate. Apply the formula to the facts given. Remember that salvage value is not used with this method in calculating amortization in the early years of the asset's life.

Constant Percentage x Book Value at Beginning of the Year = Amortization

$\frac{100\%}{\text{Life}} = \frac{100\%}{5 \text{ years}} = 20\%$ 20% x 150% = 30% constant percentage

30% x $900,000 = $270,000 First year of life
30% x (900,000 – $270,000) = $189,000 Second year of life
1/2 x $270,000 = $135,000 for 2008
(1/2 x $270,000) + (1/2 x $189,000) = $229,500 for 2009

OR

30% x ($900,000 - $135,000) = $229,500 for 2009 (Solution = a.)

Question

7. A plant asset with a five-year estimated useful life and no salvage value is sold during the second year of the asset's life. How would the use of the straight-line method of amortization instead of an accelerated amortization method affect the amount of gain or loss on the sale of the plant asset?

	Gain	Loss
a.	Increase	Decrease
b.	Decrease	Increase
c.	No Effect	Increase
d.	No Effect	No Effect

EXPLANATION: An accelerated method would result in more accumulated amortization and, therefore, a lower book value. In contrast, the straight-line method results in less accumulated amortization and a higher book value. This means a lower gain or a higher loss is calculated if the asset is sold and the straight-line method is in use. One way you can prove this to yourself is to make up a set of facts (cost, service life, accelerated method to use) and assume the asset is sold for a given amount at the end of the second year. Compare that gain or loss with the gain or loss that would result if the straight-line method is used. (Solution = b.)

Question

8. Roberts Truck Rental uses the group amortization method for its fleet of trucks. When it retires one of its trucks and receives cash from a salvage company, the carrying value of property, plant, and equipment will be decreased by the:
   a. original cost of the truck.
   b. original cost of the truck less the cash proceeds.
   c. cash proceeds received.
   d. cash proceeds received and original cost of the truck.

EXPLANATION: Write down the journal entry to record the disposal of the truck and analyze its effect. Remember that no gain or loss is recorded on the disposal when the group or composite method is used.

Cash	Proceeds	
Accumulated Amortization	**Plug**	
Truck		Original Cost

In analyzing the entry's net effect on the book value (carrying amount) of property, plant, and equipment we find the following: (1) the decrease in Truck will reduce PP&E by the truck's original cost, (2) the debit to Accumulated Amortization will increase PP&E by the excess of the truck's original cost over the proceeds from disposal, (3) therefore, the net effect is to decrease PP&E by the amount of the cash proceeds from the sale. (Solution = c.)

Question

9. Which of the following uses a straight-line amortization calculation?

	Group Amortization	Composite Amortization
a.	Yes	Yes
b.	Yes	No
c.	No	Yes
d.	No	No

EXPLANATION: Both the group and composite amortization methods use a straight-line method calculation. Both methods perform one calculation for a group of assets. The group method is used for a collection of similar assets; the composite method is used for a group of dissimilar assets. Each method involves the calculation of a total amortizable cost for all the assets included in one asset account and of an estimated weighted-average useful life. (Solution = a.)

Question

10. The Schoen Company purchased a piece of equipment at the beginning of 1998 for $60,000. The equipment was being amortized using the straight-line method over an estimated life of 20 years, with no salvage value. At the beginning of 2008, when the equipment had been in use for 10 years, the company paid $10,000 to overhaul the equipment. As a result of this improvement, the company estimates that the useful life of the equipment will be extended an additional 5 years. What should be the amortization expense for this equipment in 2008?
    a. $2,000
    b. $2,667
    c. $3,000
    d. $1,867

EXPLANATION: Write down the model or format to calculate amortization whenever there has been a change in the estimated service life and/or salvage value. Fill in the data of the case at hand and solve.

Cost	$ 60,000
Accumulated amortization at 1/1/08	30,000[a]
Book value (before overhaul) at 1/1/08	30,000
Additional expenditure capitalized (if any)	10,000
Revised book value (after overhaul)	40,000
Current estimate of salvage value	0
Remaining amortizable cost at 1/1/08	40,000
Remaining years of useful life at 1/1/08	÷ 15[b]
Amortization expense for 2008	$ 2,667

(Solution = b.)

[a] Cost	$ 60,000
Original estimate of salvage	0
Original amortizable cost	60,000
Original service life in years	÷ 20
Original amortization per year	3,000
Number of years used	x 10
Accumulated amortization at 1/1/08	$ 30,000

[b] Original estimate of life in years	20
Number of years used	(10)
Additional years	5
Remaining years of useful life at 1/1/08	15

Question

11. As the result of certain changes in circumstances indicating that the carrying amount of plant assets may not be recoverable, Timberlake Company reviewed the assets at the end of 2008 for impairment. The company estimates that it will receive net future cash inflows of $85,000 (undiscounted) as a result of continuing to hold and use these assets. The fair value of the assets at December 31, 2008 is estimated to be $75,000. The assets were acquired two years ago at a cost of $500,000 and have been amortized using the straight-line method and a five-year service life. The loss from impairment to be reported at the end of 2008 is:
    a. $0
    b. $215,000
    c. $225,000
    d. $300,000

EXPLANATION: The carrying amount of the asset at the end of 2008 is $300,000 [$500,000 cost less (2 years x $500,000 x 20%)], but the recoverable amount is only $85,000. Thus, the test for recognition of an impairment loss has been met. The impairment loss is measured by the excess of the carrying amount ($300,000) over the fair value ($75,000). Therefore, Timberlake should recognize a loss of $225,000 ($300,000 – $75,000 = $225,000). (Solution = c.)

Question

12. Assume the same information as in Question 11 except that Timberlake, at December 31, 2008, discontinues use of the equipment, intending to dispose of the equipment in the coming year through sale to a competitor. The expected disposal costs are $10,000. The loss from impairment to be reported at the end of 2008 is:
    a. $0
    b. $225,000
    c. $235,000
    d. $300,000

EXPLANATION: Assuming the asset meets the criteria for classification as held for sale, the asset would be reclassified as held for sale and written down to fair value less costs to sell. Therefore the $10,000 disposal costs become relevant and the new carrying amount would be $65,000. Amortization would no longer be recorded. The amount of the loss in 2008 would be $235,000 ($300,000 –75,000+ 10,000) (Solution = c.)

TIP! If the asset above did not meet the criteria to be classified as held for sale, it would not be reclassified and would be written down to fair value. (Solution = b.) This is the situation in Question 12.

Question

13. The book value of a plant asset is:
    a. the fair market value of the asset at a balance sheet date.
    b. the asset's acquisition cost less the total related amortization recorded to date.
    c. equal to the balance of the related accumulated amortization account.
    d. the assessed value of the asset for property tax purposes.

EXPLANATION: Write down the definition for the term book value—**book value** is the asset's original cost (acquisition cost) less accumulated amortization. Look for the answer selection that agrees with your definition. (Solution = b.)

Question

14. Pantages Inc. has just sold the last asset in class 8 for $20,000. The original cost of the asset was $18,000. The UCC prior to the disposal was valued at $35,000. Pantages would report:
    a. recapture of $15,000.
    b. capital gain of $15,000.
    c. terminal loss of $15,000.
    d. terminal loss of $2,000.

EXPLANATION: Think about the definitions of the terms listed. Recapture occurs when the last asset of a class is disposed of and, after the disposal, the asset class has a negative balance. The amount would be added to income. A capital gain occurs when a company sells an asset for more than they paid for the asset (not the case here). A terminal loss occurs when the last asset of a class is disposed of and, after the disposal, the asset class has a positive balance as is the case here. ((Solution = c.)

Case Study

Laidle Disposal Limited (Part 2)

(See case in Chapter 11)

If LDL's sites are accounted for as fixed assets there is a further problem, and that is which amortization method to use. L.L. has done some research and has noted that the following methods are used by a sample of companies:

PepsiCo Inc. uses straight-line on their property, plant, and equipment.

Canadian Tire uses declining balance on their property and equipment.

L.L. estimates that the sites will take, on average, 10 years to fill up and that the amount dumped will increase, at least initially (year 1, 3% of total capacity; year 2, 5% of total capacity; year 3, 10% of total capacity), as LDL picks up more contracts. On the other hand, most contracts are annual and the possibility exists that they may also lose some. The costs of most sites average $1 million and the financing has been obtained from various sources at an average rate of 10%, which appears to be the best rate that they can get. Salvage values are not known at this time although land usually holds its value. L.L. is not sure what the difference is between these methods or what impact they might have on the financial statements. He is concerned that large amounts of amortization might make the financial statements look weak. On the other hand, the choice of amortization methods is probably arbitrary since one method is likely as good as another.

REQUIRED:

As an independent consultant to L.L., discuss the issues and provide recommendations.

Suggested Approach to Case Study

Overview

The financial statements will be used to obtain new contracts, and users will focus on financial stability and adherence to environmental standards. Management will therefore want the financial statements to show the company in the most favourable light (i.e., maximize profits and assets, and minimize negative disclosures). The statements will likely be constrained by GAAP since the government will want reliable statements.

Analysis and Recommendations

Issues: Are the landfill sites inventory (in which case they do not have to be amortized) or are they fixed assets? If they are fixed assets, which amortization method is appropriate?

Inventory vs. Fixed Assets

Discussed in Part 1 to the case in Chapter 11.

Amortization Method

Since the assets generate income through use, it would make sense to amortize them, thereby allocating the cost to the periods in which the revenues are earned under the matching principle. The question arises as to which method to use. The straight-line method will result in equal amounts being booked to expense in each year and therefore will provide consistent net income. The declining-balance method will provide for decreasing amounts of expense and is best suited to revenues that decline over time or where the assets contribute less to revenues over time (i.e., as they wear out). The sinking fund method results in increasing charges and, therefore, is suited to assets that result in increases in revenues over time.

These methods are theoretically equally acceptable and to some extent the choice is arbitrary. However, true matching would attempt to match the amortization pattern with the revenue pattern. In this case, less revenues will be generated in the earlier years according to LDL estimates (year 1, 3%, year 2, 5%, etc.). The usage will not always be increasing; however, contracts are annual and may be lost, resulting in less capacity used. Based on this, the most appropriate choice may not be one of the methods presented, but rather one based on activity (e.g., if 3% is used in the first year, then 3% of the gross cost of the assets should be depreciated, and 5% in the next year, etc.).

As a final note, the amount amortized should exclude salvage value, according to the *CICA Handbook*. In this case, the salvage value is not known, although land usually retains its value. Perhaps then there is nothing to amortize. In that case, however, the land may not hold its value to the extent that it was used as a garbage dump and is likely not located in a primary location.

Therefore, assuming that the salvage value is not estimable, it would make sense to amortize based on the amount of the assets used up each year. This will result in more favourable income statements in the earlier years since the site will be used less initially. This will meet the financial reporting objective of making the financial statements look better, at least in the earlier years.

Goodwill and Other Intangible Assets

Chapter 12

Overview

The balance sheet classification for intangible assets is used to report assets that lack physical existence and are not financial instruments. For instance (1) bank deposits and accounts receivable both are intangible by a legal definition but are properly classified as financial assets for accounting purposes, and (2) investment in shares is intangible in nature but should be classified as either a current asset or a long-term investment for accounting purposes with the further classification as to strategic investments, available for sale or held for trading. In any event, they are financial instruments. Assets such as patents, trademarks, copyrights, and franchises are intangible in nature and are classified in the intangible asset section of a balance sheet. Intangible assets derive their value from the rights and privileges granted to the company using the assets and are discussed in this chapter.

Study Steps

Understanding the Nature of Intangible Assets and Deferred Costs

Goodwill

Goodwill represents the value attributable to a company (in excess of the value of net tangible assets) because it is a successful, functioning business with customers, established suppliers, trained employees, and a good management team.

If one company purchases another, and the latter company is successful, the purchaser will likely pay more than the recorded net assets are worth at fair value (FV). The excess is due to the factors mentioned above and represents either goodwill or other unrecorded intangibles.

TIP! Goodwill is not recognized unless it is purchased by the company, i.e., another company's goodwill. This is due to the difficulty and subjectiveness of measuring a company's own goodwill.

Goodwill is not amortized. However, it is subject to an annual impairment test. This test involves the so called "two-step" impairment test. The first step requires a comparison of the fair value of the reporting unit that originally gave rise to the goodwill with the carrying amount. If fair value is greater than carrying value, nothing further is required. If fair value is less than carrying value, then the second step is performed. The second step involves a detailed analysis of the fair value of the identifiable net assets of the reporting unit. This is essentially a repeat of the purchase price equation that would have been performed upon acquisition.

Limited-life intangibles

An intangible asset with a finite or limited life is amortized by systematic charges to expense over its useful life.

As with property, plant, and equipment, if circumstances change indicating that the carrying value may not be recoverable, they are then evaluated for impairment. This involves comparing non-discounted cash flows related to the asset with the carrying value. If the expected cash flows are less, an impairment loss is recognized to the extent that carrying value exceeds fair value.

Indefinite-life intangibles

Similar to goodwill, an indefinite-life intangible is not amortized. It is subject to an annual impairment test. This involves comparing the carrying value with fair value. If carrying value is greater than fair value, an impairment loss will be recorded.

Types of intangible assets

There are many different types of intangible assets. The main headings are as follows:

- Marketing-related intangible assets
- Customer-related intangible assets
- Artistic-related intangible assets
- Contract-related intangible assets
- Technology-related intangible assets
- Goodwill

See **Case 12-1** below for examples.

Research and development (R&D)

R&D costs pose other challenges. Many successful companies in today's business environment spend significant amounts of money on research and development.

CICA HANDBOOK

Research is planned investigation undertaken with the hope of gaining new scientific or technical knowledge and understanding. Such investigation may or may not be directed towards a specific practical aim or application.

TIP!

Research is a search for new knowledge.

CICA HANDBOOK

Development is the translation of research findings, or other knowledge, into a plan or design for new or substantially improved materials, devices, products, processes, systems, or services prior to the commencement of commercial production or use.

TIP!

Development activities centre on the development of a tangible idea to the commercial production stage.

TIP!

Development activities usually begin with a tangible idea, often at the point when a prototype is developed. The distinction between what is research and what is development is not obvious and requires professional judgment.

Becoming Proficient in Calculating Goodwill

Goodwill may be initially calculated by taking the fair market value of the identifiable assets and liabilities of the purchased company and deducting this number from the purchase price. This equation is called the purchase price equation.

The concept of a purchase price equation was reviewed in Chapter 9 when calculating investment income under the equity method. The equation looks at what was paid and what the company received in return.

Amount paid to buy the company	$xxxx
Less: fair market value of identifiable net assets purchased	(xxx)
Equals goodwill	$xxxx

Therefore, goodwill is easy to quantify in situations where a company is being purchased as long as the FV of the identifiable assets and liabilities can be determined. It is simply a residual calculation.

Tips on Chapter Topics

TIP! When an intangible asset is amortized, the charge (debit) should be reported as an expense and the credit is made to the appropriate asset account. A separate accumulated amortization account should be used.

TIP! An observable market is one in which intangible assets are bought and sold, from which a market price can be observed to estimate the fair value of a similar asset.

TIP! Patents have a granted life of 20 years from the date of application. An average time from application to granting of the patent is 3 years, thus the useful life is a maximum of 17 years generally.

TIP! To record goodwill when a business is acquired, the total fair market value of the net and identifiable assets is compared with the purchase price of the acquired business. The difference is considered goodwill, which is why goodwill is sometimes referred to as a "master valuation" account. Goodwill is the residual: the excess of cost over fair value of the identifiable net assets acquired.

TIP! Negative goodwill occurs when the fair value of the identifiable net assets acquired is higher than the purchase price paid. The excess should be used to reduce the amounts assigned to given assets acquired and, if any remains, the remainder should be treated as an extraordinary gain.

TIP! The true value of goodwill may take years to "prove." It is assumed that the benefit (goodwill) is represented by excess earnings over and above the norm for the industry, with the view that any excess earnings is due to the purchased goodwill. The methods used are the excess earnings approach, number of years method, and discounted free cash flow method. Therefore, failure to earn "excess" earnings may mean goodwill is impaired.

TIP! Goodwill should be recorded on a company's books as an asset and only reduced if it is found to be impaired (test for impairment, based on a regular annual or interim basis testing), or if associated assets are sold or disposed of. Impairment losses are recognized separately before extraordinary items and discontinued operations on the income statement. The credit part of the journal entry should be to accumulated amortization, goodwill, thus bringing down the carrying value of the goodwill.

Exercise 12-1

PURPOSE: This exercise will give you practice in identifying items that are to be classified as costs associated with various intangible assets.

The Hatchling Fish Corporation incurred the following costs during January 2008:

1. Attorneys' fees in connection with organization of the corporation.
2. Meetings of incorporators, filing fees, and other organization costs.
3. Improvements to leased offices prior to occupancy.
4. Costs to design and construct a prototype.
5. Testing of prototype.
6. Troubleshooting breakdowns during commercial production.
7. Fees paid to engineers and lawyers to prepare patent application; patent granted January 22.
8. Payment of six months rent on leased facilities.
9. Share issue costs.
10. Payment for a copyright.
11. Materials purchased for future research and development projects; materials have alternative future use.
12. Costs to advertise new business.

Instructions

(a) For each item above, identify what account should be debited to record the expenditure.

(b) Indicate in which classification the related account will be reported in the financial statements.

Solution to Exercise 12-1

(a) Account Debited	(b) Classification
1. Organization Cost	Intangible Asset Operating Expense*
2. Organization Cost	Intangible Asset Operating Expense*
3. Leasehold Improvements	Property, Plant, and Equipment (or Intangible Asset)
4. Research and Development Expense	Operating Expense
5. Research and Development Expense	Operating Expense
6. Factory Overhead	Allocated to Inventory and Cost of Goods Sold
7. Patent	Intangible Asset
8. Prepaid Rent	Current Asset
9. Organizational Costs	Intangible Asset*
10. Copyright	Intangible Asset
11. Raw Materials Inventory	Current Asset
12. Advertising Expense	Operating Expense

* Canadian GAAP is moving to eliminate many deferred charges that had been allowed in the past. A new standard on Internally Developed Intangible Assets would clarify this treatment. In any event, if deferred, the organization costs would be amortized over a short, arbitrary period.

TIP! Many companies will expense organization costs due to materiality and the short time period over which they will be deemed to have future economic benefits.

TIP! Canadian GAAP is moving to eliminate the deferral of expenditures such as Organization Costs. This is in line with the objective of having a balance sheet that represents "true" assets, not necessarily assets created to merely satisfy the matching principle. The project on "Internally Developed Intangible Assets" would restrict "deferrals" to circumstances where the future benefits can clearly be identified.

Case 12-1

PURPOSE: This case will review examples of various types of intangible assets.

Although companies are permitted to capitalize certain costs to develop specifically identifiable intangible assets such as patents and copyrights, the amounts capitalized are generally not significant. Material amounts of intangible assets are recorded, however, when companies purchase (rather than internally develop) intangible assets, particularly in situations involving the purchase of another business (often referred to as a business combination).

Instructions

Give at least two examples of each of the six types of intangible assets listed below:

1. Marketing-related intangible assets.
2. Customer-related intangible assets.
3. Artistic-related intangible assets.
4. Contract-related intangible assets.
5. Technology-related intangible assets.
6. Goodwill.

Solution to Case 12-1

1. **Marketing-related intangible assets:**
   Trademarks, trade names, non-competition agreements, newspaper mastheads, Internet domain names and non-competition agreements.

2. **Customer-related intangible assets.**
   Customer lists, order or production backlogs, and both contractual and non-contractual customer relationships.

3. **Artistic-related intangible assets.**
   Ownership rights to plays, musical works, pictures, photographs, video and audiovisual material, literary works. Protected by copyrights.

4. **Contract-related intangible assets.**
   Licencing arrangements, leaseholds, construction permits, broadcast rights and services or supply contracts.

5. **Technology-related intangible assets.**
   Patents, trade secrets.

6. **Goodwill.**
   By definition, not separately identifiable. It is attached to the acquired business as a whole. It is the residual after all of the above intangibles have been identified.

TIP! It is extremely difficult not only to identify certain types of intangibles but also to assign a value to them in a business combination. As a result, the approach followed is to record identifiable intangible assets that can be reliably measured. Other intangible assets that are difficult to identify or measure are recorded as goodwill.

Exercise 12-2

PURPOSE: This exercise will review the accounting guidelines related to three types of intangible assets—patent, franchise, and trademark.

Information concerning Linda Heckenmueller Corporation's intangible assets follows:

1. Heckenmueller incurred $85,000 of experimental and development costs in its laboratory to develop a patent which was granted on January 2, 2008. Legal fees and other costs associated with registration of the patent totalled $16,000. Heckenmueller estimates that the useful life of the patent will be 8 years.
2. On January 1, 2008, Heckenmueller signed an agreement to operate as a franchisee of Cluck-Cluck Fried Chicken Inc. for an initial franchise fee of $150,000. Of this amount, $30,000 was paid when the agreement was signed and the balance is payable in four annual payments of $30,000 each, beginning January 1, 2009. The agreement provides that the downpayment is not refundable and no future services are required of the franchisor. The present value at January 1, 2008, of the four annual payments discounted at 14% (the implicit rate for a loan of this type) is $87,400. The agreement also provides that 5% of the revenue from the franchise must be paid to the franchisor annually. Heckenmueller's revenue from the franchise for 2008 was $1,800,000. Heckenmueller estimates the useful life of the franchise to be 10 years.

3. A trademark was purchased from Wolfe Company for $64,000 on July 1, 2005. Expenditures for successful litigation in defence of the trademark totalling $16,000 were paid on July 1, 2008. Heckenmueller estimates that the useful life of the trademark will be 20 years from the date of acquisition.

Instructions

(a) Prepare a schedule showing the intangible asset section of Heckenmueller's balance sheet at December 31, 2008. Show supporting calculations in good form.

(b) Prepare a schedule showing all expenses resulting from the transactions that would appear on Heckenmueller's income statement for the year ended December 31, 2008. Show supporting calculations in good form.

Solution to Exercise 12-2

(a)

Linda Heckenmueller Corporation
INTANGIBLE ASSETS
December 31, 2008

Patent, net of accumulated amortization of $2,000 (Schedule 1)	$ 14,000
Franchise, net of accumulated amortization of $11,740 (Schedule 2)	105,660
Trademark, net of accumulated amortization of $11,671 (Schedule 3)	68,329
Total intangible assets	$ 187,989

Schedule 1: Patent

Cost of securing patent on 1/2/08	$ 16,000
2008 amortization ($16,000 x 1/8)	(2,000)
Cost of patent, net of amortization	$ 14,000

Schedule 2: Franchise

Cost of franchise on 1/1/08 ($30,000 + $87,400)	$ 117,400
2008 amortization ($117,400 x 1/10)	(11,740)
Cost of franchise, net of amortization	$ 105,660

Schedule 3: Trademark

Cost of trademark on 7/1/05	$ 64,000
Amortization, 7/1/05 to 1/1/08 ($64,000 x 1/20 x 2.5)	(8,000)
Book value on 1/1/08	56,000
Cost of successful legal defence on 7/1/08	16,000
Book value after legal defence	72,000
Amortization, 1/1/08 to 12/31/08 (Schedule 4)	(3,671)
Cost of trademark, net of amortization	$ 68,329

(b)

Linda Heckenmueller Corporation
EXPENSES RESULTING FROM SELECTED INTANGIBLES TRANSACTIONS
For the Year Ended December 31, 2008

Interest expense ($87,400 x 14%)	$ 12,236
Patent amortization (Schedule 1)	2,000
Franchise amortization (Schedule 2)	11,740
Franchise fee ($1,800,000 x 5%)	90,000
Trademark amortization (Schedule 4)	3,671
Total expenses	$119,647

Schedule 4: Trademark Amortization

Amortization of original cost ($64,000 x 1/20)	$ 3,200
Amortization of legal fees ($16,000 x 1/17 x 6/12)	471
Total trademark amortization	$ 3,671

APPROACH: The ideal approach would be to prepare the journal entries associated with the facts given and post them to T-accounts to determine the balances to be reported on the income statement for the year ending December 31, 2008, and on the balance sheet at December 31, 2008. Under some circumstances (such as exam conditions), time may not permit these additional steps. You should at least think about and visualize the flow of the information through the accounts. This will greatly aid the successful completion of the schedules required.

EXPLANATION:

1. Research and development costs are to be expensed in the period incurred. Thus, the $85,000 of experimental and development costs incurred in developing the patent would have been expensed prior to 2008. Legal fees and other costs associated with obtaining the patent should be matched with each of the 8 years estimated to be benefited; therefore, the $16,000 of legal fees and registration costs should be capitalized and amortized.
2. The franchise rights will benefit future periods. Therefore, the costs associated with obtaining those rights should be capitalized and amortized over future periods. The acquisition cost is determined by the cash given (down payment of $30,000) and the cash equivalent of the related payable (present value of the four annual payments at 14%—$87,400). The fact that "the down payment is not refundable and no future services are required of the franchisor" has no impact on how the franchisee accounts for the franchise. The provision in the agreement which calls for the franchisee to pay 5% of the annual revenue from the franchise to the franchisor does not initially require any accounting treatment; an expense accrues as revenues are earned from use of the franchise. The capitalized franchise costs are to be amortized over the useful period of 10 years. The interest expense resulting from deferred payment is to be recognized annually by applying the implicit interest rate of 14% to the outstanding payable balance.
3. The purchase price of the trademark ($64,000) was capitalized in mid-2005 when the trademark was acquired. That cost is being amortized over the 20-year useful life. (Note that only one-half year of amortization was recorded

in 2005.) Expenditures of $16,000 for successful litigation in defence of the trademark rights are to be charged to the Trademark account because such a suit establishes the legal rights of the holder of the trademark (which benefits future periods). Because the litigation was settled in the middle of 2008, only one-half year of amortization of these legal costs is recorded for 2008. The $16,000 is to be amortized over the remaining useful life of the trademark (17 years in this case).

Exercise 12-3

PURPOSE: This exercise reviews the subject of leasehold improvements.

On January 1, 2008, Mr. Howard Anderson's Prize Paints entered into a lease contract with the Regency Mall Corp. The agreement provides for a 10-year lease on store space in a suburban mall. Mr. Anderson is leasing the space for his wholesale paint business. In order to prepare the facilities for his purpose, Mr. Anderson constructed several partitions at a cost of $3,200 and lowered the ceiling at a cost of $1,400. The partitions and ceiling revert to the owner of the property at the end of the lease term. Mr. Anderson assumes they will last as long as the building, which he estimates to have a 20-year life. The company uses a calendar year reporting period.

Instructions

(a) Prepare the journal entry to record the payment to the builder who put in the partitions and ceiling.
(b) Identify the period of time over which the improvements should be amortized. Explain why.
(c) Prepare the related adjusting entry (if any) at December 31, 2008.
(d) Explain how the improvements would appear on the balance sheet at the end of the third year of the lease.

Solution to Exercise 12-3

(a)

Leasehold improvements ($3,200 + $1,400)	4,600	
Cash		4,600

(b) Leasehold improvements are to be amortized over their useful life or the remaining term of the lease, whichever is less. In this scenario, the remaining term of the lease is 10 years, which is less than the 20-year useful life of the improvements. The 10-year period should be used.
(c) The adjusting entry to amortize the improvements at December 31, 2008, would be:

Amortization of Leasehold Improvements Expense	460	
Leasehold Improvements ($4,600 ÷ 10 years = $460)..........		460

(d) Leasehold Improvements would most likely appear in the property, plant, and equipment section of Prize Paints' balance sheet at an amount of $3,220 [$4,600 – (3 x $460) = $3,220] at the end of the third year of the lease, although some accountants would prefer to report this item in the intangible asset classification.

Exercise 12-4

PURPOSE: This exercise will give you practice in identifying activities that constitute R & D activities.

Listed below are four independent situations involving research and development costs:

1. During 2008 Bebe Co. incurred the following costs:

Research and development services performed by Way Co. for Bebe	$ 325,000
Testing for evaluation of new products	300,000
Laboratory research aimed at discovery of new knowledge	375,000
Research and development services performed by Bebe for Elway Co.	220,000

How much should Bebe report as research and development expense for the year ended December 31, 2008?

2. Holly Corp. incurred the following costs during the year ended December 31, 2008:

Design, construction, and testing of preproduction prototypes & models	$ 220,000
Routine, on-going efforts to refine, enrich, or otherwise improve upon the qualities of an existing product	250,000
Quality control during commercial production including routine testing of products	300,000
Laboratory research aimed at discovery of new knowledge	360,000
Conceptual formulation and design of possible product alternatives	100,000

What is the total amount to be classified and expensed as research and development for 2008?

3. Polanski Company incurred costs in 2008 as follows:

Equipment acquired for use in various R & D projects (current and future)	$ 890,000

Amortization on the equipment above	135,000
Materials used in R & D	300,000
Compensation costs of personnel in R & D	400,000
Outside consulting fees for R & D work	150,000
Indirect costs appropriately allocated to R & D	260,000

What is the total amount of research and development expense that should be reported in Polanski's 2008 income statement?

4. Liverpool Inc. incurred the following costs during the year ended December 31, 2008:

Laboratory research aimed at discovery of new knowledge	$ 175,000
Routine design of tools, jigs, molds, and dies	60,000
Radical modification to the formulation of a chemical product	125,000
Research and development costs reimbursable under a contract to perform R & D for Johnathon King, Inc.	350,000
Testing for evaluation of new products	275,000

What is the total amount to be classified and expensed as research and development for 2008?

Instructions

Provide the correct answer to each of the four situations.

Solution to Exercise 12-4

1.

Research and development services performed by Way Co. for Bebe	$ 325,000
Testing for evaluation of new products	300,000
Laboratory research aimed at discovery of new knowledge	375,000
Total R & D expense	$ 1,000,000

TIP! R & D costs related to R & D activities conducted for other entities are classified as a receivable (because of the impending reimbursement).

2.

Design, construction, and testing of preproduction prototypes and models	$ 220,000
Laboratory research aimed at discovery of new knowledge	360,000
Conceptual formulation and design of possible product alternatives	100,000
Total R & D expense	$ 680,000

TIP! Routine, ongoing efforts to refine, enrich, or improve an existing product is not considered R & D. Similarly, quality control is a regular operating expense of production.

3. Amortization on the equipment acquired for use in various R & D projects

Amortization on the equipment acquired for use in various R & D projects	$ 135,000
Materials used in R & D	300,000
Compensation costs of personnel in R & D	400,000
Outside consulting fees for R & D work	150,000
Indirect costs appropriately allocated to R & D	260,000
Total R & D expense	$ 1,245,000

TIP! Equipment, facilities, and purchased intangibles that have **alternative future uses** (in other R & D projects or otherwise) are to be **capitalized**; the **related amortizations are to be classified as R & D.**

4.

Laboratory research aimed at discovery of new knowledge	$ 175,000
Radical modification to the formulation of a chemical product	125,000
Testing for evaluation of new products	275,000
Total R & D expense	$ 575,000

APPROACH: Read the requirement of each situation before you begin detailed work on the first one. Notice that all four items deal with research and development costs. Therefore, review in your mind the definitions of the words "research" and "development." Recall what you can from the list of activities considered to be R & D and the list of activities which are **not** considered to be R & D. Think of why the items logically appear on a particular list. It is important to think about these items **before** you dig into the questions because details in the situations may mislead you. To minimize confusion, organize your thoughts and recall what you know about the subject before you begin to process the data at hand.

EXPLANATION: To differentiate research and development costs from other similar costs:

> **Research** is planned search or critical investigation undertaken with the hope of gaining new scientific or technical knowledge and understanding. Such investigation may or may not be directed toward a specific practical aim or application.
> **Development** is the translation of research findings or other knowledge into a plan or design for new or substantially improved materials, devices, products, processes, systems, or services prior to the commencement of commercial production or use. *CICA Handbook*, Section 3450.02.

Many costs have characteristics similar to those of research and development costs, for instance, costs of relocation and rearrangement of facilities, start-up costs for a new plant or new retail outlet, marketing research costs, promotion costs of a new product or service, and costs of training new personnel. To distinguish between R & D and those other similar costs, the following schedule provides (1) examples of activities that typically would be included in research and development, and (2) examples that typically would be excluded from research and development.

1. R & D Activities

(a) Laboratory research aimed at discovery of new knowledge.
(b) Searching for applications of new research findings.
(c) Conceptual formulation and design of possible product or process alternatives.
(d) Testing in search for or evaluation of product or process alternatives.
(e) Modification of the design of a product or process.
(f) Design, construction, and testing of preproduction prototypes and models.
(g) Design of tools, jigs, molds, and dies involving new technology.
(h) Design, construction, and operation of a pilot plant not useful for commercial production.
(i) Engineering activity required to advance the design of a product to the manufacturing stage.

2. Activities Not Considered R & D

(a) Engineering follow-through in an early phase of commercial production.
(b) Quality control during commercial production including routine testing.
(c) Troubleshooting breakdowns during commercial production.
(d) Routine, on-going efforts to refine, enrich, or improve the qualities of an existing product.
(e) Adaptation of an existing capability to a particular requirement or customer's need.
(f) Periodic design changes to existing products.
(g) Routine design of tools, jigs, molds, and dies.
(h) Activity, including design and construction engineering, related to the construction, relocation, rearrangement, or start-up of facilities or equipment.
(i) Legal work on patent applications, sale, licencing, or litigation.

TIP! Disclosure should be made in the financial statements (generally in the notes) of the total R & D costs charged to expense each period for which an income statement is presented.

Case 12-2

PURPOSE: This case is designed to give you practice in differentiating expenditures that are classified as research and development costs from expenditures that are not included with R & D.

Instructions

Various types of expenditures are listed below. Indicate the accounting treatment appropriate for each type of expenditure listed.

Type of Expenditure	Accounting Treatment
1. Construction of long-range research facility for use in current and future	

projects (three storey, 400,000-square-foot building).
2. Acquisition of R & D equipment for use on current project only.
3. Acquisition of machinery to be used on current and future R & D projects.
4. Purchase of materials to be used on current and future R & D projects.
5. Salaries of research staff designing new laser bone scanner.
6. Research costs incurred under contract with another corporation and billable to that company monthly.
7. Material, labour, and overhead costs of prototype laser scanner.
8. Costs of testing prototype and design modifications.
9. Legal fees to obtain patent on new laser scanner.
10. Executive salaries.
11. Cost of marketing to promote new laser scanner.
12. Engineering costs incurred to advance the laser scanner to full production stage.
13. Cost of successfully defending patent on laser scanner.
14. Commissions to sales staff marketing new laser scanner.

Solution to Case 12-2

Accounting Treatment

1. Capitalize and amortize as R & D expense.
2. Capitalize and amortize as R & D expense.
3. Capitalize and amortize as R & D expense.
4. Inventory and allocate to R & D projects; expense as consumed.
5. Expense immediately as R & D.
6. Expense as operating expense in period of related revenue recognition.
7. Capitalize as development costs if all criteria are met, otherwise expense.
8. Capitalize as development costs if all criteria are met, otherwise expense.
9. Capitalize as patent and amortize to overhead as part of cost of goods manufactured as used.
10. Expense as operating expense (general and administrative).
11. Expense as operating expense (selling).
12. Capitalize as development costs if all criteria are met, otherwise expense.
13. Capitalize as patent and amortize to overhead as part of cost of goods manufactured as used.
14. Expense as operating expense (selling).

TIP!

Development costs must be expensed unless all of the following criteria are met:

1. The product or process is clearly defined and the costs attributed to it can be identified.
2. The technical feasibility of the product or process has been established.
3. The enterprise management has indicated its intention to produce and market or use the product or process.
4. The future market for the product or process is clearly defined or, if it is to be used internally rather than sold, its usefulness to the enterprise has been established.
5. Adequate resources exist or are expected to be available to complete the project. Furthermore, the total amount of development costs deferred must be limited to the extent that their recovery can reasonably be regarded as assured. *CICA Handbook*, Section 3450. 13.

TIP!

Refer to item 6 above. Sometimes one enterprise conducts R & D activities for other entities under a contractual arrangement. In this case, the contract usually specifies that all direct costs, certain specific indirect costs, plus a profit element, should be reimbursed to the enterprise performing the R & D work. Because reimbursement is expected, such R & D costs should be recorded as a receivable. It is the company for whom the work has been performed that reports these costs as R & D and expenses them as incurred.

Illustration 12-1

Determination of Goodwill and Purchase Price (Excess Earnings Approach)

Step 1: **Determine normal earnings.** Multiply *the industry average rate of return on net assets times the fair market value of the identifiable net assets* of the company.

Step 2: **Determine an estimate of future average annual earnings.** This is usually done by calculating the adjusted (normalized) average net earnings of the company in the past, (usually 6 years). Adjust for accounting changes, extraordinary items, and other such special items.

Step 3: **Determine excess earnings.** This is the average earnings from Step 2 less the normal earnings from Step 1.

Step 4: **Determine the value of goodwill.** This can be done by using an appropriate discount rate and choosing the number of periods for which the excess earnings will be maintained. It could be treated as a perpetuity by capitalizing the excess earnings (dividing excess earnings by an appropriate capitalization rate). Alternatively, the number of years method could be used.

Exercise 12-5

PURPOSE: This exercise illustrates the steps in estimating the value of goodwill.

Mr. Lastman is contemplating the sale of his business, Classic Vettes. The following data are available:

Book value of tangible and identifiable intangible assets less liabilities	$ 185,000
Market value of tangible and identifiable intangible assets less liabilities	$ 200,000
Estimated average future annual income for Classic Vettes	28,000
Normal rate of return for the industry	10%

Instructions

(a) Calculate the estimated value of goodwill if excess income is capitalized at a 10% rate.

(b) Calculate the estimated value of goodwill if excess income is capitalized at a 25% rate.

Solution to Exercise 12-5

(a) $200,000 x 10% = $20,000 normal earnings
$28,000 – $20,000 = $8,000 excess earnings
$8,000 ÷10% = $80,000 goodwill

EXPLANATION: Perform the applicable steps described in **Illustration 12-1**:

Step 1: Determine normal earnings. Multiply the industry average rate of return times the fair market value of the identifiable net assets of the firm.
10% x $200,000 = $20,000 Normal earnings

Step 2: Determine an estimate of future average annual earnings. This is given data in the exercise at hand—$28,000.

Step 3: Determine excess earnings. Deduct normal earnings from future average annual earnings.
$28,000 – $20,000 = $8,000 Excess earnings

Step 4: Determine the value of goodwill. Capitalize excess earnings by dividing excess earnings by the chosen capitalization rate.
$8,000 ÷ 10% = $80,000 goodwill

(b) $200,000 x 10% = $20,000 normal earnings
$28,000 – $20,000 = $8,000 excess earnings
$8,000 ÷ 25% = $32,000 goodwill

TIP! The higher the capitalization rate, the lower the resulting value for goodwill.

TIP! Excess earnings are often referred to as superior earnings.

TIP! Net identifiable assets are determined by deducting total liabilities from total identifiable (tangible and intangible) assets.

TIP! Fair value, market value, and fair market value are terms which are often used interchangeably.

TIP! Goodwill can only be accurately determined when there has been a transaction between two (or more) unrelated parties. It is interesting to note that initial "goodwill" will be influenced by negotiating skills and certain terms of the agreement. However, on an ongoing basis, the value of goodwill must be "proven" by the excess earnings referred to above.

Exercise 12-6

PURPOSE: This exercise will provide an example of how to use the present-value method to estimate the value of goodwill.

As president of Winnie Audio Corp., you are considering purchasing Winkle Video Corp., whose balance sheet is summarized as follows:

Current assets	$ 400,000	Current liabilities	$ 400,000
Fixed assets (net of amortization)	800,000	Long-term liabilities	500,000
		Common shares	300,000
Other assets	200,000	Retained earnings	200,000
Total	$1,400,000	Total	$ 1,400,000

The fair market value of current assets is $700,000. The normal rate of return on net assets for the industry is 15%. The average expected annual earnings projected for Winkle Video Corp. is $160,000.

Instructions

Assuming that the excess earnings continue for 5 years, determine the value for goodwill by use of the present-value method.

APPROACH: Apply the steps listed in **Illustration 12-1**.

Step 1:	Fair market value of net assets	$ 800,000*
	Normal rate of return	15%
	Normal earnings	$ 120,000

Step 2: Average expected annual earnings are $160,000 (data given).

Step 3:	Expected earnings	$ 160,000
	Normal earnings	(120,000)
	Excess earnings	$ 40,000

Step 4:	Excess earnings	$ 40,000
	Present value of an annuity of 1 factor, 5 years @ 15%	3.35216
	Estimated goodwill	$ 134,086.40

* Book value of total assets	$ 1,400,000
Excess fair market value over book value of current assets	300,000**
Fair value of total assets	1,700,000
Total liabilities ($400,000 + $500,000)	900,000
Fair market value of net identifiable assets of Winkle	$ 800,000

** Fair market value of current assets	$ 700,000
Book value of current assets	400,000
Excess fair market value over book value of current assets	$ 300,000

TIP! You should also be able to calculate the purchase price that would result if both parties agree with the estimated goodwill figure calculated above. The fair value of the net identifiable assets ($800,000) plus the value of the unidentifiable asset (goodwill of $134,086) equals a total fair value of $934,086 for Winkle Video Corp.

TIP! You should also be able to record the purchase of Winkle Video Corp. if Audio Corp. pays $934,086 to purchase it. The identifiable assets would be recorded at their fair values ($1,700,000), Goodwill would be debited for $134,086, the liabilities would be recorded at their fair values ($900,000) and Cash would be credited for $934,086.

Analysis of Multiple-Choice Questions

Question

1. Innoventions Inc. acquired a patent from Whizkid Inc. on January 1, 2008, in exchange for $7,000 cash and an investment security that had been acquired in 2004. The following facts pertain:

Original cost of investment	$ 14,000
Carrying value of patent on books of Whizkid Inc.	4,500
Fair market value of the investment security on January 1, 2008	23,000

The cost of the patent to be recorded by Innoventions Inc. is:

a. $7,000.
b. $11,500.
c. $21,000.
d. $30,000.
e. none of the above.

EXPLANATION: Recall the guideline for determining the cost of any intangible asset. The cost of an intangible asset includes all costs incurred to acquire the asset. The historical cost principle dictates that cost be measured by the fair market value (i.e., cash equivalent value) of the consideration given or by the fair market value of the consideration received, whichever is the more objectively determinable. Innoventions Inc. gave $7,000 cash plus the investment security with a fair market value of $23,000 at the date of the exchange. The cost of the patent is, therefore, $30,000. (Solution = d.)

Question

2. The adjusted trial balance of the Laventhal Corporation as of December 31, 2008 includes the following accounts:

Trademark	$ 30,000
Discount on bonds payable	37,500
Organization Costs	12,500
Excess of cost over fair value of identifiable net assets of acquired business	175,000
Advertising costs (to promote goodwill)	20,000

What should be reported as total intangible assets on Laventhal's December 31, 2008 balance sheet?

a. $205,000
b. $230,000
c. $217,500
d. $275,000

EXPLANATION: Identify the classification of each item listed. Sum the ones you identify as being intangible assets.

Trademark	$ 30,000
Organization Costs	12,500
Excess of cost over fair value of identifiable net assets of acquired business	175,000
Total intangible assets	$ 217,500

Discount on bonds payable is to be classified as a contra liability. Advertising costs incurred are to be reported as an expense on the income statement. The costs to develop, maintain, or restore goodwill are not to be capitalized. Only the costs to acquire goodwill with a going business can be recorded as goodwill. The "excess of cost over fair value of net identifiable assets of acquired business" is a technical term referring to goodwill. (Solution = c.)

TIP! The Organization Costs referred to in Question 2 may also be expensed.

Question

3. A patent with a remaining legal life of 12 years and an estimated useful life of 8 years was acquired for $288,000 by Bradley Corporation on January 2, 2004. In January 2008, Bradley paid $18,000 in legal fees in a successful defence of the patent. What should Bradley record as patent amortization for 2008?

a. $24,000
b. $36,000
c. $38,250
d. $40,500

EXPLANATION: Analyze the Patent account. Use the data given to calculate the amounts reflected therein and the resulting amortization for 2008.

Cost at beginning of 2004	$ 288,000	
Amortization for 2004-2007	(144,000)*	
Book value at beginning of 2008	144,000	
Legal fees capitalized	18,000	
Revised book value, beginning of 2008	162,000	
Remaining years of life	÷ 4	
Amortization for 2008	$ 40,500	(Solution = d.)

* Beginning of 2004, patent cost	$ 288,000
Estimated years of service life	÷ 8
Annual amortization for 2004-2007	36,000
Number of years used	4
Total amortization 2004-2007	$ 144,000

Question

4. On January 1, 2008, Teeple Corporation acquired a patent for $30,000. Due to the quickly changing technology associated with the patent, Teeple is amortizing the cost of the patent over 5 years. What portion of the patent cost will Teeple defer to years subsequent to 2008?
   a. $0
   b. $6,000
   c. $24,000
   d. $30,000

EXPLANATION: $30,000 ÷5 yrs. = $6,000 amortization per year.

If $6,000 is amortized, then the amount to defer is calculated as follows:

Total patent cost	$ 30,000	
Amount amortized in 2008	(6,000)	
Amount to defer to subsequent periods	$ 24,000	(Solution = c.)

Question

5. The legal life of a patent is:
   a. 17 years.
   b. 20 years.
   c. 40 years.
   d. the life of the inventory plus 50 years.

EXPLANATION: A patent offers its holder an exclusive right to use, manufacture, and sell a product or process over a period of 20 years without interference or infringement by others. It is not subject to renewal. (Solution = b.)

TIP! Patents should be amortized over their useful life—which in many cases will be far less than their legal life.

Question

6. The cost of permits and licences are material to the entity for whom you are accounting. The cost of these items should be:
   a. expensed in the period acquired.
   b. expensed over the useful life of the items.
   c. charged against paid-in capital.
   d. capitalized but not amortized.

EXPLANATION: Licences and permits offer the holder certain rights. Like all other intangible assets, the cost of these items should be matched with the periods benefited. Permits and licences are often for a definite period and should be amortized over that period—not to exceed their useful life.(Solution = b.)

TIP! Permits and licences may have an indefinite life. In this case they would not be amortized but would be subject to an annual impairment test.

Question

7. The costs of intangible assets which are internally created are typically:
   a. capitalized but not amortized.
   b. capitalized and amortized over a long period of time.
   c. capitalized and amortized over a short period of time.
   d. expensed as incurred.

EXPLANATION: The following is helpful to keep in mind:

	Manner Acquired	
Type of Intangible	Purchased	Internally Created
Specifically identifiable intangibles	Capitalize	Expense, except certain costs
Goodwill-type intangibles	Capitalize	Expense
Deferred Charges	Capitalize restricted amounts	Capitalize restricted amounts

If you purchase a patent from an inventor or an owner, the cost of that patent is capitalized. If you develop (internally generate) a product yourself, the research and development costs related to the development of the product or idea that is subsequently patented must be expensed unless the specified criteria are met. However, other costs incurred in connection with securing a patent, as well as attorney's fees and other unrecovered costs of a successful legal suit to protect the patent, can be capitalized as a part of the patent cost—subject to recoverability of course. (Solution = d.)

TIP! Deferred charges may only be capitalized in very limited circumstances–specifically when the future benefit has been clearly identified. Most items that would have qualified for deferred charge treatment in the past would now be expensed.

Question

8. The costs of organizing a corporation include legal fees, fees paid for incorporation, fees paid to underwriters, and the costs of meetings for organizing the underwriters. These costs are said to benefit the corporation for the entity's entire life. These costs should be:
   a. capitalized and never amortized.
   b. capitalized and amortized over 40 years.
   c. capitalized and amortized over 5 years.
   d. expensed as incurred.

EXPLANATION: Although it is difficult to exactly determine the length of benefit, costs incurred in establishing an organization are deferred as organization costs. Amortization costs are normally short (5 years maximum) as a conservative approach. (Solution = c.)

TIP! Many entities may choose to expense Organization Costs.

Question

9. Windsor Corporation was organized in 2007 and began operations at the beginning of 2008. Prior to the start of operations the following costs were incurred in 2007:

Attorneys' fees for assistance in obtaining corporate charter and drafting related documents	$ 33,000
Meetings of incorporators	14,000
Improvements to leased office space prior to occupancy	21,000
Fees to underwriters to help locate buyers for Windsor's common shares	$116,000

   What should be the balance of the Organization Cost account based on the above?
   a. $21,000
   b. $33,000
   c. $163,000
   d. $116,000
   e. None of the above.

EXPLANATION: Before reading through the list of costs incurred, define "organization costs" and think of the most common examples. Organization costs are costs incurred in the formation of a corporation such as fees to underwriters, legal fees, federal fees of various sorts, and certain promotional expenditures. They are often deferred—however, many companies choose to expense them.

Windsor should charge the following to Organization Cost:

Attorneys' fees for incorporation	$ 33,000
Meetings of incorporators	14,000
Fees to promoters	21,000
Total organization costs	$ 68,000

(Solution = c.)

TIP! The $21,000 of improvement to leased office space prior to occupancy should be recorded in the Leasehold Improvements account.

Question

10. Motts Corporation purchased the following items at the beginning of 2008:

Materials to be used in R & D activities; these materials have alternative future uses and they remain unused at the end of 2008.	$ 50,000
Materials to be used in R & D activities; these materials do not have alternative future uses and $12,000 of them remain unused at the end of 2008.	33,000
Equipment to be used in R & D activities; this equipment was used in one R & D project during 2008 and is expected to be used in other R & D projects to be undertaken over the next 5 years. It has no residual value. Motts normally uses the straight-line amortization method for equipment.	100,000
Total	$ 183,00

Based on the above information, Motts should report R & D expenses for 2008 of:

a. $183,000.
b. $103,000.
c. $53,000.
d. $21,000.
e. none of the above.

EXPLANATION: Mentally review the proper accounting treatment for materials and equipment acquired for use in R & D activities. The cost of materials acquired for use in R & D activities should be expensed in the period acquired unless the items have alternative future uses (in R & D projects or otherwise); then they should be carried as inventory and allocated to R & D expense as used. The cost of equipment and facilities acquired for use in R & D activities should be expensed in the period acquired unless the items have alternative future uses (in R & D projects or otherwise); then they should be capitalized and amortized as used (the resulting amortization should be classified as R & D expense). Thus, Motts would have the following R & D expense for 2008: (Solution = c.)

Materials acquired, no future alternative use	$ 33,000
Amortization on equipment used in R & D activities ($100,000 ÷ 5 years)	20,000
Total R & D expense for 2008	$ 53,000

Question

11. The total amount of patent cost amortized to date is usually:
   a. shown in a separate Accumulated Patent Amortization account which is shown contra to the Patent account.
   b. shown in the current income statement.
   c. reflected as credits in the Patent account.
   d. reflected as a contra property, plant, and equipment item.

EXPLANATION: In accounting for intangible assets, the amortization of an asset is usually credited directly to the Accumulated Amortization, Patent contra asset account. (Solution = a.)

Question

12. Gates Inc. develops computer software to be sold to the general public. The costs incurred in creating a new piece of software should be:
   a. charged to R & D expenses.
   b. capitalized and amortized.
   c. charged to R & D expense when incurred until technological feasibility has been established for the product; the costs incurred after this point are to be capitalized.
   d. charged to cost of goods sold expense.

EXPLANATION: Costs incurred in creating computer software to be sold to external parties should be charged to research and development expense when incurred until technological feasibility has been established for the product (which occurs upon completion of a detailed program design or working model). Costs incurred subsequent to this point are to be capitalized and amortized to current and future periods. (Solution = c.)

Question

13. The owners of Tellmart Shoe Store are contemplating selling the business to new interests. The cumulative earnings for the past 5 years amounted to $750,000, including extraordinary gains of $25,000. The annual earnings based on an average rate of return on investment for this industry would have

been $115,000. If excess earnings are to be capitalized at 15%, then implied goodwill should be:

a. $175,000.
b. $233,334.
c. $200,000.
d. $725,000.

EXPLANATION: Follow the steps in **Illustration 12-1**.

Step 1:	Normal earnings = $115.000.	
Step 2:	Cumulative earnings over the past 5 years	$ 750,000
	Extraordinary gains included in above	(25,000)
	Total earnings excluding extraordinary items	725,000
	Number of years included above	÷ 5
	Average earnings in past 5 years assumed to be average annual earnings	$ 145,000
Step 3:	Expected average earnings	$ 145,000
	Normal earnings	(115,000)
	Excess earnings	$ 30,000
Step 4:	Excess earnings	$ 30,000
	Capitalization rate	÷ 15%
	Estimated value of goodwill	$ 200,000

(Solution = c.)

Question

14. Which of the following would not be included as research and development?
    a. Routine or periodic alterations to existing products, production lines, manufacturing processes, and other on-going operations.
    b. Depreciation of equipment being temporarily used for R&D.
    c. Laboratory research aimed at the discovery of new knowledge.
    d. Testing in search for, or evaluation of, product or process alternatives.

EXPLANATION: These would not be included since the expenditures are routine or periodic adjustments/alterations to existing operations. Basically, R&D is focused on new technology or alternatives to existing technology. (Solution = a)

Question

15. Which of the following criteria is the overriding requirement for deferral for development expenditures?
    a. financing available
    b. product technically feasible
    c. product defined and related costs identifiable
    d. development costs do not exceed expected related net income from future commercial sale of product/process

EXPLANATION: The overriding factor would be the ceiling test which prohibits any non-recoverable development costs from being capitalized. (Solution = d.)

Question

16. Purchased goodwill should be:
    a. amortized over its useful life.
    b. written off immediately due to the uncertainty as to future value and to ensure consistency with internally generated goodwill which is expensed.
    c. charged to shareholders' equity on the basis that, unlike other assets, goodwill is not separable from the business and cannot be sold separately.
    d. capitalized and not amortized.

EXPLANATION: Goodwill should be capitalized as an asset and not amortized. It should be tested for impairment annually. (Solution = d.)